DARK CARNIVAL

DARK CARNIVAL

THE SECRET WORLD OF TOD BROWNING

Hollywood's Master of the Macabre

DAVID J. SKAL AND ELIAS SAVADA

ANCHOR BOOKS   NEW YORK LONDON TORONTO SYDNEY AUCKLAND

An Anchor Book
PUBLISHED BY DOUBLEDAY
a division of Bantam Doubleday Dell Publishing Group, Inc.
1540 Broadway, New York, New York 10036

Anchor Books, Doubleday, and the portrayal of an anchor are
trademarks of Doubleday, a division of Bantam Doubleday Dell
Publishing Group, Inc.

Frontispiece photo: *The British Film Institute.*

Book Design by Gretchen Achilles

Library of Congress Cataloging-in-Publication Data

Skal, David J.
  Dark carnival : the secret world of Tod Browning—Hollywood's
master of the macabre / David J. Skal and Elias Savada. — 1st ed.
    p.   cm.
  Includes bibliographical references and index.
  1. Browning, Tod, 1882–1962—Criticism and interpretation.
2. Horror films—History and criticism.   I. Savada, Elias.   II. Title.
PN1998.3.B773S53   1995
791.43′0233′092—dc20   95-14870
                                                         CIP

Dedicated
to the memories of
GEORGE C. PRATT
who taught me how to be
spellbound in darkness

—E.S.

and
ROBERT BLOCH
who couldn't wait to read it.

—D.J.S.

CONTENTS

PROLOGUE

THE DIRECTOR VANISHES

Lon Chaney, with a missing friend, in West of Zanzibar *(1928)*.
(Elias Savada collection)

It was perhaps fitting that a man who had loved baseball for at least seventy of his eighty-two years should die in the middle of the World Series, the game tied 1–1 between the Yankees and the Giants. As a long-naturalized Californian, Tod Browning might be expected to favor the Giants. In fact he preferred Cincinnati, but was never one to let sentiment influence his bets.

In his carefully guarded private life, Browning adored animals and schmaltzy figurines, but when it came to the sphere of public spectacle, his approach was clinical and unsparing. As a director of motion pictures, he forged a reputation as the "Edgar Allan Poe of the cinema," a Hollywood prince of criminality, darkness, and the grotesque. His foremost concern as a storyteller was the plight of outsiders, at first depicted as garden-variety criminals, but, as his career progressed, in fantastic distortions worthy of Dorian Gray's infamous portrait. The criminal-outsider, played as often as not by the protean silent-film actor Lon Chaney, Sr., began to display physical anomalies reflective of disordered inner states: characters in Browning films wouldn't be merely wronged, guilty, or vengeful; they would also be scarred, crippled, or spectacularly mutilated. Eventually, Browning's cast-asides would include real sideshow freaks, who, through accidents of birth, surpassed anything Lon Chaney could accomplish with rubber humps and harnesses—as well as utterly fantastic alien strangers like the predatory Count

Dracula. *Freaks* and *Dracula* would, in fact, be his two most famous films, fascinating audiences more than six decades after their initial releases as timeless evocations of otherness, alienation, and dread.

Tod Browning had one of Hollywood's most singular careers, with a tremendous shaping influence on two significant American genres: the gangster picture and the horror film—not to mention their stylish cinematic nuptials in *noir*. His firsthand knowledge of the industry and its personalities, from D. W. Griffith's pioneering Biograph Company to the sophisticated dream factory of Louis B. Mayer's M-G-M, would have been the material of a terrific Hollywood memoir.

But Tod Browning didn't like to talk—not about his career, at least. Now, lying in his coffin in a Santa Monica funeral home, he was dead of a wasting illness that had, finally, deprived him of any possibility of speech. It was a grimly ironic comment on the life and death of a man who had made his fortune as a silent-film director, but who had had considerable difficulties in adapting his talents to the medium of talking pictures. He would become angry, in his final years, whenever a person he had allowed to become intimate would begin to press for details about his life in Hollywood.

There was much to be curious about. Few directors had displayed such a singular preoccupation with the grotesque—his *Freaks* had been one of the biggest disasters of the early talkie era, repulsing and infuriating audiences and critics with its unprecedented display of real human deformities, and had been banned in some parts of the world for thirty years. There was his legendary collaboration with the equally secretive Chaney, the "Man of a Thousand Faces" who never revealed his own. There was *Dracula* with Bela Lugosi. And whether his subject was the criminal underworld or the nether realm of the undead, Browning's films are filled with repeated, almost interchangeable, themes, characters, and compositions that impress the viewer with the disturbing power of recurrent dreams. As critic Stuart Rosenthal noted in 1975 in the only substantial critical essay ever published on Browning's work, "Although the work of any *auteur* will repeatedly emphasize specific thoughts and ideas, Browning is so aggressive and unrelenting in his pursuit of certain themes that he appears to be neurotically fixated on them. . . . Browning expresses his obsessive content in a manner that may be properly described as compulsive.''

But while Browning reveled in disturbing and provoking the public, he did so from a position of obsessive privacy. Unlike other Hollywood movers and shakers of his generation, he seemed to care nothing for posterity, or even publicity over which he was not completely in control. He never gave a retrospective interview, dying before the advent of film studies as a respected academic discipline.

Even if an army of credentialed film historians had approached him during his lifetime, it is doubtful that Tod Browning would have been willing to talk. He left the world no papers, kept no diaries, affecting an indifference to the film medium that approached outright contempt. ''When I quit a thing, I quit,'' he was said to have told a friend. ''I wouldn't walk across the street now to see a movie.'' Yet one of his favorite pastimes in his final years was watching old movies in the privacy of his home on the new medium of television.

Finally, in October 1962, he was in no position to reminisce about everything, embalmed in a box and awaiting cremation. Boxes and their secrets had figured with a dark prominence throughout his life. His career began, he claimed, with a turn-of-the-century carnival scam, where, as the Living Hypnotic Corpse, he had allowed himself to be repeatedly buried alive in a ventilated coffin. Later, in vaudeville, he became acquainted with all the tricks of magicians' trunks and cabinets, a theme he would resurrect in picture after picture. His most famous film, *Dracula,* dealt with a perambulating Transylvanian vampire and his hiding boxes of native soil. From time immemorial boxes have symbolized secrets, the unconscious, and the occult. And Tod Browning, perhaps more than any Hollywood director, had chosen to repeatedly exploit this symbol, while jealously guarding secrets of his own. His real name, for instance, wasn't Tod, but the professional alias couldn't have been better chosen—in Old English, the name means ''fox'' or ''trickster''; in German, it is the word for death.

Visiting hours were over in the slumber room at the funeral

home of Gates, Kingsley & Gates, but one mourner remained, bringing forth a special box of his own. At the dead man's request, the visitor was to be permitted to spend the night and perform a final ritual. The man, as far as anyone could remember, was called Lucky; he knew little about Browning's life in Hollywood, making his acquaintance as a house painter and drinking buddy. The box he brought with him was nothing mysterious or occult: it was a case of Coors beer. Before he died, Browning had asked Lucky to sit up with him and polish off a final batch. In another show of legerdemain, Browning presented himself as a "recovered" alcoholic who nonetheless consumed, quite openly, prodigious quantities of brew for the rest of his life. It was said, though never really substantiated, that he received a case a month as a perpetual personal gift from Adolph Coors—the result of a favorable comment Browning had once made about the product to Coors himself at a racetrack, unaware of the beer magnate's identity. Drinking, in Tod Browning's life, amounted to more than just a personal weakness; it precipitated two catastrophes that not only affected his own life but set in motion changes in a career that would have an outsize impact on the future of American film.

To Lucky, Tod Browning was a kindly and generous man who displayed no signs of the dark sensibility revealed in his films. He was a garrulous old man who lived on the sun-drenched beach at Malibu, raised dogs and ducks, and loved nothing so much as preparing gourmet meals in his well-equipped kitchen. But to others, he was a classic Hollywood son of a bitch with a morbid streak a mile wide, who used the film medium to indulge his unhealthy obsession with physical disability and human predation. Hollywood veteran Budd Schulberg, author of the caustic classic *What Makes Sammy Run?*, lived near Browning in the Malibu colony in the 1930s, and considered the director an out-and-out sadist. Browning's critical reception was, and is, equally mixed: to some, he was an unassailable *auteur* of cinematic darkness; to others, he was a cynical hack, who mined the same thematic material over and over, not to any artistic purpose, but simply out of creative laziness. His most controversial film, *Freaks,* has been just as often praised as a compassionate masterpiece as it has been damned for its tasteless, exploitative excesses. One veteran executive at M-G-M, who did not want to be identified, offered the following, icy appraisal: "As a director, he was terrible . . . as a person, he was nothing."

Neither statement is true, but establishing the facts of Browning's life and the meaning of his work presents special problems to would-be biographers, film historians, and critics. Andrew Sarris, in 1968, cited Browning as one of several directors who were "subjects for further research," but research materials remained maddeningly elusive, and no biography appeared, even with Browning's elevation to cult-director status with the 1970s revival of *Freaks* on the art-house circuit. *Dark Carnival* intends to fill the gap in the understanding of Browning and his career by drawing on dozens of unpublished interviews with the director's co-workers and friends, most now deceased, and new revelations from surviving, recently located family members and from previously untapped archives.

A good biographical subject ideally maintains a certain core of impenetrability, and Browning is no exception, but the present book should at least create a more multidimensional portrait of Browning than has ever been attempted. In a town that has traditionally worshiped fame, self-aggrandizement, and the glare of publicity, Browning's reclusive career and its dissolution amounted to one of Hollywood's most mysterious vanishing acts. *Dark Carnival,* the authors hope, will shed some illumination on its methods and machinations.

In October 1962, when Tod Browning died, America was less interested in pondering the metaphors of stage magic than it was in the more tangible escape exploits of myriad tunnelers under the Berlin wall. The cold war was growing warm, and in a few short weeks the dark rite of the Cuban missile crisis would plunge America into a collective ritual more terrifying than anything Browning had ever depicted in a film. Count Dracula's sarcophagus had long been replaced by the fallout shelter as a cultural locus of dread, and, unlike the vampire, the atom bomb didn't evaporate at dawn.

A quaintly morbid trickster forgotten in an impersonal age of mass destruction, Tod Browning vanished from this world with an intimate flourish of macabre celebration. For the dead man and his loyal friend in the Santa Monica slumber room, only one trick remained: making the final case of Coors disappear.

ONE

CERTIFIED PUBLIC SPECTACLES

Tod Browning as a blackface comedian. (Courtesy of Chatty Eliason)

Charles Albert "Tod" Browning was born in Louisville, Kentucky, on Monday, July 12, 1880, the second son and third child of Charles Leslie Browning and his wife, Lydia Jane Fitzgerald Browning. Charles Leslie was a remarkably thin man, mustachioed, and of average height; Lydia, by contrast, was imposing not only in pillowy girth but in towering stature as well. Not even old age would stoop her: the undertakers who eventually took measurements for her coffin recorded her height in death at six feet three inches. Tod Browning would take after both his parents, resembling his mother in height and his father in bony angularity.

His parents, both Louisville natives, had been born and raised on the near west side of the bustling port city, coming of age during the tumultuous years of the Civil War. Favorably situated between the industrial North and the agricultural South, postbellum Louisville was a boomtown during the years of reconstruction and reconciliation, its population swollen to 174,000 from about 50,000 before the war. But the city fathers ascribed the city's good fortune to its citizens' character rather than any accident of geography. "Louisville has possessed few of the natural advantages of a commanding port," the introduction to *Caron's Louisville Directory* for 1880 explained. "A river town with less push than its pretentious rivals"— Cincinnati, evidently, caused the most consternation—"she has grown slowly, solidly . . . her people have always been painfully modest, and have neglected opportunities which other cities would have given much to have. The great expansion of the city's population and trade in the last two decades has given the people both courage and energy, and there is a more confident and aggressive spirit taking the place of shyness and caution."

As a nonsecessionist slave state, Kentucky had divided allegiances during the Civil War, and gave sons to both the Union and Confederate causes. Born in Danville, Kentucky, in 1826, the family matriarch, Mary Jane Browning, *nee* Sheppard, was a southerner through and through, and flew the Confederate flag proudly from her home when the Union troops marched through Louisville in 1861. The state did not require formal registration of vital statistics before 1911, but Mary Browning's family can nonetheless be reconstructed through a patchwork of census data, burial records, commercial city directories, and hints provided by newspaper clippings containing references to the Browning clan. Mary had seven children by her husband, Samuel (1814–75), a well-known lumber merchant and grocer. Their four sons were Charles Leslie Browning (1850–1922), Henry D. Browning (1853–1911), Samuel L. Browning (c. 1857–1900), and Louis Rogers "Pete" Browning (1861–1905); their three daughters were Florence Bell Browning (1851/52–1935), Fannie E. Browning (c. 1859–1907), and Blanche Browning (1854/55–61/65), who died in childhood. Florence married, and was widowed by, a certain John Ramsey of Louisville, but Fannie never took a husband.

Little is known about the fortunes of Henry and Samuel, Jr.— Henry worked as a woodcarver and lottery dealer, Samuel as a plumber, fireman, and barkeeper—but Mary's two other documented sons couldn't have presented a stronger study in contrasts. While Charles pursued conventional livelihoods, as a bricklayer, carpenter, and machinist, primarily for the firm of B. F. Avery and Sons, a world-renowned manufacturer of plows and agricultural equipment, "Pete" Browning stubbornly refused to conform. He hid the schoolbooks his mother bought him under the porch and refused to attend classes, spending his days instead shooting marbles (he became a local legend), spinning tops, and, most of all, playing ball. Pete suffered from severe ear infections which left him hard of hearing from an early age; the condition was so painful that he couldn't endure one of the central childhood pleasures of a sweltering Louisville summer—swimming with his friends in the Ohio River, just a few blocks from his home. The hearing disability interfered with his education as much as any marble playing, and he never learned to read or write. As if in the belief that everyone else was as deaf as he, he would, for the rest of his life, carry on ordinary conversations in the stentorian manner of an auctioneer.

Nonetheless, Pete Browning found a way to distinguish himself professionally, eventually becoming one of Louisville's most colorful and recognizable citizens during the 1880s, living proof of the city's trumpeted reaction against shyness. Whatever his other shortcomings, Pete Browning knew how to do one thing very well: he could hit a baseball, very hard and very far. He was, in fact, one of the most outstanding natural hitters in baseball history, compiling a lifetime .341 batting average, thirteenth highest in the annals of the sport and just a single percentage point below Babe Ruth. His career lasted from 1882 to 1894, primarily with Louisville in both the American Association and, later, the National League. The bat now known as the Louisville Slugger was originally custom-made for Browning in 1884, after he had broken his favorite, paddle-style bat. A fan and apprentice woodmaker named John Hillerich fashioned a new, rounded bat on a lathe in his father's woodworking shop, which had, until then, specialized in bedposts, table legs, and butter churns. The success of the new bat changed both the way baseball was played and the fortunes of the woodworking shop; today Hillerich & Bradsby is still one of the most recognizable trademarks in sporting equipment.

To call Pete Browning a "colorful" character would be an injustice. He was something of a one-trick pony, interested in power batting over almost every other aspect of the game, and was considered an atrocious outfielder. The press, nonetheless, followed his every exploit, and he earned numerous sobriquets, including the Gladiator, Glad, Gladdy, Old Pete, and Pietro.

He enjoyed his notoriety and did everything he could to attract the attention of the press, both on and off the ball diamond. It wasn't difficult. For one thing, he drank, and not a little—the most famous, if saddest, quote ever attributed to him was "I can't hit the ball before I hit the bottle." One of the local papers was fond of calling him "Pietro Redlight District Distillery Interests Browning," and his relationship with the press developed into something of a feud. Baseball historian Philip Von Borries suggested that a turning point was reached when Browning, informed of the death of President James A. Garfield in 1881, responded to an astonished newspaper reporter with a flip, or drunken, "Yeh? What league was he in?" "The remark undoubtedly convinced the press that Browning's ability to put his foot in his mouth was exceeded only by his ability to tilt a glass in the same direction, a habit they had previously tolerated," wrote Von Borries. "The press spent more than a decade jousting with him in their sports pages about his chronic drunkenness and frequent 'lost weekends,' his inability to read or write, and his difficulty in catching routine fly balls. In time, the celebrated battles and not his prodigious hitting ability, earned him the moniker of 'The Gladiator.' "

Legend has it that, during the early games Browning played with a local amateur nine, a keg of beer was routinely placed at third base as both an enticement and a reward. "Pete knocked so many three-baggers and home-runs that little beer was left for anyone else," the *Louisville Times* reported. In the professional leagues during the 1880s, it was not unheard-of for players to hide alcohol behind billboards during games. Things became so bad that the *Sporting News* took to attacking drunken players by name in an effort to protect the game's image from the increasing pressure of temperance groups. Drinking as part of the baseball ritual was hardly limited to the players; soccer-style melees among inebriated spectators were common. In 1886 Chicago White Stockings owner A. G. Spalding offered a $350 bonus to players who would voluntarily stop drinking. The bribe had no takers, so Spalding sent the entire team to the steaming waters of Hot Springs, Arkansas, in order to "boil out the alcoholic microbes," as he explained the matter to the press.

Pete Browning was largely unrepentant, however, even when, too drunk to make the train, he was left behind by his team in St. Louis in 1887. Still under the effects of his debauch, Browning made it back to Louisville on his own to play a game against Cincinnati—and promptly fell asleep about fifteen feet off second base, "to the intense disgust of the spectators," according to a newspaper report. Beyond his drinking, the Gladiator's other peculiarities were equally legendary. He held some strange superstitions about his eyes, or "lamps," as he liked to call them. While on the road, he would stick his head out the windows of trains in order that fly ash from the locomotive would blow into his eyes and make them water; somehow, he thought this would improve or maintain his vision. He liked to stare directly, if briefly, into the sun each morning, as if this would somehow magically energize his eyes. On the field he was afraid of sliding, crossing mud puddles, or of being run into by another player—he would often stand in the outfield, storklike, one knee held out like a defensive battering ram (this latter peculiarity might also be ascribed to his fear of being trampled and spiked by onrushing players he could not hear).

All in all, Browning was a Louisville original, a certified public spectacle if there ever was.

Pete broke with Louisville in 1889, playing for Pittsburgh, Cleveland, and Cincinnati before retiring in 1894 at the age of thirty-three. He played for a few seasons in the minors and tried, unsuccessfully, several other careers, including saloonkeeping and cigar selling. Never married, Pete lived his entire life with his mother but was nonetheless well acquainted with Louisville's demimondes. The city's higher-class whorehouses lined Tenth Street just a few blocks from his home, and syphilis, then incurable, significantly exacerbated his health problems. In July 1905 he was committed to the Central Asylum for the Insane at Lakeland, Kentucky, suffering from paresis and a massive ear infection. The mastoid condition that had plagued him from childhood had worsened, necessitating surgery; briefly improved, he was released from the asylum, but within a few months he began a rapid deterioration. He died on Sunday, September 10, 1905, in the City Hospital, members of his family at his bedside. The official cause of death was "asthenia," a basically meaningless euphemism that, like "exhaustion," was often applied to turn-of-the-century deaths caused by tertiary syphilis.* He was forty-four years old.

Nothing is known about the extent of Tod Browning's boyhood dealings with his uncle Pete, though it is impossible to believe that the bellowing, carousing Louisville legend who lived just two houses away did not make some significant impression on his nephew. (If nothing else, the boy did develop a passionate, lifelong interest in baseball.)

Tod had a sister he never knew: Octavia F. Browning, his parents' first child, was born in the summer of 1874, but died of paralysis just shy of her year and one-half birthday in the early afternoon of November 14, 1875. The tragedy followed the death, from ulceration of the stomach, of the family patriarch, Samuel Browning, a few weeks earlier. Tod's older brother, George Avery Browning (evidently middle-named after his father's longtime employer, B. F. Avery), was conceived in the immediate aftermath of these family misfortunes and born on Sunday, August 13, 1876. He became a coal merchant, eventually founding the Louisville company of Bowser and Browning. Avery—as George preferred to call himself—is remembered as the tallest member of the family, almost six and one-half feet, and an obsessively organized personality, with a lifelong aversion to being touched. He was also phobic about germs. His nieces recalled, more than a half century after the fact, his wary response to their offering him a piece of homemade fudge: "Is it *clean?* Is it *clean?"* Avery preferred having most of his food prepared by his mother alone, and well into adulthood made a daily ritual

---

* *In an apparent effort to place the best possible spin on the case for Browning's inclusion in the Baseball Hall of Fame in the early 1980s, partisans laid Browning's mental degeneration entirely on a chronic mastoid infection, which was also held responsible for his alcoholism. The issue of syphilis went discreetly unmentioned, despite a direct reference to paresis in documents included in Browning's file at the Baseball Hall of Fame, Cooperstown, New York. Notwithstanding a batting average that rivaled that of Babe Ruth, Pete Browning has never been elected to the Baseball Hall of Fame, owing, perhaps, to the unsavory aspects of his reputation. Nonetheless, in 1984, the City of Louisville, in cooperation with the Hillerich & Bradsby Co., erected a commemorative plaque over Browning's grave on the seventy-sixth anniversary of his death, formally honoring his remarkable career achievements. An earlier grave marker had misspelled his real first name as "Lewis."*

trip home to eat Lydia Browning's never-changing lunches of roast beef and homemade bread. Avery favored long dark overcoats, which he wore regardless of the season, and constantly puffed odiferous cigars. He had an aversion to driving. Family members recalled that he stopped attending church at the age of sixteen. He never married, and his social life centered around his lodge, where, as a member of the Ancient and Accepted Scottish Rite, he achieved the rank of a 32nd-degree Mason.

In addition to his older brother, Tod had a younger sister, Virginia "Jennie" Cook Browning, born in Cincinnati on Saturday, February 17, 1883. Jennie was actually the daughter of Lydia's brother and his wife, both Kentucky natives who had moved upriver to Ohio; for now-obscure reasons, Lydia and Charles Leslie Browning took her into their home at 1433 West Jefferson Street at a very early age and raised the red-haired girl as their own daughter. While the Brownings never formally adopted Jennie, their bond was sufficiently close that Jennie's own children did not learn until later in their lives that Lydia and Charles were not their natural grandparents.

Tod, like his uncle Pete, reveled in public attention; at an early age, he began producing shows—"performances to astound," as the *Louisville Herald-Post* later described them—in an old shed in back of his family's second house at 2227 West Main Street, a residence occupied by the Browning family on March 7, 1887. In lieu of pennies, he charged the neighborhood children five pins for admission, recalled the *Herald-Post*. "This little fellow was a go-getter," the paper reported:

> Every show he gave proved a dazzling success. And he gave many, sometimes five in a single vacation season . . . later on, he passed from pins to pennies. He gathered about him a greater and more glittering galaxy of neighborhood talent, with himself, of course, "doubling in the brass," this being to enact the principal roles in whatever drama or comedy chanced to be on any bill, and to keep a weather eye cocked to the box office. For he was a precocious youngster, a Barnum, perhaps, in the making.

A "sprightly boy," the paper called him, "bright as a dime and keenly alert to the main chance. . . . That was why Tod Browning's penny shows always drew better crowds than the rival penny shows in the neighborhood. He put on something better. He knew his public and studied their wants—and gave them what they wanted."

Mildred McAuliffe, the daughter of one of Tod's first cousins and still a Louisville resident in 1994, recalled a specific detail of the boy's repertory, passed down as family lore: with the help of his father, who fashioned him wooden figurines, he would fill a washtub and stage a kind of Lilliputian aquacade. Browning also had a distinct talent for singing, and was a member of the Christ Church Cathedral choir, where he was held by some to be "an infant phenomenon."

Information on Tod's religious upbringing is scant. He was received for baptism at the 26th and Market Street Baptist Church on Sunday, February 15, 1891, and, in the presence of a full chapel, was officially baptized a month later at this then branch of the 22nd and Walnut Street Church. On April 5 Tod's father took the plunge. Although Lydia (and Avery, until his midteens) attended regularly, they were not active in other church activities, and when the branch organized as an independent church in March 1893, the Brownings transferred back to the mother church. While her mother stayed home tending to the needs of her growing family, Jennie Browning's daughter Helen Polsgrove recalled attending church with her grandmother regularly, until Lydia became incapacitated in the mid-1920s.

There was much in Louisville to impress Tod in the way of popular entertainment and show. An annual city event of the early 1890s that could not have escaped the boy's attention was a spectacular carnival called the Satellites of Mercury, evoking all the splendor and pageantry of Mardi Gras with its parades, floats, and exotica. Owing to Louisville's natural river link to New Orleans, amusements in Louisville often reflected the carnivalesque atmosphere of the gaslit French Quarter. Like many port cities, Louisville had a raffish riverfront culture and a plethora of legitimate playhouses offering melodrama, burlesque, and prestigious touring companies from New York and Europe.

For its geographical location, Louisville was remarkably cosmopolitan, with a flair for elegance and show, for "strong wine, fast music, and blooded horses," according to historian Peter Chew. In the mid-1870s, a flamboyant promoter named Meriwether Lewis Clark proposed an annual event to compete with the rival Cincinnati's acclaimed music festival or New Orleans' Mardi Gras. The end product of Clark's efforts was the Kentucky Derby, inaugurated in 1875, and a fixture of both Louisvillan and American culture ever since. The Derby evolved quickly into a vast cultural spectacle far beyond the confines of Churchill Downs, annually attracting to Louisville an extraordinary cross section of humanity, ranging from European royalty to riverboat gamblers to the proverbial ragtag assortment of Gypsies, tramps, and thieves. Kentucky's homespun philosopher Irvin S. Cobb, asked in the 1930s why the Kentucky Derby was so special, replied, "If I could do that, I'd have a larynx of spun silver and the tongue of an angel," but nonetheless asked his readers to "imagine a track that's like a bracelet of molten gold encircling a greensward that's like a patch of emerald velvet. . . . But what's the use? Until you go to Kentucky and with your own eyes behold the Derby, you ain't never been nowheres and you ain't never seen nothin'!" According to an unsourced article in *Louisville* magazine, Browning was especially attracted to the Gypsy encampments the derby always drew, fascinated with their nomadic culture and disdain for the restrictions and conventions of the outside world.

Another riveting spectacle that came within Browning's childhood purview elicited quite a different emotional response.

On the evening of March 27, 1890, when Tod was nine years old, a devastating tornado swept through the Brownings' neighborhood on the west side of Louisville, destroying five churches, the railroad depot (which it lifted off its foundation and dumped into the Ohio River), three schools, thirty-two factories, and over five hundred homes. Seventy-five people died. The massive funnel, a full block and a half wide at its base, roared within blocks of the

Browning homestead on West Main Street, which, owing to the characteristic caprice of tornadic winds, was spared. Elsewhere in the neighborhood, mangled bodies lay under smashed and splintered houses and on the streets, including one man described tersely as having his "head cut in twain." The sky cleared immediately after the storm, eerily bathing the devastated city in bright, almost theatrical moonlight. The disaster made national headlines for days and etched itself permanently into Louisville's memory.

Browning was educated in the Louisville public school system, though, like his uncle, was less interested in a formal education than in outside pursuits, and the full extent of his schooling is open to question. Although he claimed to have attended Louisville's high school, later known as the Male High School, surviving records contain no mention of Charles Albert Browning beyond elementary school. When Browning himself filed a formal birth certificate in 1947,* he presented the Kentucky Registrar of Vital Statistics a Louisville public school document dated September 2, 1889, giving his age as nine years. This is the sole piece of documentary evidence regarding his education. The high school, in any event, would hardly have been to the young Tod's liking; the school had been traditionally inhospitable even to athletics, much less the kinds of extracurricular distractions the boy found appealing. As Pendleton Beckley, a member of the class of 1895, recalled, the principal was Maurice "Ole Hoss" Kirby, who "thought that all hours of school should be consecrated to American History, English literature and Shakespeare." The end of Browning's documented education nearly coincided with the tornado, just two and one-half years after the family's move to its "shotgun" row house on Main Street farther west of downtown, on the edge of the factory district.

By this time Browning had begun to dream of a world beyond working-class Louisville—in particular, the world of riverboats, carnivals, and music halls. A book published the year after he was born continued to cast a spell over his generation, and for all practical

---

*At the time of Browning's birth, the state of Kentucky did not maintain a centralized registry of vital statistics.

purposes invented the notion of "running away with the circus." James Otis Kaler's *Toby Tyler, or, Ten Weeks with a Circus* (1881) enjoyed tremendous popularity as both a magazine serial and a novel, telling the story of an ingenuous boy who, unhappy with the small portions of food he is receiving at home from his uncle, a strict deacon, seeks a better deal elsewhere and runs away with the traveling show. Life as a candy seller in the circus proves more difficult than Toby bargained for; he is beaten and abused by his jailerlike employer but finds friendship in a pair of circus freaks, Lilly and Samuel Treat, the troupe's resident fat lady and human skeleton. The Treats accept Toby as one of their own and fete him at a Thanksgiving feast of freaks, including a sword swallower, a snake charmer, albino children, and a chimpanzee named Mr. Stubbs, who becomes his closest companion. In the course of his adventures Toby picks up a good deal of incidental knowledge about the circus trade, some of it cynical: Mrs. Treat, for example, weighs four hundred pounds but "of course" is advertised as weighing six hundred. The lemonade is heavily watered but dressed up with lemon peels to fool the rubes. Customers, Toby finds, are wont to pass off lead slugs for coins. In the course of the plot, Toby also enjoys some prepubescent romance and performs as a horseback rider but soon starts dreaming again of running away, this time back home. Following the accidental death of Mr. Stubbs, Toby breaks with the circus for a sentimental reunion with his uncle, his heart considerably softened by the near loss of his young charge.*

Browning may or may not have been directly influenced by *Toby Tyler* (he would, in later life, name one of his own beloved animal companions Toby), but he nonetheless began to plan an escape from his parents, whose own Jack Sprat marriage may well have evoked a certain aura of sawdust and tinsel. As Browning related the story to a friend in 1958, he began earning money surreptitiously by tending the horses of amorous couples making use of a

*Toby Tyler *is best known today in the 1959 film version produced by Walt Disney, which considerably sanitized the story, omitting the novel's Dickensian level of child abuse and replacing the freaks with normally proportioned circus characters. The 1923 adaptation starring Jackie Coogan called* Circus Days *was truer to the novel and retained Toby's relationship with the fat lady and human skeleton.*

park near his home. To be sure his stash would not be discovered, he stored it not in his room, but in a box kept secreted in the rafters of the family outhouse. Every night, ritualistically, he would add to his fortune, counting and recounting the money, anticipating the day he would flee Louisville to find a real fortune.

Finally, the day was at hand. He had saved enough to make his escape. Trembling, he reached for the box one last time. It slipped —and his entire savings disappeared down the outhouse's reeking hole.

Browning finally did escape Louisville, though the break may not have been as decisive or dramatic as he later described. Since almost all accounts of Browning's entry into show business originated with Browning himself, or with studio publicists in the bally-hoo-heavy 1920s, they need to be evaluated with a certain skepticism. For instance, he told his longtime friend William S. Hart, Jr., son of the famed western-film actor (another friend), that he first ran away from home with a carnival at the age of twelve, which would make him almost a literal Toby Tyler. He also told Hart that his real birth date was 1874, not 1880, and that he claimed the later date for professional reasons, in order to appear younger in Holly-wood. But that assertion is contradicted by the aforementioned 1947 birth certificate and its supporting documentation.

Browning's self-proclaimed story of his early professional experience is indeed colorful, but largely unverifiable by independent means and often contradicted by surviving archival data. According to the legend, as first put forth in friendly newspaper interviews in the *Louisville Herald-Post* and in studio handouts, a street fair came to Louisville in 1898 and Browning fell under the spell of one of the dancers. The show left town, and so, supposedly, did Tod. When his parents next heard from him, he was a ballyhoo artist, or spieler, with something called the Manhattan Fair and Carnival Company. "He became one of the best known barkers in the white-top business," his publicity would later maintain, "with a string of vivid adjectives and a rolling delivery that were the envy of his barking brethren." According to the *Herald-Post,* "His infatuation with the side show queen wore off but the carnival spirit had entered his blood and his days at the family fireside were over. He remained with the carnival the remainder of the season 'barking' for a 'Wild Man of Borneo'—the 'wild man' being a Mississippi negro in makeup."

"Wild men" were a favorite offering of sideshows in Europe and America from the Victorian age onward; the late nineteenth century, disturbed by the theories of Darwin and their rapid cultural acceptance, found a strange gratification in gazing upon beings who seemed to blur the distinctions between humans and lower animals. At first, retarded individuals, especially those afflicted with microcephaly—"pinheads" in popular parlance—were displayed as evolutionary missing links, the last surviving members of ancient races, at first identified as "Australian," but later more commonly as "Aztec." Joseph Merrick, England's world-famous Elephant Man, was another variation on the theme during the 1880s, although his disfigurement, called multiple neurofibromatosis, had no evolutionary basis.

In America by the turn of the century, the demand for sideshow attractions by traveling carnivals outstripped the supply of real human oddities, and "gaffed," or fraudulent, freaks of the kind ballyhooed by the young Tod Browning, became increasingly common. The wild man was typically displayed not on a stage but in a "pit," a freestanding, waist-high enclosure around which the customers could freely circulate after paying their admission to the tent. Just below the wild man on the carnival's evolutionary ladder was the "geek," usually an end-stage alcoholic willing to bite the heads off snakes, rats, or chickens for a pittance in salary—or more likely, just for his next drink. According to his later publicity, Browning's carnival days included a geeklike turn as Bosco the Snake Eater.

Browning's baptism into carnival culture was a significant juncture in his life, for it gelled a particular worldview that impressed him deeply and later fueled his best film work. The carny ethos divided the world into rigid camps: show people and everyone else—"suckers," "marks," and "rubes." The worldview had a certain basis in the very real difficulties show people traditionally endured:

"running away with the circus" was hardly the carefree lark as held in the popular imagination. As sideshow historian Robert Bogdan described the condition of the amusement worker at the turn of the century, "Showmen knew they were not trusted. They were well aware of their dubious status in the communities they worked. What they had to offer—the excitement, the entertainment, the fun, the bribes—was enough to compensate the hosts. But although the showmen were allowed to practice their trade, they were never accepted—they were merely tolerated." Bogdan adds that show people's low community esteem derived from a well-deserved, if highly self-rationalized, reputation for being swindlers, thieves, and grifters; the exhibition of freaks per se found no widespread objection until relatively recent times.

It is impossible to reconstruct Browning's relationship with his family—why he felt the need to run away from their home, why he rejected their traditional work ethic, or why he refused to use his real first name. Lydia Browning was recalled by her foster grand-daughters as a sometimes perfectionistic "snooty" woman. William S. Hart, Jr., a longtime friend of Browning's and part heir to his estate, said that Browning was "proud" of his parents and had a close relationship with them. But another late-life acquaintance had the impression that Browning had been on better terms with his grandmother than with his immediate family. No evidence exists to determine exactly when he began to use the name Tod, whether it was a family nickname or represented a self-bestowed identity. A son who rejects his father's name might suggest a significant generational conflict, but no documentation survives that can shed light on Charles Albert's relationship with Charles Leslie. But a lonely, restless sense of flight pervades the accounts of Browning's early days of independence, the calliope music beckoning in a distinctly minor and discordant key.

Browning's subsequent adventures in show business, at least according to his later publicity, included work as a Ringling Bros. clown, followed by employment as a handcuff-escape artist, a contortionist, a ringmaster, and—most improbably—as a jockey at Churchill Downs as well as for a "prominent southern turfwoman" named Virginia Carroll, whose name has somehow evaded the chronicles of horse racing. Browning, though quite thin as a young man, was nonetheless six feet tall—hardly jockey material. He also claimed to have spieled for a carnival attraction known as the Deep Sea Divers, and photographs exist of him in costume as a blackface comedian in a vaudeville act known as "Lizard and Coon," with Roy C. Jones, a former spieler Browning met at the 1904 St. Louis World's Fair.

But without question, the apex—or nadir, depending on one's perspective—of Tod Browning's purported early career was his role as the Hypnotic Living Corpse with a carnival river show that traversed the mythical waters of the Ohio and the Mississippi sometime around the turn of the century. The demise of one century and the beginning of another was an especially appropriate time for a death/rebirth ritual, and our hero apparently made the most of it. The earliest account of Browning's hypnotic corpse routine appeared in the magazine *Reel Life* in 1914:

> When the celebrated hypnotist, with whom he had formed a partnership, fixed upon him his mesmeric gaze, he would fall into a trance. Then he would be lowered several feet under the ground and the earth thrown over him. A wooden shaft permitted the wonder-struck crowd, one by one, to gaze down upon his inert form in the bottom of the pit—and incidentally supplied him with air. Sometimes, during an exhibition, he would have to stay buried forty-eight hours at a time.

Long a fixture in the repertoire of Hindu fakirs, live burial acts found their way West during the late Victorian era when mesmerism, spiritualism, and other occult fads provided a measure of reassurance against the dehumanizing materialism of the industrialized nineteenth century. The ritual was often begun on a Friday and finished on a Sunday, a freak-show travesty of Easter weekend. As explained by the great stage magician Joseph Dunninger, the traditional Indian version of the stunt involved a specific trick: "The coffin . . . was not as ordinary and crude, as our Hindoo entertainer would have us believe. The lower, inner edge of the molding, which seemed to act as a reinforcement for the box, was a sliding tube. As the coffin was being covered with sand, the man of mystery, upon the inside, was secretly sliding this tube, out from the coffin." The tube either reached the surface of the ground on its own or joined with a buried ventilation duct.*

In Asia and Europe the emphasis was placed on the fantastic possibility of death and resurrection; in America the obvious, air-providing periscope pretty much demolished the illusion, the emphasis shifting from the intimations of the miraculous to Yankee ingenuity and endurance. (Houdini, had he lived, would have performed a live burial trick on stage using a huge tank of earth; an atmospheric poster had already been printed at the time of his death from peritonitis in 1926.)

"When I heard the dirt come crashing down on that coffin, I actually shivered," Browning told a reporter twenty years later. His subterranean sustenance consisted of malted milk pellets concealed in his shirt and drink lowered to him by a string during the periods when the crowd thinned out. Save for a brief reference to an empty water bottle, excretory details went discreetly unmentioned by the writer for the *Herald-Post*. But whatever his level of physical discomfort, the paper maintained that "he became accustomed to the performance and was able to almost enjoy the confinement." The long hours wiled away in the grave "were conducive to thought and Mr. Browning made the most of the opportunity. That period of intensive thought did much to shape Tod's destiny and was the cause of awakening the spark of genius lying dormant within him."

Perhaps. But Browning's eventual genius for creating macabre spectacles far grander than any Hypnotic Living Corpse was not to be immediately realized. The show was ultimately busted by local authorities in Madison, Indiana, for violating the Sabbath, and the

---

* *Coffin acts proved remarkably resilient in the carnival world, persisting even a half century after Browning's final disinterment. One of the present authors witnessed an exact re-creation of the routine in Ohio during the mid-1960s, where, as part of a drive-in theater's promotion for Roger Corman's* The Premature Burial, *a young man was "hypnotized," boxed, and buried in the drive-in's parking lot for the duration of the weekend. Persons wishing to get a closer look could pay a small fee to enter a tent erected over the gravesite and peer down a periscope at a quadrant of the man's face in the coffin. Sepulchral sound effects were piped in over a hi-fi set, and the young man's family sat around on folding lawn furniture, looking rather bored.*

company was fined every cent its members had—a grand total of $14.07. After two years with the river show, Browning teamed with the vaudevillian Roy C. Jones for touring of a more conventionally entertaining sort—circus stunts, buck-and-wing routines, blackface comedy, slapstick, and burlesque. After they split, Browning worked as a single-turn artist for a year but eventually reteamed with Al West, a vaudeville pairing that lasted for three seasons. He also claimed to have had legitimate stage experience, appearing with Anna Held in Florenz Ziegfeld's *Mam'selle Napoleon* (1903), a legendary disaster that helped set in motion Ziegfeld's financial ruin. Browning, however, is not listed in any surviving programs of the elaborate costume drama about a famed actress of the Comédie-Française, which played Philadelphia, New York, and Chicago—although it is certainly possible he used a stage name.

Far more significant in light of Browning's later professional work was his claimed association with the celebrated magician Leon Herrmann (1867–1909). The French-born illusionist, especially popular in the American South—he played Louisville annually each January from 1903 to 1906—was stage-magic royalty, nephew of the magicians Carl and Andre Herrmann ("Herrmann the Great"), who bore such a striking resemblance to his namesakes that the three were often confused in the public mind. Leon frequently appeared with his aunt, Adelaide Herrmann, an accomplished illusionist in her own right, known for her spectacular sense of theater. A 1902 account of a Boston appearance describes her fantastically embroidered kimono: "On black satin are entwined snakes upon snakes, each one more brilliant in color than the last . . . the effect in the lime light is beyond description."

The male Herrmanns, in contrast, favored austere evening dress and cloaks, a costume convention that would ultimately survive in popular entertainment primarily in the mesmeric persona of Count Dracula. A Herrmann performance always emphasized gorgeous painted scenery depicting exotic locales—Oriental gardens and French court scenes were favorites. In addition to such familiar specialties as the trunk escape and the Hindu basket trick, the Herrmanns were the foremost interpreters of the "bullet catch" illusion, a somewhat nerve-wracking trick in that it required the audience's marking of live ammunition and the split-second, sleight-of-hand removal of shells and the substitution of blanks by not one person, but a series of people. Houdini himself considered the trick too dangerous to perform. In the Herrmanns' version of the illusion, flattened bullets were deflected off a china plate held like a shield in front of the targeted illusionist; in other variations of the act, the bullet would seem to be caught in the performer's teeth. In the hands of lesser artists, or fumbling assistants, this act could—and occasionally did—prove fatal.

A 1905 publicity photo of Herrmann and his assistants shows a young man who may be the twenty-five-year-old Tod Browning, glaring straight ahead, arms akimbo, doing his best to look mysterious. According to William S. Hart, Jr., Browning said he also worked for a time with a renowned Chinese magician noted for his ability to produce goldfish bowls out of the air. Hart did not recall the magician's name, but the field is fairly narrow. The goldfish trick was first popularized by a turn-of-the-century Mongolian conjurer named Ching Ling Foo, who toured extensively in the United States. But since Foo's entourage consisted primarily of family members, it is unclear how Browning could have assisted him, except perhaps as an employee of one of the many theaters booking Foo's act.

Browning's published recollections of this period suggest a romanticized break with his hometown and family at the age of sixteen or eighteen, but the Louisville city directory for the year 1901 shows him employed, mundanely, as a clerk for Harbison & Gathright, a wholesale saddlery company, and for several years afterward as a boarder in his family's home, with an entrance at 2229 West Main Street. In all likelihood, Browning maintained Louisville as a base of operations for many years, returning home after his various theatrical tours.

One of the most excessive pieces of puffery about his early career appeared in *The New York Times* in 1926, claiming that "he has appeared before the footlights in almost every city of importance in this country and also in a vast number of places in Europe, Africa, and Asia." Describing his work with the Willard and King Company ("a spectacular act which originated in Europe"), the *Times* reported that upon the death of Willard, junior partner of the company, Browning replaced him, "doing a special contortionist act." The thirty-seven-member troupe then spent more than a year touring Europe, "playing in London, Paris, Madrid, Berlin, and Rome. . . . After Europe the company went to the Far East, where they saw life in Calcutta, Bombay, Shanghai, Peking, and other cities. Then they went to Africa, and following an engagement in Capetown the company returned to the United States." Unfortunately, there is no record of Browning's ever having applied for a passport until 1927.

In short, most of the "record" of Tod Browning's early career cannot be confirmed by documentary evidence, and is likely an uneasy amalgam of truth, half-truth, embellishment, and, in some cases, outright fabrication. Obviously, show business pulled Browning powerfully, and from an early age, but the full nature and extent of his apprenticeship is far from clear. There is, however, substantial documentation of a less glamorous phase of his private life in Louisville from 1905 to 1909.

Like innumerable show folk who made their living on the road, he claimed to have been working in San Francisco at the time of the 1906 earthquake, although a close examination of San Francisco newspapers and playbills in the weeks before the cataclysm revealed no attractions to whose name Browning's has ever been linked. Furthermore, by the spring or summer of 1905, Browning had fallen in love with Amy Louise Stevens, a twenty-three-year-old Louisville native, the daughter of a New England–born pawnbroker and later prominent jeweler named Fred E. Stevens, Sr. (whose storefront was less than one block away from Avery Browning's office) and his wife, Emma. He had met Amy three years earlier—at least, that is when Amy's parents first made his acquaintance. It was a meeting they would live to regret.

A photo of Amy from the period shows her to be a classic "Gibson Girl" beauty with piles of dark, luxuriant hair. Not surprisingly, Tod Browning wasn't the only young man in Louisville expressing interest in her. He had a rival in one Milton Meffert, the twenty-seven-year-old son of a local stockbroker, Colonel William Meffert. Milt's interest in racing would lead him to an apparently profitable career as a traveling auditor and racing official (a newspaper clipping would eventually describe him as "the Andrew Mellon of racing activities about Havana" who "had more friends probably than any one person connected with racing in the country").

The present race, however, had nothing to do with horses. On September 8, 1905, Milt wrote in longhand on the letterhead of the American Tobacco Company, 111 Fifth Avenue, New York:

My Dear Amy,

Don't know what you will think but must write, and remind you that you and I have gone together a long while and think lots of one another. I know I may not have acted exactly right—in fact neither one of us. I know I care just as much for you as I ever did, and there is no getting around the fact, although I have tried not to awfully hard. Now honey what I want you to do is cut out the other party—altogether—neither to write him—or let him call on you—and you and I be good old friends once more—just like we used to be in days gone bye, if you think you can do this, let me hear from you, but if such is not the case—don't answer—or say anything about it to any one, and above all don't write and say you will do this and then turn around and in the course of time, let him call on you, as that would not be right to either one of us—and it's really not right now—as we both care for one another—and you are not acting just right towards him. You don't know, honey, just what this costs me to write this way—but I realize there is no use—in spoiling three lives. Think over what I have written—and make up your mind one way or the other, provided it is not already made up.

With love, I remain
As ever
Milt

When, exactly, Amy made up her mind isn't known, but on March 24, 1906, the Saturday evening edition of the *Louisville Times* announced the impending nuptials of Miss Amy Louise Stevens and

Mr. Charles Albert Browning, to take place the following Wednesday evening. The bride was given a linen shower by the members of her Thursday Afternoon Euchre Club. "She will also be given a handkerchief shower on next Tuesday," the *Times* added. A marriage license was issued the day of the wedding, March 28, and a small, families-only ceremony was held in the pastor's study of the First English Lutheran Church, the Reverend Dr. S. S. Waltz officiating. Immediately following the ceremony, "the young people went East on a wedding trip," the *Louisville Courier-Journal* reported on April 1. "After April 15, they will be at home with the bride's parents. Mrs. Browning is a strikingly handsome brunette. Mr. Browning is an employee of the L. and N. Railroad."

Clearly, Browning's show business aspirations took a temporary backseat to the need to support his wife. The fact that the couple started their marriage under Fred and Emma Stevens' roof at 1950 Sixth Street suggests that Browning's earnings were inadequate to support a household. Emma Stevens later would state that the couple lived together under her roof for three years, "except when they were traveling with a show or out on the road." Amy's effects from this period (later passed on to her niece) include photos of Browning as a vaudevillian and blackface comedian, indicating that conventional employment with the L. and N. Railroad was only a passing fancy. Browning's unorthodox vocational goals and unreliable income quickly generated tension in the Stevens household; on ten occasions in March and April of 1907, Browning borrowed sums of money totaling $130.90 from his mother-in-law, which he failed to pay back; additionally, it fell to Emma Stevens to pay off in installments a clothier's bill of $100.75 for wardrobe items purchased by her daughter. Browning promised to reimburse her but never did. Emma claimed that she and her husband became the couple's primary means of support, that her son-in-law "was a shiftless man—was too lazy to work. Sometimes he would work in [an] Amusement Park in the summer and when winter would come he did not work."

The amusement park was, in all likelihood, Fontaine (pronounced "fountain" by most Louisvillans) Ferry Park, a classic turn-of-the-century "trolley park" on the river in Louisville's far west end—the park's rides and brilliant lights were fueled by excess direct current from the city's electric trolley system. From its inauguration in 1905, Fontaine Ferry Park contained numerous attractions, including a "Gypsy village," a sprawling "scenic railway" (a prototype roller coaster), and a bicycle racetrack with a covered grandstand resembling the grander Churchill Downs. Browning was, no doubt, also intimately acquainted with Fontaine Ferry's rival amusement center, White City, founded in 1907 and known as Riverview Park during its final year of operation in 1910. Across the Ohio River in New Albany, Glenwood Park offered more traditional carnival attractions and tent shows of the kind that would figure with a dark prominence in Browning's Hollywood films. Louisville's vaudeville venues in 1906 included two major houses, the Buckingham and the Hopkins.

These parks and theaters were available to provide Browning with dreams and distractions, if not a living wage, during the collapse of his youthful, disastrous marriage to Amy Stevens. Little tangible evidence of their union remains today: a handful of photos, including a portrait of Browning cut in a circle and evidently once set in a locket; their wedding invitation; and, perhaps most sadly, Milt Meffert's 1905 pathetic, pleading letter, preserved by Amy along with newspaper accounts of Meffert's death in the late 1920s. According to a statement given by Emma Stevens during Amy's 1910 divorce proceeding, the breakup of the marriage was "all [Browning's] fault. . . . He can blame no one but himself, as she made him a kind, dutiful and affectionate wife." According to Mrs. Stevens, Browning abandoned his wife and left Louisville in June or July of 1909. "Because he refused to provide and support his wife I had to do that . . . he has not contributed anything towards her support and maintenance since he abandoned her." Asked about Browning's whereabouts, Mrs. Stevens replied, "I don't know where [the] defendant is now. It has been over a year since we heard from him." The last record of any communication between the couple, in fact, is a photograph signed "With Love, Tod," the day before Halloween 1909, suggesting that the June or

July "abandonment" was not quite as decisive as Emma Stevens asserted. Nonetheless, the marriage was indeed finished, and Amy Stevens was granted a divorce decree on Christmas Eve 1910. She never remarried, using the name Mrs. Amy Louise Stevens until her death in 1956 in Louisville at the age of seventy-three. Her death certificate noted her marital status as "single," instead of the more truthful "divorced."*

The next few years of Browning's life are less well documented. Mildred McAuliffe recalled impressionistic family stories that he had "lived with a woman in Chicago" for a time. Chicago was a prime center for vaudeville around 1910, the largest showcase outside of New York, with a dozen major houses. It was also the home base of the powerful Orpheum circuit (which had booked Leon Herrmann's American tours until his death in 1909). Actress Mary MacLaren, who worked with Browning in several films for Universal in the late teens, related a story told to her by Browning about his touring days, revealing the darker side of theatrical boardinghouses and their sometimes desperate denizens.

Browning was lodging at a hotel in a midwestern city—MacLaren vaguely recalled that it was Cleveland—when he found the door to his floor's shared bathroom closed for an unusually long time. After knocking, and receiving no answer, he opened the door. His impatience turned to horror when he discovered that the occupant, a destitute mother at the end of her wits, had appropriated the bathroom to rid herself of her family.

"She had two little children," MacLaren recalled Browning telling her. One was already lying dead on the floor. "She was holding the other little child, with the blood pouring out of its throat, into the tub." Browning told MacLaren he was "absolutely frozen." The woman "was completely oblivious. She didn't hear him knock; she had probably lost her mind then and there." Browning said he was torn between feelings of horrific revulsion and compassion for the "poor soul, to think what she had been through, to force her to do

* Amy's niece Marie Louise Stevens (1909–81) made a much happier show business marriage than her aunt. As Stevey Stevens, she appeared as a showgirl in the Ziegfeld Follies of 1931–33, and in 1934 married the silent-film actor William "Buster" Collier (1902–87). She was later well known as a San Francisco society hostess.

such a terrible thing." Browning quietly closed the door and called the police. The woman never looked up.

At the time of his grandmother's death at the age of eighty-five in April 1911, the *Louisville Courier-Journal* mentioned among her survivors "Tod Browning, a vaudeville performer, now playing in New York City." His next documented employment was a season-long stint with a variety burlesque show called *The Whirl of Mirth,* which debuted at the Casino Theater, Brooklyn, in August 1912. Like Browning, *Whirl* had a Louisville connection; its producer, the Whallen and Martell Company, was co-owned by Harry Martell and John H. Whallen, the latter a Louisville resident and a founder of the Empire Circuit Company, also known as the Western Burlesque Wheel. Whallen, who died in late 1913, was additionally a prominent Louisville businessman, former chief of police, and Democratic political figure. He also owned the Buckingham Theater, one of Louisville's two major vaudeville houses.

The Whirl of Mirth was an unusually elaborate production for the burlesque circuit; according to the *New York Clipper,* "a better dressed show [has] rarely hit the burlesque boards." The center-piece of the show was an opening act called "In Cartoon Land," wherein popular newspaper strips were brought to life. The most successful strip of the day was Bud Fischer's *Mutt and Jeff*—the char-acters were cultural superstars, having even been enshrined as wax-works at the Eden Musée. It fell to Browning to play the part of the racetrack habitué A. Mutt, his nose elongated with outlandish makeup. *Variety* praised his performance: "Browning is the best sub-ject," the trade paper opined on August 23, 1912. "His gaunt ap-pearance in the burlesque was good for a laugh all the time." The *New York Clipper* called Browning's performance "extremely funny," generating "an abundance of laughs." Elsewhere in the show, Browning took on the roles of "Silk Hat Harry" and "Sherlocko."

The Whirl of Mirth clocked nearly forty separate engagements in New York, Boston, Newark, Paterson, Philadelphia, Scranton, Balti-more, Washington, Cleveland, Cincinnati, Chicago, Milwaukee, Minneapolis, Omaha, Kansas City, St. Louis, Indianapolis, Detroit, Toronto, and Buffalo. But perhaps the biggest impact Browning made, on a personal level, was in his hometown of Louisville, where *The Whirl of Mirth* was booked for a week at John Whallen's Buckingham Theater in January 1913. The *Louisville Courier-Journal* noted that "Tod Browning, the 'Louisville Boy,'" was "very amusing," sharing honors with the show's headliner, Eddie B. Collins.*

The Whirl of Mirth evidently withstood a court challenge by Gus Hill, producer of the licensed stage musical *Mutt and Jeff,* claiming a copyright infringement in September 1912. The cartoon characters were still part of the show when it appeared in Louisville four months later.

Among the people taking note of Browning's return to Louisville was his former mother-in-law, Emma Stevens, who had not forgotten his desertion of her daughter. Nor had she forgotten his specific financial debts to her, and enumerated them all in an affidavit filed in the Louisville courts on January 17, 1913. So great was Emma's obsession that it included sums as small as one dollar loaned six years earlier, aggregating $231.65 in cash loans to Browning and clothing purchases for her daughter. Browning, however, escaped the Louisville limelight for an engagement in Indianapolis before the Jefferson County Circuit Court could take action against him.

The Whirl of Mirth returned Browning to Brooklyn in the spring of 1913, where his well-honed burlesque routines brought him to the attention of the comedian Charlie Murray, a former circus performer then working for Biograph Studios in New York, cranking out one-reel nickelodeon comedies for an up-and-coming director named David Wark Griffith.

Much like Tod Browning himself, the motion picture had worked its way up from carnival roots; early magic-lantern displays had been part of the repertoire of the famed French magician Robert-Houdin, and later formed a part of P. T. Barnum's "black tent" circus sideshow. That a link would be forged between vaudeville and the early motion picture was inevitable, given the short

---

* Collins, who moved into motion pictures in the mid-1930s, provided movement cues to Walt Disney animators for the dwarf Dopey in Snow White (1938). Among the supplemental material included on the Snow White Deluxe LaserDisc Edition (1994) is live-action test footage of Collins later rotoscoped for use in the animated feature.

length of the typical vaudeville skit and its emphasis on broad physical comedy, both of which were ideally suited to the technological capacities of the early film medium.

Like Browning, D. W. Griffith was a son of Kentucky; the two men had, in fact, been enrolled in the Louisville public school system at the same time, although there is no documentation that they knew each other at the time (Griffith was four years Browning's senior). Both men, however, made their first forays into show business in 1890s Louisville—Griffith in a local theater company and Browning in a carnival. Charlie Murray, later a popular member of Mack Sennett's roster, introduced Browning to Griffith, who immediately hired him to appear with Murray in a pair of Biograph comedies, *Scenting a Terrible Crime* and *A Fallen Hero,* both released in October 1913.

Scenting a Terrible Crime was a farce about an odiferous tub of sauerkraut and the comic chain reaction it sets in motion. Browning made his screen debut as an undertaker—an appropriate thematic harbinger of the directorial career that was to come. *A Fallen Hero* featured "queer make-up effects and grotesque characters," according to *Moving Picture World,* in a story concerning a rivalry for a judgeship.

Tired of a grinding production schedule—he directed some 450 pictures for Biograph from 1908—and the studio's resistance to anything longer or more ambitious than formula one-reelers, Griffith broke with Biograph in the fall of 1913, relocating to California to assume directorship of the Reliance-Majestic company. Reliance-Majestic was one of several production units under the umbrella of the Mutual Film Corporation, which would also distribute the famous Keystone Comedies and, beginning in 1916, make Charles Chaplin its biggest star ever.

Before his break with Biograph, one of Griffith's ongoing problems was the unreliability of his actors, many of whom felt that screen acting was beneath contempt from an artistic standpoint, but nonetheless provided easy money between "legitimate" assignments; whenever Broadway beckoned, their interest in the bastard medium of film would summarily evaporate. Additionally, film's emphasis on the visual aspect of performance at the expense of speech and elocution made it possible to successfully employ players who would be laughed off the stage in a traditional theatrical venue. Griffith had a tense relationship with Mary Pickford, for instance, whose fealty could never be taken for granted. If, as Mary later wrote, "a little girl fresh from a department store could give a performance as good or better than any of us who had spent years mastering our technique, then pictures were not for me. I would return to the theater, where the years of study and effort were a safeguard against the encroachment of amateurs." Pickford, of course, eventually found her greatest success in the movies, but her ambivalence about the "amateur" aspects of the cinema were not unusual.

In Tod Browning, Griffith found a reliable player without high-falutin ambitions in the theater. Another loyal performer, first hired in 1911, was Lionel Barrymore, whose theatrical career had capsized despite his membership in America's most illustrious family of thespians. Browning and Barrymore would later have a sustained, if sometimes testy, professional relationship at Metro-Goldwyn-Mayer, but for the moment they were both aspiring hopefuls under Griffith (who used Barrymore, at first, only as an extra).

Both actors followed Griffith to Los Angeles, where he set up operations at the former Kinemacolor Studios at 4500 Sunset Boulevard. The Reliance-Majestic amalgamation included a subsidiary, the Komic Company, which would provide Browning with steady employment through the spring of 1915. He acted in nearly fifty Komic pictures, all one-reelers that gave him ample opportunity to develop his comedic talents. As Griffith assistant cameraman Karl Brown recalled, "Tod Browning used a cane as his trademark and spent most of his time thinking up new ways to get tangled up in it."

Browning's first West Coast picture, *An Interrupted Séance,* amusingly anticipated the phony-medium theme he would summon up repeatedly in his later years as a director. In the film, two out-of-work friends decide to try for an easy buck as clairvoyants, but their facility for creating spirit-rapping on the ceiling is so energetic that it results in an avalanche of plaster, powdering the investigating landlord beyond recognition. Judging from trade press accounts of these early films, most of which are now lost, the endless reaching for new forms of physical comedy sometimes crossed the line between the merely broad and the downright crude. Browning had top billing in *Nell's Eugenic Wedding* (1914), written by the precocious teenage scenarist Anita Loos—later world-famous for *Gentlemen Prefer Blondes*—which drew the following terse notice from *Moving Picture World*: "There is nothing funny or elevating in having a man eat soap and vomit all over creation as a result of his diet. Because most people will take this view it may be said that *Nell's Eugenic Wedding* does not belong."

Another 1914 production starring Browning was *Victims of Speed,* in which a pair of hoboes, Weary Willie (Browning) and Dusty Rhoades obtain "speed germs" from a nutty doctor enabling them to perform ordinary tasks in comically accelerated time. The now-lost film presumably made use of a slow-cranked camera to give the illusion of dizzying energy. For director Edward Dillon, Browning also created the continuing role of attorney James Hadley (The Boss) in a newspaper-originated series featuring the character Bill the Office Boy (portrayed by the celebrated New York gate-crasher Tammany Young). Fay Tincher, another Komic regular, appeared as Ethel the Stenographer in this series. Known for her humorous exaggeration and outlandish fashion sense, Tincher, a trade magazine noted, "does not hesitate to make herself grotesque, and actually repulsive, for art's sake. She thoroughly enjoys the reputation of being awkward and hideous on the screen." *Bill's Job,* the first of the seventeen episodes in which Browning appeared, was released on July 5, 1914.

Griffith himself was no longer personally directing one-reel comedies; he was immersed in the production of an epic called *The Clansman* (later retitled *The Birth of a Nation*), which bore as much relationship to the Biograph one-reelers as a moon landing did to Kitty Hawk.

It is difficult to understate the impact Griffith had on the emerging film medium; although he was sentimentally attached to the conventions of nineteenth-century melodrama, he had an instinctive grasp of film's need to break away from proscenium-stage compositions. Thomas Edison's original dream of the motion picture anticipated vivid reproductions of stage dramas and operas, right down to the drop curtain, recorded by a camera in a fixed position. Griffith had a more fluid conception of the camera's role, although some viewers thought he was insane when they saw his first experiments with close-ups, medium shots, and rapid montage. How could audiences ever accept actors cut off at the waist, or pictured as grotesquely looming, disembodied heads? But Griffith's visionary technical innovations were offset by mawkishness and questionable taste; *The Birth of a Nation,* with its perverse glorification of the Ku Klux Klan, may have been a true reflection of Griffith's sentiments as a southerner, but was distinctly out of the mainstream of American opinion fifty years after the end of the Civil War.

Despite such miscalculations, Griffith was a feisty, charismatic presence in American culture. "He must have been in his early thirties," recalled Anita Loos, "but he had an authority that seemed to deny that he had ever been young. His high arched nose belonged to some Roman emperor; his pale eyes, in sharp contrast to the tan of his complexion, sparkled with a sort of archaic amusement, as if he were constantly saying to himself, 'What fools these mortals be.' " Tod Browning's fiercely independent grandmother, waving the Confederate flag from her homestead in Louisville, no doubt would have been his ideal audience.

Browning's romantic companion at the time he went to work for the Griffith organization was a pretty, wide-eyed young woman from Missouri named Alice Lillian Houghton, an actress whom he had met and toured with in vaudeville. Alice had relatives in Chicago, but the extent to which she toured theatrically is not clear. Whatever the circumstances of their meeting, and whatever initial basis of their attraction, they did share one thing in common: both had survived early, premature marriages by walking out on their respective spouses.

On June 14, 1887, in O'Fallon, Missouri, thirty miles west of St.

Louis, Alice Houghton was born into a family that later achieved social prominence in the piano trade in Helena, Montana—at least judging from the profusion of details that accompanied the *Helena Daily Independent*'s reporting of her March 1907 wedding to J. Douglas Wilson, Jr., of Portland, Oregon. The romance may have been largely a schoolgirl infatuation; a later, Hollywood acquaintance remembered that Alice had attended an exclusive women's school in the Pacific Northwest. The air of gaiety that surrounded the nuptials—several card parties and luncheons in Alice's honor; a surprise dousing of the bride by a bag of rice suspended from the ceiling; gifts of hand-painted cologne bottles (Alice's handiwork) to the assembled guests; her wedding gown of white crepe de chine over white silk, the veil held in place by natural orange blossoms; the beautiful gifts of silver and cut glass—gave no hint of the unhappy union that was to follow. The final documentation of Alice Houghton's marriage to Douglas Wilson is the *Daily Independent*'s description of the bride's going-away gown, "green and plaid, with hat to correspond," as the newlyweds departed for a brief honeymoon stop in Butte.

The details of Douglas Wilson's eventual complaint against his wife, filed in the divorce proceeding he undertook in San Francisco in 1915, have long since been destroyed by the courts. Only the judgment has survived, but it makes clear that on May 5, 1914, Alice Wilson "willfully, without cause and against plaintiff's consent, with the intention of so doing, deserted and abandoned plaintiff and has ever since such date continued willfully, and with such intent and without cause to so desert and abandon him and to live separate and apart from him without his consent." The couple claimed as joint property a six-room house with furnishings at 397 46th Street North in Portland. Despite her desertion of Wilson, and failure to answer his divorce action, the court nonetheless awarded her half the property. Exempt from the joint property decree was a piano belonging to Alice.

Alice Wilson worked professionally under her married name as well as the stage name Alice Rae. George Marshall, an extra who would become one of Hollywood's most prolific directors, lived with Wilson and Browning in an apartment house called the Reiter Arms on a hilltop at the intersection of Sunset and Hollywood boulevards, across the street from the Reliance-Majestic studios. He was unaware that they were unmarried. "She was always Alice Browning to me," he remembered. But William S. Hart's wife, Winifred Westover, remembered that Alice lived in a separate apartment in the building with her parents, Effie and George Houghton, relocated to California. Director Allan Dwan, who also knew the couple at the time, recalled in 1972 that Browning had an earlier major involvement with a woman named Alice Ladley, before meeting Alice Wilson.

Also living at the Reiter Arms was Frank Borzage, another character actor who would find his real career as a director, and George Siegmann, who created the role of the mulatto in *The Birth of a Nation*. George Marshall recalled the "big family" atmosphere of the house, and the frequent parties and card games, often lubricated with generous amounts of liquor. Strip poker was a popular pastime, and Marshall remembered how actress Dorothy Davenport, framed by the other players, artfully retained her decorum by careful arrangement of her abundant, waist-length hair. Davenport's husband, Wallace Reid, like George Siegmann, had done memorable work in *The Birth of a Nation*, but unlike his other housemates with promising futures, Reid's would be cut short by head injuries sustained in a train accident on the way to a film location in 1919. Reid survived the accident, but excruciating headaches left him hopelessly addicted to painkillers. He would finally die in an asylum.

Of the 1914 housemates, Tod Browning had begun to display evidence of the same substance-abuse problem that had overwhelmed his uncle Pete. Director Raoul Walsh, then also a member of the Reliance-Majestic Company, recalled Browning in a 1978 interview at the age of ninety. "When Tod first came to the Griffith organization, he was a pretty good comedian," Walsh said. "He was known as a daring guy. He'd take a chance with anything." Walsh knew Browning was from Kentucky "because he was always talking about Kentucky whiskey . . . he always had a bottle of laughing water with him." In Walsh's view, "he never got drunk. . . . never lost control of himself. He'd stay up half the night, drinkin' and playin' cards and then come to the studio in the morning looking fresh as a daisy," the director remembered. "He had a thing for flashy cars, too. I guess that went with the whiskey."

Browning's car habits were noted by a trade magazine in the summer of 1914. "Tod Browning, comedian of the Komic-Mutual combination, bought a French racing car three weeks ago," *Reel Life* reported. "Since buying the machine Browning has ridden in it four times and has had four accidents. His speedometer shows that he has traveled a fraction over twenty-one miles in the car. The machine has been out of the repair shop only one day." In spite of the apparent jinx on the machine, or the owner's ability to drive it, "Browning still persists [*sic*] that he has a good car and promises to demolish some speed records as soon as he gets out of the garage and the automobile gets out of the hospital or vice versa, which is the way Browning and the car have been most of the time he's had it." Another *Reel Life* profile the same year suggested that the hand-cuff-escape tricks he had learned in his carnival days might still be useful should his "speeding mania" ever get him into trouble.

Browning had graduated from acting at Komic to directing for Reliance-Majestic, and completed eleven one- and two-reelers between March and June 1915. His first directorial effort, anticipating the tone of much of his later output, was a "crook" story called *The Lucky Transfer,* about a female reporter who uncovers a jewel theft, followed by lurid-sounding titles like *The Slave Girl, The Spell of the Poppy, The Living Death,* and *The Burned Hand.* These last two are especially important as harbingers of his future work. *The Living Death* was a grim drama about an overprotective doctor and father who deliberately misdiagnoses his prospective son-in-law's poison ivy as leprosy to prevent his daughter's marriage. *The Burned Hand* also centered on a semi-incestuous theme: a divorced man kidnaps his daughter, burning her sweetheart's hand when he attempts to rescue her, but the sweetheart's best friend also brands himself with fire in an effort to conceal his pal's identity. Both *The Living Death* and *The Burned Hand* introduced two leitmotifs of the later Browning oeuvre: tense, obsessive relationships between fathers and daughters and the omnipresent threat of physical mutilation or branding.

Actress Miriam Cooper, who starred in *The Burned Hand,* remembered Browning as "a tall, skinny, very remarkable man" who had the habit of pronouncing her first name as if it rhymed with "Hiram." " 'Hi, Miram, how the hell are you.' That would shock me in those days. I thought, 'What a horribly common man,' and I didn't even answer him. Then he would yell it again as loud as he could, 'How the hell are you, Miram.' Browning was himself, and he didn't care what anyone else thought about him."

Also completed in the spring of 1915 was *The Highbinders,* the first of many Browning melodramas with Chinatown settings, and *The Woman from Warren's,* in which a shop girl, betrayed by a seductive villain, foils his plan to similarly exploit another. *Little Marie,* the last picture he would direct for Reliance, was a prototype Browning revenge melodrama, wherein an Italian laborer, attempting to kill the employer who fired him, nearly dynamites his own beloved daughter instead.

On top of these many seminal projects, Browning also found time to assist D. W. Griffith with *The Mother and the Law,* a modern melodrama which would be the cornerstone of Griffith's four-story masterpiece *Intolerance.* Additionally, Browning appeared in the film as the owner of an automobile who lends his car to save a wrongly condemned man in a last-minute, breakneck race.

But shortly after playing an automotive Good Samaritan on-screen, he would enact a cruel travesty of the role in real life.

TWO

SHADOWS OF BABYLON

Browning (with megaphone) directing Under Two Flags *(1922) on location at Oxnard, California.* (Elias Savada collection)

PART TWO

BRANCHES OF FASHION

After hours, Browning and members of the Griffith company enjoyed cutting loose at watering holes like the Watts Tavern and the Vernon Road House, each requiring a significant commute by car in a time when "designated drivers," much less speed limits and even driver's licenses, were unheard-of. Sometimes the California nights were so foggy that one of the passengers would have to get out and walk in front of the car to be sure the way was clear. On the return route from the Vernon Road House was a "very bad crossing," remembered Allan Dwan, where freight cars painted black would stop across the road without signals.

On the night of June 16, 1915, Browning led a party of friends to the Vernon nightspot, where the drinking continued far after midnight. Among the revelers was a charismatic young comedian named William Elmer Booth,* who, under the professional name of Elmer Booth, had joined the Komic Company as Browning's replacement in the *Bill* pictures with Tammany Young only three months earlier. The thirty-two-year-old Booth, a compact performer with highly expressive features, had already made motion picture history by appearing as the first gangster ever identified as such in

---

* *Booth, a Los Angeles native, had a younger sister, Margaret Booth, who would later be employed by Griffith as a film cutter and who would eventually become one of M-G-M's most respected film editors, her credits ranging from* Mutiny on the Bounty *(1935) to* Annie *(1982).*

Griffith's *The Musketeers of Pig Alley,* opposite Lillian Gish in 1912. He had made a stage hit with Douglas Fairbanks in *The Cad,* on tour with the comedy *Stop, Thief,* and during the slow summer theatrical seasons had filmed numerous shorts for Griffith in New York, appearing in films with Mary Pickford and May Irwin. His move to Hollywood was widely considered to be the beginning of an enormously promising film career.

Booth sat next to Browning on the foggy drive home from Vernon, and no one bothered to walk ahead of the car. Also in the vehicle, or the one following, was a Booth relative named Edward Joseph Booth, as well as George Siegmann. Browning, apparently, drove as fast as he could manage under the circumstances, and when the car reached the blocked railway intersection at Santa Fe Avenue and the Salt Lake tracks, he collided at full speed with a flatbed car loaded with iron rails. They connected with Elmer Booth's face with the force of a stamping press, killing him instantly. "The impresses in his skull," the *Los Angeles Times* reported, "were as even and regular as the design of a waffle off the grill." George Siegmann suffered four broken ribs, a deep laceration on the thigh, and internal injuries. Of the survivors, Browning was hurt the worst, his right leg fractured in three places below the knee, his upper body pinned and crushed, with unspecified internal injuries that, according to the *San Francisco Chronicle,* made his recovery "doubtful." The *Los Angeles Times,* milking the story for a sex angle, included the question "Were any women in the car when actor was killed?" in its stack of headlines, stating that spectators had reported females of "mysterious identity" as "members of the merry party returning from the roadhouse revels."

Director Allan Dwan was a member of the party that night, though he was traveling in a separate car. "I wasn't far behind him," Dwan said, "and remember we came up to the excitement and panic and wondered what the hell it was." To Dwan's horror, "We discovered it was our friends. . . . they were picking pieces of them up here and there." Dwan didn't qualify his description, and it is possible that Booth's body, ripped from the car by the force of the collision, was mutilated far beyond the already-unpleasant description given by the press. It is also possible that some of the "pieces" lying about were Browning's teeth. Browning wore full dentures from an early age, something he would sometimes attribute to being "kicked by a horse." The dentures never fit properly and caused him considerable discomfort, which he later complained about endlessly, and which suggests a somewhat more complicated initial trauma than a simple loss of teeth. In any event, it is more than likely that Browning carried a painful oral reminder of the night of June 16, 1915, for the rest of his life. In the years following the accident, the bristling mustache he had previously worn only sporadically became a permanent facial fixture, one that he never stopped twirling, touching, and teasing. Dentofacial injuries tend to have significant psychological ramifications, and for a man, teeth have a primal symbolic resonance with hardness, aggression, and maleness—the loss of teeth can be experienced as a kind of emasculation. But aside from complaints about his false teeth, Browning never talked about the accident or his injury to any of his colleagues interviewed for this book; nor did he seem to have ever openly communicated feelings of responsibility for Elmer Booth's death.

Booth's funeral on June 18 was attended by virtually the entire Reliance-Majestic Company and required an entourage of twenty-eight automobiles. D. W. Griffith gave a moving, impromptu eulogy at the grave. Browning and Siegmann did not hear it, of course; Siegmann was treated at the Receiving Hospital for his injuries and released to recuperate at home, but Browning would remain in the California Hospital for weeks. A coroner's inquest was held on the day of Booth's funeral, which ruled the death accidental, due to "lack of precaution by both parties," referring to Browning and Los Angeles Street Railway conductor H. H. Jones, who nonetheless stated that he had been waving a signal lantern at the time of the crash.

The exact length of Browning's hospital confinement can be only vaguely determined from trade paper press reports of his recuperation, but the accident seems to have laid him up for most of the summer of 1915. Actress Mary MacLaren, who later worked in four films for Browning, remembered that "he was in bed for almost a year . . . it must have been ghastly for him." The Louisville city directory for 1916 (compiled in 1915) lists him as a boarder in his family's home, suggesting that he spent at least part of his recovery period in Kentucky.

The first news reports of his returning to work, in Griffith's scenario department, appeared in September. Browning must have been amazed when he returned to 4500 Sunset Boulevard and first encountered the monumental Babylonian sets that Griffith had constructed for *The Mother and the Law,* which had grown, since the spring, from a modest modern melodrama into a sprawling, multinarrative historical epic. The sets weren't just big—they were, and remain, some of the most imposing structures ever built for a motion picture, towering nearly 150 feet in an architectural delirium of columns, friezes, and statuary, including a full squadron of thirty-foot-high, rearing plaster elephants.

Griffith, impressed (and not a little threatened) by the historical Italian film epic *Cabiria,* decided that it would be a mistake to follow up his own epic, *The Birth of a Nation,* with a film as limited in scale as *The Mother and the Law.* He devised a complex narrative employing three additional stories—French, Judean, and Babylonian—each echoing the themes of the others through elaborate cross-editing. Griffith intended to produce the most dazzling motion picture to date, and succeeded, at least from a technical standpoint. Ultimately titled *Intolerance* (partly as an oblique reference to the lack of tolerance that greeted *The Birth of a Nation* in many quarters), the film proved confusing to audiences and was not the box-office hit that had been expected. The production was largely —and complexly—financed by the coffers of Reliance-Majestic, which enjoyed a positive cash flow from its prodigious output of small-scale pictures, such as those assigned to Tod Browning.

As Browning returned to work under the surreal shadows of Babylon, the hot, powerful Santa Ana winds also made a comeback, seriously threatening to topple the *Intolerance* sets. Battleship moorings anchored to buried railroad ties (picturesquely called dead men) stabilized the Babylonian edifices as Browning himself began to rebalance his professional life in the less physically demanding role of a screenwriter. During the first eleven months of his re-employment, he was credited with only three scripts, *The Queen of the Band, Sunshine Dad,* and *The Mystery of the Leaping Fish*—the first two of which may have been completed before the accident—strongly suggesting that his full recuperation was nowhere as rapid or robust as trade paper items indicated. Allan Dwan noted that Browning's overall level of physical activity was permanently limited after the crash, and that he never again participated in sports or exercised even mildly.

The two-reel *Queen of the Band* and the five-reel *Sunshine Dad* were both jewel-heist stories; *The Mystery of the Leaping Fish* was an outrageous farce in two reels with Douglas Fairbanks in the role of an eccentric scientific detective named Coke Ennyday, who, true to his name, uses cocaine injections to help him nab an opium smuggler. Fairbanks' laboratory is a cartoonish set recalling the decor of Georges Méliès' turn-of-the-century trick films; the actor wears a clownish checked suit and drives a matching automobile, and lives by a clocklike device whose hand points in turn to the words DOPE, SLEEP, DRINKS, and EATS. The film's use of stylized sets and costumes, while interesting, is inconsistent, and the paradoxical theme of one addictive drug being used to suppress another is handled without any sense of irony.

Griffith had by this time entered into a complicated partnership with Mack Sennett and the dynamic producer-director-screenwriter Thomas Ince, who had launched the film career of western star William S. Hart. The new venture, in which the three producers maintained autonomous studios, was called Triangle, and, for the year it lasted, Browning worked for the subsidiary called Triangle–Fine Arts. By the summer of 1916 he was ready to direct again, and his comeback effort was a stylized experiment called *Puppets,* featuring live actors in the puppetlike costumes of a harlequinade, and sets graphically rendered in minimalist black and white. Two other short programmers followed, *Everybody's Doing It,* about a crook who manipulates a society youth into committing a bold robbery by making the boy believe he is aiding a damsel in distress, and *The*

Deadly Glass of Beer, about the temptation of a young man who stands to inherit a fortune provided he doesn't touch a drop of brew before the age of twenty-one.

One of Browning's closest friends in the late teens was William S. Hart, who counted Browning among the most memorable of the dozens of film folk who frequented an eatery called the Hoffman Café, "that was real 'Bohemia.'" Included among the habitués were Mack Sennett; Mrs. Talmadge and her up-and-coming daughters, Norma, Constance, and Natalie; director Chester Franklin; actor (and later producer) Raymond Griffith; George Siegmann; and many others. Hart recalled that the Hoffman had a round table designed to seat seven people. "From 6 to 9 P.M. there were seldom less than fourteen dining at it. It did not matter if your tip was a dime or two bits (there were certainly none higher), Fritz, the waiter, played no favorites." Fritz often got in on the conversations himself, until one of the "family" would ask pointedly whether their order of pig's knuckles and sauerkraut would arrive in time for dinner, or breakfast.

Browning's first feature-length directorial assignment came in early 1917 with *Jim Bludso,* based on the celebrated ballad by John Hay, the secretary of state under Presidents William McKinley and Teddy Roosevelt, and its stage adaptation by I. N. Morris. In the original Hay ballad, Bludso was the brave captain of a burning steamboat who sacrifices his life in order that the passengers may escape with theirs. By way of the theater and Hollywood, however, the brief, tragic poem was thoroughly subverted as a full-length romantic melodrama in which the martyr Bludso would manage to escape with both his life and his girl. Despite the liberties taken with the original story, *Jim Bludso* was nonetheless a critical triumph for the director. "The production given it by Tod Browning is quite without the limits of adverse criticism," *Motion Picture News* opined. Reviewers were mightily impressed by the spectacles of a bursting levee, an ensuing flood, and the burning of the steamboat *Prairie Belle,* all accomplished on location without the aid of miniatures or studio effects.

It is, perhaps, significant that Browning's first major production took place in the riverboat milieu that had been so much part of his youth. "The charm in the story of *Jim Bludso* lies not so much in the plot as in the witchery of the river scenes with which it is surrounded," wrote the *New York Dramatic Mirror*. "You feel that the river is personified as a member of the cast; it is a benevolent friend of the hero in its milder moments and a fierce and vindictive villain when it overflows and wrecks the little village on its banks." Winifred Westover Hart, who acted in the film, recalled that it was filmed in San Francisco, Rio Vista, and a marshy area outside Los Angeles then called Nigger Slough, California.* Two full-scale riverboats were used, one operable and one a wreck that could be completely destroyed by fire. Special state permission was required to perform such stunts on the navigable waters of the Sacramento River, and was obtained with some difficulty. Wilfred Lucas, the actor who played Bludso, is frequently listed as co-director with Browning, but Hart remembered clearly that the shared credit was at the "pushy" insistence of the star, who "didn't direct *Jim Bludso* any more than I did." In Hart's memory, the entire production went smoothly and, more important, convivially, with Browning at the helm. Al Joy, a cartoonist from the *San Francisco Examiner,* was allowed to play a riverboat gambler, "just for fun." When the production wrapped, Browning, a devoted orientalist since his early days in stage magic, who could speak Chinese to some degree, personally supervised an elaborate celebratory dinner for the entire company at a nearby Mandarin settlement.

Browning directed two more productions for Triangle, *A Love Sublime,* a modern interpretation of the Orpheus legend (in which Alice Wilson had a supporting role), and *Hands Up!,* a convoluted crime melodrama based on an original story by a convicted felon. But when D. W. Griffith left the Triangle combine in 1917, Browning also departed, contracting his services to Metro Pictures for five films, most of them to be produced in New York. Alice Wilson followed Browning east, and they were married at the Salem Baptist Church in New Rochelle, New York, on June 11, 1917. Alice's lack

---

* *Now the Los Angeles Harbor Park Golf Course in Torrance.*

of divorce papers from her brief first marriage may have delayed their nuptials, but Winifred Hart's father, the president of the San Francisco Press Club, undertook a West Coast search for a copy of the decree, and was successful, allowing the couple to obtain a New York marriage license.

Browning's first two Metro films, *Peggy, the Will o' the Wisp* (1917), and *The Jury of Fate* (1917) both starred Mabel Taliaferro— the screen's reigning ingenue before the dawn of Mary Pickford. *Peggy* concerned a modern-day female Robin Hood, and *Jury* was a cleverly conceived trick film set in the Canadian north woods, in which Taliaferro played opposite herself through double-exposure techniques that were quite ambitious for the time. Browning's growing sophistication in the use of cinematography is reflected in a *Moving Picture World* interview about *Peggy*, in which he called for a move to "rational lighting," that is, identifiable sources of illumination. "The day for magical light is over," he said, almost anticipating his later reputation as a partisan of cinematic shadows. "What could be more foolish than a flood of light, either on stage or screen, when a painted 'set' reveals a cloudy sky, and yet that is the way it almost invariably appears in dramatic presentations of all kinds. Light should come from natural sources and should not, as if by magic, appear for no reason, equally strong at all points."

Browning's third Metro outing was *The Eyes of Mystery,* a melodramatic offering filled with sliding doors, secret stairways, "seeing" portraits, and similar gothic gadgetry.

In 1918 the New York–based Metro, energized by $2.6 million in recapitalization, leased the old Quality studios in Hollywood in order to begin West Coast operations. The whole industry was by this time consolidating in Los Angeles where, among other things, outdoor shooting could proceed year-round (winter effects could be improvised anywhere, but no one could convincingly fake summer). In addition, land was available for expansion; in 1915 a one-time immigrant haberdasher named Carl Laemmle incorporated a 250-acre municipality, Universal City, for the express purpose of making motion pictures.

Browning returned to California to direct two more features. *The Legion of Death,* recounting the real-life story of female Russian revolutionaries, was intended as a splashy inaugural showpiece for Metro's California operation, and was well received. *Revenge,* released a few weeks later, was a small-town melodrama set in Arizona, in which a woman tracks down the murderer of her fiancé. By this time a distinct pattern had appeared in his post-accident body of work distinguishing it from the comedy that had been his specialty before 1915. Now his focus was moralistic melodrama, with recurrent themes of crime, culpability, and retribution.

In the spring of 1918, Browning left Metro when the studio's plans to have him direct two prestige pictures in New York starring either Ethel Barrymore or Alla Nazimova failed to materialize. He collaborated on the continuity for a standard crime drama, *Which Woman?,* for Bluebird, a Universal production unit, but was handed the directorial megaphone when the film's first director, Harry Pollard, fell ill during production.

Next, he was paired with a rising Universal ingenue named Priscilla Dean for *The Deciding Kiss,* a romantic society drama which showed off to good advantage Dean's striking, almost patrician face. But her screen image was highly dependent on camera angles and costuming, which could mask qualities that would have sunk the career of a stage performer. "She had tremendous legs," recalled veteran Hollywood story editor Samuel Marx, then working at Universal. But he didn't mean "tremendous" as a compliment. According to Marx, Dean's ample appendages caused her so much grief that she submitted to a surgical operation in an attempt to reduce them. Dean's somewhat haughty air was not everyone's cup of tea, but it suited her well for the roles of lady thieves, guttersnipes, and adventuresses that would soon become her specialty in Browning-directed productions.

Without Dean, Browning directed another heiress film, this one a light melodrama called *Set Free,* about a bored, rebellious young woman of means (Edith Roberts) who runs away from her family disguised as a Gypsy. Once more, Browning coscripted a story about a flight from comfortable, conventional life into a carnivalesque world of tricksters and con artists—a theme distinctly echoing his own experiences.

At Universal, Browning met the two men who, together and separately, would have the greatest shaping influences on his career. Universal's studio manager from the end of 1918 was a twenty-year-old "boy wonder" from Brooklyn named Irving G. Thalberg, who had, within the space of a year, risen from the position of Carl Laemmle's private secretary to that of the studio's chief decision-maker. Outwardly, it was a perfect success story for the age of Horatio Alger, but the glamorous legend had its dark side. Thalberg's burning ambition for early success may well have had its roots in his own lifelong sense of impending doom. Thalberg had been born a blue baby, and doctors held out little hope that he would achieve a normal life span. Thalberg's physique would remain painfully underdeveloped, almost stunted, all his life. His fiercely protective mother nursed him through a sickly childhood and adolescence, but at the age of sixteen, a lengthy bout with rheumatic fever further damaged his heart and dashed his plans for college. Thalberg's grandmother had a summer cottage on Long Island, next to one owned by Carl Laemmle, who projected all his latest films on a sheet hung outdoors. The boy, who had no particular ambitions in motion pictures, nonetheless impressed Laemmle, who offered him a job, first in Universal's New York office and then in Hollywood. As Laemmle's personal secretary, Thalberg soon had a comprehensive overview of the studio's operations. When he suggested to Laemmle that Universal might need a general manager, Laemmle gave the job to Thalberg, then twenty-one years old. Thalberg recognized and encouraged Browning's flair for underworld pictures and was responsible for his pairing with Priscilla Dean.

The other shaping influence on Browning's career was a then-obscure young actor with haunted, working-class features. His professional name was Lon Chaney. Leonidas (later Leonard and finally Lon) Chaney was born on April 1, 1882, in Colorado Springs, Colorado, the second of five children born to Frank and Emma

Chaney. Both parents were deaf. Frank, a barber, was known with backhanded affection as Dummy Chaney to his loyal patrons in Colorado Springs, which had a thriving deaf community and was home to the Colorado School for the Deaf. Emma Chaney was bedridden for several years after the birth of her last child, and Lon, then about twelve years old, acted as her link to the larger world, using sign language and pantomime to relate the day's news. It has always been part of Chaney's legend that the practical requirements of communicating with his parents also provided basic training in theater. Throughout his adolescence, Chaney worked as a prop boy and stagehand at the Colorado Springs Opera House, but also, more prosaically, as a wallpaper hanger and carpet layer. He made his debut as an amateur actor at the age of nineteen. Within a few years he was touring extensively with often threadbare troupes, making a name for himself as a song-and-dance man, primarily in venues west of the Mississippi. In many ways his early professional career paralleled that of Tod Browning, who was touring in vaudeville around the same time.

In 1905, while performing in Oklahoma City, Chaney met a sixteen-year-old singer named Cleva Creighton. A romance and pregnancy ensued, and the couple was finally married on May 31, 1906, three months after the birth of their son, Creighton Tull Chaney, later known professionally as Lon Chaney, Jr. The marriage proved shaky—Cleva was alcoholic and emotionally unstable—and reached a breaking point on April 29, 1913, in Los Angeles when Cleva, standing in the wings of the Majestic Theater while Chaney stage-managed a performance, attempted suicide by swallowing a vial of bichloride of mercury. She survived, but the poison permanently damaged her vocal cords and her singing career was destroyed. Later in the year Chaney filed for divorce, charging his wife with adultery, "habitual intemperance," and the infliction of mental anguish. Chaney was finally awarded custody of their son, whom he placed in a foster-care facility while trying to stabilize his career in the burgeoning motion picture industry in Los Angeles.

The date of Chaney's first appearance in film is not known, but his biographer, Michael F. Blake, speculates that his first bit roles probably occurred around 1912. Chaney had filled character parts in at least seven pictures for Universal beginning in 1913 with IMP/ Universal's *Poor Jake's Demise*, but had backslid to the properties department when he came to the attention of director Allan Dwan. "He used to be my property man at Universal, and he'd come around with these spiky teeth and things on his face, for no reason. And I said, 'What the hell is all that for? You want to be an actor?' " Chaney told Dwan of his previous acting experience and his eagerness to act again. "I stuck him in a couple of things and let him wear some of those teeth," said Dwan, "and people began to notice him." In reality, Dwan used Chaney in a total of seventeen Universal two-, three-, and four-reelers from late 1913 to late 1914.

Tod Browning's first encounter with Lon Chaney no doubt took place in the fall of 1918, shortly after Browning began directing for Universal's Bluebird brand. Their first picture together was *The Wicked Darling* (1919), a pickpocket melodrama that established Priscilla Dean firmly as a new kind of film heroine, one who managed to live on both sides of the law, titillating audiences with a kind of vicarious criminality for several reels before making a virtuous turnabout in the last. Chaney played Dean's pickpocket cohort, "Stoop" Connors. *The Wicked Darling* was also significant in teaming Browning for the first time with scenarist Waldemar Young, with whom he would later create some of his most successful films for M-G-M. But the first professional association of Browning and Chaney did not lead immediately to an ongoing collaboration; Chaney left Universal for Paramount to play a role that would transform his own career and, six years later, profoundly influence Browning's.

The part that attracted Chaney was Frog, the bogus cripple of George M. Cohan's 1914 Broadway hit *The Miracle Man,* based on the novel by Frank L. Packard. The story was being adapted and directed for Paramount by George Loane Tucker, who originally planned to use an experienced contortionist for the character, who fakes a miraculous recovery as part of a faith-healing scam. But Tucker found that real contortionists couldn't act, and selected Chaney instead. The actor's corkscrew-limbed, rolling-eyed inter-

pretation of the character proved more than convincing, drawing
extravagant critical attention and setting the mold for the kinds of
roles that would propel him to 1920s superstardom.

Browning continued at Universal with a series of fairly undistin-
guished but nonetheless profitable six-reelers in 1919, including
another Priscilla Dean "supercrook" vehicle, *The Exquisite Thief,*
and four pictures starring Mary MacLaren: *The Unpainted Woman,* a
rural social drama; *The Petal on the Current,* based on the novelette
by Fannie Hurst about a young girl unjustly accused of a crime;
Bonnie, Bonnie Lassie, a change-of-pace comedy drama set in the
Scottish highlands; and *The Pointing Finger,* which Browning produced, with Edward Morrissey and Edward Kull directing.

Mary MacLaren had a positive, admiring opinion of Browning
—at least until she worked with him on *The Petal on the Current.*
"Tod I could never forget," she said in a 1972 interview. "He was
wonderful, but he was a skunk as well. He played a very, very dirty
trick on me," she said, recalling the San Francisco location shoot
for *Petal.* On the occasion of her twentieth birthday, "my mother
and sister Katherine [MacDonald, also a film actress] had given me
a beautiful diamond sapphire bar pin—bar pins were very much in
the vogue. We were staying at the St. Francis Hotel . . . Tod took
me out to a couple of nightclubs. We had a few drinks and I was
afraid to go back to the hotel—I knew my mother would scold me."
Tod suggested they take a drive. They did, and in the process, Mac-
Laren said, she felt the director unclasping her new gift.

The shock of the thievery sobered her instantly, but she was too
humiliated and confused to immediately confront him. Browning
was staying on the same floor at the St. Francis as MacLaren and
her mother, and when he called for the actress in the morning, she
demanded the return of her jewelry. Browning flatly denied he had
taken it. In terms of their friendship, "Well, that was the end of Tod
and me."

But it wasn't the only incident recalled by MacLaren related to
the loss of jewels and the Browning name. In 1920 her sister starred
in a film entitled *Passion's Playground,* in which Alice Browning
played a supporting character called Dodo Wardropp. MacDonald

had a diamond ring worth $15,000, MacLaren said, and one day in the middle of production, the ring was gone. "There was hell to pay," MacLaren said. "My sister called in the studio guards . . . they decided they would hold everybody. No one would be able to go off the set until the ring was found." The missing item rapidly reappeared, "but we knew it was Alice who had stolen it," Mac-Laren added, "because they were both thieves."

In fairness to the memory of Alice Browning, it needs to be said that MacLaren's account was completely atypical of most stories regarding her character, which emphasized Alice's volunteer work and charitable activities. But Tod Browning's recurrent use of the jewel heist as a critical plot element, and his general fondness for tricks and scams, raises the question of whether such incidents involving him might be considered bad private jokes, perpetrated not for any criminal gain, but simply for the excitement of the challenge and deception. A 1932 newspaper interview described Browning using carny techniques to shortchange the teller in the M-G-M commissary.

David Butler, who acted in *Bonnie, Bonnie Lassie,* recalled Browning's emerging directorial technique. Other directors, like W. S. Van Dyke, Butler remembered, "walked up and down" the set, and "never sat down at all." Raoul Walsh, by comparison, "used to stand way in the back—you'd never know he was the director." But Browning would sit in his chair, giving occasional instructions, and preferred to remain stationary on the set, rather like a member of the audience, watching the story unfold. Nonetheless, he had a tendency toward imperiousness. According to Butler, Browning was always "very cordial" off the set, "but on the set he was king."

Browning's work for Universal had sufficiently impressed Irving Thalberg for the executive to entrust him with a Universal "Jewel De Luxe" production: *The Virgin of Stamboul,* a massive undertaking which, at least according to its most extravagant publicity, required eighteen months of preparation (the actual production schedule was eighteen weeks) at a cost of a half million dollars—an extraordinary sum in 1920 terms, more than the actual cost of *Intolerance* five years earlier. A few months prior to its release, Universal gave the cost of *Virgin* as something closer to $250,000.

Whatever the real cost, the picture was indeed elaborate. Alternately known during production under its final release title as well as *Undraped* and *The Beautiful Beggar, The Virgin of Stamboul* was based on a story by H. H. Van Loan about a beggar girl (Dean) who falls in love with a dashing young American soldier of fortune named Pemberton (Wheeler Oakman, Dean's real-life husband). Sari witnesses the murder of another American by a powerful sheik, Achmedt Hamid (Wallace Beery), who decides to silence her by adding her to his already-swollen harem. Pemberton marries Sari himself in a clever proxy subterfuge, which only angers the sheik, who kidnaps them both to his desert home. Sari escapes and brings troops to the rescue in a final, spectacular struggle. Browning adapted the story himself, in collaboration with William Parker, and it was filmed in late 1919 at Universal City and on location in the Gila Desert, Arizona.

Over forty individual sets were constructed, including several streets in Constantinople, a full-scale bazaar, the Sultana Gardens, and a detailed reproduction of both the interior and the exterior of the Hagia Sophia. For Universal, the film posed unprecedented challenges in art direction and effectively served the studio as a dress rehearsal for its extravagant re-creation of Monte Carlo for Erich von Stroheim's *Foolish Wives* (1922). Stroheim, like Browning, was a former assistant director to D. W. Griffith, but the two men couldn't have had more antithetical working relationships with the studio, and with Irving Thalberg in particular. Browning advanced his career by careful adherence to budgets and schedules; in later years he would typically negotiate salary bonuses for pictures brought in on time and/or below budget, and would almost always collect. Stroheim perversely built his own reputation by antagonizing the front office with absurd cost overruns; *Blind Husbands* (1919), the picture he had completed just as Browning was beginning *The Virgin of Stamboul,* was reported to have cost ten times its budget, and *Foolish Wives,* a near-million-dollar debacle, was only barely profitable for Universal because of its inflated cost. Clearly, Browning was far more astute, politically, than Stroheim was. Nonetheless, Samuel Marx recalled that Browning was somewhat jealous of Stroheim's ability, while it lasted, to have Universal expensively indulge his whims, and often made sarcastic cracks about his one-time Griffith co-worker. Stroheim had a far more visible public profile than Browning ever would, but his spendthrift proclivities—particularly with *Greed* in 1925—effectively ended his career as a director. He was later a character actor and sometime scenarist, and one of his last screenwriting credits would be, ironically, for Browning's horror fantasy *The Devil-Doll* (1936).

The script of *The Virgin of Stamboul* called for a camel race, Browning not reckoning on how stupid and stubborn the animals could be—and were. Unlike Stroheim, who was said to have held up a production for weeks waiting for a flock of wild geese to assume a formation he had in mind but could not communicate to them, Browning took a more practical approach. He noticed the camels' tendency to flock together like sheep and decided on a slightly cruel experiment. He separated a baby camel from its mother, who was herded with a group of other adults about a thousand feet from the camera, where the baby was held captive. With the cameras rolling, the camels were released, and the mother "bore down on her captive infant with all the speed in her power, the others sweeping behind her like the tail of a comet," according to an account of the incident in the *New York Tribune*. But a camel got the better of Browning as it refused to turn its eye and wink at Priscilla Dean for a gag scene; rather than cut the shot, a ready crew camped with the obdurate beast for three days until it finally turned and winked in the proper synchronization.

Priscilla Dean, of course, was hardly the image of a Turkish beggar, but "a healthy Californian," according to *Photoplay,* who nonetheless conveyed that "she knows more about the Orient than a Cook's Tourist could tell you." Of course, the whole point of pictures like *Virgin* was to provide American audiences with a familiar point of identification while titillating them with stories whose events and emotions would seem ludicrous in an American setting.

Exotic melodramas in Eastern locations became a staple commodity in Hollywood, and the success of *The Virgin of Stamboul* no doubt had a significant bearing on Paramount's decision to film *The Sheik* with Rudolph Valentino the following year. The delirious melange of architectural styles—Egyptian, Moorish, Chinese—that distinguished movie palace architecture of the 1920s and 1930s also owed much to the popularity of Middle and Far Eastern themes in Hollywood productions in the years immediately following World War I.

Universal used extraordinary methods to publicize *The Virgin of Stamboul,* including the planting of a phony sheik in a Manhattan hotel who successfully hoodwinked the *New York Times* into running the following story on March 8, 1920:

SHEIK SEEKS $100,000,000 GIRL

Fiancee of Amir of the Hedjaz
in an Arabian Nights Elopement with an American

WORLDWIDE SEARCH BEGUN

Father, "the Rockefeller of Turkey," Dies of Grief
After the Disappearance from Constantinople

Ben Mohamet, a Sheik of Arabia and brother of the Amir of Hedjaz, arrived at the Hotel Majestic yesterday, with a tale fit to be added to the Arabian Nights. In brief, his story is that he and his party have come to America to search for Sari, fiancee to his brother, the Amir, and daughter of Hadahismo, one of the richest men in Turkey, who died in grief over her disappearance just after the Armistice and left her about $100,000,000. . . .

The absurd story, concocted by Harry L. Reichenbach, one of the most colorful press agents known to show business, and abetted by a squadron of thoroughly domestic Arabs recruited on Washington Street, nonetheless kept New York reporters dancing for several days. As *Moving Picture World* noted, "The reporters, overlooking the fact that no follower of Islam would affront the Prophet by using the feminine spelling of his name, with an 'et' instead of an 'ad,' hotfooted it to the subway and presently were in the august presence. They had not the slightest difficulty in gaining an audience." Soap-opera developments were added daily. The missing girl was reported to be found with an Armenian family, washing dishes to support herself in the best Cinderella fashion. She had escaped to Canada, the story went, with an AWOL marine she met in Constantinople, who himself had now disappeared. And on and on. While some of the other papers made straightforward news of the hoax, the *Times* never directly admitted its complicity in the scam, merely noting in its final story that the manager of the Majestic finally evicted the entire party, suggesting that "Sari" "could recover from her hysteria in a motion picture studio just as well as in the hotel."

By this time, however, the story had penetrated the wire services and was an effective component of Universal's national publicity campaign. All across America, theater lobbies were transformed into harem tents, and Browning devised a live stage prologue with music for the film's New York premiere. *The Virgin of Stamboul* did holdover business nearly everywhere it played, quickly recouping the studio's investment and furthering Browning's standing at Universal. The critics, while generally complimentary, were not uniformly impressed. The *New York Times* gave *Virgin* qualified praise:

> Those who like their movies in unmitigated melodramatic reels, with electrified heroes, heroines, villains and their variously assorted associates speeding through scene after scene of "action," not bothered by logic or any necessity for being lifelike, should find much to entertain them in this production of the motion-picture mill. It is the old wine of the long-familiar Western poured into a new bottle of Eastern setting. Its characters race against each other with all of the thrills that may be derived from a race of the wooden horses in Steeplechase Park, which go at high speed along fixed grooves to a predetermined result.

The *Bioscope,* a British film magazine, noted that "the film cannot be regarded very seriously as a picture of Oriental life and character, but it makes fine entertainment of a popular type. . . . Massively staged interiors, colorful street pictures and delightful glimpses of the gleaming desert are all presented with a thoroughly sheik-like disregard for expense and prodigality of display.''

Profitable prodigality, of course, is never a transgression in Hollywood, and Browning was rewarded for his work with not just a new office, but a five-room chatelet on the Universal lot including editing facilities. (The studio was dotted with homey bungalows, many of which served as real homes for relatives of Universal president Carl Laemmle, who, as Ogden Nash memorably phrased it, had a ''very large faemmle.'') Browning worked best at night and had taken to working on scripts from 6:00 P.M. to 6:00 A.M., a practice he called ''burning moonlight.''

In his new, nocturnal, working environment, Browning developed the script for a picture that would reunite Priscilla Dean with Lon Chaney for maximum box-office punch. Browning had planned to pair Dean and Chaney again after *The Wicked Darling* in another crime programmer (most likely *The Exquisite Thief*) but released Chaney from the commitment, enabling the actor to accept his career-making role in *The Miracle Man*. *Outside the Law* was shot partially in San Francisco but primarily at Universal City, where sets were backed with glass-backed, oversize panoramic photos of San Francisco, through which projected light could realistically approximate any hour of the day or night. The process was a forerunner of Hollywood's ubiquitous process screen, used for all manner of camera effects. Reviewers praised the realistic evocation of the city by the Bay, though San Francisco critics in particular bridled at the title cards referring to ''Knob'' Hill and, horror of horrors, ''Frisco.''

The story for *Outside the Law* strongly echoed *The Exquisite Thief*, with Dean once more cast as a thief who crashes a society party to get the goods. But *Outside the Law* marked a significant turning point in the development of the crime drama with its emphasis on character psychology. At the beginning of the film, Dean's character, Molly ''Silky Moll'' Madden, is introduced as the daughter of a former crook, ''Silent'' Madden (Ralph Lewis), who has followed the straight and narrow herself since her father's conversion. Both have found a moral compass in the Confucian wisdom of a Chinatown sage, Chang Low (E. A. Warren). When her father is framed for a shooting and railroaded to a penitentiary, Molly assumes he is guilty and that the virtuous path is, therefore, hopeless. She commits a jewel heist for "Black Mike" Sylva (Lon Chaney), the gangster who framed her father and wants to railroad her as well. Learning of his plans, Molly and a disenchanted gang member, "Dapper Bill" Ballard (Wheeler Oakman), give Chaney the slip, hiding out in a Nob Hill flat with the stolen jewels. There the psychological pressure builds as Chaney stalks and finds them, with a final confrontation in Chinatown where Chaney, in a secondary, Chinese role, shoots and kills his Black Mike persona in a split-screen tableau. Chaney had already begun to play multiple roles in his films, such as Jacques Tourneur's *Treasure Island* (1919), extending his already-growing reputation as the Man of a Thousand Faces beyond mere makeup versatility from film to film to the more novel possibility of playing opposite himself in the same film, and even in the same frame.

Leo McCarey, later the director of *Duck Soup* (1933), *Going My Way* (1944), and *The Bells of St. Mary's* (1945), began his film career as Browning's assistant director on *The Virgin of Stamboul* and *Outside the Law.* On the former, McCarey remembered, "It was my duty to remember whether or not the hero had a cigarette hanging from his lip in the scene that preceded the one we were shooting, so that when the whole thing was glued together, a butt wouldn't fly out of his lips, like a hummingbird, right in the middle of a scene." On the latter, "Browning was ill, so the studio sent me to San Francisco to direct Chaney. At night, a thousand people gathered in the street to watch me direct him," McCarey told interviewer Peter Bogdanovich. "I walked back and forth, a little like De Mille. I was finally somebody. I went over and said, 'Lon, at least give the appearance of listening to me.' We had a little conference and I suggested he light a cigarette or something. . . . But I gave the appearance of directing him for three nights in a row, and made a big impression on the crowds."

McCarey had been trained in law at the University of Southern California and "had developed quite a vocabulary, and the heads

of studios in those days didn't have the advantage of advanced education. . . . they thought I was brilliant because I used big words.
So they made me a director at the end of one picture! I was a 'script
girl,' and at the end of the picture they were measuring me for
jodhpurs."

Thus, through the medium of adventure and crime films, Chaney obliquely introduced the essentially uncanny themes of the
shape-shifter and the doppelgänger to American popular culture—
motifs being addressed more directly in European horror films like
The Student of Prague (*Der Student von Prag;* Germany, 1913), *The
Royal Life* (*Az Elet Kiralya,* an adaptation of Oscar Wilde's *The Picture
of Dorian Gray;* Hungary, 1917), and *The Head of Janus* (*Der Janus-
kopf,* based on Stevenson's *Dr. Jekyll and Mr. Hyde;* Germany, 1920).
In an America still very much in the thrall of Horatio Alger, themes
of transformation were treated largely in terms of material acquisi-
tion (legal or otherwise); in Europe the metamorphoses tended to
be physical and/or metaphysical. Lon Chaney was one of the first
Hollywood stars to systematically exploit the public's powerful
yearning for transformation and transcendence. In the words of
film historian David Thomson, "There is not a screen performer
who so illustrates the fascination for audiences of the idea, promise
and threat of metamorphosis. Why do we go to the cinema, sit in
the dark before overwhelming fantasies that appear real? To share
in these plastic moments, to change our own lives, and to encourage the profound spiritual notion of our flexible identity."
American society after World War I was making innumerable adjustments, not the least of which was to the peculiar schism between
the Puritanism that drove Prohibition and the characteristic, almost
reflexive testing of boundaries that was a hallmark of the looming
jazz age. Lon Chaney was himself a living, breathing assault on the
boundaries of human personality, experience, and identity as they
were commonly understood; films like *Outside the Law* made glamorous, and even sympathetic, modes of existence outside the moralistic mainstream. The laissez-faire twenties would be a time of personal and social experimentation, and, to a considerable degree,
the "Man of a Thousand Faces" describes the moviegoer him/

herself, eager and ready to perceive reality from a kaleidoscopic multitude of moral and cultural perspectives.

The New York premiere of *Outside the Law* capitalized on the implicitly protean themes by opening in not one, but four Broadway theaters, at least for the first day (three of the theaters were legitimate houses, momentarily available for a film screening). The facades of all three houses were covered with painted canvas flats simulating the exterior of a prison—a peculiar come-on, but an effective one nonetheless. *Outside the Law* was given generally positive reviews but generated extraordinarily good box office. It may be something of a testament to the charisma of its stars that, six years later, when Universal revived the film, a print missing its last reel did clean-up business in Pittsburgh, with nary an audience complaint, despite the unresolved climax.

Part of the American public's fascination with criminality as evidenced by the popularity of *Outside the Law* may have had something to do with enduring the first year under Prohibition, which overnight turned millions of previously law-abiding citizens into instant transgressors, and set in motion the biggest wave of organized crime the country had ever seen as bootleggers and mobsters began staking out their territories.

The advertising campaign for *Outside the Law* didn't address Prohibition directly, but it came close: the drive for Sunday blue laws, fueled by the same forces that had closed the saloons, was exploited by four different billboard messages that sprang up around New York shortly in advance of the film's opening. "Do You Motor on Sunday? You are OUTSIDE THE LAW." "Do You Work on Sunday? You are OUTSIDE THE LAW." And so on. The New York blue law partisans, feeling that their position was being distorted, countered with a billboard campaign of their own, and the war of signs received saturation coverage in the press.

Universal announced that Browning would adapt *Outside the Law* as a stage production—an interesting idea, given the stagelike mise-en-scène of the hideout setting in which most of the drama takes place—but a theatrical version of the film never came to fruition. (Universal would continue to announce impending stage adaptations of various pictures off and on throughout the twenties, though perhaps just for publicity value.)

Following the enormous success of *Outside the Law*, Browning acted as producer only for *Society Secrets* (1921), directed by his assistant Leo McCarey. ("He didn't put his name on it, and I don't blame him." Asked if *Society Secrets* was a comedy, McCarey answered, "Yes." Asked if the film was any good, he answered, "No.") Immediately following, Browning codirected the film version of Edna Ferber's best-selling novel *Fanny Herself*, an unabashed tearjerker about a Jewish woman's sacrifices for her family. Universal retitled the film *No Woman Knows* (1921), despite the high recognition value of Ferber's original title—a move that raised eyebrows in the publishing industry and amounted to a new boldness in the studio's willingness to alter aspects of established literary works for perceived commercial reasons. Following the Ferber adaptation, Browning took on a pair of "Universal Special Attractions" into which he had no story input at all, suggesting some distraction or necessity to curtail his activities. *The Wise Kid* (1922) was a nondescript romance set in a cafeteria, and *The Man Under Cover* (1922), a crime drama, scored publicity points by being based on a story written by a life-sentence inmate of the Arizona State Penitentiary.

Between the release of *The Wise Kid* and *The Man Under Cover*, the illness and death in Louisville of Charles L. Browning may have taken an emotional toll on his son, inhibiting his productivity. The elder Browning had been in frail health following a debilitating stroke. His foster daughter's children remembered that he had two activities that provided some measure of physical therapy: endlessly shelling peanuts in the parlor, his lap covered with heavy blankets, and painstakingly papering the walls of the bathroom with identical red-and-green two-cent postage stamps, steamed from envelopes of mail received. He finally died at home from arteriosclerosis at the age of seventy-two on March 31, 1922.

Although there is no record of film activity that would have prevented Tod from traveling to Louisville to be with his family, he did not attend his father's funeral. He would not, in fact, see any members of his family for several years to come. Avery Browning and his foster sister, Jennie (then Mrs. William E. Block, Jr., of Louisville), made all burial arrangements. A funeral service was held at the family home at 2227 West Main Street, and Charles L. Browning was buried on Saturday, April 22, 1922, at Eastern Cemetery, Louisville, under a temporary marker bearing the inscription "Papa."

Browning's failure to pay his respects to the family raised eyebrows in the west end of Louisville, according to Jennie's daughters. It might have been excused, in the long run, but it would not be the last time Tod Browning failed to join his family in a time of grief. And it would not be the last time a family death presaged a difficult period for Browning, emotionally and professionally. He began drinking heavily—at least, more heavily than his norm, which was heavy enough. And, as had been the case almost ten years earlier, when coworkers wondered at his ability to "hold" his liquor, there was at first no perceptible effect on his work.

Browning's return to full-scale production came with *Under Two Flags,* a desert melodrama with Priscilla Dean which capitalized on the earlier success of *The Virgin of Stamboul* as well as the subsequent popularity of Valentino's *The Sheik* and similar sand-dune sagas like *Burning Sands* (1922). *Under Two Flags* was based on the 1867 novel by Ouida (the pseudonym of Marie Louise de la Ramée), which had been profitably adapted to the stage by David Belasco in 1901 and had been previously filmed by Fox in 1917 as a vehicle for Theda Bara. This time, Dean played the role of Cigarette, a French-Arabian daughter of the regiment stationed in Algiers who becomes involved in desert intrigue and makes the ultimate sacrifice by taking a bullet intended for her lover. The production, like the plot, was not without twists and complications. As Samuel Marx recalled:

> A disaster overtook *Under Two Flags* on location at Oxnard, north of Los Angeles, where the sandy beach resembled the Sahara, provided the camera didn't pick up the adjacent Pacific Ocean. To add reality to Priscilla Dean's camel ride across this desert setting, director Tod Browning transported a number of engines fitted with airplane propellers to simulate a fierce windstorm. But God trumped man's efforts—a real sandstorm buried the wind machines. Thalberg had to decide whether to return the troupe

to the studio or wait out the elements. He brought them back. It took weeks to unearth the machines and get them working again.

The critical reception of *Under Two Flags* was not quite up to the level of *The Virgin of Stamboul,* but the film was nonetheless a box-office hit and, the wind-machine debacle notwithstanding, was efficiently produced at a final cost of $222,522. Browning was firmly established at Universal as a dependable director of large-scale spectacles. In late 1922 the studio began to prepare what would be its most ambitious production to date: an adaptation of Victor Hugo's *Notre-Dame de Paris* starring Lon Chaney as the hunchbacked bell-ringer, Quasimodo. No expense would be spared in the re-creation of the sumptuous Parisian settings and the telling of Hugo's tale; Universal's prestige was frankly on the line. And so it came as an extraordinary vote of confidence by the studio when it announced in its trade publication, *Universal Weekly,* that *The Hunchback of Notre Dame,* a "Universal Super-Jewel Production" starring Lon Chaney, would be directed by Tod Browning.

It was the first, and last, announcement. The addiction that had destroyed the career of his uncle Pete had taken its toll on Browning, who had drifted into a deep alcoholic stupor. *White Tiger,* a picture he had just completed, would go unreleased for over a year —a highly unusual practice for the time, and a strong indication that the film was unreleasable in the form Browning had delivered it. *White Tiger* once again paired Priscilla Dean and Wallace Beery in what Thalberg, evidently, felt was a safe project for his once trust-worthy, now dissipated and erratic director. Oddly worded trade paper items reported that Thalberg and Browning required a "heart-to-heart" talk about the assignment, and, with "Thalberg at the urging point," Browning agreed to make a formula crook story "for old-times sake." *White Tiger* doggedly repeated familiar Browning themes: a pair of crooks running a scheme to bilk society types of their jewels. Browning concocted the story himself, and the means by which the swindle is facilitated is a clever update on the magic cabinet tricks of his stage days. Dean and Beery play a pair of Limehouse crooks who import a "mechanical chess player" to New

York where it gains them access to fashionable homes; in reality, the machine houses a hidden confederate who calls the moves and slips out of the box to rob the nearest safe. The remainder of the picture deals, rather statically, given the convoluted melodrama, with Dean falling in love with one of the intended victims and her realization that one of the other crooks is her long-lost brother and that the other killed her father. Fate allows for the evil one's disposal and the reformation of the others. Browning and his company trained East for the production; much of the film was shot on location in Manhattan and at Coney Island in the late summer of 1922.

When the film was finally released, it received extremely mixed notices, and many critics found it downright puzzling. The *Chicago Daily Tribune* found the story illogical and confusing, and suggested that Browning had "started something he hadn't the remotest idea how to finish." The film was pulled from Chicago theaters within three days of opening.

Dean was Universal's major star at the time, "the queen of the lot," in the memory of Samuel Marx, and Thalberg decided that her next film with Browning would go more smoothly if it was an adaptation rather than a Browning original. He chose a play, *Drifting,* cowritten by his closest personal friend at the time, John Colton, who was also his roommate, according to Marx. Colton, a playwright and scenarist, was the coauthor of the celebrated Sadie Thompson drama *Rain* and, as Marx noted elsewhere, "a world-weary homosexual who could be persuaded over drinks to discuss revealing intimacies of love between males."

Since there is no documentation that Thalberg himself was homosexual (he later married the actress Norma Shearer), his living arrangements with Colton suggest, at the very least, an uncommon open-mindedness for the time and a sympathy for the social outsider—a quality Thalberg would demonstrate time and again in the melodramas he would develop at M-G-M for Tod Browning and Lon Chaney.

Drifting, however, was not a success. "It is a hard, rather unwomanly role," wrote *Moving Picture World* of Priscilla Dean's performance. "Possibly because of the direction, her interpretation seems at times unnecessarily fierce, particularly in the scene where she resists the child who is clinging to her for protection. It is not the type of role which popularizes a star, even though there is some really effective acting."

The *New York Tribune* called *Drifting* "dull and incoherent" in an unusually blunt headline. "If we remember correctly, *Drifting* was not received with any great enthusiasm when it was presented here on the stage," the *Tribune* noted. "We did not see it, but if it was half as dull as the picture, which opened yesterday, we have no regrets on that score. . . . Priscilla Dean, that vituperative heroine of the screen, leaves us as cold as lemon ice, no matter what she does." The *Tribune* went on mercilessly:

> When the chief character in the story is so disagreeable that you don't care in the least whether she is captured by the Manchus or incinerated, you can't take much interest in this picture, but that is not why we dislike her. No, indeed. She portrays women totally lacking in humor or humanness. Her heroines are sharp, spiteful, without repression or subtlety. She has but two moods—pleasant and ugly. Her heroines are rather hefty, physically, too; but not nearly so hefty physically as they are mentally.

The *Tribune*'s reviewer confessed that she watched dispassionately when Dean was locked in a burning bungalow, and, "in reality, we were slightly wishing that she would get burned up and leave the hero for Anna May Wong. There is an actress with charm and imagination! She is really quite wonderful, besides being extremely decorative."

The decorative, delicate beauty was not always known as Anna May. Born in Los Angeles in 1907, Wong Liu Tsong (literally, "Frosted Yellow Willow") was the daughter of a Chinatown laundryman but was thoroughly Westernized at an early age and spoke excellent, unaccented English. She was especially entranced by the motion pictures that seemed to be in production on every empty lot in Los Angeles during World War I. By the age of twelve she began to do extra work, a move that was first welcomed by her family as a means to supplement the household income, but which may have also precipitated an adolescent nervous breakdown, forcing her to withdraw from school. When her aspirations to really act became apparent, her parents were horrified. In the Chinese tradition, the idea of an "actress" was tantamount to that of a courtesan —female parts in the Chinese theater were always played by men. Her parents were also concerned about the intentions of powerful white men in the motion picture industry—agents, producers, and directors—especially in light of their daughter's hauntingly fragile beauty. She was a Hollywood victim waiting to happen. Anna's father insisted on a traditional, arranged marriage.

But Anna rebelled. Steady extra work led to a featured role in M-G-M's first Technicolor feature, *The Toll of the Sea* (1922). One of the industry people who seemed to believe in her talent was Tod Browning, whose interest in Asian culture proved somewhat more than just professional. Wong recalled that on the day she met Browning to test for the part, she wore a fetching fur coat, not counting on being caught in a downpour. She arrived for the audition looking something like a drowned seal, but Browning saw beyond the wet fur, and she got the part. His casting her in *Drifting* was an important career break that would lead directly to an even bigger break—the slave-girl role opposite Douglas Fairbanks in *The Thief of Bagdad* the following year. Wong would eventually become one of the few Asian-American performers to achieve steady employment and notoriety in the Hollywood studio system, and she responded to Browning's early interest with gratitude. He responded to the teenager with something more, his judgment, no doubt, clouded by almost unimaginable blood levels of alcohol. Allan Dwan recalled that Browning was so far gone that he kept a bottle of hard liquor under his bed "so that he could have a swig when he got up in the morning." Browning's affair with the underage Wong was common knowledge in the industry, and not all viewed it cynically. "He was in love with her," said M-G-M production manager J. J. Cohn. David Butler, however, saw the interracial liaison as "typical" of Browning's constant need for "something different."

Finally, "Universal laid him off," Allan Dwan remembered, because "he got to a point where he was quite unreliable." "I made an ass of myself," Browning later admitted. An interviewer recalled one of Browning's most memorable debauches, a New Year's Eve party at the St. Francis Hotel in San Francisco (later notorious as the site of the Fatty Arbuckle scandal). An assistant manager tried repeatedly to persuade Browning to lower the decibel level of the revels. "As the evening waned, the animosity waxed," writer Fred Pasley reported. Finally, "Tod yanked out his false teeth—uppers and lowers—and hurled them at the A.M. with the suggestion: 'Go bite yourself!' "

For Alice Browning, it was all too much. An affair might be tolerated by some Hollywood wives under some circumstances, but a drunken dalliance with a teenage girl was more than just a fling—it was statutory rape. Samuel Marx recalled her desperate attempts to confiscate and hide bottles, trying to convince herself that she could somehow circumvent his own unwillingness to change his behavior. Alice was in a trap personally, having given up her own career a few years earlier to help support Browning's—ironically, one of her last acting roles was in a film called *What's Your Husband Doing?* But she still had her family to support her, and in late 1923 she made the only decision possible, and walked out the door.

THREE

"MURDEROUS MIDGETS, CRIPPLED THIEVES, AND POISONOUS REPTILES, ALL SINISTER AND DEADLY IN A MURKY ATMOSPHERE OF BLACKNESS AND UNHOLY DOOM"

The menacing shadows of Lon Chaney, Harry Earles, and Victor McLaughlin in
The Unholy Three *(1925).* (Courtesy of Philip J. Riley)

Following his soggy fall from grace at Universal, Browning didn't hit bottom immediately; still drinking, he managed to negotiate a one-picture deal with Goldwyn Pictures, with an option on three additional films. The first picture was salaried at $15,000; the additional photoplays, if they materialized, would pay him $20,000 apiece plus twenty percent of the net profits. If the first option went smoothly, Goldwyn was willing to pay Browning $25,000 a picture, again with twenty percent of the profits, for four more projects. Goldwyn set a cap of $135,000 on any of the pictures; overruns were to be deducted from Browning's share of the profits.

All in all, it was an astonishingly good contract for a director deemed dysfunctional by a rival studio, offering him an easy shot at a $100,000 annual salary. It was a far cry from his vaudeville days of skipping town on debts to his mother-in-law and sharing lodgings with desperate, infanticidal women. Instead of being buried alive in carnival river silt, he was being offered the opportunity to be buried alive in money. Needless to say, he had to actually produce the pictures and forge a congenial relationship with Goldwyn in the process. But in his present alcoholic state of mind, it was impossible.

The December 1925 issue of *Picture Play* magazine presented the closest thing to a candid account of Browning's smashup and recovery that has survived. Except for the occasional, opinionated newspaper reviewer, there were no really independent film journalists at the time, and certainly no investigative Hollywood reporting; the fan magazines existed primarily as adjuncts to the studio publicity mills, and stories like Myrtle Gebhart's "Because a Woman Believed" were highly controlled exercises in public relations—hardly investigative reporting. But because the article remains the single seeming example in Browning's career of a self-revelatory interview (however guarded and studio-sanitized), it still commands interest and is worth citing at length.

"Two years ago, I went to smash," Browning told the *Picture Play* reporter. "Temperament, impulse, wanting my own way, stubbornness—there were a number of contributing factors." He admitted to having "rows" with "the company with which I was then associated." Browning believed he might have been "partly in the right" in these fights with Goldwyn (Gebhart doesn't mention the studio by name), "for at that time they were in a grand, internal mix-up, changing executives, each man bringing in ideas of his own. There were a dozen people a director had to please, with little chance of doing anything the way he wanted." Trouble began with his first Goldwyn assignment. June Mathis, a senior scenarist—who had just been assigned the task of cutting von Stroheim's eighteen-reel *Greed* (1923) down to size, and would be a major creative force on *Ben-Hur* (1925)—listened politely to Browning's idea for his first picture. Although she called his original story concept "very excellent," Mathis nonetheless "suggested to him that with all the other directors doing stories that were well-known, I thought for his own sake it would be very foolish for him to do a story that was unknown, and he agreed with me." Mathis was pushing for Browning to direct a Goldwyn property called *The Captain of Souls,* based on Charles Tenney Jackson's 1910 novel *The Day of Souls,* a redemption story set in turn-of-the-century bohemian San Francisco. The rights to the story had been purchased for an extremely high sum—over $20,000—and the studio was eager to make use of it. Browning resisted, telling Mathis that he liked the story but wasn't sure it was the commercial knockout he wanted his first picture for Goldwyn to be, but would like to consider it for the future. Mathis gave him an alternative script with the unpromising title *The Gambling Chaplain*, as well as synopses of properties with the similarly unappetizing titles of *It Is the Law, Those Who Dance,* and *The New Deluge.* Two days later, another Goldwyn executive expressed skepticism that Browning was being straight with Mathis. "Sometime at your convenience, I wish you would find out from Tod Browning, whether he really has any eagerness for ever doing *[The] Captain of Souls,*" Abraham Lehr wrote to Harry Edington. "I may be wrong, but I suspect he is trying to let down Miss Mathis as easy as he can on a story he assumes she is crazy to have him do," Lehr wrote. "I know you will handle this diplomatically."

In the end, Browning was thrown together with Mathis, who, with coscenarist Katherine Kavanaugh, wrote him a faith-healing melodrama called *The Day of Faith* (1923), based on the novel by Arthur Somers Roche, originally serialized in *Collier's.* Browning managed to have the film's budget increased to over $250,000. Browning was forced to edit the film repeatedly to please the front office, presenting it in three versions of twelve, nine, and ten reels during August 1923. Starring Eleanor Boardman and Tyrone Power, Sr., *The Day of Faith* received mixed, often lukewarm reviews, though Boardman's performance was especially praised. (In 1972 Boardman remembered only that "I was brand new, scared and found Mr. Browning unattractive.") Goldwyn had drawn blatant comparisons in its advertising to Lon Chaney's similarly themed *The Miracle Man* and thus let itself wide open for the *New York Herald*'s critical salvo: "There was a great deal of slush in *The Miracle Man* but it was so completely disguised that the most carping observer could not easily resent it," the paper noted. However, "*The Day of Faith* . . . has borrowed all the slush from *The Miracle Man,* but has neglected to take with it any of the sincerity. The result is a picture that is preachy without being convincing; it aims at the emotions of its audience but is utterly unable to stir them." Other reviewers did manage to deem the drama stirring, but one senses their critical judgments were informed less by the merits of the film than they were polarized on the moral-values politics then dividing Prohibition-era America. (An example of the film's acerbic dialogue, as a worldly gentleman chides the ingenue: "You modern flappers don't even know what needles are for." Her reply: "Why, I do too! They're for phonographs!") A film that extolled the value of faith must be good, ipso facto.

The *Herald* review concluded that *The Day of Faith* was "a sorry mess," a phrase that also described Browning's relations with Goldwyn. In the *Picture Play* interview, Browning admitted to a "reputation of being contrary and temperamental and uncertain. The rumor got around that I had a nasty disposition—and let me tell you, it was true!" He had grown used to autonomy on the lot. "I had always got what I wanted before. I wouldn't listen to reason. I was as stubborn as a mule—I wouldn't budge or make concessions, even when I knew inside that I was wrong. I quarreled constantly with the various and assorted swivel-chair bosses, and finally blew up and stalked out." Needless to say, Goldwyn exercised none of their contractual options on Browning's services.

Browning had hit bottom. He didn't acknowledge drinking as a contributing factor to his smashup, though it was clearly recognized as such by all around him. Instead, he claimed to have "suddenly got sick of pictures, work, people, life, everything—and most of all myself. I didn't care what became of me. I drifted. . . ." He recalled once having stayed "shut up in the house, alone, for three weeks, with scarcely anything to eat, barricaded by a sort of self-hatred. At times I would write feverishly—the melos I'd always wanted to write, with strange characters in unusual situations. Then, in a fit of despair, I would throw them into the wastebasket."

When his wife finally walked out ("There is just so much that a sensitive, well-bred woman will stand"), he missed her at first, in "practical" terms:

When you've been married to a woman for seven years, you get to take her presence and her work for granted. It was vaguely annoying, after she had gone, that my clothes weren't in shape, the house disorderly, and meals irregular. When things are going well, you never really notice the woman's efficient hand oiling the wheels out of sight. Men are animallike in the way they snuggle into comfort, but it seldom occurs to them to consider the work that goes into making their surroundings pleasant.

Beyond the household disorganization, Browning began to miss Alice in deeper ways, "her helpful talk, her suggestions, herself. I wanted to ask her advice about stories, and she wasn't there. And I thought of our years together, of those fine dreams we had started out with, of her hopes in me and what a mess I had made of them."

When Browning finally acknowledged his alcoholism, he painted it, with no small measure of denial, as the result of his personal and professional problems, not a proximate cause. (Several years later he would make a more straightforward press statement about his attempt to drink up "all the bad liquor in the world.") One night, Browning told *Picture Play*, he was "moody, sunk in gloom. I got out a bottle of whiskey, and was just pouring a drink, when it suddenly occurred to me, 'No wonder Alice left a weak specimen like you.' "

In a moment of temperance-novel transformation, Browning said he "threw the bottle against the radiator, smashing it, said one brief prayer, 'God, help me to pull myself together!' and turned over and went to sleep. That sounds like a scene from an old melodrama, but it actually happened." Although he identified the incident as the beginning of his "a man's regeneration," he added that he didn't like the term because it was "usually applied to moral ruckers. Fortunately, I hadn't any immoral tendencies. . . ." Needless to say, the subjects of Anna May Wong, and marital infidelity in general, never came up in the studio-sanctioned *Picture Play* interview. In the cleaned-up version of the story, Browning went to Alice the day following his whiskey-bottle epiphany and asked her to take him back.

"If you want me," she told him, "you've got to prove it. I'll help, but it's up to you. I don't care to go down with a sinking ship." Browning had no choice but to court his wife all over again. She "let me call to see her, and take her to the theater." He be-

came melodramatic in his resolve to woo her. "My trouble assumed, in my eyes, the proportions of a tragedy. Anyone connected
with the make-believe professional world is subconsciously an actor.
I was sincere, mind you, but I was sensitized to feel things in an
exaggerated dramatic pitch." But Alice Browning didn't need his-
trionics. "She only smiled—that slow, lazy smile—and yawned,
'Why make a mountain out of a molehill, Tod? Surely, you'll make
good. When you stop orating and get down to brass tacks again, I'll
be waiting. In the meantime, let's have supper.' "

"By making it all prosaic," Browning said, "she brought me
back to realities—the actualities upon which the only worthwhile
life can be built." He admitted that he was only beginning dimly to
sense the emotional pain that Alice "must have concealed to keep
things on a casual plane."

The *Picture Play* piece turned on a sentimental note of reassurance—rather like a formula Hollywood screenplay. In this case, the
formula was the myth of the quietly powerful woman standing in
the shadow of the successful man. "Women are much stronger than
men, only it's a different strength," Browning said. "We men, physically powerful, swagger in this masculine braggadocio, believe we
control things. But a frail little woman can make or break any one
of us. The strongest man is a child, compared to a woman's spiritual
backbone."

Alice Browning, in her husband's public recollection of the
events, provided the strength and determination to reestablish him
in Hollywood. ("From outward aspects, she is the sort that a man
would feel needed protecting and babying," Browning said. "But
under that sweet femininity, there is a firmness like granite. . . .")
With Alice's support, he managed to find employment from spring
to fall of 1924 with FBO Studios, a small operation adjacent to
Paramount's lot which later became more famous as RKO Radio
Pictures, as director of *Dollar Down,* a preachy story on the virtues of
thrift, starring Ruth Roland and Henry B. Walthall, and *The Dangerous Flirt,* starring Evelyn Brent. (*The Dangerous Flirt*—ironically a
story on the dangers of sexual naïveté—may have been an unfortu-

nate title; Mrs. Lucien Andriot, wife of the film's cinematographer, remembered Browning as a moral rucker despite his newfound sobriety. "He was quite a lady's man," she recalled. Browning, she stated, was dating a woman other than his wife and other than Anna May Wong during the FBO period. Mrs. Andriot declined to give the woman's name, but recalled her clearly as a friend of hers given acting bit parts by Browning. Tod and Alice's marriage may have continued to have problems besides his alcoholism.)

Neither of the first two FBO pictures made waves; the second picture was, in fact, shelved for over a year, finally receiving a limited release to less than enthusiastic reviews. Nonetheless, Evelyn Brent recalled that Browning was impressive as a director. "I was scared when I first worked with him, because I'd heard the stories," she said. Her husband, Bernie Fineman, was a good friend of Browning's and also an executive at FBO, and had personally decided to give the director a second chance in the business. But Brent was relieved by the sobriety, courtesy, and professionalism Browning exhibited at all times. Alice was at her husband's side constantly, a "very steady" presence, Brent remembered. "She kept her eye on everything," and even accepted an acting role in Browning's third and final FBO film, *Silk Stocking Sal,* a crook drama again starring Evelyn Brent. Alice played a gang moll named "Gina, the wop." Brent noted that "Tod Browning was the first director who made you use voice when you worked." In the silent films Brent had earlier worked in, "the actors would make up lines, just say anything, throw it away." But Browning, audaciously, asked actors to speak lines that corresponded with the story. "He was a good director," Brent said, "a damned good director."

The critics agreed with her, at least in terms of *Silk Stocking Sal.* Armed with tangible evidence of her husband's reliability, Alice went directly to the most powerful man in Hollywood who might be in a position to help her husband get back on his feet with a major studio.

Irving Thalberg, who at Universal had initially championed Browning as director of *The Hunchback of Notre Dame,* had quit Carl

Laemmle's employ when the mogul's attempts to arrange a marriage between Thalberg and his moonstruck daughter, Rosabelle, were rebuffed. According to Samuel Marx, Thalberg wasn't particularly interested in Rosabelle in the first place; his protective mother, Henrietta, opposed a wedding partly because of fears that "the sexual requirements of marriage would exhaust his fragile strength."

Laemmle was outraged at Thalberg's rejection of his firstborn child.* He responded by denying Thalberg a long-promised promotion and raise. Thalberg responded by accepting a new position with Louis B. Mayer Productions, founded two years earlier. While Mayer was hardly Laemmle's equal, Thalberg's timing was fortuitous: Mayer's own company was on the verge of a monumental merger with the Metro Picture Corporation and the Goldwyn Picture Corporation, which, under the control of the theater-chain giant Loew's, Inc., would result in the most powerful, glamorous, and ultimately legendary motion picture studio in Hollywood history—Metro-Goldwyn-Mayer.

In order to feed the ever-expanding empire of Loew's theaters with weekly products, M-G-M became an enormous consumer of literary properties. The story that Browning was keen to sell to Thalberg was a curious, though best-selling, novel by Clarence Aaron "Tod" Robbins, first published in 1917. *The Unholy Three* had languished in Hollywood, however, due to its outré subject: a triumvirate of sideshow denizens—a midget who masquerades as a baby, a strong-man giant, and a cross-dressing ventriloquist—social outsiders all, who join forces to create a crime syndicate in miniature. Hollywood's hesitation to capitalize on Robbins' tremendously popular book may be attributed to the novel's failure to conform to crook-story conventions in the cinema, or to the mystery-melodrama formulas then all the rave in the theater. Browning later related that he had been told, "You can't make an audience seriously believe in a crook dressed up as an old woman and a dwarf

---

* *According to Samuel Marx, Rosabelle Laemmle's charms proved far from lethal, and Thalberg ultimately carried on an affair with her in the late twenties, just before his marriage to Norma Shearer.*

disguised as a baby . . . the stuff's comedy. Mack Sennett might use it and get a million laughs, but for the mystery drama—impossible.'' But Browning, who deeply believed in the book's potential, thought otherwise.

Upon the novel's initial publication, the *New York Times Book Review* noted that, while undeniably a crime tale, *The Unholy Three* ''is not a detective story. The reader is almost immediately let in on the secret, so that its discovery in the end awakens no thrill of surprise.'' The *Book Review* predicted that the novel would appeal less to mystery aficionados than to ''those who find enjoyment in tales of blood-freezing, if incredible, vindictiveness.''

The Unholy Three recounts the story of a trio of dime-museum denizens: Tweedledee, a midget; Hercules, a strong man; and Echo, a ventriloquist whose identity is psychotically blurred with that of his dummy. Tweedledee, seething with rage at the injustice of being trapped in a ''child's'' body, enlists the other two—both truly child-like and easily controlled—in a campaign of criminal retribution against the ''normal'' (i.e., adult) world. Tweedledee assumes the guise of a helpless baby; Echo dresses as a kindly grandmother, the better to catch victims unaware. Hercules provides the muscle to carry out their schemes. Together they constitute a composite master criminal—one mind, one body, and one voice.

The opening chapter of *The Unholy Three* is still powerful in its evocation of pure spleen:

All that he asked—all that he had ever asked—was to be taken seriously; and yet no one had granted him this simple wish. Most had laughed, some had pitied, but none had understood—none had looked upon him as a human being, like themselves. No, he had been a doll, a plaything for all these vulgar children of the world—children who paid to see him move his head, open his mouth and speak—children quite careless of the inner workings of their doll—children of the materialistic world. And, as he had grown older, the inner workings of this doll had changed; strange transformations had taken place; the springs of good had corroded with rust; and soon the green mould of evil covered everything.

The midget is especially revolted by children, who reflect him-self as in a glass, darkly: "Their piping voices, their pointed fingers, their curious eyes—all filled him with a nauseating hatred hard to bear. At the sight of them, he felt tempted to spring forward, to dig his finger-nails into their soft flesh, to hurl them to the ground to stamp them into unrecognizable bloody heaps."

It is hard to read these passages from a book that so seized Browning's imagination without wondering at their resonance with his own childhood, when Tod himself strutted on a backyard stage, projecting an assumed persona for public approval; when he was touted to all the world as an "infant phenomenon" for the delecta-tion of judgmental noninfants. Children will do almost anything to bargain with the unmitigated power adults wield over them. The smile reflex in infants, for instance, is not so much an expression of affection as it is a mindless Darwinian trait: babies who smile—or, by extension, who sing, or tap-dance, or otherwise entertain—are cared for better, and so have improved their chances of survival in a hostile world of "giant" adults. Infant phenomena often perform against a live-or-die backdrop of raw, existential panic. Browning's description of his frustration with studio authority figures strongly echoes the perverse power dynamic of the midget Tweedledee in his volcanic contempt for the very notion of audience approval: "It grew warm in the tent. It was as though these people, this herd of sweating animals, were sucking the precious air through their great, gaping mouths; were taking it from Tweedledee. His breast rose and fell; he leaned back, sick and dizzy. . . . he felt that his over-strained nerves were giving away."

Browning's nerves, finally, had given way, in part from his thwarted attempts to deal with the quasi-parental authority of the studios, in part from an infantilizing, oral addiction to alcohol. The 1915 car accident had left him with a baby's toothless mouth, which he would never outgrow, as well as other injuries, which, according to George E. Marshall, to some extent inhibited his physical activi-ties as an adult. It is hardly surprising that Browning found the story of entertainment outcasts in *The Unholy Three* powerfully attractive as he tried to reassert his own power and influence in the film industry.

Thalberg also liked *The Unholy Three* and purchased the screen rights for $10,000. (John Robbins, son of the novelist, insisted in 1972 that his father was actually paid half that amount, and that the sale was facilitated by Tod Robbins' boyhood friend, M-G-M art director Cedric Gibbons. The younger Robbins said his father "was never within 3,000 miles of Hollywood in his lifetime" and never met or corresponded with Browning, even after the huge success of the picture.) The producer had lavished tremendous attention on Lon Chaney's *The Hunchback of Notre Dame* at Universal, and knew the box-office value of grotesque themes just as surely as he recognized the public's craving for glamour.

In all likelihood it was Thalberg who had originally thought of pairing Browning and Chaney for *Hunchback*. Physically limited himself, Thalberg "may have come to think of himself as something of a freak," according to his biographer, Roland Flamini. Freakishness, deformity, and disability had taken root as a staple of American entertainment in the years following World War I; it is difficult to ignore the parallels between the cinema's ongoing obsession with disability and the real social problem of a quarter million disabled American soldiers who returned to find limited employment opportunities in an otherwise thriving economy. A sense of "disability" also pervaded the ranks of noninjured veterans, who as a group were disproportionately unemployed during the twenties; the plight of "the forgotten man" would not be effectively addressed by the government until the onset of the Great Depression. Lon Chaney's seething depictions of maimed and marginalized characters reflected the resentment of a significant population segment; on a broader level, Chaney's endlessly metamorphosing persona touched millions more who struggled with their own sense of identity in a decade of bewildering and rapid social change.

Thalberg warily offered Browning a one-picture contract to direct Lon Chaney in *The Unholy Three* at a salary of $6,500—less than half his compensation at Goldwyn—payable $750 a week for six weeks, with the $2,000 balance due upon the film's completion. An incentive bonus of $3,500 was added, provided Browning completed the picture within the twenty-four allotted shooting days and within the studio's estimated budget of $103,192.37. If Browning satisfactorily fulfilled the contract, the studio had the option to contract him for three additional films on the same terms, and a second option for four additional pictures at an increased salary of $10,000 per picture with a completion bonus of $5,000 for each film.

At Metro, Thalberg was able to follow his original instinct at Universal to pair Browning with Lon Chaney—the actor had just finished principal photography on Universal's *The Phantom of the Opera* when he signed a long-term agreement with M-G-M. But *The Unholy Three* presented certain script difficulties. In order to function as a star vehicle for Lon Chaney, the narrative focus needed to be transferred from the midget to a character that Chaney could plausibly perform: in this case the cross-dressing ventriloquist, Echo. Waldemar Young's screenplay transformed Echo from a split personality who could only speak through his false personae, to the story's calculating mastermind.

Beyond this essential transposition, much of Robbins' original nastiness was maintained. In the opening scene in the dime museum, there is some surprising pre–Production Code double entendre; a hoochy-koochy artist, for instance, is introduced as a girl who "broke the Sultan's thermometer." And the scene in which the ill-tempered Tweedledee (Harry Earles, stage name of the German midget actor Kurt Schneider) kicks a gawking child in the face, bloodying him, still shocks. The threesome was completed by actor Victor McLaglen as Hercules ("the mighty . . . marvelous . . . mastodonic model of muscular masculinity," according to the film's sideshow spieler).

The plot of *The Unholy Three* concerns the trio's scheme to rob wealthy victims by establishing the front of a pet store, run by Echo in old-lady drag, who pushes around an equally bogus infant (Earles) in a pram. They sell phony talking parrots, made voluble only by Echo's ventriloquial art; their "speech" is amusingly indi-

cated by the superimposition of comic-strip-style dialogue balloons
(anticipating the graphically rendered onomatopoeia of television's
Batman four decades later). The birds' failure at utterance provides
a convenient excuse for Echo and Tweedledee to make personal
visits to the complaining owners—and to case their homes in the
process.

But the first crime, a Christmas Eve theft of jewels from a pillar
of the community named John Arlington (Charles Wellesley), goes
horribly awry. Arlington's infant daughter (Violet Crane) discovers
Hercules and Tweedledee in front of the Christmas tree. "Oh,
Santa Claus," she exclaims happily to the strong man in Young's
first draft of the script, "you brought me a little bruvver!" The
"bruvver" is not amused, however, and when the girl tries to kiss
him, violently chokes her in front of the Christmas tree. The scene
was filmed as scripted, but finally cut by Metro before release on the
grounds that it was too intense for 1925 audiences. The excision of
the scene, however, paradoxically made it all the more comfortable
for Metro to indicate—via the insertion of a newspaper headline—
that the little girl had actually been killed, rather than merely in-
jured, as in Young's original scenario.

The unwholesome threesome frames the pet store's book-
keeper, Regan (Matthew Betz), with whom Echo's pickpocket moll,
Rosie O'Grady (Mae Busch), has forged a romantic attachment.
Although Echo also is in love with Rosie, he realizes the evil of his
ways and uses his ventriloquial powers to project exculpatory testimony into the mouth of his rival Regan during his trial. Hercules
and Tweedledee, holed up in a mountain cabin, are dispatched by a
crazed ape, one of the pet store's disgruntled denizens.

The Unholy Three proved a box-office sensation. "Not often does
one see so powerful a photodrama as *The Unholy Three*," wrote
Mordaunt Hall of the *New York Times,* which later selected the film
as one of the ten best of 1925. Hall called the film "a startling
original achievement which takes its place with the very best productions ever made." It was only the beginning of a deluge of uniform raves. The *New York Sun* praised the film's "wealth of cinematic imagination. . . . *The Unholy Three* is atmospheric, striking,

and gorgeously exciting.'' The *New Yorker* gave Browning an especially warm vindication of his comeback vehicle, the impact of
which it compared to:

> a kick equivalent to a cocktail concocted from red-eye, coal-dust,
> and squirrel whisky . . . To Mr. Tod Browning, all honor. His
> direction is replete with the gruesome, the humorous, and the
> plain hardboiled. He has distilled grotesque melodramatic com-
> edy and has deftly built up a thing that kaleidoscopes a ghoulish
> combination of cruelty and hard laughter, irony and action. And
> how easily he might have fallen into the ordinary cinema traps
> and made of the picture mere crook junk! In fact, he has risen far
> above the story, which is, especially at the end, as full of holes as a
> sieve and again has proved the old Shakesperian adage that ''the
> direction's [*sic*] the thing.''

The Unholy Three's production cost of $114,000 yielded M-G-M a
spectacular profit of $328,000, even after deduction of general stu-
dio overhead. The film generated a total of $704,000 in domestic
and foreign rentals, instantly reestablishing Browning as a commercial player in Hollywood.

The film's popularity is not surprising, given the sheer novelty
of the story and the audacity of its telling. In terms of American
popular culture, the freak-show outlaws of *The Unholy Three* are significant precursors of the bizarrely theatrical villains of *Batman* and
Dick Tracy. As Tweedledee, Harry Earles is especially impressive, his
sudden shifts from squalling infant to cigar-chomping gangster simultaneously hilarious and appalling. Earles is perhaps at his
creepiest in the scenes where the mask of a smiling baby blurs with
true, criminal countenance—as in the moment where he gestures
greedily from his baby carriage for an emerald necklace incau-
tiously dangled in his direction.

On another level, Chaney, emasculated in geriatric drag, may
have provided a kind of moral bulwark for the masses who didn't
live in cosmopolitan centers like New York or Hollywood, in a sense
guarding them against the threatening tide of moral license that
American show business was everywhere else extolling: Chaney's

appeal was, to a large extent, based on a martyrdom of enforced chastity. Unlike virtually every other male star in Hollywood, Chaney almost never got the girl. The commercial glue that held Browning and Chaney together for the next four years was their mutual interest in themes of boiling sexual frustration and concomitant, visceral revenge. Together they would provide the free-spirited jazz age with a profoundly reactionary shadow-ethos. Irving Thalberg, in essence, recognized the profitability of Hollywood assuming the role of moral good cop and bad cop, playing not only to the public's appetite for extravagant sex fantasy but to its puritanical resistance as well.

On March 2, 1925, M-G-M exercised its first, three-picture option on Browning's services, raising his per-picture salary to $10,000 ($6,500 plus $3,500 bonus). Shortly thereafter, Tod and Alice made a whirlwind pilgrimage to Louisville, the only confirmed visit with his family following his Hollywood success. Jennie Browning Block's two surviving children, Helen Polsgrove and Alice Carnell, recalled that they and their older siblings received cash gifts from the Brownings ranging between five and fifteen dollars. ''We thought we were millionaires.'' Tod presented his mother with a fur coat, as well as one of the first commercially manufactured radio receivers. Alice Carnell described Alice Browning's shopping spree at a local store called Sellman's: ''She bought three long dresses and paid two hundred dollars apiece for them—we never heard such a thing in our lives!'' The Block sisters recalled that Tod and Alice ''stayed no longer than two or three days'' before flying directly back to Los Angeles. And they were left with a sense of a jealous estrangement between their mother and Tod and Avery—an emotional issue that Jennie never discussed with her children. She only told them that Charles and Lydia Browning had taken pains to treat their foster daughter as an equal member of the family—an evenhandedness, perhaps, that the brothers resented, feeling they were entitled by birth to more. Following their father's death, Tod and Avery convinced Jennie to sell them her equity in what would eventually be the siblings' estate when Lydia died. With the family residence, a flat building up the block at 2221–2223 West Main Street (where

Jennie raised her family) and a one-fourth interest in property handed down from Samuel Browning, the value of the family real estate alone was $8,900. Jennie accepted a flat payment of $1,900 for her future claim sometime before June 2, 1923. Legally, they now owed her nothing.

Back in the film colony, his family obligations to some extent fulfilled, or at least endured, Browning launched his next project, *The Mystic.* Using an original story by Browning, screenwriter Waldemar Young recycled plot elements that had made such a hit in *The Unholy Three,* most notably the basic setup of carnivalesque criminals involved in a highly theatrical scam. Michael Nash (Conway Tearle), an American crook in Hungary, induces Zara, a carnival fortune-teller (Aileen Pringle), and her followers to accompany him stateside to bilk an heiress out of a fortune. Their technique: a phony séance in which the girl's dead father "instructs" her to turn over her securities and jewels. Following several showy sequences demonstrating the elaborate methods of fraudulent mediums, Nash renounces criminality and manages to escape with Zara back to Hungary.

The Mystic was especially distinguished by the costumes of the famous French designer Romain de Tirtoff—otherwise known, internationally, as Erté. Later memorably described by a *New York Times* retrospective as "an Aubrey Beardsley who mastered the Foxtrot and occasionally broke into the Charleston," Erté had been imported by Louis B. Mayer at great expense to create costumes and decor for two planned films, *Paris* and *Monte Carlo.* Mayer took extraordinary pains to make the artiste comfortable: one was the detailed re-creation on the M-G-M lot of Erté's atelier in Sèvres, down to the smallest architectural details; another was a gift of a Packard autocar. According to Mayer biographer Charles Higham, "Despite the fact that Erté was, to say the least, outré, Mayer was fascinated by him. Erté turned up at the studio in rose and gray crepe de chine or crimson and black brocaded coats and gold pants, or gray suits with red stripes. . . ."

Erté wasn't the only dandy on the M-G-M lot. Tod Browning

himself had become a sartorial peacock, favoring boldly patterned suits, berets and bowler hats, two-toned shoes, and a theatrically waxed mustache in the manner of Agatha Christie's Hercule Poirot. When the scripts for *Paris* and *Monte Carlo* failed to materialize on schedule, Erté had nothing to do besides designing some specialty costumes for *Ben-Hur* (1925). Mayer finally threw both his leading fashion plates together, assigning Erté to Browning's unit for *The Mystic.*

"Half the clothes were to be gypsy costumes," Erté recalled; "the others were elaborate and sumptuous gowns." But as executed by M-G-M's costume department, the finished product met with Erté's disapproval. "I felt the clothes lacked allure," he wrote. Mayer responded by setting up a workshop dedicated to Erté's designs alone. "He found the most marvelous woman to run it. Although her name was Madam Van Horn, she was thoroughly French; everything she touched emerged incredibly chic. The workshop was staffed by Mexicans whose work was superb."

Since *The Mystic* was being filmed in black-and-white, it made sense to Erté that he should provide black and white designs. But here he discovered a Hollywood peculiarity: "It seemed that actors became bored if they were not surrounded by colours, and their boredom would be reflected in their eyes." He relented, and executed color renderings which he viewed through a tinted blue glass to gauge their effect in monochrome.

Like Tod Browning, Erté was powerfully drawn to the cinema's potential for the strange and unreal. As he wrote in his autobiography:

> My dream was to make a film fantasy. After all, hadn't the cinema evolved from that series of bizarre pictures which had originated in the fertile imagination of Georges Méliès, pioneer film-maker, inventor and magician? But it was *The Cabinet of Dr. Caligari,* produced by Erich Pommer in Germany in 1919, that had first fired my enthusiasm for the possibilities of the film medium, especially in the realm of fantasy.

Unfortunately, a shared interest in the fantastic did not foster a good relationship between Browning and the designer. According to Aileen Pringle, Erté knew about dresses, but not about pictures, and Browning didn't know anything about dresses. The designer concocted a fanciful creation in black satin, including a dramatic jet hoop and tassel. The effect was visually stunning, but sadly impractical; when she attempted to act, the whole thing ripped after she took a single step. Browning started screaming, calling Erté a "fucking incompetent fairy," Pringle recalled. The director chased the designer off the set and the actress never saw Erté again.

Browning's work, beginning with *The Unholy Three* and continuing with *The Mystic,* showed abundant signs of *Caligari*'s influence. The German film, produced by Pommer and directed by Robert Wiene, had been released in the United States by Samuel Goldwyn in 1921; its dreamlike story of a carnival mountebank who carries a murderous zombie from town to town in a coffin crate was unlike anything American audiences had ever seen. For Browning, of course, *Caligari* could not fail to have resonated with his own history as the Living Hypnotic Corpse of the Ohio and Mississippi rivers. With its daring expressionistic settings—still, arguably, the most instantly recognizable designs in the history of film—*Caligari* created a tremendous early-1920s debate over the artistic future of motion pictures. The Europeans had gravitated toward the uncanny from the cinema's inception; in America, however, where movies owed more to vaudeville traditions than to the legitimate theater or to literature, cinema seemed stalled at a window-on-the-world kind of literalism. The motion picture itself had originally been a turn-of-the-century tent-show attraction, its appeal based on novelty, strangeness, an encounter with the uncanny. Hollywood, nonetheless, continued to resist symbolic, supernatural themes: throughout the twenties, the appearance of magical events, ghosts, or monsters would almost always be "explained away" as the materialistic machinations of some master criminal, a plot to steal an inheritance, etc. It was Tod Browning who almost single-handedly— if with a frequent assist from Lon Chaney—would push the envelope of the weirdly impossible to its acceptable outer limits in the commercial studio system of the 1920s. *The Mystic,* though it purported to "expose" spiritualism, nonetheless capitalized on the public's persistent interest in occult themes. In effect, the reductionistic dynamic of the machine age was being teased from both ends—a cynically materialistic worldview versus a desperate craving for spiritual transcendence. The numbing horrors of World War I had introduced a deep note of cultural pessimism/nihilism into the twenties, with results ranging from the fractured nightmares of surrealism to the frantic, live-it-up ethos of the jazz age.

The designer Erté, whatever he thought of the director personally, was amazed by the surreality of Tod Browning's Hollywood. The studios constituted "a world of fantasy in themselves. There were royal facades without palaces; sumptuous interiors without walls, kings and queens in full regalia eating sandwiches in the cafeteria with beggars in rags." He wondered at the Prohibition-era spectacle every weekend, when "half the population of Hollywood set off for the Mexican frontier town of Tijuana . . . to get drunk. The road from the border to Hollywood on a Sunday evening had to be seen to be believed; it was crowded bumper to bumper with cars manned by inebriated drivers." In addition to the partying, there was also a fair deal of orgying. "I went only to one but I left sickened—and I'm no prude," he recalled in his memoirs. Erté also noted "a great deal of drug-taking."

Willard Sheldon, a then-recent high school graduate getting his first taste of feature film making with *The Mystic,* served as assistant cameraman to cinematographer Ira H. Morgan. In a 1994 interview he recalled his youthful baptism in the pre-union rigors of M-G-M, where twelve-to-fourteen-hour days were considered the norm. Willard said that "many days I slept in the prop room where the beds were." The grueling hours, of course, enabled M-G-M to deliver a new motion picture every week, fifty-two weeks a year. "If you collapsed, they'd just bring in someone else and keep shooting," Sheldon said. Browning could be pleasant enough off the set, but at work he was "like an iron man. I still remember the way he paced back and forth, staring at you." Sheldon characterized Browning as "a man who knew what he wanted, and got what he wanted." He remembered the director as being "a rough man to work with . . . he never wanted to break for lunch. When he got hungry—that's when we would break for lunch, sometimes it would be as late as four o'clock in the afternoon. There were no unions then and a director could do exactly what he wanted." *The Mystic* achieved Browning's goal of maintaining his viability as a contract director at M-G-M, though just barely. While the film did better than break even, its profit of $52,000 amounted to barely a quarter of *The Unholy Three*'s thundering success. Nonetheless, the press response was fairly laudatory—save for the *New York Herald-Tribune*'s particularly nasty pan, calling the film "one of the dullest, most annoying pictures we ever sat through."

"The amazing events which take place during the seances make very good screen material," noted the *New York Evening Post,* "and melodrama, as many people have said week in and week out until their throats are beginning to hurt, is something the screen should do more often, but doesn't seem to do very well even when it tries. Perhaps Mr. Tod Browning will be able to put film melodrama on a new basis. He has an excellent start."

Following *Variety*'s suggestion that *The Mystic* might make an excellent stage melodrama, *Moving Picture World* reported that New York producers were indeed negotiating with Browning and M-G-M for legitimate rights, though nothing ever came of the story. For a time, in the twenties, Hollywood seemed enamored of the notion that it might be able to profitably sell stage rights to its successful films; Universal, for instance, announced that Lon Chaney was preparing to tour on stage in *The Hunchback of Notre Dame* following the success of the 1923 film. But given the financial realities of the theater versus those of Hollywood, one must wonder if these kinds of announcements were made only for publicity purposes. That a star of Lon Chaney's magnitude would even consider touring from city to city, nightly repeating the physical tortures of his *Hunchback* characterization, defies credibility.

Browning again teamed with Chaney for *The Black Bird* (1926), in which Waldemar Young's screenplay, based on a story by Browning, once more played to the public's appetite for Chaney in states of disability and disfigurement. Chaney's films, it should be noted, are not the only examples of disability-drenched cinema in the 1920s. John Barrymore's peg-legged Ahab in *The Sea Beast* (1926) and his hunchback in the *Francesca da Rimini*-inspired *Drums of Love* (1928) are two examples; characters and/or plots hinging on paralysis, blindness, and twisted spines were featured variously in films like D. W. Griffith's *The Orphans of the Storm* (1921), Henry King's *Tol'able David* (1921), Rex Ingram's *The Four Horsemen of the Apocalypse* (1921) and *The Magician* (1926), Frank Capra's *The Strong Man* (1926), and even Herbert Brenon's *Peter Pan* (1924), with the villainous amputee Captain Hook providing a sugarcoated counterpoint to Lon Chaney's stock characterizations.

The Black Bird is another crook-scam story, this time set in the seedy Limehouse district of London and featuring Chaney as a master criminal called the Black Bird. He covers his crimes by assuming the identity of a "twin brother" known as the Bishop, the kindly, cruelly palsied head of a mission who uses the charity operation and his faked disability as elaborate fronts for the Black Bird's crimes. The Black Bird and another crook, West End Bertie (Owen Moore), vie for the affections of a music-hall performer, Fifi (Renée Adorée); the ensuing melodrama takes an O. Henry turn when the Black Bird is actually paralyzed in a police raid, and dies having truly become his false persona.

As in *The Unholy Three*, Browning managed to transform preposterous premise into convincing entertainment, at least for the space of an hour. In many ways, Browning's plots resembled traditional tall tales, the success of which was judged not on inherent plausibility, but rather on the teller's skill in distracting an audience from the essential irrationality of the narrative.

In other words, Browning's success—much like that of his characters—was knowing how to put over a con job. To this end, he favored a complete artificiality in art direction, lighting, and photography. The *New York Sun* praised *The Black Bird*, noting the director's growing penchant for a dark, controlled ambiance: "It has been pointed out before that Mr. Browning, in order to keep his little crime waves in a shadowy fantastic key, pictures all the action

in front of dimly lighted sets, against shadowy walls. . . . there is
not a touch of Mother Nature, not a hint of sunshine, or sky or
trees. . . ."

Despite a fair amount of favorable critical attention, *The Black
Bird,* like *The Mystic,* failed to repeat the success of *The Unholy Three*
and posted a profit of $263,000, good but nowhere near the levels
of other Chaney vehicles at Metro like Victor Seastrom's *He Who
Gets Slapped* (1924, $349,000), *The Unholy Three,* and, most spectacu-
larly, Universal's *The Phantom of the Opera,* which ended $539,682 in
the black. Part of the problem with *The Mystic* and *The Black Bird*
may have been the ultimately mechanical nature of Browning's self-
developed stories. Much of his best work had derived from novels,
stories, and plays with far more fully realized characterizations and
literary textures than he was capable of generating on his own.
Despite his taking frequent credit for original stories, no treatment
or manuscript has yet come to light that is solely Browning's work.

But to whatever extent he shaped his scripts, he was unique
among directors of the period. Agent Phil Berg, who represented
most of M-G-M's directors in the late twenties (though not Browning), offered that "Tod was one who really looked for material
. . . most of the bunch never looked for a story . . . they were
only assigned [a script], sometimes only three weeks before they
started shooting." Berg felt that "Tod was a very peculiar guy" for
not having an agent, but admitted that there was little an agent
could do for a director who wasn't interested in branching out from
a narrow groove of offbeat films.

Nonetheless, Browning had an unerring instinct for building
the big, melodramatic moment and a clear understanding that
audiences would respond predictably to tense, exaggerated situations. Sometimes he pushed too far: *The Black Bird*'s cleverness in
particular veered dangerously close to farce, with Chaney's relentless quick-change transformations taking place frantically behind
slamming doors.

Metro nonetheless was sufficiently impressed with Browning's
work to renegotiate his 1924 contract, more than doubling his com-
pensation. On January 8, 1926, Louis B. Mayer signed a new agree-

ment for five additional photoplays, guaranteeing Browning $20,000 per picture, plus a $5,000 bonus for each project delivered on time and within budget. Buoyed by Mayer's faith and money, Browning seems to have been freed to follow his own instincts to a greater extent than ever before, inaugurating the most personal, obsessive, and bizarre chapter in his career.

For his next project, Browning had a story collaborator whose contributions may have had a lasting salutary effect on the remainder of the Browning-Chaney oeuvre. Herman J. Mankiewicz, the New York journalist, theater critic, and member of the celebrated Algonquin Round Table, had accepted a position with M-G-M as a scenario writer. Mankiewicz was one of several writers of the *New Yorker*/Algonquin axis who gravitated to Hollywood in the twenties; others included Charles Brackett, Robert Benchley, Dorothy Parker, and Nunnally Johnson. As Pauline Kael observed, Hollywood was probably an inevitable destination for the Algonquin group, who were ''fast, witty writers, used to regarding their work not as deathless prose but as stories written to order for the market. . . .'' Mankiewicz initially expected to write a screenplay based on his wartime experiences in the Marines. The *New York Times* noted the ''perverseness'' of the studio's decision to put another writer on the war story once Mankiewicz had arrived, ''as though the studio authorities were utterly surprised that Mr. Mankiewicz should want to write about something with which he was familiar.'' Instead, he was assigned to work with Tod Browning, whose improvisatory methods of concocting screen stories must have struck the Manhattan literateur as proof positive that the words ''Hollywood writer'' constituted an oxymoron. Indeed, he was informed that prose of any kind—deathless or not—might not even be a consideration on a Browning film. Howard Dietz, then M-G-M's head of advertising and exploitation, recalled a meeting between Mankiewicz and Browning in which the director half described and half acted a scene for a proposed Chaney vehicle (''This is going to be the greatest movie I've ever made'') that never came to fruition. Browning knew the kinds of images he wanted—the story was to concern the transplanting of women's heads onto apes, and vice

versa. The problem was, he didn't have a scrap of narrative rationale for the outlandish theme.

Dietz remembered Browning's pitch to Mankiewicz: "You don't
have to write anything—just answer one question correctly and
you'll get screen credit."

Browning then related the scene:

> It opens with Lon Chaney wearing a white wig and an inverness
> cape, playing "The Last Rose of Summer" on the violin. He is
> blind and has a tin cup hooked onto him, and the crowd divides
> before him as he slowly walks into a measured tempo while
> scratching away at his fiddle. He continues on his way and sud-
> denly darts down five or six steps in front of a brownstone house.
> He taps a mysterious code on the door and rings a doorbell in
> between taps. The door is opened. We hear strange screams from
> inside. [Metro, by this time, was recording synchronized music
> and sound effects for its silent films.] Lon Chaney removes his
> white wig and inverness cape and appears in a complete surgical
> outfit. He enters the room from which the screams emerge, the
> screams get louder and Chaney gets covered with blood. The
> prison-like cells are filled. We see him cutting off the heads of a
> dozen nude ladies. He also cuts off the heads of a dozen apes.

The director's dilemma: *"What business is he in that he wants to do
this?"*

The writer, apparently, had no answer—one can only speculate
on the tart retort Dorothy Parker might have mustered—and the
film was never made. (It was just about this time that Mankiewicz
sent a telegram to his friend Ben Hecht in New York: "Millions are
to be grabbed out here and your only competition is idiots. Don't
let this get around.") In place of the monkey business, Mankiewicz
shared an original story credit with Browning for *The Road to Mandalay* (1926)—a pretentiously named film if there ever was, having
nothing at all to do with the celebrated Rudyard Kipling poem of
the same title, but obviously happy to bask in its reputation. But *The
Road to Mandalay* nonetheless proved a creative turning point in
Browning's career, in which the stock elements of his previous work
—exotic locales, criminality, secret identities, love triangles, and the

all-important element of a physical anomaly—were given a dark psychological resonance Browning had not been able to achieve since *The Unholy Three*. Mankiewicz possessed both the cynical literary sophistication of a mid-twenties Manhattanite and an awareness of the literary/dramatic implications of Freudian theory. Mankiewicz, with his younger brother, Joseph, had lived in Berlin during the 1920s and was "familiar with the currents of psychoanalytic thought swirling about the German capital," according to Stephen Farber and Marc Green, authors of *Hollywood on the Couch* (1993).

Indeed, *The Road to Mandalay*—crafted into a final screenplay by Elliot Clawson and Waldemar Young—is invigorated by a Freudian ambiguity about the relationship between Singapore Joe (Chaney), a whoremaster with a startling dead eye, and his daughter (Lois Moran), raised in a convent with no knowledge that the disturbing man who visits her Mandalay curio shop is in reality her own father; instead, he becomes a vague but insistent threat of imminent sexual predation. The daughter falls in love with the admiral, one of Joe's formerly disreputable, though now regenerate, partners (Owen Moore); Joe, outraged that the reprobate desires his daughter, refuses to acknowledge the man's reformation and kidnaps him to Singapore to prevent a marriage. The daughter follows, is trapped by another of Joe's enemies—an Oriental who attempts to rape her —and finally stabs her own father to death in a climactic melee, never aware of his identity or his misguided efforts to protect her.

The film colony of the late twenties, like much of America, had begun to notice Freud, at least in the half-baked form his theories had taken "after being filtered through the successive minds of interpreters and popularizers and guileless readers and people who had heard guileless readers talk about it," according to 1920s historian Frederick Lewis Allen. "New words and phrases began to be bandied about the cocktail-tray and the Mah Jong table—inferiority complex, sadism, masochism, Oedipus complex." Freud's message about the dangers of repression was interpreted, with a typically American pragmatism, as a simple green light for makin' whoopee on a grand scale. Samuel Goldwyn, with considerable hoopla, announced that he was traveling to Vienna to offer Dr. Freud, the expert on eros, $100,000 to concoct a tremendous "love story" for the screen. Freud, needless to say, declined to even meet with the producer.

As transmuted into an American fad, Freud's science verged on pseudoscience, holding the promise of a near-magical cure for all human discontents. Twenties-style psychobabble thus overlapped with the quintessentially Browning milieu of faith healing and occult hucksterism: at least one Santa Monica boardwalk astrologer was observed displaying a shingle offering "Psychoanalysis, Readings." Freud was appalled at the transatlantic excesses perpetrated in his name. As he once wrote, only half facetiously, "America is a mistake; a gigantic mistake, it is true, but nonetheless a mistake."

But Browning, with an assist from Mankiewicz, was not mistaken in his understanding that overt manipulation of disturbing sexual symbolism was a sure way to rivet an audience's attention. *The Unholy Three* had turned on a naïve Oedipal triangle—the hypermaternal image of a "grandmother," a hypermasculine "strong man," and a hyperfrustrated "baby"—but *The Road to Mandalay* went much further, consciously teasing viewers with an unsettling parent-child melodrama, in which Singapore Joe's attempts to protect his daughter from the admiral becomes an emotional rivalry with the admiral. Accepting Freud's dictum that the unconscious mind equates the eyes in the plural with the testicles and in the singular with the penis—a theory put forth in his influential 1919 essay "The 'Uncanny' "—Chaney's dead eye further colors Joe's estrangement from his child as a kind of incestuous sexual deprivation. "A study of dreams, phantasies and myths has taught us that anxiety about one's eyes, the fear of going blind, is often enough a substitute for the dread of being castrated . . . the threat of being castrated in especial excites a particularly violent and obscure emotion . . . [that] gives the idea of losing other organs its intense colouring."*

---

* *Chaney's clouded eye in* The Road to Mandalay *was one of the earliest practical applications for the contact lens, which, perversely, had not yet been perfected for ordinary optometric purposes. The* Mandalay *eye shield was made of glass and completely covered the visible sclera; it was the handiwork of Dr. Hugo Kiefer, a leading Los Angeles optician.*

The Road to Mandalay was Mankiewicz' last association with Browning, although a Broadway play he coauthored with Marc Connelly the following season—*The Wild Man from Borneo* (1927)—paid a perhaps intentional homage to the turn-of-the-century world of carnival scams and traveling charlatans that had shaped Browning's career. Though based on a skit Connelly had originally written for W. C. Fields and Beatrice Lillie, the story contained so many Browning-like elements, including a dime-museum setting, a freak-show father who hides his identity from his daughter, and a theatrical landlady who once toured as "Lady Dracula" (Bram Stoker's novel had been recently adapted for the stage in England and attracted both Chaney and Browning at this time), that Mankiewicz' interest in such a story so shortly after working with Browning seems more than an accident. *The Wild Man of Borneo* was a flop, however, and closed after fifteen performances. Fired by the *New Yorker,* Mankiewicz returned to Hollywood, becoming one of the most prolific scriptwriters in the business, and ultimately one of the most lauded, winning an Academy Award for *Citizen Kane* in 1941.

The Road to Mandalay did good business and posted a $267,000 profit despite dismissive reviews. "The picture is quite tedious," wrote Mordaunt Hall in the *New York Times,* "and it strikes us that Mr. Browning did not quite know what to do with the players in a number of scenes. They show themselves and talk to one another, employing conventional actions that are helped out by the title writer." *Variety* called it "a slumming party abroad screened with a sugarcoating to make it respectable to America, which includes censors and reformers," but admitted that "the film has a large-sized dramatic punch, which, after all, was the thing aimed at and achieved, and which will sell the picture to exhibitors and to the public."

If Tod Browning's films favored themes of visceral, sex-charged resentment and revenge, they were nothing compared to the real-life psychosexual warfare that raged throughout the twenties between Louis B. Mayer and one of his leading contract stars. The darkly handsome actor John Gilbert had rocketed to major stardom in M-G-M vehicles like Victor Seastrom's *He Who Gets Slapped* with

Lon Chaney (1924), Erich von Stroheim's *The Merry Widow* (1925), and King Vidor's *The Big Parade* (1925). But Gilbert clashed repeatedly with Mayer over offscreen issues of sex, mothers, and whores. In fact, they hated each other, so much that they actually came to blows. Their first major altercation had erupted over Gilbert's desire to film John Masefield's *The Widow in the Bye Street;* Mayer exploded when he learned the epic poem featured the character of a prostitute: "You want me to make a film about a whore?" "Why not?" Gilbert said, adding truthfully, "My own mother was a whore." Apoplectic, Mayer threatened to "cut off his balls" for making such a comment. Gilbert laughed and told the producer to go ahead—he'd still be the better man.

Another fracas ensued when Gilbert became infatuated with Greta Garbo, his costar in the highly successful *The Flesh and the Devil* (1926). When Garbo didn't show up for their wedding, Mayer, one of the guests, compounded Gilbert's humiliation by gleefully slapping him on the back with the suggestion: "What do you have to marry her for? Why don't you just fuck her and forget about it?" Gilbert responded by pushing Mayer into a bathroom and slamming his head against the tiles. The men were pulled apart. In the presence of several guests, including the actress Eleanor Boardman, Mayer vowed to destroy Gilbert's career, even "if it costs me a million dollars."

The incendiary animosity between Gilbert and Mayer was reminiscent of any number of Tod Browning's smoldering revenge melodramas, and it was perversely appropriate that Mayer used a Browning film to punish his volatile contract star. Although the literal castration he had threatened was not a practical possibility, Mayer retaliated with a figurative emasculation: he cast Gilbert to star in Tod Browning's latest production as a despicable character named Cock, faced with the imminent threat of losing his head.

Cock o' the Walk was based, extremely loosely, on the Charles Tenney Jackson novel *The Day of Souls,* which Goldwyn had expensively acquired in the early twenties and was determined to use, one way or another. The studio also quashed Gilbert's ambition to star in a film adaptation of Ferenc Molnár's romantic stage fantasy

Liliom (1909); the script for *Cock o' the Walk* blatantly appropriated the Hungarian carnival setting of the play (which had nothing whatsoever to do with the Jackson novel, set in bohemian San Francisco), going so far as to costume Gilbert in the striped carnival barker's sweater worn by Joseph Schildkraut in the Theater Guild's acclaimed 1921 revival of the Molnár play. *Cock o' the Walk* was released in the spring of 1927 under the decidedly more prosaic title *The Show.* Cock Robin (Gilbert) is the spieler in a Hungarian freak emporium called the Palace of Illusions. Most of the attractions consist of women with lower-body anomalies or radical amputations: a mermaid, scaly from the waist down; a truncated half-girl; and a disembodied head trapped in a giant spiderweb. The sideshow's pièce de résistance, however, is a grisly playlet depicting Salome's dance of the seven veils and the decapitation of John the Baptist (played by Gilbert). After Herod, played by an actor known as the Greek (Lionel Barrymore), performs the clever illusion, involving trap doors, the substitution of a fake sword, etc., Salome (Renée Adorée, one of Gilbert's real-life romantic attachments) receives the head on a silver charger. It opens its eyes and declares, "Salome, thou art a wicked woman!" before she silences it with a languorous kiss.

The freak-show exposition contains some remarkable double entendres of the kind that enraged moral reformers of the Prohibition era: as Cock displays Zela, the bottomless woman, he winkingly reassures the crowd: "Believe me, boys—there's no cold feet here to bother you." He plunges even further with the phony mermaid: "Now I know why the divers go down!" a gawker guffaws. (By the time Salome osculates the bodiless Baptist, one fully expects Browning to propose a new meaning for the phrase "giving head," but somehow he passes on the opportunity.) Cock, we learn, is a sexual opportunist who has no difficulty in extracting money from the young girls who are smitten with him. One, the daughter of a shepherd whom the sinister Greek had killed for a roll of money that was actually in the girl's possession, gives the cash to Cock for supposed safekeeping. To complicate matters further, Salome, whom the Greek has been keeping as a mistress, is really in love with Cock and begs him to return the shepherdess' money. The Greek becomes jealous and decides to exact his sexual revenge by actually chopping off Cock's head—onstage. He is not successful, and Cock escapes with Salome into a clumsily appended subplot (the only part of the film taken from Jackson's novel) in which the barker redeems himself by posing as the long-lost son of Salome's blind, delusional, dying father whose real son is being hanged in the square outside. The old man dies, believing he has been reunited with his child. His good deed done, Cock is now ready to be a true moral foil for the Greek, who tries to kill him with a giant, poisonous reptile he has borrowed from the sideshow. In the final, wildly melodramatic fracas, the Greek is trapped in a closet with the deadly animal and fatally bitten. Cock and Salome are reunited on the sideshow platform, life's strange carnival marching on.

By pushing grotesque imagery and improbable plot twists to extreme limits, *The Show* achieves a dreamlike plateau previously unattained in the American cinema; it is arguably the closest approximation of *Caligari*'s expressionism that Hollywood had yet attempted, even if the effects were highly diluted. The truly fantastic and surreal was still verboten in the American cinema, but Browning was nonetheless able to "sell" his fascination with grotesque visuals by simultaneously debunking them as cynical sideshow illusions. In its emphasis on images and evocations of below-the-waist mutilation, *The Show* again echoes Freud's essay "The 'Uncanny.' " One image that opens the film, a disembodied female hand that collects tickets from patrons as they enter the tent, seems almost a verbatim borrowing from Freud's observation that "dismembered limbs, a severed head, a hand cut off at the wrist . . . all these have something peculiarly uncanny about them, especially when . . . they prove capable of independent activity in addition. As we already know, this kind of uncanniness springs from its proximity to the castration complex."

Browning's perennial fascination with sexually charged mutilation imagery led to a completely unsubstantiated but nonetheless long-standing Hollywood rumor that he had himself suffered a disfiguring genital trauma in the car crash that killed Elmer Booth.

The story was—to say the least—psychologically naïve; the exhibition of castration anxiety, to Freud, was evidence of a universal unease, not a telltale symptom of individual anomaly. The wide popularity of Ernest Hemingway's *The Sun Also Rises* (1926), with its story of wartime emasculation, is evidence for the general public's built-in receptivity to such themes.

The Show received mixed reviews—many critics complained about John Gilbert being cast in a largely unsympathetic role. "This one starts off like a house afire but turns out to be much smoke and little flame," the *New York Morning Telegraph* complained, citing "inserts of the most puerile, milk-and-water sequences"—the Jackson material—"ever alleged to be pathos." The *New York Daily Mirror* disagreed, calling *The Show* "snappy and unusual" and thanked heaven that the film's characters lacked the "syrupy virtue" so common in Hollywood pictures of the time. "Any one who is tired of drawing room dramas that are intensely unreal despite the fact that nothing particularly remarkable happens in them will have a wonderful time at *The Show*," opined the *New York Evening Post,* "for here all sorts of remarkable things happen in the most convincing manner possible." The *New York Times* managed, stingingly—if inadvertently—to illuminate an aspect of Browning's films harking back to his vaudeville-era marriage to Amy Stevens: "Like most of Mr. Browning's heroes, Cock Robin escapes the penalty of the law for taking money from a nice little girl."

Richard Watts, Jr., film critic for the *New York Herald-Tribune,* gave *The Show* a positive evaluation. "It has been one of the less desirable results of current cinema development that the individuality of directors is suppressed before the standardization of picture making. . . . Only Tod Browning stands for the moment aloof from the blandishment of imitators and the bludgeons of those who would change his intent." According to Watts, "Browning is the combination Edgar Allan Poe and Sax Rohmer of the cinema. Where every director, save Stroheim, breathes wholesomeness, out-of-door freshness and the healthiness of the clean-limbed, Tod Browning revels in murkiness. . . . His cinematic mind is a creeping torture chamber, a place of darkness, deviousness and death."

The critic noted, with pleasure, that "there is no reason to think that Mr. Browning is in immediate danger of becoming a director of clean-limbed photoplays. His next production bears the gratifying title of *Alonzo the Armless,* and it is not too difficult to imagine the sort of merry tale it is likely to be."

In Browning's next project, Freudian theory would be bizarrely literalized into a weird and spectacular circus attraction. Based on an original story by Browning, *Alonzo the Armless* was a vehicle for Lon Chaney that would prove to be one of the darkest carnivals of the entire Browning canon. Its title changed—rather vaguely—to *The Unknown,* the film's release in New York coincided with Charles Lindbergh's triumphant homecoming, but it could not have provided a more antithetical cultural counterpoint to the celebratory mood of June 1927. Nevertheless, *The Unknown* managed to find a huge audience.

"This is a story they tell in old Madrid . . . the story, they say, is true" reads the opening title, urging us to suspend our disbelief as we enter a world of heightened unreality. The setting is a Spanish circus, featuring an armless entertainer named Alonzo (Chaney), a precision knife-thrower and sharpshooter who handles blades and bullets with his bare feet. In the opening scene, Alonzo demonstrates the prowess of his aim: seated at one end of a rotating platform, he propels a phallic barrage of knives and ammunition unerringly at his beautiful assistant, Nanon (Joan Crawford).* Articles of her clothing fall away, their stays severed by Alonzo's wildly sublimated ardor.

Alonzo actually has arms, a fact known only by his dwarf assistant, Cojo (John George), who daily laces him into a cruel leather corset to maintain the illusion of amputation. Cojo's name, in proper Spanish, means "lame"; in the vernacular, it also conjures

---

* *A small mystery still exists over the name of the Crawford character in the original release prints of* The Unknown. *In the script, in studio publicity material, and in reviews of the film that appeared in* The New York Times, New York Herald-Tribune, San Francisco Chronicle, Moving Picture World, *etc., the character is called Estrellita (Spanish for "little star"). Variety, however, referred to the character as Nanon, a name that also appeared on the original musical cue sheets for theatrical accompanists. The present titles that appear on M-G-M's restored print of the film were translated from a French print, and also call the character Nanon.*

cojones, or testicles. Alonzo has two reasons for his disguise: first, it hides his link to previous, unidentified crimes; second, it keeps him in favor with Nanon, who is possessed by a bizarre phobia, a repulsion to men's upper extremities ("Men! The beasts! God would show wisdom if he took the hands from all of them!"). Alonzo may have arms, but he's still a freak, possessed of a double thumb on one hand. In the original story, Browning and scenarist Waldemar Young intended a more hideous physical deformity along the lines of a claw. The double thumb seems yet more evidence of the possible influence of Freud's essay 'The Uncanny' "; doubling is viewed by Freud as an imaginative defense against the feared loss of the self, or a part of the self.

Although Alonzo restricts his pining for Nanon to a platonic plane, he draws the wrath of her father, owner of the circus. One dark night, arms unlaced, he strangles the man outside of his wagon. Nanon, peering from a window, does not see the killer's face, but she does glimpse the unforgettable double thumb as it crushes her father's windpipe.

While Alonzo broods over the problem of how best to win Nanon without letting her learn his secrets, the girl is pursued, far more conventionally, by a strong man named Malabar (Norman Kerry). Alonzo, crazed with jealousy, blackmails a surgeon into actually removing his arms. But when he returns to the circus after his recuperation, he finds that Nanon has shaken off her phobia and is now happily engaged to Malabar. The truth dawns on Alonzo in a long, cruelly teasing sequence in which he mistakes the couple's talk of marriage with his own nuptial fantasies. The film reaches a climax when Alonzo attempts to sabotage Malabar and Nanon's crazy specialty act: a pair of white stallions on treadmills are whipped into a frenzy by a scantily clad Nanon while Malabar restrains them. Knowing that a failure of the treadmills could cause the horses to rip Malabar's arms from their sockets, Alonzo proceeds to make the necessary mechanical adjustments. Just before Malabar is torn apart, Alonzo falls onto the treadmill and is delivered to his death beneath the horse's punishing hooves.

The story is preposterous, yet it obeys its own obsessive dream logic so rigorously that it can keep even today's sophisticated audiences spellbound and appalled. Unlike many of Browning's films, *The Unknown* is single-minded in its brutal momentum, unencumbered by distracting subplots and unconvincing last-minute repentances. Like the stage contraption that kills Chaney at the film's conclusion, *The Unknown* itself is a perfectly constructed torture machine and arguably Browning's most accomplished film.

The sadomasochistic tone pervading the Browning-Chaney collaborations raises legitimate questions about the private psychologies that together generated such cruel public spectacles. Chaney, according to screenwriter-director Curt Siodmak, who worked with the actor's son in numerous films for Universal in the forties, "seemed to have been a sadistic character, the way he treated Lon [Jr.] as a child and young man." In Siodmak's account, the younger Chaney survived his father's maltreatment "a tortured person." Siodmak hinted that he knew more about the relationship but found public airing of such matters distasteful. It should be noted, however, that however he behaved in his private life, Lon Chaney's coworkers (unlike Browning's) typically praised him for his numerous considerations and kindnesses on the set.

Joan Crawford, who was eighteen at the time of *The Unknown*, had few memories of Browning but vividly recalled Chaney's self-punishing behavior. "I was so eager to learn my craft in those early days . . . that I did more observing of acting than I did of directors and directing techniques." Nonetheless, she could remember "how very soft-spoken, quiet and sensitive Tod Browning was, and how very knowledgeable." She recalled Chaney's ordeal with his leather harness as "agonizing. . . . when he was not before the camera, Mr. Browning would say to him, 'Lon, don't you want me to untie your arms?' And Lon would answer, 'No, the pain I am enduring now will help the scene. Let's go!' " Crawford remembered Chaney keeping his arms bound one day for five hours, "enduring such numbness, such torture, that when we got to this scene, he was able to convey not just realism but such emotional agony that it was shocking . . . and fascinating." The actress found Chaney to be "the most tense, exciting individual I'd ever

met, a man mesmerized into his part.'' When he acted, ''it was as if
God were working, he had such profound concentration. It was
then I became aware for the first time of the difference between
standing in front of a camera, and acting.'' In Crawford's recollection, Browning was ''concerned that all of us were comfortable in
our scenes. . . . he was very patient with me, a newcomer.'' Chaney also offered Crawford a combination of technical and emotional assistance:

> I'll never forget one incident with Lon when we were filming *The
> Unknown.* I was having trouble crying, which is one of the hardest
> jobs we have anyhow. I felt more like laughing, and Lon saw it. He
> came over and put his hand on my shoulder and said, ''Every-
> thing's just all right.'' The words didn't mean anything, but the
> sympathy in his voice and the understanding in his action was
> enough. I started to cry, and cried all through the scene. I love
> working with Lon, and speaking of crying, we have stood around
> and cried at him when he is doing a sad scene, and you don't
> forget it.

It is clear that Lon Chaney projected the image of physical suffering as both the definition and price of his stardom; exactly why
he chose to is not so clear and, since he left no revealing journals or
correspondence on the matter, may forever remain obscure. On
one level he offered his large working-class audience a grotesque
exaggeration of the Puritan work ethic: he toiled hard, he suffered,
he succeeded—and so, by extension, might they. In the populist
cathedral of the American cinema, Chaney was a martyr saint, his
celebrity maintained as a kind of crucifixion in progress. ''When
we're getting ready to discuss a new story,'' Browning told an interviewer, Chaney would ''amble into my office and say, 'Well, what's it
going to be, boss?' I'll say, 'This time a leg comes off, or an arm, or
a nose'—whatever it may be.''

There were limits, of course, to Chaney's somatic flexibility—he
was in no sense a trained contortionist. In *The Unknown* he was
forced, for the first time, to employ a double. The upper half of his
body hidden from camera view, a real armless man named Paul

Dismute provided the dexterous footwork for scenes in which Chaney smoked, mopped his brow, etc. But however accomplished the illusions, the overall sickliness of the Browning-Chaney formulas and their resemblance to a public flogging were making a growing number of critics truly queasy.

Richard Watts, Jr., writing in the *New York Herald-Tribune,* observed that "the case of Mr. Tod Browning is rapidly approaching the pathological. After a series of minor horrors that featured such comparatively respectable creations as murderous midgets, crippled thieves and poisonous reptiles, all sinister and deadly in a murky atmosphere of blackness and unholy doom, the director presents us now with a melodrama that might have been made from a scenario dashed off by the Messrs. Leopold and Loeb in a quiet moment." Watts conceded that, given a cinema otherwise so completely devoted to red-blooded values and "general aggressive cleanliness," films of the sort Browning championed might provide "a valuable counteracting influence." Nonetheless, he felt a trifle repelled by *The Unknown.* "What amazes me," he wrote, "is that those careful custodians of public squeamishness, Mr. Hays and Mr. Thalberg, allowed the director to go on. . . . compared to Tod Browning, the morose Erich von Stroheim is the original apostle of sweetness and light." Watts was referring to Will H. Hays, the former U.S. postmaster general who had been named head of the Motion Picture Producers and Distributors of America (MPPDA), an industry self-regulatory organization founded in wake of such scandals as the Roscoe "Fatty" Arbuckle sex-murder trial. At the time, however, the MPPDA existed at the pleasure of the studios and didn't have any real regulatory power, functioning largely as an industry public relations buffer.

Reflecting the growing public alarm over the moral tone of motion picture entertainment in the late twenties, *The Unknown* was the first Browning-Chaney film to be frankly and aggressively attacked in the press for its melodramatic morbidity. The *New York Sun* assured readers that "the suspicion that the picture might have been written by Nero, directed by Lucretia Borgia, constructed by the shade of Edgar Allan Poe and lighted by a well-known vivisectionist was absolutely groundless. . . . *The Unknown* is merely one of the cute little bits of lace designed and executed by Tod Browning. . . ." The *Sun* admitted that *The Unknown* "may be just what the public wants. If it is—well, the good old days of the Roman Empire are upon us." The New York *Daily Mirror* suggested that "if you like to tear butterflies apart and see sausage made you may like the climax to *The Unknown*. . . . typical Chaney fare spiced with cannibalism and flavored with the Spanish inquisition." The *New York Evening Post* observed that "Mr. Chaney has been twisting joints and lacing himself into strait-jackets for a long time—so long, in fact, that there is almost nothing left for him now but the Headless Horseman. No doubt that will come later." The *Evening Post* called *The Unknown* "a remarkably unpleasant picture, which can hardly be recommended as even moderate entertainment. A visit to the dissecting room in a hospital would be quite as pleasant, and at the same time more instructive." The conservative *Harrison's Reports* was particularly disturbed:

> One can imagine a moral pervert of the present day, or professional torturers of the times of the Spanish Inquisition that gloated over the miseries of their victims on the rack and over their roasting on hot iron bars enjoying screen details of the kind set forth in *The Unknown,* but it is difficult to fancy average men and women of a modern audience in this enlightened age being entertained by such a thoroughly fiendish mingling of bloodlust, cruelty and horrors. . . . Of Mr. Chaney's acting it is enough to say it is excellent, of its kind. Similar praise might well be given the work of a skilled surgeon in ripping open the abdomen of a patient. But who wants to see him do it?

"Despite the popularity of the Chaney distortions," the *New York Telegram* wrote, "it is rumored that this will be the actor's last film of this sort for some time. The "don't step on it" ["it might be Lon Chaney"] jokes, combined with a poisonous Broadway rumor that Chaney's next film would be entitled *Teddy the Torso,* have apparently pierced deeply into Hollywood hearts."

In Europe, however, Browning was taken far more seriously by cineastes still under the spell of a fantastic expressionism that had still only partially penetrated America. Browning "is an unbridled romantic," wrote the French critic Jacques B. Brunius in 1929, "and even when making box office pictures for the average cinemagoer he does not conceal the fact that he is influenced by German romantic-expressionism—even when he uses, as in this case, a psychological situation as a springboard, he feels no compulsion to stay on this plane." Brunius admitted that *The Unknown* contained "more than the usual ration of extravagance . . . fit[ting] with Tod Browning's relish for freaks, monsters, and extravagant situations—enough for aesthetically minded people to be squeamish and patronizing about it. What does it matter for those who, like myself, discover in Tod Browning's films an undefinable poetry, an uncanny charm, probably irrelevant to the canons of Great Art, I confess, but nonetheless effective and disturbing."

The Unknown was thought to be a lost film for many years, until a print was discovered, misplaced, in a French archive. Amusingly, its translated title, *L'Inconnu,* had robotically relegated it to the section of canisters marked "Inconnu," containing unidentified reels of film.

Browning's next story, filmed as *The Hypnotist* and released as *London After Midnight,* was most likely an attempt to capitalize on the 1927 London stage success of Bram Stoker's *Dracula,* dramatized by Hamilton Deane and revised for Broadway by John L. Balderston, London correspondent for the *New York Sun* and joint playwright, with J. C. Squires, of the supernatural fantasy *Berkeley Square* (1928). Stoker's widow was jealously guarding motion picture rights to *Dracula*—she had been burned by the German plagiarism called *Nosferatu* (1922)—but at the moment the American studios weren't interested in a frankly occult tale. In the Hollywood scheme of things, supernatural spectacles were acceptable only if they could be explained away as the machinations of mere mortals, usually part of a criminal conspiracy. Browning, of course, was perfectly at home with such an approach, which he had previously exploited in *The Mystic* and other films. But he also wanted very much to do a straight adaptation of *Dracula,* with Chaney in the title role. The

New York Times reported, nine years after the fact, that "Chaney wanted to act Dracula and often discussed the part with Tod Browning. . . . Both men believed the American public to be 90 per cent superstitious and ripe for horror films. Chaney had a full scenario and a secret makeup worked out even at that early date. . . ." With its spectacular bat, wolf, and mist transformations, all accomplished by a five-hundred-year-old title character who grows younger as he drinks human blood, Dracula would indeed offer Chaney his ultimate challenge in cinematic metamorphosis. But Metro, as in the matter of *Liliom,* decided it would be better to imitate *Dracula* than to purchase it.

Browning's story borrowed brazenly from the stage version of *Dracula,* escaping charges of plagiarism by debunking its second-hand vampire trappings as part of a criminal investigation. It featured an English heroine named Lucy (Marceline Day), who lives next door to a spooky, ruined estate housing a vampiric specter in white tie and black cloak, known as the Man in the Beaver Hat (Chaney), along with his thoroughly original bat-girl assistant, Lunette, played by Edna Tichenor.* Both stories recounted ancient vampire lore, the protective aspects of garlic, etc.; featured an authoritative middle-aged investigator (Van Helsing in *Dracula;* Chaney in a second role as Inspector Burke of Scotland Yard) who employs hypnotism; eerie entrances via clouds of mist; an ineffectual juvenile lead (the character Jonathan Harker in *Dracula;* actor Conrad Nagel in *London After Midnight*); and highly theatrical bat transformations.

Chaney's beavered bogey was patterned, rather obviously, after the figure of Werner Krauss as the cloaked, behatted, shock-haired carnival mountebank in *The Cabinet of Dr. Caligari;* whether or not Browning had input into this aspect of the character's appearance can't be authoritatively documented, but the costuming and makeup nonetheless provide an important iconographic link between the predatory con men who populated the films of Browning's early career and the preternatural vampires who inhabited

---

* *"Lunette," despite its sound, is not a proper name; rather, it is the French word for the wooden neck restraint of the guillotine.*

his later work. In Browning's story, as scripted by Waldemar Young, the vampires are merely stooges employed by the Scotland Yard inspector to trap a murderer, but they allowed Browning to push his dark reveries considerably beyond the confines of commonplace crook melodramas into cobweb-festooned realms of the ultimate social outsiders: the living dead. Chaney's makeup caused him only minimal discomfort; in addition to ghastly whiteface and sharklike dentures (outfitted with protruding hooks that lifted the sides of his mouth into a death rictus), the actor employed loops of wire fitted into the skin around his eyes like monocles, and expanded to pull open the lids: the film reportedly featured close-ups of the bloodshot, watery orbs, their irises rolling like loose egg yolks. Forrest J Ackerman, one of the country's leading collectors of fantasy-film memorabilia, saw the film as a boy in San Francisco during its initial release, and likened Chaney's bizarre, scuttling posture to a macabre variation on Groucho Marx. The late horror writer Robert Bloch, who also saw the film as a child, recalled one of Browning's oddest bits of atmosphere: a pride of scurrying armadillos, hardly indigenous to London, but glimpsed nonetheless through the cobwebs of the vampire's mansion.

London After Midnight was released in December 1927, two months after *Dracula* had proved a Broadway hit. Today, it remains one of the two "lost" Browning-Chaney films and is considered by the American Film Institute—not to mention hordes of film historians and fans—to be one of the most important missing-in-action pictures of the silent era. Periodic reports of its discovery still have the power to set phone lines buzzing from coast to coast as film buffs spread and embellish the rumors. Part of the phantom film's enduring mystique is undoubtedly attributable to its being the first American "vampire" film—vampirism, by the Anne Rice–saturated 1990s, having become a prevalent cultural theme—but also to the fact that *London After Midnight* proved the most profitable of all Browning-Chaney collaborations for M-G-M, grossing more than a million dollars in worldwide rentals, with a profit of $540,000.

The *New York Herald-Tribune* noted that "the distinguished talents of Lon Chaney, Tod Browning, and the late author of *Dracula* are shrewdly combined in the picture . . . the scenes are so imaginatively done and Mr. Chaney's passion for grotesque makeup is so effective, that you feel that shortly both director and star will be hard at work making the real Dracula—a 'movie' property if there ever was one." *Harrison's Reports* called Chaney's makeup "hideous —enough to make one sick in the stomach."

But in England the courts had to consider whether Chaney's makeup was enough to incite murder.

On October 23, 1928, a twenty-nine-year-old Welsh carpenter named Robert Williams and a twenty-two-year-old Irish housemaid named Julia Mangan were found in London's Hyde Park, their throats slashed by a razor. Mangan died before reaching St. George's Hospital, but Williams survived. He was subsequently charged with murder and attempted suicide; a first trial ended in a hung jury over the question of his sanity. During Williams' second trial, the defense asserted that just before the killing, the prisoner was possessed by a vision of Lon Chaney. According to the London *Times*, "The prisoner, in the witness box, said that, while he was talking to the girl in the park noises came into his head, and it seemed as if steam was coming out of the sides of his head, and as if a red-hot iron were being pushed in behind his eyes. He thought he saw Lon Chaney, a film actor, in a corner, shouting and making faces at him. He did not remember taking a razor from his pocket, or using the razor on the girl or on himself. The next thing he remembered was a nurse washing his feet at the hospital." A doctor called as a defense witness gave the opinion that Williams suffered from a form of epileptic insanity. Justice Travers Humphreys, while admitting that Chaney's makeup in *London After Midnight* presented a "horrifying and terrible spectacle," and that members of the jury who had seen the film, or even advertisements for *London After Midnight,* might themselves be horrified, pointed out that simply being frightened by a characterization meant to be frightening, and recalling it in a moment of emotional excitement, hardly indicated insanity or epilepsy. The jury agreed, and Williams was sentenced to death on January 10, 1929. But three weeks later, on the advice of the home secretary, the condemned man was issued a reprieve on medical grounds.

Browning and Chaney's next project—their second "lost" film —was a calculated attempt to break the mold of grotesque masquerade; the publicity for *The Big City,* released in early 1928, emphasized that Chaney would appear wearing his own face—one of the few real novelties left to the actor and to his audience. The story was another crook caper, with Chaney as a dapper criminal don named Chuck Collins involved in double-crossing intrigue and schmaltzy reformation against a colorful nightclub setting (Browning attempted to engage Sophie Tucker for some atmosphere but was put off by her $5,000 demand for thoroughly silent song-styling). Chaney acted opposite two proven costars, Marceline Day from *London After Midnight* and Betty Compson, who last acted with Chaney in his first hit, *The Miracle Man.* Betty Compson recalled her role as "trite and uninteresting," an assignment with Browning "completed so quickly that it was impossible for me to know him even slightly." Compson played a hard-boiled moll (the antithesis of Day's wide-eyed ingenue) who helps Chaney execute a convoluted jewel robbery involving a specialty act of "headless" dancers (who might have waltzed in from the set of *The Show*) and the concealment of the loot in a plate of spaghetti right under the nose of the law. (Hard-core Freudians, fishing for revealing resonance, might well consider the larger connotations of "family jewels," endlessly dangled and jeopardized in one Browning film after another.)

The film did well, posting a profit of $387,000. But reviews of *The Big City* reflected the increasing polarization of critics on the subject of Tod Browning. The *Chicago Sunday Tribune* called him "a wiz of a director, and exceedingly wizzy in this number." But the *Film Spectator* felt that Browning had "directed wretchedly." "Every situation in *The Big City* is a manufactured one. . . . One absurd scene follows another until the only feature of the picture that is entertaining is the speculation it arouses as to how long the absurdities can last." Richard Watts, Jr., a critic who followed Browning's

Hollywood progress with particular acumen, sensed that the essence of the Browning-Chaney mystique was beginning to wobble, and commented in the *New York Herald-Tribune:*

> The Clean Love of a Good Woman is hard at work reforming Mr. Lon Chaney this week, but the result, somewhat to the discredit of virtue, is rather a disastrous one. The demands of cinema censorship being what they are, it is only natural that crime pictures should be softened into anemia by the necessary last-reel reformation of the hero-crook, but it hardly seems necessary to sentimentalize this surrender in the ecstatic way resorted to in the film. . . . This orgy of reform is all the more surprising because the picture was both written and directed by Tod Browning, ordinarily the most uncompromising of the screen's devil worshippers. . . . the sight of the First Diabolist of the Cinema concerned in the reformation and marriage of all his characters at the same time is a disconcerting one.

Following the completion of *The Big City,* Tod and Alice Browning took a six-week vacation in Europe, at least part of which was devoted to seeking out story material. Despite earlier publicity stories implying he had toured the world as a circus performer in his youth, the only documentation of a passport in Browning's name is one issued in late 1927, and the trip was, in all likelihood, Browning's first trip abroad.

He could afford such luxuries now. By 1927 the Brownings owned an impressive Tudor-style mansion on a triangle of land opposite the Beverly Hills Hotel, and were building a second, beachfront residence at Malibu. Additionally, Browning had invested in a vineyard near Emeryville, California. By today's standards and tax rates, his salary of $100,000 a year plus bonuses made him the equivalent of a millionaire. All in all, he had come a long way from the cramped house in working-class Louisville, from carnival tents, and from boardinghouses.

The degree to which he kept in touch with his family can't be determined, but Helen Polsgrove, his foster sister's daughter, recalled that Lydia Browning was always proud of her son and visited their house to read his letters whenever they arrived. Still, he never returned home, and the whirlwind visit after the success of *The Unholy Three* would prove to be the last time he saw his mother, alive or dead. One day in 1927, Polsgrove remembered, Lydia "was hanging clothes out in the backyard, fell and broke her hip, and went to Highland Baptist Hospital where she stayed for one year. She came home with a nurse in uniform, and got pneumonia and died." Despite her recollections, the official cause of Lydia Browning's death was a cerebral hemorrhage on May 24, 1928. Jennie Block's daughters remembered how Avery Browning let them know of his mother's passing—not in person, or by a phone call, but by the solemn formality of three signaling knocks on their front door.

Although Browning had no production immediately in progress —his next film would not begin shooting for a month after his mother's death—he did not make the trip to Louisville for his mother's funeral or at any time thereafter to be with his family in their grief. Funeral arrangements were made by Jennie, who selected a plain silver-gray casket and matching burial clothes. Only a dozen folding chairs were required for the wake. Five limousines, including the hearse, were needed for the funeral, held May 28 at the Baptist church at the corner of 22nd and Walnut streets. Interment was at Eastern Cemetery, under a temporary burial plate marked "Mama."

Avery Browning paid the bill: $423, roughly one percent of his brother's per-picture salary under a new contract with M-G-M, which once more doubled his salary. His production in preparation, an adaptation of the lurid Broadway play *Kongo*, by Charles de Vonde and Kilbourn Gordon, was, perhaps coincidentally, the most extreme depiction of parent-child alienation Browning had yet attempted. Retitled *West of Zanzibar*, the film was Browning's first project under an arrangement with Metro that increased his salary to $45,000 a picture, with a contingent bonus of $5,000. *Kongo* told the sordid story of a stage magician who, grappling with a rival for his wife's affections, is paralyzed in the altercation. The magician's wife disappears, and he assumes she has run away with his rival, an ivory trader. A few years later, she returns, with a daughter, but dies before she is able to talk to him. He takes the child and vows his vengeance, following the hated rival to Africa. He sets himself up as a wheelchair-ridden god to the natives, who do his bidding. For his revenge, he consigns the child to a whorehouse in Zanzibar, where she contracts syphilis. He summons his wife's lover, contriving to have him shot by the natives after their meeting, knowing that it is their custom to burn alive the wife or daughter of men who have died. But the rival presents his own surprise—the girl is not his, but the magician's, who has in his blind thirst for vengeance mistakenly consigned his own child to a hideously fatal sexual disease. The natives kill the rival and demand the live cremation of the girl. The magician, using some of his old stage tricks, helps the girl escape with a derelict doctor who can offer her medical assistance, and is himself sacrificed on the natives' pyre.

The stage play, presented in New York with Walter Huston as the crippled avenger, was initially deemed too hideous for any type of Hollywood adaptation, but Browning managed to soften the script considerably—primarily by substituting alcoholism for syphilis—and ultimately circumvented the Hays Office's objections. As the magician Phroso, a.k.a. ''Dead Legs'' Flint, Chaney was able to essay a crippled role without reliance on painful harnesses or extreme makeup, but merely the ability to project hate while letting his lower limbs go rubbery. Lionel Barrymore played Chaney's nemesis, and Mary Nolan was given the role of the degraded daughter (who, in classic Browning fashion, never recognizes her natural parent).

But for many critics, *West of Zanzibar* was the final straw in the Browning-Chaney freak circus. *Harrison's Reports* not only panned the film but ran a lead editorial entitled AN OUTPOURING OF THE CESSPOOLS OF HOLLYWOOD! expanding on its outrage. ''How any normal person could have thought that this horrible syphilitic play [*Kongo*] could have made an entertaining picture, even with Lon Chaney . . . is beyond comprehension. But here it is, a Metro-Goldwyn-Mayer picture, which you will be compelled to show to the people of the United States as entertainment.'' *Harrison's Reports* urged individual theater owners to marshal the moral support of civic and religious groups to resist films like *West of Zanzibar.* "The stupidity of some of the producers seems to be unbounded. . . . In no other industry do the manufacturers insist on producing an article that the consumers do not want. Only in the moving picture industry this thing happens."

In reality, motion picture consumers—at least those who actually bought tickets, resulting in worldwide billings of $921,000 for *West of Zanzibar*—were sending a different message entirely. But many critics had begun to resist Browning and Chaney's increasingly formulaic concoctions on artistic grounds. "It's getting so that Lon Chaney's name warns theatergoers of a bad picture, and with Tod Browning atrocity is assured . . . it would be a good idea if Browning let someone else play his malignant cripple for a change," Donald Beaton wrote in the *Film Spectator.* "There are a lot of people who are getting sick of seeing Chaney gulp over some girl half his age who is ungrateful enough to love someone else or set his jaw while another girl who doesn't know she is his daughter tells him that he is a low form of life. . . . Chaney's once considerable acting ability has been atrophied by the parts he has to play until he has about three expressions left. . . ."

Irving Thalberg may well have begun to have doubts about the long-term viability of the Chaney-Browning pairings, despite their profitability. The looming specter of talking pictures posed a challenge and a threat to everyone who had achieved success in the silent period; although a nontalkie, *West of Zanzibar* had included a synchronized orchestral score with sound effects as a sop to audiences already exposed to and excited by *The Jazz Singer* (1927) and the noisy cinematic future it foretold.

Neither Browning nor Chaney was comfortable with the prospect of a talking screen; their art, after all, was firmly grounded in the tradition of pantomime melodrama, with little grounding in the nuances of vocal projection beyond their early work in vaudeville. To the public, however, Chaney's virtuosity in previous screen portrayals implied that he might be just as protean in the talkative hereafter. But Chaney's contract made no mention of any vocal requirements—and the actor held fast to the letter of his obligation.

By 1928 the question of the continued viability of Chaney and Browning as a team must have occurred to Thalberg; Chaney's biggest hit of all had been *Tell It to the Marines* (1927), a straight dramatic picture directed by George Hill, devoid of disability and mutilation, that had nevertheless shown a profit of $664,000, dwarfing even the estimable earnings of *London After Midnight*. *Mr. Wu* (1927), directed by William Nigh, showed an above-the-line figure of $439,000. *While the City Sleeps* (1928), with Jack Conway directing Chaney in a sympathetic, girl-getting role, ended up $399,000 in the black. *Laugh, Clown, Laugh* (1928), inspired by *I Pagliacci*, with Chaney opposite a fourteen-year-old Loretta Young, showed a profit of $450,000.

In other words, Browning's partnership with Chaney was hardly sacrosanct from Metro's standpoint; the actor frankly earned better for the studio without the director: non-Browning films with Chaney between 1924 and 1928 showed an average profit $30,000 higher than films with Browning at the helm. And the lack of documentary evidence for the standing legend of a dedicated creative relationship between the men is, to say the least, striking. Chaney's only published comments on Browning were politely dismissive: he told a writer for *Photoplay* that while he respected Browning, and understood that many people had come to think of him as "the Chaney director," the selection of directors was almost a matter of indifference to him. Following Chaney's death, the writer Adela Rogers St. John asked Browning about their working relationship. "Never said anything to me on the set except, 'Yes, boss,' " he replied. "We used to argue a bit before and after hours. But on the set he was a good soldier." But St. John seemed to have information of her own. "Argue!" she wrote. "They fought like a couple of sea lions. They yelled and cussed each other out plenty. But just let anyone else interfere. Let any executive or writer attempt to take advantage of the apparent friction. They soon found out it was a very private fight. Tod and Lon instantly ganged up on the intruder, who decided that he would be better occupied elsewhere." Other observers formed their own impressions. To agent Phil Berg, "Tod and Chaney were very simpatico," though both men could be enigmatic. (Berg hosted a noontime "director's table" for his clients and their stars, but "Chaney would very rarely come to lunch with us—and when he did, he wouldn't say anything!") Film editor Errol Taggart, who cut *The Black Bird* and *The Road to Mandalay* and coedited *London After Midnight,* once commented that the director and actor "weren't exactly bosom buddies."

Whatever the nature of the men's private relationship, their public collaboration was limping toward its final hour.

Browning and Chaney's last picture, *Where East Is East* (1929), proved an anemic retread of characters and plot devices from earlier films. One again senses their mutual hesitation at taking on talkies, resorting to another synchronized music track with sound effects to appease the box office and looking profoundly backward in the attempt to create a story. In a story by Browning scripted by Waldemar Young, Chaney played "Tiger" Haynes, an animal trapper in Indo-China who wears his résumé on his deeply scarred face (an effect achieved with nonflexible collodion, a liquid still used by makeup artists, which puckers the skin as it dries). Tiger has a charmed, if perhaps overly playful, relationship with his effervescent daughter Toyo (Lupe Velez) interrupted by the appearance of a suitor, Bobby (Lloyd Hughes), and the reappearance of Toyo's dragon-lady mother, the sloe-eyed Madame de Silva (Estelle Taylor, real-life wife of former heavyweight boxing champion Jack Dempsey). In a psychosexual configuration even Freud would have been hard-pressed to unravel, the mother decides to torture the father by seducing the daughter's fiancé—and raising the wrath of the animal kingdom in the process. For in the intervening years, we learn, Tiger has kept a resentful, abused gorilla in his menagerie, who remembers Mama's transgressions from way back when. At the climactic moment, he releases the ape to pay a midnight visit to Madame de Silva's boudoir. She opens the door eagerly, expecting Bobby's embrace—but instead meets a crowd-pleasing death in the best tradition of Poe's "Murders in the Rue Morgue."

Reviewers had wildly divergent responses to *Where East Is East*. The *Film Spectator* ran two notices, the first calling it "the best job that Tod Browning has ever done," a "succession of beautiful exotic, and romantic scenes." Chaney was commended for making "no attempt to disguise himself as either a beetle or a battleship." But the reviewer protested Browning's "giving us many close-ups of kisses, a beastly exhibition of poor taste entirely out of keeping with the artistic standard of the production as a whole." A few weeks later, the publication saw fit to run a second, thoroughly stinging review, noting that "Lupe Velez plays one of those bounding halfcaste girls whose very appearance on the screen makes the hand itch for a fly swatter. . . . Screen writers, for some reason, have the idea if the girl has the blood of two races in her veins, she must go nutty and leap around as if she were weaned on a pogo stick." The *New York Times* praised "several shrewdly photographed and exciting episodes" but found the story "more than slightly incredible."

Where East Is East is a fairly ridiculous film, with Chaney wasted in an oddly passive role requiring him primarily to stand on the sidelines, glowering his disapproval. But the picture is nonetheless significant in its recapitulation of essential themes of the Browning canon: marital estrangement; family secrets; sexual revenge; semi-incestuous arrangements between parents and children; degraded, "animalized" protagonists (with names like Tiger, the Black Bird, Cock Robin), often deprived of normal human attributes like upright posture.

The summer of 1929 was a turning point for both Chaney and Browning. Chaney had come down with a nagging respiratory infection in the spring while completing location work in Wisconsin for the railroad drama *Thunder* (1929), directed by William Nigh. The underlying cause of Chaney's illness was lung cancer—the actor had long been a heavy smoker—and on July 25 his contract was suspended on grounds of incapacity. The full gravity of his illness was a closely kept secret, and he remained in seclusion for most of the summer and fall of 1929.

Browning had begun preparing the final picture of the three-project contract that had begun with *West of Zanzibar*. The agreement hadn't specified that Browning deliver a talking picture, much less a talking and silent version of the same picture, but that is exactly what M-G-M had in mind for his next production, an adaptation of Bayard Veiller's 1917 stage melodrama *The Thirteenth Chair* (which had earlier been filmed as a silent by Pathé in 1919). The additional payment of $25,000 Browning received from Metro on April 10, 1929, may reflect the added responsibilities of supervising two separate productions for separate markets.

In the spring of 1929 he entered into new contract negotiations with M-G-M, and it was soon announced in the trades that his next film would be *The Sea Bat*, a "weird story of tropical life and jungle voodoo." Lon Chaney was named as star, but plans for the picture were put on hold as his health worsened. Beyond *The Thirteenth Chair*, Browning's future at M-G-M became suddenly murky.

The original stage production of *The Thirteenth Chair* had starred the playwright's wife, the British-born, American-trained actress Margaret Wycherly, as a medium named Madame La Grange, who helps trap a murderer among the diplomatic set in Calcutta. Wycherly played the part against type, as a dowdy Irishwoman (in London, the redoubtable Mrs. Patrick Campbell interpreted the role, to great acclaim, in her usual grande dame manner), and re-created the role in Browning's film, her first screen assignment. Leila Hyams and Conrad Nagel provided the love interest.

The cast had originally included Hollywood newcomer Joel McCrea in the Nagel role, but the engagement didn't last. Hyams remembered McCrea as "an unknown, a sort of cowboy come off the range." For the opening scene, the actor was squeezed into an ill-fitting tuxedo. "The sleeves were too short, his hands were too big," Hyams said. "He didn't know how to handle himself at all. The first couple of scenes were so bad they had to take him out."

Hyams recalled that Margaret Wycherly was so intent on upstaging her coplayers that it created a problem on the set. "She was full of all the old theatrical tricks, and it was very difficult to play a scene with her." Browning took her aside. "Is she upstaging you? We can't get your face in the camera." Hyams confirmed his suspicions and asked what she could do. Browning told her not to worry.

They rehearsed the scene again, and when Wycherly started her tricks again, Browning told her, "Margaret, that isn't your camera," and asked her to play to an alternate lens. The camera was hidden in a soundproof box, and Wycherly never knew it wasn't running.

In the role of the mercilessly interrogative police inspector, Browning cast the Hungarian actor Bela Lugosi, who had just scored a tremendous stage success in New York and California in the Hamilton Deane and John L. Balderston adaptation of *Dracula*. *The Thirteenth Chair* is of particular interest to Lugosi aficionados in that it is probably the best documentation of the actor's acting style during his stage *Dracula* period. Browning's casting of Lugosi is almost perversely inappropriate, unless he was colluding with the actor to produce a screen test for the film version of *Dracula*, which M-G-M and several other studios were then considering. In fact, this may have been exactly the case. There is nothing in the script of *The Thirteenth Chair* to suggest that the police inspector has the temperament and demeanor of a Transylvanian vampire, but that is just how Lugosi played the part, evidently with Browning's full approval. The actor's makeup is aggressively, unnaturally stylized; his eyebrows are pencil-sharpened precisely as they were for the theatrical vampire role; he wears semiformal attire and seems on the verge of hypnotizing everyone in sight. Casting Lugosi was a real stretch in terms of the play—his character, named Delzante in the film to accommodate his accent, was called Donohue in the original script, and provided considerable comic relief. But it is apparent from the actor's first appearance that Browning is intending to showcase Lugosi as a discovery or revelation. The actor stands with his back to the camera, a conspicuous mystery as another detective speaks on the phone. He finally turns to reveal his face, delivering an absolutely ordinary line as if he were lost in darkest Shakespeare.

The buildup is inexplicable in dramatic terms but suggests a significant effort on Browning's part to promote the oddly magnetic performer. Browning offered an explanation in the film's press materials: "On the stage," he said, "the inspector's role had comedy in it, but by playing him as a mysterious figure, dominant and dangerous, I think we enhanced the sense of mystery. Every play has to have comedy, even a mystery drama, but to get it from a central figure in a mystery plot destroys, to my mind, the usefulness of that figure as a mysterious point. . . ."

The Thirteenth Chair is a perfect example of the wax-museum "staginess" that plagued early talkies, although to be fair it must be said that the static qualities evidenced in these films had less to do with any prevailing style of the legitimate theater than to the simple inability of silent-movie directors to handle dialogue. Nowhere in the professional theater did actors speak so slowly or portentously as they did in *The Thirteenth Chair;* as Edward Wales, the story's amateur sleuth who comes to a bad end in the middle of a séance, John Davidson gives a zombielike delivery that almost rivals Lugosi's evocation of living death. And perhaps the greatest howler in the script, given Lugosi's accent-smothered diction, is his commanding assertion, "Madame, my words are perfectly clear!"

The newly formed Motion Picture Producers and Distributors of America, convened as an industry watchdog to anticipate and avoid the banning or mutilation of films by state, city, and international censor boards, found Lugosi's performance troubling. W. F. Willis, advising M-G-M on behalf of the MPPDA, was concerned about the inaccurate depiction of a Scotland Yard investigator's actual power of authority in India: ". . . we have an Inspector, of less rank than the Superintendent, far outside the bounds of authority, coming into the residency of Sir Roscoe, and Sir Roscoe far outranking [Lugosi] politically. And yet the Inspector's attitude is insolent all the way through. His accent betrays him as a Continental, and not British, and to me this aggravates the offence." Willis could not imagine that "a Continental could have risen to an inspectorship without a better sense of the deportment expected in the drawing room of a gentleman in Sir Roscoe's position." There was a practical basis to his concern:

> . . . the falseness of the character . . . makes all other characterizations false. And perhaps this *may* have a censorship bearing in the British countries. I do not know *how,* or even *that* it will, but I will not be surprised if it does. We have had troubles in the past

when we have ad-libbed too much in matters of foreign custom and characterization.

But Willis' most intriguing recommendation to M-G-M is probably the earliest example on record of a now time-honored, if supremely cynical, Hollywood practice—the deliberate planting of extraneous, objectionable material, simply to allow censors to feel that they have accomplished something:

> I have an uncertain feeling regarding the possible attitudes of the censors regarding [*The Thirteenth Chair*]. I cannot see a single point to which I believe they will have reasonable objection, and yet I have the fear that some of them will think they must do something to it. I cannot even guess what. It is a freak picture, and whatever the censors may do will be freak action. Here is a case where I think it will be wise for us to give them something definite to do. Perhaps they will try to create objection to the scenes of Edward Wales when his corpse sits in the chair for the climax. . . . Therefore I suggest the inclusion of the most ghastly close-up we may have if it can be done without interfering with the sound record.

The Thirteenth Chair, released on Friday the 13th of December 1929, showed only half the profit ($148,000) of Browning's recent pictures with Chaney. It no doubt dawned on Browning that the new Hollywood would force him to share creative responsibilities in ways that were alien to him. He had created his most striking effects working directly and intimately with actors versed in pantomime; now layers of skilled intermediaries were required: screenwriters and sound technicians had almost as much influence as the director. Dialogue couldn't be doctored after the fact by a title-card writer—it had to be right the first time, on the set. But Browning wasn't a stage director and could offer little technical advice in matters of vocal projection and pacing. His most bankable collaborator was as reluctant to do a sound picture as he had been, and was gravely ill to boot; their plans for *Dracula* seemed a pipe dream at best. A vast migration of stage-trained actors from the East had already begun, and the stock market crash of October 1929 had shaken the New York theater world further, forcing another wave of talkative talent westward. Browning was at a crossroads, and for the moment chose not to make a decision. He was drinking again, though not as self-destructively as he had before; press statements that he "hasn't touched a drop of liquor in years" were technically true, but only if one made a distinction between alcohol derived from hard spirits and that obtained from beer, his new drink of choice.

He picked up his last salary from M-G-M at the end of August and took an extended trip to Europe with Alice. He was not offered, or did not sign, a new contract with M-G-M. For the first time in five years, he was without a film, a studio, or a paycheck.

FOUR

TRANSYLVANIA

Bela Lugosi, caught in the web of Dracula. (David J. Skal Collection)

he word "Transylvania" means "across the forest," and the next chapter of Tod Browning's career proved a trip into the woods on any number of levels.

A few months before Browning's contract lapsed at M-G-M, the new head of production at Universal Pictures, Carl Laemmle, Jr., began negotiations with Metro for a loan-out of Lon Chaney for a talking-film version of *Dracula*. Though the studio hadn't yet purchased the rights to the 1897 book and 1927 stage play, it had already leaked press stories to the effect that it had, further suggesting that the German actor Conrad Veidt would wear the cape of the master vampire. Veidt had already begun doing Chaney-like parts for Universal and proved his facility for projecting a frightening orality; in the studio's lavish adaptation of Victor Hugo's *The Man Who Laughs* (1928), he played a character whose face had been horribly disfigured in childhood, the sides of his mouth slit open to create a permanent, deathly grin. As the zombie sleepwalker in *The Cabinet of Dr. Caligari,* Veidt was already established as one of the cinema's leading interpreters of macabre roles. His casting as Dracula was championed by Universal associate producer Paul Kohner and by director Paul Leni, the studio's German-born mystery specialist who had overseen one of the studio's great silent hits, *The Cat and the Canary* (1927).

But Leni died suddenly from blood poisoning in September

1929, Veidt returned to Germany rather than risk talkies with his shaky English, and Kohner's career rise at Universal was derailed by the ascendancy of Carl Laemmle's twenty-one-year-old son, Julius Laemmle, who assumed control not only of the studio but of his father's first name as well. *Dracula* appealed powerfully to Junior Laemmle's postadolescent imagination; the stage play, starring Bela Lugosi, had been a hit in Los Angeles the previous summer, and may first have come to his attention. Kohner was taken off major projects and put in charge of producing foreign-language versions of Universal's talkies, a common practice in the early sound era, before dubbing was the norm.

At the end of June 1929, M-G-M was willing to draft a contract agreement for Universal to borrow Chaney for *Dracula,* and their lawyers forwarded paperwork to Laemmle. Most intriguing, their correspondence of June 25 referred to discussion of Chaney's playing a dual role in the film; one can only surmise that Universal toyed with the idea of Chaney playing both Dracula and his nemesis, Professor Van Helsing, in the same way he had played both the "vampire" and police investigator for Browning in *London After Midnight.* Metro's draft contract allowed Universal to require Chaney to submit to a physical examination, and for the studio to purchase its own health insurance policy for the actor during the course of the production.

Within a month, however, the prospect of Chaney working for anyone was in doubt. Carl Laemmle, Jr., seems to have gotten wind of the impending suspension of Chaney's contract and briefly considered offering the actor a personal, rather than a studio, contract (an uncommon but not unknown practice among producers at the time); since Chaney's agreement with M-G-M made no provision whatsoever for talking pictures, he theoretically could have made an arrangement to do a talkie with whomever he pleased. On July 22, M-G-M's lawyers emphatically advised Laemmle against making a contract with Chaney personally; regardless of the legal aspects, they regarded such a move highly objectionable from the standpoint of business ethics.

Scenario department readers had been giving very negative

feedback to Universal's top brass regarding *Dracula,* despite its lu-
crative track record as a stage play and its worldwide fame as a
novel. (The studio had, in fact, toyed with the idea of a film *Dracula*
as early as 1915, the year of Universal's inception.) Typical of the
1927 readers' reports on the book and play was one by Steve Miranda, written on the heels of the successful London stage production and in anticipation of the reworked version on Broadway:
"While this may have a fantastic opening [on stage] and be very
engrossing for those who like the weird, I cannot possibly see how it
is going to make a motion picture. It is blood—blood—blood—kill
and everything that would cause any average human being to revolt
or seek a convenient 'railing.' Sorry but I cannot see where there is
anything in this. . . ."

Another silent-era reader for Universal, George Mitchell, Jr.,
noted that "we all like to see ugly things . . . we are all attracted,
to a certain extent, to that which is hideous. (For instance, the big
appeal in *The Phantom of the Opera.*) But when it passes a certain
point, the attraction dies and we suffer a feeling of repulsion and
nausea." Mitchell wrote that *Dracula* "passes beyond the point of
what the average person can stand or cares to stand. . . . it would
take a thousand titles to tell the people what it was
about . . . . . and then they wouldn't know!"

Junior Laemmle, who had scored big with his first major effort,
a triumphantly successful adaptation of Erich Maria Remarque's *All
Quiet on the Western Front* (1929), and felt he should be able to pick
his own projects, clashed repeatedly with his father over the matter
of *Dracula.* The elder Laemmle felt the whole subject of vampirism
was morbid in the extreme, and disagreed strenuously with his son
that the Stoker novel was a fit subject—much less a profitable prospect—for the screen. Other studios, however, including Fox, Pathé,
Columbia, and M-G-M, were actively considering *Dracula,* and Universal kept its options open. Finally, Laemmle Sr. gave the project a
guarded go-ahead, with the proviso that the vampire be played by
Lon Chaney—a virtual guarantee of box-office success.

In January 1930 the Laemmles signed Browning to what was
heralded in its publicity as a "five-year contract." Although *Dracula*

may well have been the main reason for Browning's engagement, the studio had not yet acquired the rights to the novel or play, nor the services of Lon Chaney. It was instead announced to the press that Browning would direct *The Scarlet Triangle,* "a sensational crook melodrama for which Browning will supply the story and dialogue as well as wield the megaphone," but shortly thereafter a newspaper item appeared stating that the director would instead do a talking remake of his 1920 Universal success *The Virgin of Stamboul.*

Paralleling Browning's negotiations with Universal, Chaney, who had rallied from cancer treatments, signed a new contract with M-G-M, agreeing to a talking remake of *The Unholy Three,* obviously without Browning.

While the *Dracula* negotiations languished, *The Virgin of Stamboul* remake fell by the wayside, and Browning instead directed a talkie version of his early Universal success, *Outside the Law,* with Edward G. Robinson interpreting the role first created by Chaney. With Universal scenarist Garrett Fort, Browning made numerous changes to the original story: Chaney's "Black Mike" Sylva became Robinson's "Cobra" Collins, and both the San Francisco locale and Chinatown subplot were completely deleted. The shell of the plot remained, however: A pair of crooks, Connie (Mary Nolan) and "Fingers" O'Dell (Owen Moore) hide out in an apartment, pursued by Collins, who wants a cut of the loot from a bank robbery. They befriend a toddler (Delmar Watson) who lives next door, not knowing his father is a policeman. The officer is critically wounded in a gun battle that ends in Cobra's death, but the couple redeem themselves by saving the cop's life.

In addition to recycling one of his proven crime plots, Browning managed to work a sideshow motif into the picture, having Fingers O'Dell pose in a bank window as a carnivalesque mechanical man, the better to case the joint. (The director had used a related device for Universal almost a decade earlier—the phony mechanical chess player employed by the crooks of *White Tiger.*)

Typically—for Browning—the critics were irreconcilably divided over *Outside the Law.* The *New York Herald-Tribune* called it "a good picture" and—while conceding that it was "old fashioned"—

"alluring." But *Variety,* in one of the most devastating appraisals ever given a Browning film by a major trade publication, called it "one of the worst pieces of clap trap since sound came in. . . . players obviously as bewildered as the director."

Today, *Outside the Law* is an often excruciating film to sit through, its poorly paced scenes further attenuated by endless pauses and stilted dialogue, frequently delivered "crook style" out of the corners of the actors' mouths. As *Variety* noted in its withering pan, "The crazy-quilt theme and the anemic direction permit the players to run wild. . . . Any kind of filler was used to drag out [the story] into feature length. Yards of film deal repetitiously with stupid conversation. . . ."

Part of the disparity in critics' responses may have had less to do with the film itself than with a fascination for the novelty of talkies, counterbalanced by a discomfort with the unfamiliar new cinematic grammar dictated by sound. *Variety,* like some of Browning's detractors in the late twenties, disapproved of his penchant for close-ups, which were held to break up the "natural" rhythms of stagebound pictorial pantomime. While today's audiences are conditioned to expect frenetically fragmented montage, it is instructive to consider that at one time the mere inclusion of a close-up was considered by many viewers and critics to be a grotesque intrusion.

Browning's general difficulties with sound were, perhaps, summed up by one painfully emblematic encounter with the new technology. According to the film's pressbook:

> The massive metal "mike" had been suspended at an unusually low elevation, to "pick up" the voice of four-year-old Delmar Watson, sitting on the floor surrounded by half a dozen puppies. Having instructed the youngster in the action of the scene about to be "shot," Browning sprang to his feet, intent on hurrying back to his seat in the directorial chair. But his head came into violent contact with the microphone, and the director fell to the floor with a resounding thud.

"I can't fight all you guys at once," said Browning thickly, slowly coming out of a daze, "but I'll take you one at a time."

Following the accident, Browning suggested that all microphones on film sets henceforth be marked with conspicuous red warning flags.

Whether or not the incident happened quite the way the studio publicist described, it ironically underscored Browning's basic discomfort with sound. When he last worked at Universal, in the early twenties, he preferred to work imagistically, avoiding even titles if he could manage it. "The unnecessary subtitle is an abomination upon the face of the silver sheet," he told an interviewer for *Moving Picture World.* "The novelist works with words, but the director works with expressions." The lack of dialogue, or its titled facsimile, allowed him to do much of his creative work after principal photography was completed. "The director does the real writing of his story in the cutting and projection rooms," he said. But with talkies, the tables were turned: dialogue sequences could not be so easily cut and rearranged.

Dracula, Browning's next assignment, was a wordy book and a talky stage play, but its profusion of disturbing imagery—centuries-old crypts from which the "undead" rise nightly to feed on the living; the spectacle of beings who transform themselves into wolves, bats, and mists; the vampire's grisly destruction via the wooden stake—finally made the story irresistible to the cinema.

Securing rights to the story was another matter. Universal had to contend not only with Bram Stoker's widow but with the playwrights Hamilton Deane and John L. Balderston as well. All three were often at odds. Deane's original stage version of *Dracula,* which Florence Stoker had licensed to him in 1924, did not completely please her; when Deane brought his play to London after three seasons of provincial touring, she undercut him by privately commissioning another adaptation from the playwright Charles Morrell. It was produced briefly, in September 1927, while Deane's play was still performing strongly in the West End, and served the evident purpose of preserving some of the literary values of the Stoker original that Deane had jettisoned. These included primarily long speeches—too long for the stage—taken almost verbatim from the novel, that contained pretentious theatrical overtones, most notably influences of *The Tempest*. Dracula, in Stoker, is a bargain-basement antithesis to Prospero, who drives the elements, causes shipwrecks, and, crucially, has an animalized servant at his disposal—Caliban in Shakespeare, Renfield in *Dracula*.

Bram Stoker was in many ways a frustrated playwright, who spent the best years of his life in well-paid servitude to the celebrated actor-manager Henry Irving, for whom he wrote *Dracula*, hoping that Irving would play it on the stage. Irving scorned it, but *Dracula* earned an amazing afterlife as a popular distillation of high villainous archetypes like Mephistopheles in *Faust*—another favorite Irving role, qualities of which Stoker intentionally incorporated into his book.*

By the time *Dracula* reached Universal Pictures and Tod Browning for its sacramental transmigration to the screen, it was a property encumbered by personalities, pretension, prior adaptations, and litigation. Florence Stoker had spent eight years in legal wrangles with the producers of *Nosferatu,* the unauthorized German adaptation. The German courts had ordered the negative of the film destroyed, but many prints had escaped—one resurfacing in a Greenwich Village art cinema at the height of the delicate negotiations with Universal. Agent Harold Freedman, who represented Mrs. Stoker and the playwrights (and who had also made a personal trip to Los Angeles in an unsuccessful attempt to persuade Lon Chaney to accept Universal's offer), managed to buy off the New York exhibitor and deliver the infringing print of *Nosferatu* to Universal "for purposes of destruction." The flamboyant impresario of the Broadway production, the publisher-producer Horace Liveright, had signed away screen rights but nonetheless threatened a suit on the basis that a film would unfairly compete with his stage rights. Liveright was finally paid off to avoid nuisance litigation. The sale of the book and stage adaptations was completed in the

---

* *In 1928, when the Deane and Balderston version of* Dracula *opened in Chicago, the veteran drama critic Frederick Donaghey (who knew Stoker from years earlier when he had toured the states with Irving) recalled the author's explanation of the character of Dracula vis-à-vis Irving: "The Governor as Dracula would be . . . a composite of so many of the parts in which he has been liked—Matthias in* The Bells, *Shylock, Mephistopheles, Peter the Great, the bad fellow in* The Lyons Mail, *Louis XI, and ever so many others, including Iachimo in* Cymbeline. *But he just laughs at me!"*

summer of 1930; Browning was formally assigned to the picture in mid-July, and *Nosferatu* was handed over to Universal on August 15.

Just after naming Browning as director, Universal announced that the Pulitzer Prize–winning novelist Louis Bromfield would adapt *Dracula* to the screen. Two treatments had already been attempted, one by Fritz Stephani and the other by Louis Stevens. Stephani's was a workmanlike combination of both the book and play that went over the top with only one image: a bat-winged airplane Dracula uses to transport his coffin boxes from Transylvania to England between the hours of dusk and dawn. Deane and Balderston had referred to an airplane in their adaptation, but not to any avian abnormalities. One of Stephani's inventions would find its way into the final picture, however: the vision of a flapping bat leading a driverless carriage through the treacherous roads leading to Dracula's castle.

Bromfield, a novice to Hollywood who would shortly return East, discouraged and disgusted, wrote a lavish first treatment, doing his best to reconcile the continuities of the novel and the stage play—which, he discovered, were different animals indeed. Commercial expediency dictated that *Dracula* conform to the conventions of a drawing room mystery melodrama, and Deane and Balderston had, therefore, thrown away the most dramatic sequences of the book: the opening chapters in which the young solicitor Jonathan Harker finds himself a prisoner in Transylvania, as well as the novel's climax, in which the English protagonists mount a chase back to the count's ancestral home, where the demon has been driven after his unsuccessful attempt to make Britain a vampire colony.

Bromfield composed a remarkably cinematic opening based on the novel. His hero, renamed John Harker, is transported to Castle Dracula during a snowstorm, training a revolver on a pack of wolves who pursue the sleigh. Both the muffled sleigh-driver and mysterious footman who takes his luggage bear a strange resemblance to his host, Count Dracula, whom Bromfield introduces as a disembodied voice as Harker peers out the window at a sheer, yawning abyss. "It is a long drop, nearly two thousand feet," the voice intones, and Harker whirls to confront the master vampire, whom Bromfield conceived as a clever amalgam of Stoker's ancient, ungroomed satyr and the stage play's music-hall Mephisto: "a tall man, dressed in musty, and unpressed, trousers and morning coat. He has a very pale face with drooping white moustache and long, unkempt white hair. Yet he has a distinction of bearing. He wears, also, a long black cape, which floats about him as he moves forward to greet Harker."

Bromfield was less successful with his approach to the second, stage-based part of the story. Deane and Balderston understood that the repulsive, largely offstage phantom of Stoker's book had to be cleaned up considerably to be presentable in the theater; but where their Dracula was sociably unctuous, Bromfield's went so far as to play bridge with a fat, wealthy widow—only to be revealed as a monster when he fails to reflect in her makeup mirror during a powder break.

One senses that Bromfield grew less interested in the assignment as it progressed; Universal's financial situation was worsening daily in the wake of the stock market collapse, and a straightforward, budget-minded adaptation of the stage play became a more attractive option than Bromfield's evocative, but expensive, approach to Stoker's novel. Dudley Murphy, later the director of *The Emperor Jones* (1933), wrote the first full-length script on which Bromfield received cocredit, although it used almost none of the novelist's material. It was Murphy who seems to have struck on the idea of using Renfield as the real estate lawyer who travels to Transylvania, in place of Harker.

Browning had been accustomed to developing scenarios at Metro in a close relationship with the story department and a handful of trusted writers; at Universal he had to contend not only with testy literary negotiations but with volatile father-son politics and the studio's vain desire to force a "prestige" novelist on the project—not to mention money problems. According to William S. Hart, Jr., Browning leaned heavily on his earlier relationship with Laemmle *père* to wrest some measure of control over the project.

Using Murphy's script as the backbone, Browning worked on three more drafts in collaboration with Garrett Fort, combining material from Stoker, Deane and Balderston, Morrell, and Stephani. Carl Laemmle, Jr., asked for numerous changes that Browning was able to resist: the elimination of Dracula's classic line "To die—to be really dead—that must be glorious. There are far worse things awaiting man—than death."

Laemmle was also uncomfortable with the implicit suggestion of Dracula's bisexuality. "Dracula should only go for women and not men," he commented in the margins of the scene following Dracula's decimation of the crew of the ship that has transported him to England. Browning kept the material, and pushed the envelope of polymorphous perversity even further by having Dracula vampirize Renfield, rather than leaving it to his wives as the script dictated.

The final script credited both Browning and Fort with "Adaptation and Dialogue," though Browning's and Murphy's names would be dropped from the on-screen credits, with only Fort given billing. The final, budget-minded script eliminated completely the exciting overland chase back to Transylvania, relocating the climax to the catacombs of Dracula's English residence, Carfax Abbey.

There is evidence that Browning favored casting Bela Lugosi from the very start—possibly from the time (coinciding with the onset of Lon Chaney's cancer) that he first worked with Lugosi in *The Thirteenth Chair*. Lugosi insinuated himself into the film negotiations—conceivably at Browning's prompting—by corresponding directly with Florence Stoker, doing his best to bring down her asking price. On April 8, 1930, Lugosi wired Harold Freedman, the New York agent representing Stoker, Deane, and Balderston: HAVE EXCELLENT REPUTABLE DIRECTOR WITH BIGGEST STUDIO HERE WILLING TO BUY AND DO DRACULA WITH ME AS STAR, asking Freedman to quote his LOWEST PRICE QUICK. On June 25 Lugosi followed up with another telegram to Freedman: SPENT MANY

MONTHS TO PROMOTE DRACULA SPENT MANY CABLES WITH LON-
DON TO BRING DOWN PRICE WILL YOU PLEASE EXPRESS OPINION
TO UNIVERSAL FOR ME BEING THE LOGICAL CHOICE TO BE CAST
FOR DRACULA. On July 8 he wrote to Freedman on the stationery of
the Leamington Hotel, in Oakland, California:

> Dear Mr. Freedman,
>
> I have your letter of June 26th in response to my wire, and
> wish to thank you very much for your kind effort in suggesting
> that I play the part in "Dracula" when it is filmed. I am sure the
> success of this enterprise will be largely due to your endeavors,
> which I very much appreciate.
> Hoping we may have future business interests together, and
> thanking you again, I remain,
>
> Yours very truly,
> BELA LUGOSI
>
> N.B. If you have plays in which there are great character parts
> suitable to my kind of ability, I would appreciate it if you would
> send me copies: my permanent address is 1146 North Hudson
> Avenue, Hollywood, California.

At this point, while Lugosi's casting was not a fait accompli, it
was certainly close. Universal's final choices during August 1930
boiled down to Lugosi; Ian Keith, a well-regarded, Shakespearean-
trained actor, then the husband of actress Blanche Yurka; and William Courtenay, a distinguished stage actor who had successfully
toured the country as a caped magician in *The Spider*. As early as
July 2, Browning told the *Los Angeles Examiner* that he favored "getting a stranger from Europe, and not giving his name." Other actors considered by Universal included John Wray, Chester Morris,
and Paul Muni. Harold Freedman, negotiating for Mrs. Stoker and
the playwrights, initially favored the romantic lead Joseph Schildkraut. (The occasionally heard suggestion that John Barrymore was
considered is interesting but has not been documented.) Of the
rival studios, Columbia Pictures had considered Raymond Huntley,

who had played the role both in London's West End and on tour in America.*

On August 26, Lon Chaney died of cancer in Los Angeles. Radium treatments had only resulted in anemia, and his death followed a series of bronchial hemorrhages, unstoppable despite the offers of hordes of fans to donate their own blood to the man who might have been Dracula.

Browning served as an honorary pallbearer in an entourage that included Louis B. Mayer; Nicholas Schenck, president of Loew's, Inc., M-G-M's parent company; Irving Thalberg; General Smedley D. Butler; actors Harry Carey, Lionel Barrymore, Wallace Beery, Ramon Novarro, William Haines, and opera singer/actor Lawrence Tibbett; *Ben-Hur* director Fred Niblo; writer-director Edgar Selwyn; comedian Jack Benny; and dance director Sammy Lee.

Chaney was buried in Forest Lawn Cemetery in Glendale, on August 28, the ceremony accompanied by a Marine honor guard. Their presence was the result of Chaney's acclaimed performance in *Tell It to the Marines* (1928), which had struck a deep chord among military men; but on a deeper level, Chaney's parade of disfigured and disabled characterizations may have provided the larger public with ritual engagement, and exorcism, of the tangled emotions surrounding the mass maiming of World War I.

Browning never made a public comment on his private reaction to Chaney's death, although one might assume it was complex. Browning's departure from M-G-M had coincided with Universal's attempts to borrow Chaney for a film they both wanted to do. Despite his health problems, Chaney had backed out of Universal's offer and gone on to do M-G-M's talking remake of *The Unholy Three* (1930), directed by Jack Conway instead of Browning. Instead of improving his grip on sound films within the more familiar and supportive environment of M-G-M, Browning was thrown into the notoriously less structured atmosphere of Universal, where Chaney essentially had abandoned him. Regardless of their personal regard for each other, Chaney had been Browning's major collaborator for

---

* *Huntley had taken over the part of Dracula from actor Edmund Blake, who originated the role in Hamilton Deane's 1924 stage play, which toured the British provinces for three seasons before opening in London on February 14, 1927.*

the five most successful years of his career, but now was gone forever.

Browning returned to Universal City to finish preparations for *Dracula*. Casting had begun in earnest, and within two weeks most of the cast had been announced. Edward Van Sloan was engaged to repeat his Broadway role of Professor Abraham Van Helsing, Dracula's nemesis. Also from the New York cast, Herbert Bunston was assigned the role of Dr. Seward, father of the imperiled heroine, Mina. For the female lead, Browning chose the twenty-year-old New York stage ingenue Helen Chandler, a delicate beauty who had already begun a slide into drinking and drug addiction that would ultimately kill her. Frances Dade, a smoky-voiced starlet from Philadelphia, and granddaughter of the model for the face on the Liberty dollar, was cast as Lucy Weston, Mina's doomed friend. Dwight Frye, another transplanted Broadway actor, was chosen to interpret the film's plummiest part—the wide-eyed, cackling, insect-eating Renfield.

Given Renfield's ascendancy in the plot, the nominal lead male role of John Harker was effectively reduced from protagonist to concerned bystander; despite it being a thankless part, it created the greatest casting headaches following the role of Dracula. Robert Ames and Lew Ayres were both announced, then withdrawn from the assignment (Ayres later maintained he wanted to play Renfield). Universal finally cast a borrowed leading man from First National, David Manners, who ended up the highest-paid member of the *Dracula* cast, earning $2,000 a week.

Bela Lugosi, in what was arguably one of the worst Hollywood contracts ever offered, or accepted, took the title role as a work for hire for a total of $3,500—$500 a week for seven weeks of production. Lugosi had a powerful sense of entitlement to the screen role, having played it hundreds of times on stage, and his sense of identification with the part may have blinded his judgment in the negotiations, or lack of them, with Universal. While the role established him in Hollywood, the terms on which he accepted fame served to cripple his later earning ability. A year following *Dracula*, Lugosi would find himself in bankruptcy court.

Part of Lugosi's practical difficulties in Hollywood stemmed from his fragile grasp on the English language. A 1920 political expatriate from the Hungarian theater, where he was a versatile, classically trained leading man, he forged a career on the New York stage by learning English roles phonetically. A San Francisco reporter recorded his speech patterns in 1928, as he groused about being straitjacketed into villain parts. "Amereecan people," he intoned, "I like their sportsmanship. Your theater—I like not so well. You hunt for actor types, instead of training your actors so they may play many roles." In America, Lugosi complained, "the foreigner is nearly always cast as a heavy."

Although his English improved in the 1930s, until the end of his life Lugosi was never able to think in his acquired language, "except for simple things," according to his son, Bela Lugosi, Jr. On the positive side, Lugosi's limited fluency resulted in the highly mannered and oddly inflected vocal style that became his trademark—and the very essence of vampire elocution for all time.

To the American actors who worked with him, however, Lugosi often seemed merely haughty and aloof, insulated in narcissistic reveries. David Manners, who also worked with him in two films after *Dracula,* told a friend bluntly that Lugosi was "a pain in the ass from start to finish." Manners remembered the actor pacing the Universal soundstage between scenes, velvet cape wrapped about him, posing in front of a full-length mirror while he intoned, with sepulchral emphasis, "I *am* Dracula . . . I *am* Dracula!"

Lugosi had his own side of the story. "After I had been in the play for a month," he said, "I began to 'take stock of myself' and I realized that for my own well-being I should make some attempt to conserve my mental and physical strength—to throw myself with less fervor into the depiction of the role." Lugosi decided "that if I could go through the play somewhat mechanically—somewhat more placidly within myself—there would be no lessening of the effect of my performance on the audience, but a decided lessening of the effect on my own nervous system." Nonetheless,

. . . I could not do it. The role seemed to demand that I keep myself worked up to a fever pitch, and so I sat in my dressing room and took on, as nearly as possible, the actual attributes of the horrible vampire, Dracula. And during those two years I did not speak a word to any person behind the scenes during the progress of the play. And since everyone knew of the strain I was laboring under, no one spoke to me. . . . I was under a veritable spell which I dared not break. If I stepped out of my character for even a moment, the seething menace of the terrible Count Dracula was gone from the characterization, and my hold on the audience lost its force.

For the film, Lugosi discovered that his stage technique needed to be modified severely. "In the theater I was playing not only to the spectators in the front rows, but also to those in the last row of the gallery . . . a certain exaggeration in everything that I did— not only in the tonal pitch of my voice, but in the changes of facial expression which accompanied various 'lines' or situations was necessary. I 'took it big,' as the saying is." Film, however, changed matters considerably:

But, for the screen, in which the actor's distance from every member of the audience is equal only to the distance from the lens of the camera, I have found a great deal of repression was absolutely necessary. Tod Browning has continually had to "hold me down." In other screen roles I did not seem to have this difficulty, but I have played *Dracula* a thousand times on the stage, and in this one role I find that I have become thoroughly settled in the technique of the stage, and not of the screen. But thanks to my director, I am "unlearning" fast.

Dracula was filmed between September 29 and November 15, 1930, with additional scenes and retakes on December 13, 1930, and January 2, 1931. According to David Manners, the production was "extremely disorganized." Asked about the experience of working with Tod Browning, Manners laughed and said, "It's funny you should ask. Someone asked me the other day who directed

[*Dracula*] and I had to say, I hadn't the faintest idea!'' Manners stated that ''the only directing I saw was done by Karl Freund, the cinematographer.'' The Bohemian-born Freund—famed for his German work on *The Last Laugh* (1924) and *Metropolis* (1927)—was, like Lugosi, not completely fluent in English. According to Manners, he employed a translator to help him, an extremely formal Teutonic gentleman who wore white gloves at all times.

Browning may well have been forced to delegate directorial responsibilities as the production lagged behind schedule. He conducted business in his flashy, trademark ''directorial'' garb: scarf, beret, and a bristling mustache—the jodhpurs had been retired with the twenties. But image went only so far in controlling the ungodly proceedings: despite an approved budget, the production was under continual downward financial pressure. The studio was literally at the edge of insolvency. As Lugosi remembered, ''Everything that Tod Browning wanted to do was queried. Couldn't it be done cheaper? Would it be just as effective if . . . ? That sort of thing. It was most dispiriting.''

But the ultimate insult, from Browning's perspective, must have been the indignity of having his production upstaged by Paul Kohner and his simultaneously rendered, Spanish-language version of *Dracula,* shot on the same sets* at night with a completely different cast and crew. As a Universal insider, Kohner was able, despite a minuscule budget ($68,750 versus Browning's $355,050), to martial studio resources for elaborate optical effects and a more sumptuous-looking production than Browning was able to achieve. It wasn't exactly a fair horse race, since Kohner and his director, George Melford, were able to view Browning's rushes and then add their own improvements. Nonetheless, the Spanish *Dracula* (long thought an irretrievable film, but finally restored in 1992) remains the technically superior version, marred only by the absence of Lugosi's magisterial presence.

---

* *In point of fact, one set had to be rebuilt. The Transylvanian inn, where Renfield is warned against continuing his trip to Castle Dracula, was destroyed by a fire of unknown origin on October 23, 1930, after Browning's unit had finished shooting, according to an October 25 item in the* Exhibitor's Herald-World. *The inn that appears in the Spanish film is a completely new structure.*

Browning, finally, wasn't Universal "family." The studio was infamous for its rampant nepotism (Carl Laemmle, Sr., even provided on-site housing for relatives, who bloated the payroll). Universal ended up doing almost no publicity for Browning's *Dracula* when it opened in Los Angeles; some of art director Daniel C. Hall's set renderings were exhibited (during production) at a Hollywood bank, but it was Kohner's film, not Browning's, that was rushed into a trade paper preview in January 1930, to considerable buzz. "If the English language version of *Dracula,* directed by Tod Browning, is as good as the Spanish version, why the Big U [Universal] haven't a thing in the world to worry about," noted *Hollywood Filmograph.* Lugosi somehow made his only Los Angeles public appearance in connection with *Dracula* for the premiere of the Spanish film, not his own. And so on.

The final negative cost of *Dracula* was $441,984.90—more than $85,000 over budget. The figure, drawn from Carl Laemmle's private ledger, contradicts the daily production log, which indicates that Browning brought the film in $13,858.80 *under* budget. Universal's arbitrary bookkeeping practices may have created headaches of their own for the director. Finally, the studio did not permit Browning a final cut on the film, and, according to William S. Hart, Jr., the director hated *Dracula* in its ultimate version. After the film was released to television in late 1957, he "suffered with it," complaining repeatedly to Hart that it wasn't his original version of the film, but rather (in Hart's words), "a thing put together and sold to television out of the scraps on the cutting room floor."

In reality, the version Screen Gems syndicated as part of Universal's "Shock Theater" package conformed precisely to Universal's 1931 cutting continuity, with the exception of the humorous missing epilogue with Edward Van Sloan admonishing the audience that vampires were real. (For its 1938 rerelease, the speech was cut to avoid giving offense to religious groups.) The studio actually did all its tinkering before the first theatrical release, trimming Browning's cut of the film by nearly ten percent—from eighty-four to seventy-five minutes—even while adding new footage.

Hart said he saw Browning's original cut of *Dracula* as a boy and remembered that the director's surreal sense of timing "was the most eerie thing I have ever seen. . . . It was not a horror where you saw anything. It was a horror of the unknown." According to Hart, "they didn't have as many pictures of Lugosi grimacing. . . . You hardly saw him at all. He was such a soft unknown thing that the horror was what he *might* be. . . ."

But effects Browning intended for evoking the slow-motion feeling of a nightmare were considered by Universal to be slow, period. Several soundless sequences were cut or shortened: Dracula's first scripted appearance (apparently filmed; a photograph survives), emerging from one of three travel boxes stacked in an arched alcove under his castle's great stairway, was replaced by a more dramatic sequence of Dracula arising, with his wives* and assorted opossums and bugs, from macro- to micro-sized coffins in the catacombs of Carfax Abbey (not Castle Dracula—a glaring lapse of continuity). With its prowling, dollying camerawork, the scene—shot nearly at the end of production—strongly suggests some last-minute decision-making on the part of Karl Freund, well known for his mobile lensmanship, a characteristic largely absent from Browning's work.

Other cuts seem to have come from within dialogue: Dracula's line, taken directly from Stoker, "The walls of my castle are broken —the shadows are many—but, come—I bid you welcome," was cut to the quick: "I bid you, welcome." Similarly, the vampire's leave-taking instruction, "I may be detained elsewhere most of the day tomorrow—in which case we will meet here—at sundown," was reduced to its memorable closing line, "Good night, Mr. Renfield." Some of these cuts may have intensified Dracula's unearthly presence, if only by rendering him unnaturally taciturn.

---

* *The identity of the actresses who played Lugosi's trio of wives, long a subject of speculation in* Dracula *circles, has now been established. Dorothy Tree, a well-known New York stage actress (who appeared in the original production of Philip Barry's* Holiday *in 1928), was just establishing herself in Hollywood (she was later blacklisted in the McCarthy era but made a comeback in* The Men *and* The Asphalt Jungle*). She died in 1992. Geraldine Dvorak, Greta Garbo's stand-in at M-G-M, was reportedly dismissed by Garbo after she began impersonating the star in public. She later pursued a stage career. Mildred Peirce (who used the stage name Cornelia Thaw) was a Hollywood bit player who retired from show business shortly after filming* Dracula *to marry and raise a family. She died in the early 1980s.*

Tod Browning in a 1909 portrait.
(Courtesy of Chatty Eliason)

Browning's uncle Louis Rogers "Pete"
Browning, at the height of his fame.
(Courtesy of Hillerich & Bradsby Co., Inc.)

Browning's first wife,
Amy Louise Stevens.
(Courtesy of Chatty Eliason)

Browning in his vaudeville days.
(Courtesy of Chatty Eliason)

Browning (with scimitar),
Fay Tincher, and Max Davidson
in *The Mascot* (1914).
(Courtesy of Leonard Schrader)

Browning and Fay Tincher in *Out Again—In Again. (Courtesy of Leonard Schrader)*

Actor Elmer Booth, killed by Browning's drunk driving, seen here in his 1914 stage hit, *Stop Thief. (Billy Rose Theater Collection, New York Public Library at Lincoln Center, Astor, Lenox, and Tilden Foundations)*

Browning with Hollywood associates, 1919. Left to right: Bernard McConville, Roy Somerville, and Bennie Zeidman. *(Courtesy of Ronald V. Borst/Hollywood Movie Posters)*

Wallace Beery and Priscilla Dean in *The Virgin of Stamboul* (1920). *(Photofest)*

Lobby card
for *Outside
the Law*
(1921). *(Courtesy of
Leonard Schrader)*

Priscilla Dean with
Browning on the
set of *Outside the
Law* (1921).
*(Elias Savada
collection)*

Priscilla Dean (with rifle) in a scene from *Drifting* (1923). *(Photofest)*

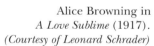

Alice Browning in
A Love Sublime (1917).
(Courtesy of Leonard Schrader)

Anna May Wong, Browning's
underage love interest.
*(Free Library of Philadelphia
Theatre Collection)*

The Unholy Three: Browning with Chaney in the guise
of an old lady. *(Elias Savada collection)*

Streetcar promotion for *The Unholy Three* (1925)
(Free Library of Philadelphia Theatre Collection)

Cut scene from *The Unholy Three:* Harry Earles attacks a child.
(Left: Elias Savada collection. Right: Courtesy of Ronald V. Borst/Hollywood Movie Posters)

Left to right: Mitchell Lewis, Aileen Pringle, and Dewitt Jennings in *The Mystic* (1925). Costume by Erté. *(Elias Savada Collection)*

Poster art for *The Black Bird* (1926).
(Courtesy of Philip J. Riley)

Lon Chaney and Renée
Adorée in *The Black Bird*
(1926). *(Photofest)*

Poster art for *The Road to Mandalay* (1926). *(Courtesy of Philip J. Riley)*

Browning and Lon Chaney between takes for *The Road to Mandalay* (1926). *(Elias Savada collection)*

Browning (top left) directs John Gilbert and Renée Adorée in *The Show* (1927). *(Elias Savada collection)*

John Gilbert in *The Show* (1927). *(Photofest)*

Lon Chaney (with leg double) and John George in *The Unknown* (1927). *(Photofest)*

Freudian focus:
Joan Crawford
in *The Unknown* (1927).
(Elias Savada collection)

Production still: Lon Chaney blackmails a surgeon into amputating his arms in
The Unknown (1927). *(Elias Savada collection)*

Lon Chaney as
the vampire in
*London After
Midnight* (1927).
*(David J. Skal
collection)*

Browning, Lon Chaney, and Edna Tichenor on the set of *London After Midnight* (1927).
(Courtesy of Michael F. Blake)

But other trims are just confusing. Renfield's comic "attack" on the fainted maid (he is finally only interested in a fly that is buzzing her) was shorn of its punch line, making the servant's subsequent, hale-and-healthy reappearance puzzling in the extreme. Scenes showing Van Helsing and Seward's discovery of one of Dracula's hiding boxes, and Renfield's role in protecting the others—the film's only explanation of precisely what services the slave is providing—simply disappeared. And the merciful staking of Lucy in her crypt is gone completely; as far as the viewer is concerned, Dracula's first English bride is still busy molesting children even as the film comes to an end.

While Browning's experience making *Dracula* may well have been stressful, he did find time for some playful self-indulgence, making a cameo appearance as the voice of the harbormaster who boards the derelict *Vesta*, discovering the maniacal Renfield lurking in the hold: "Why, he's mad—look at his eyes—the man's gone crazy." According to William S. Hart, Jr., Browning made similar visitations, in a manner anticipating Alfred Hitchcock's famous walk-ons, in "most of his films," usually as a voice, but sometimes as an extra in a crowd, or even as just a passing shadow. "He had a strange sense of humor," said Hart, and treated these flash appearances as an ongoing personal joke.

Dracula premiered in New York at the prestigious Roxy Theater on Thursday, February 12, 1931, the day moved forward for publicity reasons to avoid an "unlucky" opening on Friday the 13th. (The often-told story that the film, advertised as "the strangest love story of them all," had a macabre marketing tie-in with St. Valentine's Day, is completely without basis. Nonetheless, the anecdote is routinely repeated in almost every article or book published on *Dracula*). In its first forty-eight hours of business in Manhattan, the film sold over 50,000 tickets. In subsequent weeks it was a smash in city after city, necessitating two- and three-week holdovers, early-morning performances, and, in a few cases, even around-the-clock screenings. *Dracula* pulled in $700,000 in first-release domestic rentals, and $1.2 million worldwide, stabilizing Universal's finances and giving the studio its only profitable year during the Great Depression. It was, almost instantly, the most profitable film Tod Browning ever made for any studio, and would continue to earn handsomely during periodic theatrical rereleases in the 1930s, '40s, and '50s.

The *New York Times'* Mordaunt Hall called *Dracula* "quite an exciting Grand Guignol production" and noted the unusual audience applause "rarely heard during the showing of a motion picture" when Van Helsing repels the vampire with a crucifix. The *San Francisco Examiner* praised the film's "tragic dignity" and Browning's talents in particular: "His fertile imagination and artistic ingenuity are seemingly inexhaustible," reviewer Ada Hanifin wrote. "The photographic treatment is magnificent: the fall of light and shadows, dim forms of vaulted castles, the sudden coming on of dank mists, strange lights that illuminate the pallid fiend's eyes. . . . a well-nigh perfect thing of its kind." In late February the picture had a well-received trade preview in London. The *Era* called *Dracula* "gloominess in excelsis. . . . it is more than possible that its gruesomeness will hit a high spot among popular audiences, especially in provincial towns."

Among the dissenting voices was the *Hollywood Filmograph,* one of the few journals that noted the downhill slide of filmcraft in *Dracula,* from the atmospheric, cinematic opening scenes at the castle to the flat, stagebound mise-en-scène of the climax. "Tod Browning directed—although we cannot believe the same man was responsible for both the first and latter parts of the picture," wrote reviewer Harold Weight. But across the spectrum of critical response, Lugosi's performance was almost universally praised. "It would be difficult to think of anybody who could quite match the performance," wrote the critic for *Variety.*

For Browning, *Dracula* was the culmination of a long obsession with shadowy fantastic themes that the American cinema had long resisted—except in the oblique, "rationalized" forms Browning had pioneered in the silents. Director Edgar G. Ulmer, another dark stylist, best known for *The Black Cat* (1934), recalled that "Tod Browning was perhaps the first one to have seen what were called then 'fantasy' films—which were being made in Germany and Sweden. After the war, in Germany, there was a strong E. T. A. Hoffman influence. . . . Browning knew [Robert] Wiene's work in *Caligari* [but] began to get away from the expressionism of the period into a conception which one might call baroque." According to Ulmer, "Browning was a man of infinitely wider culture than most people. He was widely read, and not only knew Poe by heart, but all of English 'Gothic' literature."

Browning and cinematographer Freund almost certainly studied the print of *Nosferatu* Universal had captured. There are numerous direct borrowings, ranging from the parallel shots of the German Dracula (Graf Orlock, played by Max Schreck) and Bela Lugosi perusing their leases on foreign refuges, to the scene in which Renfield/Harker cuts his hand at Dracula's table, stimulating the vampire's bloodlust, to small details of decor and shot composition. (Paul Kohner, who knew *Nosferatu*'s director F. W. Murnau, then working in Hollywood, took even more visual inspiration from the German film for his Spanish-language version.)

Browning also ransacked his own earlier work for ideas; preliminary set sketches by the designer John Ivan Hoffman are obviously based on production stills of Cedric Gibbons' settings for *London After Midnight.* The director based his conception of Dracula's wives on actress Edna Tichenor's makeup as Lunette, the bat-girl in the same film, and as a final, perhaps tongue-in-cheek private joke, imported a passel of armadillos to scurry around the great hall of Dracula's castle, just as they had patrolled the shadows of Chaney's creepy house four years earlier.

While *Dracula* is unique in the Browning canon for its frankly supernatural theme, it is nonetheless linked firmly to his earlier work on a number of levels. On a technical plane, it is a film of silences, a stubborn clinging to the silent era that nourished him, and from which he was being forcibly weaned.* The film is devoid of music, save for a generically mysterious theme from Tchaikovsky's *Swan Lake* under the titles, and a few snatches of Wagner when

---

* *As a concession to theaters not yet equipped for sound, Universal prepared a silent version of* Dracula, *further condensing the film's already terse dialogue into even more taciturn title cards. No print of this version is known to have survived, but according to its cutting continuity, 197 titles were utilized—more than twice those required for Browning's most accomplished silent film,* The Unknown.

the vampire visits a concert hall. The music is arbitrary; Universal repeated the title music for *Murders in the Rue Morgue* (1932) and *The Mummy* (1933).

Thematically, *Dracula* is a rich recapitulation of the director's prior work. By patterning his Dracula not on Bram Stoker's description, but instead on the unctuous vaudeville magician conception of Hamilton Deane, Browning neatly evokes the spirit of his own early career and preoccupations. What is Dracula, after all, but a "Living Hypnotic Corpse" who daily lies buried in a coffin box? Dracula presents himself in a highly theatrical and dandified manner, falsifying his true background to advance in society. Like so many of Browning's "animalized" protagonists, Dracula can transform himself into an animal, literally. His feral, wide-eyed servant Renfield exhibits behavior recalling a sideshow geek or wild man. Like any number of the Chaney characters, Dracula is an older man who attracted younger virginal girls, but his sexuality can never be satisfied in a conventional manner—vampires are in a sense "castrated," their libidos displaced to a mouth that becomes an all-purpose sex organ, penetrating and engulfing simultaneously.

Literary critic Maurice Richardson summed up the qualities that made the character of Dracula a perhaps inevitable end point for the dark psychology that powered Browning's strongest work:

> Ambivalence is the keynote. Death wishes all round exist side by side with the desire for immortality. Frightful cruelty, aggression and greed is accompanied by a madly possessive kind of love. Guilt is everywhere and deep. Behavior smacks of the unconscious world of infantile sexuality with . . . an obvious fixation at the oral level, with all that sucking and biting. . . . Stoker makes use of all the traditional mythical properties and blends them with a family type of situation of his own contriving that turns out to be quite a blatant demonstration of the Oedipus complex.

Dracula, for all its problems, would prove a significant turning point in the American cinema, liberating the dormant irrational energies Hollywood had repressed for decades, but which were implicit in the dreamlike medium from the beginning. For Depression-era audiences, the picture may have carried all sorts of half-conscious metaphors about people paralyzed and enervated by mysterious draining forces they could not control; like Renfield on his wild trip to the castle, a large segment of the population might well have felt it was riding in a carriage without a driver. *Dracula* was a uniquely frightening picture that found its audience during a uniquely frightening year.

The final assignment of Browning's three-picture contract with Universal was *Iron Man,* a hard-boiled story about the rise and fall of a world lightweight boxing champion, based on the novel by W. R. Burnett, author of *Little Caesar. Iron Man* is the most perfunctory of Browning's talkies, a picture obviously finished to complete a contract and nothing more. Lew Ayres, who had been dropped from the *Dracula* cast, played the boxer "Kid" Mason, blind to the treachery of his beautiful, gold-digging wife, played by Jean Harlow. Robert Armstrong took the role of Mason's manager-trainer.

The *New York Times* complained that "Tod Browning has chosen to tell his story as though he was limited to the three walls of a stage set. At that, it makes good entertainment, but it is sad to reflect what a vivid piece Mr. Browning might have served up had he placed the emphasis on action instead of dialogue."

Variety noted, "As a story of the ring, it's not bad, but the trouble with these yarns is that the women have invariably looked on them as poison." The scene in which actor John Miljan, as Ayres' rival, socks Harlow squarely in the jaw raised the reviewer's eyebrows: "Pretty rough . . . it got a scream from one femme member of this audience." The *San Francisco Chronicle* praised the film as heralding "a new phase of realism in the movies." The paper applauded Browning's gritty attempt "to place on the screen some semblance of life as it is lived by you and me and the man who runs the cigar stand downstairs." And, of the luscious, up-and-coming Harlow, the *Chronicle* quipped, "[she] has one of the best figures on the screen and continues to be almost embarrassingly candid about it."

Browning didn't wait around the studio for *Iron Man* to open. On the day *Dracula* was reviewed in the *Los Angeles Times,* a small item appeared on the same page, announcing that Browning had broken with Universal, signed a new contract with M-G-M, and, following a two-month vacation in Europe, would be returning to the scene of his earlier celluloid crimes. *Dracula* had done excellent business, and it may well have occurred to Irving Thalberg that having half of the Chaney-Browning team in his pocket was better than having none of it. In addition to Browning's per-picture salary of $50,000 for three projects, Thalberg approved a $50,000 "adjustment check" for three M-G-M pictures not produced under Browning's earlier tenure through the studio's fault (these no doubt were to be Chaney pictures, starting with *The Sea Bat*).

Dracula had proven the viability of a new, more sensational kind of mystery entertainment than had ever been attempted. *Variety* reported that "U Has Horror Cycle All to Self." "With *Dracula* making money at the box office for Universal, other studios are looking for horror tales—but very squeamishly. Producers are not certain whether nightmare pictures have a box office pull, or whether *Dracula* is just a freak."

With Browning's help, Thalberg would attempt to capture the horror market for M-G-M—and in the process, show Hollywood exactly what a "freak" picture could do.

FIVE

"OFFEND ONE AND YOU OFFEND THEM ALL"

"Can a full grown woman truly love a midget?" Harry Earles and Olga
Baclanova in Freaks. (David J. Skal collection)

For his homecoming project, Irving Thalberg offered Browning a sumptuous, star-studded mystery film: *Arsène Lupin,* based on the play by Maurice Leblanc and Francis de Croisset about a master thief and the detective who outwits him. The production would bring together, for the first time and with considerable hoopla, John and Lionel Barrymore in the leading roles.

But on June 8, 1931, the day after the commencement of his new contract with M-G-M, Browning notified the studio that he was not enthusiastic about *Arsène Lupin* and would rather develop the Tod Robbins short story "Spurs," which he had convinced Metro to purchase several years earlier for $8,000. A revenge story set in a circus and centering on a midget, the tale had a natural part for the actor Harry Earles, who had made an unforgettable impression in *The Unholy Three.* Earles, in fact, had first brought the story to Browning's attention.

Robbins' original story, first published in *Munsey's Magazine* in February 1923, was set in a small traveling circus in France. The troupe's midget, Jacques Courbé, falls hopelessly in love with the company's bareback rider, Jeanne Marie, who accepts his proposal only because she has learned of his recent large inheritance. Her real lover is her partner, Simon LaFleur, whom she plans to wed after Jacques' death—she believes that midgets age and die much more rapidly than do normal people and that her wait will be mercifully brief. (Robbins: "These pygmies were a puny lot. They died young! She would do nothing to hasten the end of Jacques Courbé. No, she would be kindness itself to the poor little fellow, but on the other hand, she would not lose her beauty mourning for him.")

But their nuptials prove a fiasco. The freaks who comprise most of the wedding guests grow tipsy and querulous:

> Griffo, the giraffe boy, had closed his large brown eyes and was swaying his small head languidly above the assembly, while a slightly supercilious expression drew his lips down at the corners. Monsieur Hercule Hippo, swollen out by his libations to even more colossal proportions, was repeating over and over: "I tell you I am not like other men. When I walk, the earth trembles!" Mademoiselle Lupa, her hairy upper lip lifted above her long white teeth, was gnawing at a bone, growling unintelligible phrases to herself and shooting savage, suspicious glances at her companions. . . . Madame Samson, uncoiling her necklace of baby boa constrictors, was feeding them lumps of sugar soaked in rum.

"There can be no genial companionship among great egotists who have drunk too much," wrote Robbins. "Each one of these human oddities thought that he or she alone was responsible for the crowds that daily gathered at Copo's Circus; so now, heated with the good Burgundy, they were not slow in asserting themselves. Their separate egos rattled together, like so many pebbles in a bag. Here was gunpowder which needed only a spark."

During the feast, the drunken Jeanne Marie insults her diminutive bridegroom, declaring loudly that she could carry her "little ape" on her shoulders from one end of France to the other. A year passes, during which Jeanne Marie and her strong man are separated from one another, Jacques having retired from the circus and taken his wife to live on his large inherited estate. One day, Simon is startled to find a haggard and barely recognizable Jeanne Marie standing before his wagon door. The woman pleads with him to protect her from her midget husband, explaining that he has never forgiven her the cruel comment about carrying him on her shoulders. He has, in fact, taken her at her word. A virtual prisoner, guarded by a vicious wolfhound named St. Eustache, she has been forced daily to carry Jacques from dawn to dusk down the lonely country roads, slowly working off the equivalent of "one end of France to the other."

As Jeanne Marie concludes her woeful tale, Jacques himself enters the wagon, mounted on his canine steed St. Eustache and carrying a tiny sword. Simon tries to prevent the midget from reclaiming Jeanne Marie, but he is overpowered by the dog. Pinned to the floor by the powerful animal, Simon is silently dispatched by Jacques' penetrating blade.

Jeanne, completely humbled and resigned to her fate, places her little mate on her shoulders and weakly trudges off in the direction of their home. They are spotted in the distance by the circus owner, who is astonished: " 'Can it be?' he murmured. 'Yes, it is! Three old friends! And so Jeanne Marie still carries him! Ah, but she should not poke fun at M. Jacques Courbé! He is so sensitive; but alas, they are the kind that are always henpecked!' "

Browning had already begun developing the story for the screen by the spring of 1927. *New York Herald-Tribune* critic Richard Watts, Jr., related that "a returned visitor from Hollywood told me of an idea for another film that the director cherished. It was the story of a midget in an inevitable sideshow, who avenged himself upon a giant by leaping upon his back and riding him about Europe." The transposition of the avengee's sex indicates that "Spurs" was to be the basis of a follow-up to *The Unholy Three,* starring Chaney and Earles, alluded to in press items of the twenties.

Mayer cabled Thalberg, then himself in Europe. Thalberg was not entirely convinced that "Spurs" was screenworthy, but if the option could be exercised reasonably and if Browning was willing to gamble time on finding a compelling "human story" in the nasty vignette, then the studio would be willing to take a chance.

Thalberg assigned two scenarists Browning requested, Willis Goldbeck and Elliott Clawson. As the project, now called *Freaks,* progressed, the studio provided other writers as well: Leon Gordon,

Edgar Allan Woolf, Al Boasberg (a master of the "boffo," or comic one-liner), and, his contributions ultimately unbilled, Charles Mac-Arthur, coauthor with Ben Hecht of *The Front Page*.

Goldbeck, who called his contact with Browning "extremely limited," recalled his work on the project:

> Irving Thalberg called me into his office, after *Dracula* had been scoring heavily at the box office, and asked me to come up with a horror story more horrible than all the rest. After I sent him a finished script he called me in again and received me with his head down on his arms on the desk, as though overcome. Or about to be sick. He looked at me sadly, shook his head and sighed, "Well, it's horrible."

Goldbeck said that he had no memory of the story "Spurs" and recalled no collaborators. However, he noted that "Thalberg shuffled his writers around like chess men, without letting his rooks know what his bishops were doing. Sometimes the studio put a writer's name on a film just so they could charge off so many hours of his salary." The screenwriter's recollections are especially interesting in their indication that Thalberg, and not Browning, was driving script development.

The writer and/or writers spent a total of five months wrestling with the material, finally retaining only the married-to-a-midget motif and the idea of a raucous wedding feast from Robbins' story. But the main characters and their relationship were essentially inverted. Jeanne Marie, merely avaricious in the story, now became Cleopatra, a predatory creation who took on Jacques' propensity for murder. The midget, renamed Hans in a nod to Harry Earles' German accent, was now an innocent, thoroughly deluded victim of "the most beautiful big woman I have ever seen."

Simon became a strong man named Hercules, who plots with Cleopatra to poison Hans for his fortune. The ugly marriage between Cleopatra and Hans was offset by a normal romance between a clown, Phroso (Browning had used the name before as Chaney's magician moniker in *West of Zanzibar*), and a seal trainer, Venus.

A highlight of the story was Cleopatra's ritual initiation as "one of us" by the wedding party of freaks. They pick up a macabre chant as a dwarf dances atop the table, passing a loving cup of wine: "Gooble, gobble . . . we accept her, we accept her . . ." The drunken bride, offered the cup, is revolted and hurls the wine in their faces. "Dirty—slimy—freaks! Make me one of you, will you?" The freaks abide by a code—"offend one and you offend them all" —and they do not forget her words.

Goldbeck, during M-G-M's silent years, had fed publicity stories to the fan magazines on Lon Chaney and other stars. One article he might have had a hand in, but which almost certainly came to his attention, was called "The Most Grotesque Moment of My Life," published in *Motion Picture Classic* under Chaney's byline but undoubtedly the work of M-G-M flacks. In the story, Chaney is visited by a half dozen freaks—a war veteran with half his face blown away, a man crushed and twisted by the embrace of an anaconda, and so forth. "We have come to you tonight to offer you the greatest honor it is in our power to bestow," they solemnly tell the actor, offering him the chance to be their honorary king. The grotesque high point of *Freaks* depicted the similar acceptance of Cleopatra into freak society. Despite some brilliantly chilling moments, the script was nonetheless shaping up as something of a two-headed cow, and hardly a horror film in the manner of Universal's *Frankenstein* and Paramount's *Dr. Jekyll and Mr. Hyde,* rival projects both in preparation. The screenplay was instead structured like a surreal evening of vaudeville, the story line broken up with blackout-style comedy turns by the freaks. These were most likely the contributions of gag writer Boasberg, intended by Thalberg to soften the unpleasantness of Goldbeck's scenario.

In the final analysis, Thalberg may have been personally conflicted about a script that was the logical, if unpleasant, evolutionary stage of the special brand of disability drama that he had personally aided and abetted in the twenties. The producer was himself, after all, a physically limited individual, and the rawness of *Freaks,* using actual handicapped people instead of actors, may have been cutting too close to the bone.

According to William S. Hart, Jr., Browning disagreed with the studio over the ending of *Freaks,* and the studio won. "They wanted a macabre ending, and he just wanted to have kind of a sad ending." Browning's melancholy fade-out would underscore "the sadness of the poor people that couldn't ever be part of all other people. And then they forced on him . . . this wild revenge to make a macabre ending." But given Browning's stock-in-trade propensity for revenge stories and macabre climaxes, it is difficult to imagine him shying away from what would transpire at the end of *Freaks.* The approved shooting script featured a blood-and-thunder finale in which the freaks take their revenge on Cleopatra and her strong-man boyfriend, bestially mutilating them during a violent rainstorm. The haughty trapeze artist is revealed as a squawking, legless "human duck"* in a sideshow pit of sawdust; Hercules, the strong man, is on display nearby, newly corpulent and singing soprano.

Thalberg intended to star M-G-M newcomer Myrna Loy as the villainess and Jean Harlow as the good-girl foil, Venus.† Possibly recognizing the built-in problems of the script and sensing the troubles ahead, Thalberg pulled back from the idea of major and/or upcoming stars for *Freaks.* The Cleopatra role instead went to Olga Baclanova, former star of the Moscow Art Theater nearing the end of her Hollywood career, and Harlow was replaced by Leila Hyams, an attractive and dependable contract player but hardly a major star. Wallace Ford took the role of Phroso, British actor Henry Victor played Hercules, with the stuttering actor Roscoe Ates thrown in for dubious comic relief. Browning made use of a few familiar faces from his earlier pictures: Michael Visaroff, the innkeeper from *Dracula,* made a brief appearance as a groundskeeper horrified by trespassing freaks; and Rose Dione, a former stage associate of Sarah Bernhardt who had played the barkeeper in *West of*

---

* *Browning had originally planned a "human duck" disguise for Lon Chaney in the opening sequences of* West of Zanzibar. *Production photos show Chaney wearing a nearly identical costume to the one that appears at the end of* Freaks.
† *Some accounts have Harlow cast as the bad girl, Cleopatra, certainly a plausible move after her turn as a gold digger in Browning's* Iron Man. *But trade paper items mentioning her do not specifically name her role, and at least one states that Leila Hyams was Harlow's replacement.*

Zanzibar, interpreted the oddly affecting part of Madame Tetrallini, the freaks' motherly protector.

Casting director Ben Piazza spent nearly a month in New York and the East Coast scouting freak-show talent, collecting photographs, and even shooting on-site screen tests. Pictures and test footage were sent back to Browning in Hollywood. Leila Hyams recalled the casting process: "I was in Tod's office a lot and he had his desk piled high with photographs." One day Hyams encountered Daisy Earles (Harry's sister, who would play his fiancée in the film) critically perusing a pile of freak photos. She picked up one and clucked her tongue. "Oh my," the three-foot-high actress said to Hyams, "it must be *dreadful* to be like that." Freakishness, clearly, was a matter of perspective.

Browning selected a comprehensive conglomeration of human oddities to decorate the film, and he had enough applicants to be choosy. Among the rejects were an "elephant-skinned girl," a boy with deformed, doglike legs, a midget named Major Mite, a tattooed man, a giant, and a whole team of Pygmies. Daisy and Violet Hilton, Siamese twins joined at the hip, were familiar faces on the vaudeville circuit. In a Montreal sideshow, scouts discovered Johnny Eckhardt, professionally known as Johnny Eck, a startling "half-boy" whose body ended below the rib cage. The armless, legless Prince Randian was a native of British Guiana who could shave himself as well as roll and light cigarettes using only his mouth. Pete Robinson was a sixty-five-pound "human skeleton." Olga Roderick (real name, Jane Burnell) was a traditional bearded lady, and Koo Koo ("the bird girl from Mars") appeared to be the victim of progeria, a rare disease that causes rapid and premature aging. Betty Green, the "Stork Woman," was a physically normal but exceedingly unattractive person who chose to capitalize on her appearance. Schlitze (real last name: Metz) led a contingent of pinheads, including Jennie and Elvira Snow and the celebrated Zip and Pip (only one of whom appears in the finished film, as generic pinhead stand-in during the thunderstorm climax). Other oddities included the Austrian hermaphrodite Josephine/Joseph, two armless women, several dwarves (including Angelo Rossitto, who, alone among the freaks, would have a lasting Hollywood career), a fat lady, a "turtle girl," a sword swallower, fire eater, and so on.

Freaks began shooting in mid-October 1931. Actress Hyams was apprehensive. When she first saw "the array of freaks assembled on the set, I wondered if I could go through with it. My first reaction was a feeling of intense pity," she admitted. As she watched "the weird contortions of the Armless and Legless Wonder as he wriggled across the sound stage on his stomach or sat propped in a chair, smoking a cigarette which he had rolled with his lips—well, I'll have to confess that it made me a little ill at first." But soon she realized she was wasting her pity. "The freaks were not at all sorry for themselves . . . they might be sorry for the *other fellow* [with] an unfortunate handicap—but none of them was sorry for himself."

Art director Merrill Pye recalled that the filming was exceptionally smooth and, despite its sensational material, did not attract gawkers. In fact, a large number of people at Metro did not want to look at the freaks at all, and especially not in the studio commissary. Samuel Marx recalled that a formal protest, led by producer Harry Rapf, was staged, leading to a separate outdoor mess hall for most of the freaks "so people could get to eat in the commissary without throwing up."

One person who did throw up was F. Scott Fitzgerald, then at the end of a disastrous, drunken screenwriting stint at M-G-M. Scenarist Dwight Taylor recounted having lunch with a distraught Fitzgerald the week before he was fired. Fitzgerald and Taylor had no sooner seated themselves than they were joined at the same table by the Siamese twins. "One of them picked up the menu and, without even looking at the other, asked, 'What are you going to have?' Scott turned pea-green and, putting his hand to his mouth, rushed for the great outdoors." Fitzgerald later employed a muted reference to the commissary incident in one of his most celebrated short stories, "Crazy Sundays."

The twins and the midgets alone were spared commissary excommunication; freaks might all be different, but some were considered more different than others. Quite in contrast to the solidarity they projected in the film, the freaks proved as vain, proud, and competitive as other show people. As Tod Robbins commented in his original story, "Spurs," "There can be no genial companionship among great egotists. . . . Each one of these human oddities thought that he or she alone was responsible for the crowds. . . ."

Johnny Eck recalled the effect that Southern California had on the freaks, most of whom were being housed at the Castle Apartments in Culver City, adjacent to the M-G-M lot. They "started wearing sunglasses and acting funny," he said. "In other words, they all 'went Hollywood.' " Eck bristled at some prima donna behavior he witnessed. "In the opening sequence, at a picnic on a lord's estate, Pete Robinson, the Human Skeleton, was supposed to lie on a blanket on the grass and play a harmonica while I, the pinheads, and the dwarves danced. But Pete kept complaining that his back hurt, and Browning had to put a special mattress under the blanket before Robinson would cooperate. Jeez, if I would have had that portion of my body, I'd have gladly laid down on a Hindu fakir's bed of spikes."

In Hyams' opinion, the most temperamental of all the performers was Olga Roderick. "She was very grand and ritzy. You almost expected her to peer at you through a lorgnette." Behind her back, the rest of the cast called her the Duchess. When she first arrived on the set, Hyams recalled her having iron-gray hair and a gray-streaked beard reaching down to her waist.

"Don't do anything to that beard," Browning told her. But Olga airily informed the director that she intended "to have it touched up a bit for the picture." "Don't be silly," Browning told her. "It's absolutely perfect as is."

Olga had her own ideas, and "when the day for shooting came," Hyams said, "she appeared with her hair dyed black—and *marcelled!* Tod nearly died."

Browning later told a Los Angeles reporter that the freaks' "professional jealousy was amazing. Not one of them had a good word for the other." A typical Hollywood director might have his hands full working with an all-star cast, but "let him try these people. Each one of them had been a star in the sideshow world . . .

you seldom see more than one real monstrosity in a sideshow. The rest are minor abnormalities. I had a dozen stars, the world's greatest freaks. I had to humor them as no Hollywood actor was ever humored."

At least one of the freaks had his own very distinctive sense of humor. Willard Sheldon, who had been an assistant cameraman on *The Mystic,* was assigned as script clerk to *Freaks* during its final weeks of production. He described the fondness of Prince Randian, the human torso, for lurking in dark corners—then scaring the wits out of unsuspecting passersby with a sudden, bloodcurdling yell.

Only Schlitze, the most outgoing and affable of the pinheads, stayed clear of jests, jabs, and ego. Schlitze, who had been exhibited in carnivals as "Maggie, the Last of the Aztecs," was actually male, but for simplicity of hygiene wore a sack-like dress and was described publicly as a woman. "Here was a triumph of personality if I ever saw one," wrote film journalist Faith Service, who called Schlitze "the pet and favorite of the M-G-M lot," finding a fan even in Norma Shearer. "She makes a great to-do over new dresses, tricks of magic, gay hats, bits of string, the sword swallower, games of tag and Tod Browning." Service noted that "One of her special likes was for Jackie Cooper, much to that small trouper's terror. He did not reciprocate the affection."

"Schlitze was filthy rich," said Hyams, "very well managed, with money invested in houses and diamonds." This was probably untrue. According to sideshow veteran and historian Daniel P. Mannix, when Schlitze's manager ("or, to be more explicit about it, his owner") died, instead of coming into a fortune of jewels and real estate, Schlitze was committed to a state institution and nearly died of loneliness and neglect. The Canadian sideshow entrepreneur Sam Alexander finally arranged for Schlitze's release and the pinhead resumed touring with circuses and carnivals. Schlitze made one film, *Meet Boston Blackie,* with Chester Morris and Rochelle Hudson, for Columbia Pictures in 1941. "He lived to be eighty, dying in California," Mannix wrote.

According to Hyams, who was especially fond of Schlitze, the pinhead loved working on *Freaks* so much that even on days when he wasn't needed, he would be permitted on the set to happily watch the proceedings. Not all the other pinheads were so well behaved, however. Olga Baclanova remembered that one ''was like a monkey, she go crazy sometimes. . . . They put her in the closet and close the door.'' Browning told the *Los Angeles Times* that he ''could never tell'' what a freak might do. ''Most of them are either imbecile or abnormal and not responsible. . . . Once in a while they became upset, angry, and would try to vent their rage in biting the person nearest to them. I was bitten once.''

The director claimed to have had a recurrent anxiety dream during production. ''I was trying to shoot a difficult scene. Every time I started, Johnny Eck, the half-boy, and one of the pinheads would start to bring a cow in backwards through a door. I'd tell them to stop and the next take they'd do it all over again. Three times that night I got up and smoked a cigaret but when I went back to bed I'd pick up the dream again.''

Freaks provided a different sort of nightmare for those who worked under Browning. Film editor Basil Wrangell recalled: ''I was a very young boy at the time that I cut that picture, and my personal experiences with Tod Browning were most unpleasant.'' Wrangell found Browning an ''impossible person to work with. . . . We were working until four o'clock in the morning every goddamn day. And he would go off for dinner sometimes in the afternoon, and then we'd sit around and wait until two in the morning for him to get back.''

Wrangell described Browning as ''very much, in my book, a sadist, and I imagine that's why he picked those kind of subjects. At the time he did *Freaks* he was more or less on the downward path, compared to the other directors at Metro who were coming up, like Sam Woods and Jack Conway. While he picked the subject for its sensationalism, I think it was part of that streak in him because he always dealt with oddities—the misformed kind of people. It titillated his amusement, I think he got a bang out of seeing these crippled characters.''

The question of whether Browning took personal, even sexual gratification from the afflictions of others also occurred to Leila

Hyams and her husband, Phil Berg. Both recalled an anecdote Browning told during the making of *Freaks* when the subject of love at first sight came up in conversation. Browning described, evocatively, how he once had fallen instantly in love with a woman he saw for the first time at the bottom of a gangplank on a foggy dock. The punch line of the story was that the woman had a horribly pock-marked face. "He was very serious about it," said Hyams.

The director took a particular shine to Johnny Eck, whose deformity echoed the below-the-waist traumas that had informed so many Browning films. On the set he called Eck "Mr. Johnny" (ironically a slang term for penis, of which Johnny was devoid). "Browning was wonderful," Eck recalled. "Often he would let me ride the big camera dolly with him as he was directing a scene. . . ." Alice Browning visited the studio and posed for a comprehensive series of photographs of herself with the freaks, grouped around and posing atop an automobile, presumably Browning's.

According to film editor Wrangell, Browning made no similar effort creating a convivial atmosphere among his crew. "I thought he was sadistic in his approach to human beings and certainly had that trait in his selection of subjects," he remembered. "He was very difficult to work with, very sarcastic, very unappreciative of any effort, and very demanding." Wrangell found Browning "a completely impossible person from many standpoints, very inconsiderate, and he was very, very difficult to please. I don't think he did a very good job of directing [*Freaks*] in the first place, so it was a question of trying to make the film say something after it was finished."

If Browning was abrasive and demanding of his crew, he displayed a completely different attitude toward the freaks themselves. "Tod just loved being around them, loved talking to them," Wrangell said, adding dryly, "Of course, they didn't really talk back."

Wrangell recalled that "Browning had pretty much of a free hand" in shooting *Freaks,* and "it wasn't until it was completely put together that anyone really looked at it, and by that time there was a great deal of dissension on the lot." Several executives wanted the film shut down entirely, and Louis B. Mayer himself was said to be outraged that Thalberg was going ahead with production. But Thalberg held his ground, and Browning was given a long leash.

"It was obvious from the way that he handled the main scenes in *Freaks* that sound threw him," said Wrangell. To simplify the shooting of the wedding feast scene, Browning shot it almost as a silent film, leaving it to the editor to reconcile the wild (i.e., unsynchronized) sound track of chanting freaks. The entire sequence, Wrangell remembered with exasperated hyperbole, "took 15,000 hours to put together." In the finished film, the scene would be introduced with a silent-movie-style intertitle: "The Wedding Feast."

David S. Horsley, later a special-effects cinematographer who assisted Merritt Gerstad on the lensing of *Freaks,* recalled the film as "the toughest one I've worked on, without exception. Tod Browning was a bastard as far as his crews were concerned. Those of us who worked at the 'jute mill' (as we called the M-G-M studio in those days) would try to escape being assigned to one of his productions, because he would work us to death." Horsley recounted, with some exaggeration, that "I hardly had eight hours off" during the entire production period of mid-October to Christmas 1931.

On the technical end, Horsley remembered that the electrical equipment on *Freaks* was dangerously "hot." As he explained it, "There was a discrepancy in the ground system, and every time you'd touch something you'd get a shock. . . . it was possible to actually go to the hospital as a result."

Script clerk Willard Sheldon oversaw continuity for two weeks and was present for the filming of the storm-swept climax. "Browning wanted rain and lightning," Sheldon said, the latter effect being achieved with a device called a lacapodium. "The base of the thing was like a big vase," according to Sheldon. It held a load of aluminum powder, detonated by an electrical charge. Unfortunately, the device would sometimes store energy rather than release it, and could create a real, rather than merely theatrical, explosion.

One night, "Tod called for lightning and the thing didn't go," Sheldon remembered. "We waited, waited. Then the electrician shouted 'Watch it! It's going to blow!' " Although Sheldon and his fellow crew members were trapped between the pyrotechnic device and a high, sheer wall of rock, somehow they scrambled out of harm's way. Only afterward, when they examined the location, did they realize that they had performed a physically inexplicable feat in their panic—there was no real way to escape the imminent blast save for levitation.

In the final analysis, Horsley regarded Browning as "hardworking" but "pitiless." "He was out to get everything he could on the screen, and he didn't care how long it took in getting it there."

As today, preview screenings were an important component of the post-production period. "They would set a preview," Wrangell recalled, "and at the very last minute they would still be making changes in the picture. So the cutter would be sitting there, the splicer standing by, and a car standing by. And I remember that we would have previews where we would send the first three reels to start the show, followed by a relay car. That's the kind of pressure you worked under then."

Wrangell didn't recall seeing the preview of *Freaks,* held in early January 1932 in either San Diego or Huntington Beach. But Merrill Pye remembered the evening well. "Halfway through the preview, a lot of people got up and ran out. They didn't walk out. They *ran* out." Production manager J. J. Cohn remembered that a woman who had attended the preview tried to sue the studio, claiming the film had induced a miscarriage.

A decision was made to radically cut *Freaks* from its running time of nearly an hour and a half to just over an hour. The truncated version jettisoned the horrifying details of the mud-dripping freaks swarming over the tree-pinned Olga Baclanova and pouring into a circus wagon to castrate her lover. Several comic scenes were eliminated, including one of the turtle girl being amorously pursued by a seal. A rambling epilogue set in a second-story London dime museum called Tetrallini's Freaks and Music Hall (an elaborate, lighted facade was designed, down to the ground-floor touch of "Austin Ried Outfitters" window displays) was completely discarded, save for the final shot of Cleopatra quacking; instead a new prologue was added, featuring a spieling barker (dressed, rather uncannily, like Browning in any number of his publicity photographs) who introduces "the most amazing, the most astounding human monstrosity of all time." And finally, a second epilogue, evidently intended as a happy (or at least happier) ending, depicted the reconciliation of the midget lovers in Hans' palatial estate, approvingly witnessed by Phroso and Venus. Actress Louise Beavers originally played the midget's maid in this sequence, but her contributions were cut, or simply replaced by a butler who appears in the restored version of the film.

On February 10, the mutilated version of *Freaks* premiered at the Fox Criterion in Los Angeles, where, despite an extremely favorable review from the influential columnist Louella O. Parsons, the film died a slow, two-week death. Chicago was equally unenthusiastic. But in some locations, the film did surprisingly well. Cincinnati's UFA-Taft grossed five times its normal take with *Freaks,* and the Court Street Theater in Buffalo attracted twice its usual business. Boston, Cleveland, Houston, St. Paul, and Omaha pulled record audiences. But the regional business failed to compensate for major venues like Los Angeles, where the film bombed, and San Francisco, where it never played at all.

All across America, well-heeled, reform-minded women who wore their rectitude like fox stoles were making their displeasure with Hollywood known through volunteer organizations and by pressure on elected representatives. For those who suspected the film industry was a cesspool, Tod Browning and *Freaks* were the final proof. *Freaks* was a particularly blatant example of a studio using double-entendre dialogue to technically circumvent weakly enforced Production Code restrictions on what could be literally depicted on-screen. Secondary meanings weren't shown, after all; they were apparent only to those with dirty minds. "Feel like eating something?" the ravenous Cleopatra asks Hercules, after provocatively enticing him into her wagon. When he asks for eggs, she lets her robe fall open and, hands on hips, asks with a smile, "How do you like them?"

Mrs. Ambrose Nevin Diehl, head of the standing committee on

motion pictures for the National Association of Women, favored boycotts and direct pressure on film studios, rather than government intervention, as an answer to falling moral standards on the screen. On February 26, 1932, shortly after the picture opened in the nation's capital, she wrote to Will H. Hays, "about that offensive film *Freaks* which seems to be causing us all so much concern and embarrassment." Diehl opposed the federal-regulation fires being fanned by the Republican senator Smith W. Brookhart.

"How stupid to release it in Washington, of all places, the week Brookhart was due to explode . . . ," Diehl wrote. "We have just been having so much to say about the great improvement in film entertainment [when] this picture undoes much of our progress and of course discredits the industry far more than the financial return to the producers can possibly justify." Diehl informed Hays that her association had planned to publish a scathing review of *Freaks,* but pulled the piece at the last moment for fear that attention would only encourage calls for official censorship. Diehl's review questioned how M-G-M, "a producer with the vision that offers an *Emma* with its thought of service[,] will stoop to the disgrace of making money out of hurt, disfigured and suffering humanity."

The killed review, a galley of which Diehl sent to Hays, concluded with the opening lines of the "Litany for Hurt Things," by Katherine Burton ("commendable reading in this connection"):

> Your pity for the hurt ones, Lord, whom time will not make whole
> (Disfigured limbs may not be hid as can a broken soul).

Not everyone, however, thought Browning was guilty of a heartless abomination. Producer Louis F. Edelman, who was offered and turned down the chance to produce *Freaks* for Thalberg ("I didn't think I could take it"), nonetheless remembered Browning as "a great humanist." While conceding that many people wouldn't agree with him because of the director's "relationship with the abnormal," Edelman remembered that "Tod treated anything human with dignity." But some M-G-M staffers began to treat Browning as a kind of freak himself. "Tod was a guy you could easily hurt . . . sometimes he couldn't take it."

M-G-M, clutching at straws, tried to make the case that *Freaks* was a compassionate human story, resulting in some bizarre ads with a jumbled, defensive tone:

A LANDMARK IN SCREEN DARING!

The inside story of the making of a picture that was debated for four years—the picture that is a challenge to the world!

At every story conference the question was brought up "Do we dare tell the real truth on the screen? Do we dare hold up the mirror to nature in all its grim reality? Do we dare produce FREAKS?"

WHAT ABOUT ABNORMAL PEOPLE? THEY HAVE THEIR LIVES, TOO!

What about the Siamese twins—have they no right to love? The pinheads, the half-man half-woman, the dwarfs! They have the same passions, joys, sorrows, laughter as normal human beings. Is such a subject untouchable? While we hesitated, a great story, thoroughly planned, waited the word to go ahead. Finally TOD BROWNING cut the Gordian knot of indecision. . . .

Motion Picture Daily took note of the studio's panicky humanitarian posturing and rejected it. "The picture is unkind and brutal," the trade paper maintained, and could not simultaneously capitalize on human misfits and pretend to pity them. *Motion Picture Daily* followed the fortunes of *Freaks* closely and ran the following account of a New England contretemps over the film:

TONE DOWN 'FREAKS,' WOMEN ASK POLICE

PROVIDENCE (R.I.), Feb. 28—*Freaks* is too gruesome for the Better Films Council of Rhode Island, a woman's organization, and they protested to Capt. George W. Cowan, police censor, to see if the film couldn't be toned down. Capt. Cowan, however, said he had seen the film three times and that it was okay as far as he was concerned.

But in Georgia, a week later, the Atlanta Board of Review was successful in barring *Freaks* from its scheduled run at the Fox Theater. Mrs. Alonzo Richardson, secretary of the board, called the picture "loathsome, obscene, grotesque and bizarre." (The *Atlanta Journal,* after previewing the film, had already printed its opinion that *Freaks* "transcends the fascinatingly horrible, leaving the spectator appalled.")

The board took the matter to court on the morning of the scheduled premiere, and a judge decreed that *Freaks* indeed violated a city law. Loew's, Inc., made no recorded complaint on grounds of free speech, but rather on the fact that they had spent $2,500 in Atlanta advertising the film. *Freaks* was replaced by another, lighter M-G-M product set in a big top, *Polly of the Circus,* starring Marion Davies and Clark Gable. (Ironically, Browning had originally been announced as the director of *Polly* in 1926.)

John C. Moffitt, critic for the *Kansas City Star,* was especially caustic. "There is no excuse for this picture," he wrote. "It took a weak mind to produce it and it takes a strong stomach to look at it. The reason it was made was to make money. The reason liquor was made was to make money. The liquor interests allowed certain conditions of their business to become so disgraceful that we got prohibition. In *Freaks* the movies make their great step toward national censorship. If they get it, they will have no one to blame but themselves."

Elinor Hughes of the *Boston Herald* expressed the opinion that "Tod Browning can now retire in peace, satisfied that he has directed the ultimate in horrors, and any who enjoy watching the pitiful, grotesque mistakes of nature may behold them in *Freaks. . . .* it is the sort of thing that, once seen, lurks in the dark places of the mind, cropping up every so often with a direful persistence." Hughes added that "the sadistically cruel plot savors nearly of perversion."

Other critics found the film much less disturbing. Harold Hunt, writing in the *Oregon Daily Journal,* noted that "the vengeance portion of the story . . . escaped Browning's grasp and 'went Hollywood.' It meandered so far afield that there are times when it verges on the comical, though it is really intended to be horrifying." The storm scene Hunt found to be "a bit too overdone to be convincing."

The *Boston Evening Transcript* wondered if Lon Chaney's death had broken Browning's spell. "Somebody blundered," the *Transcript* stated bluntly. "Tod Browning is an able director. He has a flair for the sinister, a knack at bringing the shadowy corners of life to the screen. [With Lon Chaney] he made what in retrospect seem to be minor masterpieces. . . ." Nonetheless,

> Either by his own choice or by the desire of others there has come from his hands a picture—now at the State—which goes by the name of *Freaks.* On the face of it, there is promise of his familiar kind of entertainment. But the promise is not fulfilled.
>
> This is not the Browning we knew before. There are horrors, to be sure, but where is that sense of artistry that used to be an equal part of his trade-mark? Only at rare moments are those touches of imagination, those bits of photographic ingenuity that used to make his grotesqueries a source of pleasure. Here the outlines are sharp and hard. The backgrounds are negligible. Of half-suggestions, murky hints of terrors that cannot be plainly spoken, there is nothing. It was those things that once gave him his reputation as a magician of the macabre. Here there is only a catalog of horrors, ticketed and labeled, dragged out into the sunlight before the camera to be photographed against whatever background happens to be handy.

Harrison's Reports turned the *Freaks* controversy into a crusade, appealing to exhibitors' growing resentment over "block booking" by studios, which in some cases would require theaters to pay for *Freaks* even if they refused to show it. The publication suggested that the film be intentionally booked on a slow night. "Announce on that day that your theater will remain closed, because you are unwilling to become an instrument of demoralization among the people of your community." The publication further urged that theater managers invite selected guests for a private screening—ministers, priests, rabbis, police, and civic officials—to further fan community outrage. The Hollywood magazine *Rob Wagner's Script* made the blunt suggestion that M-G-M change its famous motto "Ars Gratia Artis"—"Art for Art's Sake"—to "Muck for Money's Sake."

M-G-M delayed the New York opening of *Freaks* until July, presumably to keep it away from the influential national media until it had effectively played the entire country. The New York State censors demanded that the shot of Cleopatra sneaking poison into a champagne bottle at the wedding feast be cut, on the grounds that it provided public instruction on the technique of crime. *Time* had already run a review, calling Browning "one of the few truly individual directors in the U.S. He is fond of anything that happens underground or in the dark, especially a murder. He prefers lovers who are physically deformed." *Time* called *Freaks* "one of the most macabre pictures ever filmed and it doubtless contains more misfits of humanity than were ever gathered together in the combined shows of Ringling Brothers and Barnum and Bailey."

Variety waited until after the New York release to file an opinion. "Planned by Metro to be one of the sensation pictures of the season, *Freaks* failed to qualify in the sure-fire category and has been shown in most parts of the country with astonishingly variable results. In spots it has been a clean-up. In others it was merely misery."

On July 23, *Motion Picture Herald* took the unusual step of running a second, positive review to offset an earlier, negative one. This time the reviewer, Charles E. Lewis, added helpful hints to exhibitors to avoid controversy: "If *Freaks* has caused a furor in certain censor circles the fault lies with the manner in which it was campaigned to the public. I found it to be an interesting and entertaining picture, and I did not have nightmares, nor did I attempt to murder any of my relatives," Lewis wrote.

The *New York Times* also ran a second, Sunday piece in a more positive vein: "The film takes a high place in the history of the pathological drama, even if not as high in that of entertainment . . . ," the unsigned piece opined. "*Freaks* is a curious affair. It is very good in spots and very bad in others. It has a pronounced anticlimax with which to crown the whole and yet moments of dramatic suspense that are excellent. There is a good deal of horror— in the strict sense of the term—and a good deal of tediousness. . . ." The *Times* noted that the producers, "apparently under the belief that the picture as it stood was a little too horrible," tacked on the "happy" ending. "As the real climax had formed the most powerful part of the picture, the addition is doubly unwelcome," the review concluded.

The *New York Herald-Tribune*'s Richard D. Watts, Jr., noted that Browning's other pictures "seem but whimsical nursery tales" in comparison to *Freaks*. "It is obviously an unhealthy and generally disagreeable work," Watts wrote, "not only in its story and characterization, but also in its gay directorial touches. Mr. Browning can even make freaks more unpleasant than they would be ordinarily. Yet, in some strange way, the picture is not only exciting, but even occasionally touching."

Freaks was pulled from circulation following its New York run. Great Britain had banned it outright, a prohibition that would remain in force for thirty years.

As much as film editor Basil Wrangell disliked working with Browning, nothing had prepared him for the director's final, scapegoating maneuver: demanding that M-G-M fire Wrangell for his part in the failure of *Freaks*. "Fortunately," said Wrangell, "I knew the front office very well by that time and had a reputation, so he didn't get away with things he tried." But the very idea that Browning would try to shift the blame for *Freaks* onto Wrangell after all the "blood, sweat and tears" he had poured into trying to improve the film left the young editor "disgusted with the man."

The picture was a commercial disaster. It cost M-G-M $316,000 and lost $164,000, more than the entire budget of *The Unholy Three,* the film that had made Browning's name at the studio. Thalberg, for his part, was able to laugh the whole thing off, according to Samuel Marx. "He was so great in his own way that it didn't really hurt him.'' Marx remembered a joke Thalberg played during a meeting a few months after the debacle took place. One of his producers made a crack about *Freaks* and Thalberg announced, poker-faced, that he had just seen the figures, and the picture was cleaning up overseas. It was a lie, of course, but to a man, the very producers who had tried to close the project down now fell in lock-step behind its newly perceived success: each had ''always known'' that the project had merit.

Browning was also disgusted, personally stung and confused by both the public and studio reaction to *Freaks*. What had gone wrong? He had pushed the boundaries of public tolerance many times before and had always landed on his feet—the success of the Chaney films had proven it before and *Dracula* proved it again, even without Chaney. Hadn't he simply continued to mine the same foolproof material that had served him so long and so well? His first sideshow film, as an actor, had been *Dizzy Joe's Career* in 1914, but his last, as a director, would be *Freaks*—a sudden, disfiguring wound from which his career would never recover.

SIX

MALIBU AFTER MIDNIGHT

Elizabeth Allan (left) and Carroll Borland in Mark of the Vampire *(1935).*
(Courtesy of Ronald V. Borst/Hollywood Movie Posters)

Although Browning's contract called for him to direct two more pictures within a year, Browning was idle for almost all of 1932, waiting for an assignment. Johnny Eck, the half-boy of *Freaks,* recalled that the director wanted to use him in another horror film. Returning to his hometown of Baltimore, "I began getting letters from the camera crew and some of the stars that worked with me in *Freaks* and in one of the letters was a news clipping on director Tod Browning [who was] planning and writing a story about experimenting with human bodies. . . ." The plot involved the creation of monster criminals from body parts and would have starred Eck and his normal twin brother, Robert.

Browning was undoubtedly familiar with the brothers' vaudeville magic act, in which the full-size Robert was planted in the audience as a stooge volunteer for a magician's sawing-in-half trick. Johnny, of course, was substituted, with a midget hidden inside an oversize pair of pants to fill out Robert's silhouette. When the magician finished his business with the blade, the half-boy leapt from the cutting table and chased his animated legs around the stage.

Not surprising, given the debacle of *Freaks,* M-G-M was in no mood for another picture spotlighting human deformity. Browning then tried to develop a film in collaboration with Gouverneur Morris, author of the novel *The Penalty*. Called *Revolt of the Dead,* the proposed project had a reincarnation theme but failed to meet with studio approval.

When Thalberg finally gave Browning the go-ahead for another film, it was for a project completely devoid of fantastic or bizarre coloration. It was not, however, a story lacking controversy.

As early as November 10, 1930, Production Code administrator Jason S. Joy gave a negative opinion to M-G-M, then considering the unproduced stage play *Rivets,* by John McDermott. A cynical, hard-edged comedy about a pair of New York construction workers and their colorful rivalry over a woman, *Rivets* was full of salty dialogue and situations. Joy warned that considerable revisions would be needed to make the story acceptable under the code. A revised synopsis, submitted a few months later by another company, was deemed "highly offensive, utterly unprincipled, vulgar in the extreme and totally unsuited to motion pictures."

An objectionable subplot involving gang activities and police fixing was excised, but code administrators continued to find fault with the script, even as shooting was about to begin. Some of the deleted material seems positively grotesque; James Wingate wrote to Thalberg on January 19, 1933: "From the standpoint of general policy, we feel it would not be advisable to show a child of five, even when accompanied by its parents, in a speakeasy, and being given liquor to drink."

The MPPDA never approved a finished script for *Rivets;* because of time pressures, rewritten sections of script were submitted to industry censors piecemeal during production. The film would be the last for actor John Gilbert under an embattled long-term contract with M-G-M; Louis B. Mayer's vendetta against Gilbert had reduced the performer to buying a trade paper ad complaining that M-G-M would not release him from his contract, nor would the studio give him work. According to his wife, Virginia Bruce, Gilbert was, by this period, despite bleeding ulcers, drinking all night and throwing up blood each morning "until he fainted."

The actor's final contract assignment, as in his previous Browning film, *The Show,* would be the portrayal of a morally lax character, sure to draw negative press criticism. Thus would Louis B. Mayer have the last, judgmental word on John Gilbert.

The film's title was changed to *Fast Workers,* with Gilbert playing Gunner Smith, a skyscraper riveter and irrepressible ladies' man, who doesn't hesitate to flip silver dollars at the heels of women who appeal to him. His most solid relationship, however, is with his coworker Bucker Reilly (Robert Armstrong), who falls for Gunner's sweetheart, a "wise girl" named Mary (Mae Clarke). Mary fleeces, then marries Bucker, but nonetheless agrees to spend a weekend with Gunner. When Bucker sees the light, he arranges for Gunner to have a high-rise accident, which nearly kills him. While he recovers, the friends reconcile, swearing off Mary for good. At the finish, the still-hospitalized Gunner flips a silver dollar at the feet of a departing nurse, blaming it all on Bucker.

Upon viewing the final film, the MPPDA objected to a line spoken by Gunner of two chummy girls in a speakeasy: "They're making it tougher for us every day." Code enforcer Wingate called the line "a definite inference of sex perversion, and as such in violation of the Code. . . ." M-G-M, rather boldly, ignored the MPPDA's opinion, and the lesbian joke stayed. Will Hays complained directly to Nicholas Schenck of Loew's, Inc., on March 24, 1933, demanding that the offending piece of dialogue be removed from circulating prints:

> The failure of the studio to eliminate this line . . . was very unfortunate. The absolutely essential element in the operation of the Resolution for Uniform Interpretation is the good faith on the part of the company in carrying out its promise either to eliminate the objectionable material requested by the Association, or to advise the Association of its disagreement. . . . There have been many differences between the studio and the Code officers heretofore but they have always been discussed out and settled. Never before has a thing like this happened, and I am sure you will want to ascertain the reason.

M-G-M's defiance of the Hays Office over *Fast Workers* was never explained, but it may have represented the studio's last, heady gasp of freedom before the strict enforcement of the Production Code began in 1934.

For reasons that are not at all evident in the finished product (the film is shot unimaginatively on simple interiors, and on an unconvincing construction-site set, utilizing uniquely inept process-screen effects), *Fast Workers* cost $525,000—the most expensive film Browning had ever made, dwarfing even the budget of *Dracula.*

It also proved Browning's most titanic box-office disaster, losing $360,000—more than twice the red ink generated by *Freaks.* Not unsurprisingly, critics commented roundly on Gilbert's smarmy characterization. The *New York Times*' reviewer summed it up: "The suspicion grows, watching Gunner Smith at his increasingly moronic tricks, that in real life Gunner would be pitched from a convenient skyscraper by his outraged fellow-workers for one-tenth the things he does in the picture."

Though finished with his Metro contract, Gilbert would return to the studio at Greta Garbo's insistence to costar in *Queen Christina* (1933). But his career was finished. Gilbert spent the next few years in an alcoholic blur, ending with his death from a heart attack in 1936, at the age of 41.

Two disasters under his belt, Browning was hardly the darling of the M-G-M brass. Where was the box-office magic of *Dracula* and the Chaney films that had been the whole point of bringing him back? Ironically, *Freaks* had driven a wedge, in the studio's mind, between Tod Browning and anything that smacked of sideshows and the macabre—previously his two surefire genres. The next project approved for him was a completely unfantastic melodrama set in Cajun country called *Louisiana Lou,* with "atmosphere" scenes to be filmed on location in the shrimp camps of Grand Isle, about a hundred miles from New Orleans.

Based on an unproduced play called *Ruby* (and, alternately, *Dance Hall Daisy* and *Bride of the Bayou*), by Lea David Freeman, *Louisiana Lou* was described in the trade press as a "vivid mystery of the Cajuns" dealing with the "weird traditions" of a "strange and little known people." Lionel Barrymore, Joan Crawford, Alice Barry, and Madge Evans were all announced as stars in contradictory 1933 press announcements. Erskine Caldwell, author of *Tobacco Road,* was assigned briefly to the project, spending time with Browning in Louisiana, but story editor Samuel Marx soon replaced him with a much grander literary lion of the Deep South—William Faulkner.

Faulkner's tenure at M-G-M in the early thirties generated some legendary anecdotes, embellished by the writer himself. Arriving at the Roosevelt Hotel in New Orleans, Faulkner reported to Browning and found a party in progress. "He told me to get a good night's sleep and be ready for an early start in the morning." For three weeks, Faulkner recalled, they made lengthy daily treks to the swampy location set, barely having time for lunch before having to head back to the city.

The *Los Angeles Times* noted "Mysterious Goings On":

Tod Browning's expedition to the bayou country . . . not only is concerned with a mystery play but is proving to be a real mystery. Story and cast is a deep-dyed secret, but it is known that William Faulkner, who wrote *Sanctuary,* is with him, and that they are being shown around by Senator Jules Fisher. They have visited Grand Isle and Bayou Lafourche. They are going into the back bay country, and studying the life and customs of the inhabitants thereof. . . .

Faulkner remembered the elaborate shrimp village M-G-M's art department erected in the bayou,

. . . a long platform on piles in the water with sheds built on it something like a wharf. The studio could have bought dozens of them for forty or fifty dollars apiece. Instead, they built one of their own, a false one. That is, a platform with a single wall on it, so that when you opened the door and stepped through it, you stepped right off into the ocean itself. As they built it, on the first day, the Cajun fisherman paddled up in his narrow tricky pirogue made out of a hollow log. He would sit in it all day long in the broiling sun watching the strange white folks building this strange imitation platform. The next day he was back in the pirogue with his whole family, his wife nursing the baby, the other children, and the mother-in-law, all to sit all that day in the broiling sun to watch this foolish and incomprehensible activity.

"I asked Browning when I was supposed to start work, and what was the story? Browning said I should go see the continuity writer and ask him. I found him, introduced myself as the dialogue writer, and said, 'What's the story?' The continuity writer said, 'Never mind about that, you go off and write some dialogue and then I'll tell you what the story is.' " Faulkner related the continuity man's response to Browning, who exploded, "Why, that son of a bitch. You tell him to tell you the story right away."

Shortly thereafter, said Faulkner, a telegram arrived from Hollywood: FAULKNER IS FIRED. "Browning blew up," the writer recalled, the director assuring him he would be reinstated. Browning filed his complaint, and another telegram arrived: BROWNING IS FIRED.

In reality, Faulkner did quite a bit of work on the film, and his departure was hardly as abrupt (or entertaining) as he recalled. Browning had already expressed reservations about Faulkner's dialogue, wiring Samuel Marx that the writer was a BRILLIANT CAPABLE MAN BUT HAD UNFORTUNATE START. Browning also told Marx that Faulkner was unwilling to come to Culver City to finish the dialogue, as his wife was expecting a baby within weeks in Oxford, Mississippi.

On May 14, 1933, Faulkner wrote Browning from Oxford, where he had returned to work. "I am going ahead with the dialogue. . . . They want to can me, and I am ready to quit; so just let it ride as it lays; you need not even tell them that I have not finished, and I'll get the rest of it done in another week." Concerning his enclosed script, Faulkner wrote, "I have left plenty of margin, so you can jot down corrections, etc., and fire it back to me. I would have had a bigger batch of mss. ready, but I held back to get your synopsis today, and had to back up and make some changes."

The writer added that he hoped to "get the rest of it done by next Sat. and in the meantime don't say anything more to the studio about keeping me on. Just let it go." Faulkner offered his regards to Alice Browning, and, in a P.S. to Tod, "You might drink a bottle of beer for me. I'm reduced to hard whiskey now, being in a prohibition state."

Marx diplomatically relieved Faulkner of the assignment in a telegram which, in addition to thanking him for his work, extended the offer WE WILL BE MOST HAPPY TO CONTINUE YOU ON STAFF HERE AT ANY TIME YOU ADVISE US YOU WILL COME TO CALIFORNIA.

M-G-M cut its losses and recalled Browning and the company to Culver City. *Louisiana Lou* was temporarily shelved and Browning removed from the project. Back in Hollywood, it became *Lazy River,* directed by George B. Seitz in early 1934. None of the material Faulkner prepared for Browning was utilized in the new film; the writer, in fact, never turned anything in to the studio. A twenty-eight-page fragment of Faulkner's script is owned by a private collector and has never been published.

Faulkner visited New Orleans a few years later "and heard that the Cajun people were still coming in for miles to look at that imitation shrimp platform which a lot of white people had rushed in and built and then abandoned."

Following the *Freaks* debacle, Browning found distraction at the nightly entertainment surrounding the round-the-clock dance marathon then drawing huge crowds at the Santa Monica Pier, not far from his Malibu home. The cruel spectacle, sometimes called the Torture Trot, had its beginnings in the Midwest during the 1920s, at first a fairly innocuous stunt, not unlike flagpole sitting or goldfish swallowing. But the onset of the Great Depression changed the coloration of the dance marathon considerably.

Browning loved spectator sports. He regularly frequented the racetrack at Agua Caliente, Mexico, and, with a number of his Malibu neighbors, including Allan Dwan, made a profitable investment in a California track. He also adored boxing, and was among the Friday night faithful at the American Legion Stadium, where the crowd was predominantly film people. According to Dwan, both Browning and his wife were enamored of sweepstakes and gambling. Dance marathons, as they metastasized across America, combined the worst qualities of racing, boxing, and games of chance.

"It's a great night's worth," wrote Arnold Gingrich in a 1933

Esquire article, "Poor Man's Nightclub," examining the marathon phenomenon (which by that time had dropped the dancing to become brutal endurance tests known as walkathons): "For forty cents, on any evening, you will see more knockdowns than a fight fan will ever see for forty dollars . . . if you are cold and lonely and out of a job, on a raw winter's night you will join an audience composed of people who appear to have every right to feel as wretched as yourself, and with them you get the thrill of being able to feel sorry for someone."

Hollywood veteran Budd Schulberg recalled that "even more appalling than the victims on the dance floor were the regulars, affluent sadists in the same front row seats every night, cheering on their favorites who kept fainting and occasionally throwing up from exhaustion." Browning, Schulberg remembered, was among the "most dedicated" of the regulars.

The prize thrill of the marathon experience, at least to the spectators, was "seeing them go 'squirrelly.' " As one journalist reported the phenomenon, "The crowd goes tense as the symptoms appear . . . leans forward, biting lips, twisting handkerchiefs, clutching, as a contestant staggers and seems about to go out." The payoff would occur when "girls, shuffling in a semi-coma, draped over their partners, suddenly start screaming and clawing. Men's red-rimmed, heavy eyes suddenly turn wild and they take a poke at somebody. Or they grin vacantly and weave like drunks, talking to themselves."

Like the down-and-out marathoners, Browning was at a professional nadir. While he had invested his substantial earnings shrewdly and was in no immediate financial danger, following two major flops and a film yanked from under him, he found himself reduced to begging for work from a studio that had once touted him as a major asset.

Another dry spell followed, lasting more than a year. Browning and his wife began spending more time at Malibu, surrounded by their neighbors: producer Robert Z. Leonard and his wife; directors Allan Dwan, George Marshall, and David Butler. The Brownings loved dogs and kept, sequentially, two Saint Bernards; the second was named Carlo, a beloved companion at both their homes. However domestic, life in Malibu was not without its eccentricities. Browning and Robert Leonard were fond of communicating with each other through the walls of their adjacent homes by shouting conversation at the top of their lungs, thus involving many other neighbors in their stentorian discussions. Allan Dwan described the punchline to a sudden electrical storm. Tod and Alice ran inside their house, only to have their chimney struck by lightning. The resulting explosion of soot left the couple looking like "blackface comedians."

But laughs and camaraderie with working film people did not compensate for Browning's sense of idleness and ostracization. Irving Thalberg, once his greatest champion at M-G-M, had suffered a heart attack and had taken an extended leave of absence. Finally, Browning convinced studio manager E. J. "Eddie" Mannix to give him another picture that would shamelessly recycle elements of his two most successful films: *London After Midnight* and *Dracula*. If that wasn't a winning combination, what was?

Mannix agreed, but the studio was unwilling to do another picture with Browning at anything more than half his previous salary. Browning agreed to $25,000 for a film called *The Vampires of Prague,* with the understanding that, should the loaned services of the film's intended star, Lionel Barrymore, be delayed by Fox, Browning, as well as Metro, would be additionally compensated. Barrymore was indeed delayed, triggering an additional $6,000 payment to the director.

The Browning oeuvre is permeated by a sense of déjà vu, but perhaps nowhere deployed with such calculation as in the film that came to be known as *Mark of the Vampire*. The basic plot—a gimmicky murder mystery in which an investigator (Professor Zelin, played by Lionel Barrymore) uses hypnotism and a troupe of phony vampires to catch a killer—was taken directly from *London After Midnight;* the vampires were of the Bela Lugosi variety, with Lugosi himself reprising his *Dracula* capework and deathly pallor. In an almost fetishistic attempt to recapture the box-office draw of *Dracula,* Browning reproduced key moments from the Universal film with obsessive fidelity, down to the use of opossums as rat stand-ins, and a flaccid rubber spider pulled up a wall on a string. The borrowing from *Dracula* in both the script and production was so heavy that E. J. Mannix received counsel that there might be infringement issues to consider. But Mannix overruled the worries as baseless.

For his main scriptwriter, Browning turned to Guy Endore, author of a ferociously lurid horror novel, *The Werewolf of Paris* (1933), who brought a psychoanalytic rationale to the plot: the vampire Count Mora, who sports a ghastly bullet wound in his temple, has joined the ranks of the undead after killing himself and his daughter, with whom he had committed incest. Endore was himself a Freudian partisan, described by a newspaper article as "a strange, wispy little man, sensitive as a violin string." Endore had his reasons: his own mother had committed suicide when he was a child. Psychoanalysis, according to an interviewer, "stopped him from going off the deep end."

Beyond his personal insights into the darker side of parent-child psychology, Endore had almost surely read Ernest Jones' pioneering study *On the Nightmare* (1932), which explained vampire superstitions as displaced incest fantasies (vampirism, in the Eastern European folk tradition, was usually a family affair). In his chapter on the vampire, Jones describes the Bohemian Mora, a creature that sucks not only human blood but milk as well. That Endore and Browning named their incestuous vampire Count Mora can hardly be a coincidence.

A younger screenwriter, Bernard S. Schubert, was also assigned to the film, and had no idea that the story was a remake of *London After Midnight*. Schubert recalled that Browning presented the plot as though it were thoroughly original, demonstrating his ideas "with much excited gesturing," going so far as to pantomime the rubbing of wolfsbane (or "bat-thorn" as it came to be called in the film) on the conference room windows. Endore listened attentively, taking tiny notes on big sheets of paper. Also contributing dialogue were H. S. Kraft and Samuel Ornitz, with a last-minute assist from John L. Balderston, co-author of the stage version of *Dracula*.

Some of the most vivid recollections of the making of *Mark of the Vampire* came from actress Carroll Borland, the twenty-year-old protégée of Bela Lugosi who had idolized him since seeing the actor in Deane and Balderston's *Dracula* at an Oakland theater in the late twenties. Borland was tapped to play Count Mora's deadpan daughter, Luna, after numerous other actresses, including Rita Hayworth, had been turned down.

"I was just down from Berkeley, where I was going to school, taking a speech arts degree," Borland said. She found herself the "pampered pet" of the set, doted on by the likes of Lugosi, Barrymore, Jean Hersholt, Lionel Atwill, and Holmes Herbert. "They were all so very avuncular and interested in what I was doing. I was reading [Emil] Ludwig's *Napoleon,* and many of them had European backgrounds. . . . it was sort of like having a circle of contributing professors or an auxiliary faculty."

Although Borland's part was mute (at least until the denouement, when she and Lugosi are revealed as the star troupers of a "Bat-Girl Theater"), a great deal of time and attention was lavished on her makeup and visual effects attending her on-screen appearances. Browning had featured shrouded vampire women with tightly wrapped hair in both *London After Midnight* and *Dracula,* but a different kind of femme fatale was sought for *Mark of the Vampire.* Lugosi had pretty much standardized the expected appearance of a male vampire, but the female conventions had not really gelled. Borland was short, almond-eyed, and had a luxurious mane of dark hair that fell halfway to the floor.

"In those days nobody had waist-length straight hair. And nobody had a square jaw and slanted eyes and a funny face. They kept trying to make me over into 'the girl of the times,' with waved hair. They'd marcel and curl it. They kept trying to give me cupid-bow lips," Borland said. Finally, she was sent to makeup artist William Tuttle for a fresh approach. Tuttle simply had her part her hair in the middle, adhered it to her forehead with spirit gum—and instantly created the lank-haired prototype of the female vampire that has haunted popular culture ever since.

But the most elaborate effect created for Borland had nothing to do with hair or makeup, but rather with bat wings. Browning wanted to re-create a moment from *London After Midnight* in which Edna Tichenor was shown suspended from the ceiling, displaying her webbed wingspan at full extension—a distinctly literal interpretation of the word "flapper," circa 1927.

Borland called the 1935 re-creation "perfectly fascinating. They built a track, like a little electric railroad—a monorail—and it was very high. Browning decided he wanted it to swoop in the opposite direction, so they tore out one side of the soundstage and built it out. . . ." A taxidermist at the corner of Fountain and Sunset was hired to outfit her with a set of spring-driven bat wings that opened like unruly automatic umbrellas. Borland was strapped onto a body-length aluminum frame, over which a gray shroud by Adrian (certainly the designer's only such creation) was draped. A pair of stage-hands was needed to stabilize the actress in flight, but their lack of coordination resulted in numerous belly landings before they got it right. The sequence took a day and a half to shoot, and lasts about five seconds on-screen.

Borland recalled the grand M-G-M style that could accompany the most mundane activities. An entire truck was required to retrieve a missing wart for the old cemetery crone who opens the picture. In order to get from one set to another, "you didn't cross the street, you took a limousine," she said. One day Borland shared a car with Browning and Douglas Shearer, the sound technician and brother of Norma. As a youngster in San Francisco, she had learned the old-fashioned seating protocol for men and women. The woman entered first, sat on the right, letting the man cross over her to the center, so that the woman would be the first to exit. Borland entered and occupied the proper position. Browning stared at her a moment, then crossed to the middle. "I didn't know anyone your age knew enough to sit on the right-hand side," he said in wonderment.

As the baby of the cast, Borland was forgiven impertinences a more seasoned performer would never attempt. Browning explained what he wanted from her in a scene when she is startled while hovering over the female lead, Elizabeth Allan. "You growl like a wolf," he said. "You know, deep in your throat." "I can see your point," Borland said airily, "but how about a hiss, like an angry cat?" "Try it," the director said, a little surprised at having his direction challenged. They shot the scene and Browning said "Print it" without additional comment. On another occasion she turned her ankle and grimaced while drifting down a narrow corridor. Browning said, "You gave me something with your mouth." Borland told him she had twisted her ankle. He suggested that she twist it again.

Browning marshaled all the studio resources at his disposal to create a gothic mood approaching parody. Mist effects involving an industrial-strength mixture of dry ice and water liquefied piles of earth used in the graveyard sets. "We worked in mud all the time," Borland laughed. "It was really messy. Every night the costume had to be cleaned. It got shorter and shorter."

Cinematographer James Wong Howe is usually given the lion's share of credit for *Mark of the Vampire*'s moody atmospherics, but it wasn't one of his favorite pictures. He called Browning "quite a character. . . . one of the old school who didn't know too much about the camera. He had the actors play 'at' the camera instead of moving around it, so the picture was very stagy and he used cutting to get him through." But M-G-M production manager J. J. Cohn wasn't particularly enchanted with the cameraman, and replaced him. "I took Jimmy Howe off the picture after a few weeks" because "he wasn't getting the effects right." Another lensman finished the picture, but Howe received sole credit contractually. In Borland's memory, Elizabeth Allan complained that Howe had been lighting scenes to favor the grotesque vampire makeup, to the detriment of her own appearance. Howe had gone so far as to set up black velvet draping to create a nonreflective look in the eyes of Lugosi and Borland, a kind of pampering that infuriated the lead actress.

Scriptwriter Bernard Schubert, who visited the set, was surprised at how brusque the director could sometimes be with his performers. Lionel Atwill, in a characteristic police inspector role, "was not pleased with Browning's attitude," said Schubert, and his sympathies went out to Lionel Barrymore, who "was already a great star when Tod Browning was chasing cows." The actors became confused at certain characters and plot elements that were never explained. A bit player named James Bradbury played a second-string vampire and appears in a number of publicity stills, though not in the finished film. Borland recalled that "somebody asked me once, 'Who was that guy?' I don't know. 'What did he do?' I don't know. He was this little man who was always there, but we didn't know what part he played, or anything else. I know that sounds absolutely idiotic, but it was as though there were two crews." Although all references to Count Mora's suicidal, incestuous past were cut during filming, the bleeding bullet hole in Bela Lugosi's right temple was never removed, and remains completely unexplained in the final cut. A full script was not distributed to the cast until midway through production, and Borland was disappointed to find she wasn't playing a "real" vampire after all. She suggested to Browning an alternate ending, wherein the police would receive a telegram from the vampire performers, apologizing for not having shown up. But Browning didn't bite.

The film received energetic ballyhoo, especially in Cleveland, where a "human trailer" was employed at the Loew's Theater the week before opening. Anticipating the famous William Castle fright-film gimmicks of the 1960s, a three-foot-wide cutout bat traveled down a wire from the projectionist's booth to the stage, accompanied by a whistle siren, gunshots, and screams. When the bat reached the stage, the auditorium was plunged into darkness. A cape-clad vampire appeared in a green spotlight to plug the film, followed by the standard trailer. A furniture store on Euclid Avenue had a "Victim of Vampire" sleeping in a display-window chair, with the public asked to guess the time of her awakening. The film itself was specially screened for the custodian of the Cuyahoga County Morgue—in the morgue. And so on.

The reviews were generally laudatory, with only a few dissenting opinions on the "anticlimactic" finish. *Mark of the Vampire,* while hardly a hit, was at least minimally profitable, earning $54,000 beyond its $309,000 cost, and served to reestablish Browning's credibility at Metro, however tenuously.

Buoyed by the seeming reversal of his downward fortunes, Browning immediately began work on a new weird tale. Inspired by the novel *Burn, Witch, Burn!,* by Abraham Merritt, *The Witch of Timbuctoo* was described in an M-G-M trade advertisement as a tale of "Fantastic Voodoo rites in Africa, the horrors of Devil's Island and the mysteries of the Paris underworld. To be directed by Tod Browning as one of the most important mystery-horror thrillers of the year."

The British Board of Film Censors, distressed by the large harvest of horror that Hollywood had produced in 1935—in addition to M-G-M's *Mark of the Vampire* and *Mad Love,* there had been Universal's *Werewolf of London, Bride of Frankenstein,* and most annoyingly, *The Raven,* a cartoonishly cruel Karloff-Lugosi vehicle which had drawn particular protest in the British press—announced that it would severely restrict horror entertainment. A strange ritual dance soon began between M-G-M and the British censors over *The Witch of Timbuctoo,* similar to the detailed Production Code Administration negotiations over script development that had become common in America.

Browning, Guy Endore, and Garrett Fort completed a script in the summer of 1935, based extremely loosely on the Merritt book. Their scenario centered on African witchcraft and a method by which human beings could be shrunken into living voodoo dolls. Duval, a revenge-seeking, wrongly convicted escapee from Devil's Island, returns with the magical secret to Paris, where, disguised as an old woman with a doll shop, shrinks a band of Parisian Apaches, who carry out telepathic instructions to murder two of his enemies and terrorize a confession out of the third. He then commits suicide.

The Production Code Administration was uneasy with the script, objecting to the suicidal plot resolution—a clear code violation—as well as the depiction of animal sacrifice during the voodoo scenes. Script-doctoring was solicited from Robert Chapin and the largely out-of-work Erich von Stroheim, whose work went largely unused. But the real challenge came in late 1935 when the British Board of Film Censors ruled out the voodoo angle entirely.

On November 11 agent Dave Blum wired M-G-M from London relating that E. J. Mannix HAD QUIET TALK WITH CENSOR WHO CONFIRMS THAT BLACK MAGIC ASSOCIATED WITH RELIGIOUS RITES DEFINITELY PROHIBITED STOP CENSOR AGREED WITHOUT COMMITTING HIMSELF THAT CONVERTING HUMAN BEINGS TO THE SIZE OF DOLLS IS LEGITIMATE DRAMA THEREFORE THIS HELPS A LOT AND OUR DIFFICULTY IS TO AMEND WAY IN WHICH IT IS DONE. The *Hollywood Reporter* got wind of the story and reported on December 10 that "once again a foreign government has stepped in to censor a Hollywood script for political reasons." As the *Reporter* described the matter, the British censors had dictated the removal of all black characters out of concern that the witchcraft scenes might "stir up trouble" among blacks then under British colonial rule.

The studio removed all references to witchcraft, substituting a science-fictional rationale. As filmed, the story recounted the bizarre revenge of the now-renamed Paul Lavond (Lionel Barrymore), a Parisian banker framed by his crooked associates and condemned to Devil's Island. He escapes in the company of a mad scientist, Marcel (Henry B. Walthall), who, with his even more unbalanced wife, Malita (Rafaela Ottiano), has perfected a human miniaturization process. Their goal is benevolent, if a bit misguided: they believe that reducing the size of people is the perfect answer to overpopulation and dwindling resources. Marcel dies and Lavond moves to Paris with Malita, planning to use mad science to aid his revenge. The perfectly shrunken homunculi have no will of their own—their brains are wiped clean in the downsizing—but they can be controlled telepathically, and carry tiny stilettos tipped with paralytic poison. Lavond assumes the disguise of an old woman, Madame Mandelip, whose toy store in Montmartre provides a perfect cover for manufacturing the deadly "devil dolls." Lavond places the creatures in the homes of his enemies, where they serve double duty as jewel thieves and paralysis-dispensing

Family poison: Lon Chaney offers a drink to Mary Nolan in *West of Zanzibar* (1928). *(Photofest)*

The Big City (1928): Browning offers Lon Chaney one of his favorite cigarettes.
(Elias Savada collection)

A vampire's "screen test" Bela Lugosi corners Helene Millard in *The Thirteenth Chair* (1929). *(Photofest)*

Poster art for *Where East Is East* (1929). *(Courtesy of Philip J. Riley)*

Edward G. Robinson, Browning, and Mary Nolan in a publicity pose for *Outside the Law* (1930). *(Elias Savada collection)*

Tod and Alice Browning embarking on a trip to Europe aboard the *Aquitania* in 1928. *(Billy Rose Theater Collection, New York Public Library at Lincoln Center, Astor, Lenox. and Tilden Foundations)*

Bela Lugosi—Public Vampire Number One. *(David J. Skal collection)*

Browning, with Bela Lugosi and Helen Chandler on the set of *Dracula* (1931).
(Courtesy of the Academy of Motion Picture Arts and Sciences)

Sign hangers in vampiresque formal wear install the billboard for *Dracula*'s
Los Angeles 1931 premiere. *(Free Library of Philadelphia Theatre collection)*

Advertisement for
Iron Man (1931).
(Courtesy of Leonard Schrader)

Studio portrait, early 1930s.
(David J. Skal collection)

Mae Clarke and Robert Armstrong challenge the Production Code in *Fast Workers* (1933). *(Photofest)*

Browning surrounded by his screenwriters for *Mark of the Vampire:* (left to right) Hy S. Kraft, Guy Endore, Browning, Samuel Ornitz, Bernard S. Schubert. *(Elias Savada collection)*

The dime-museum exterior for *Freaks* (1932), cut from the final release print. *(Elias Savada collection)*

Left to right: Browning, Johnny Eck, Frances O'Connor, Bill Robinson, and Minnie Woolsey. *(Elias Savada collection)*

Browning orchestrates the wedding feast sequence for *Freaks* (1932).
(Courtesy of Ronald V. Borst/Hollywood Movie Posters)

Newspaper advertisement for the San Diego premiere of *Freaks* (1932). *(Elias Savada collection)*

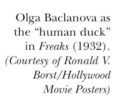

Olga Baclanova as the "human duck" in *Freaks* (1932). *(Courtesy of Ronald V. Borst/Hollywood Movie Posters)*

Browning with his Saint Bernard, Carlo, at the director's Beverly Hills home, early 1930s.
(Elias Savada collection)

Cinematographer James Wong Howe and Browning (at front of camera trolley) set up a shot of Bela Lugosi and Carroll Borland for *Mark of the Vampire* (1935). *(Courtesy of Ronald V. Borst/Hollywood Movie Posters)*

Browning and Lionel Barrymore on the set of *The Devil-Doll* (1936). *(Photofest)*

The Devil-Doll (1936): A miniaturized assassin stalks her prey. *(Photofest)*

Robert Young
and Henry Hull
in *Miracles for Sale*
(1939). *(Photofest)*

Carey Wilson, the producer who engineered Browning's dismissal
from M-G-M, dines with the director and his wife.
(Courtesy of Ronald V. Borst/Hollywood Movie Posters)

"Tod's Little Acre": Browning attends to his victory garden and menagerie in the early 1940s.
(Elias Savada collection)

Browning and his wife, Alice, not long before her death.
(Elias Savada collection)

Browning with his beloved bulldog, Dusty. *(Elias Savada collection)*

Browning's burial niche at Rosedale Cemetery, Los Angeles.
(Courtesy of Nick Bougas)

puppets to force confessions from Lavond's enemies, and exonerate him in the eyes of his daughter (Maureen O'Sullivan), who has grown up in his absence, convinced of his guilt.

By eliminating the actual possibility of murder, the original revenge story had been softened almost to the point of cuteness, but at least it could pass the censors. Barrymore's drag performance lends an additional tone of near merriment. *Time* reported the actor's exclamation, upon seeing himself in the film: "My God! It's Ethel!" Of course, he might just as well have said, "My God! It's Lon Chaney!" *The Devil-Doll* revisits several Browning films, most obviously *The Unholy Three,* in which Chaney also used an old-lady disguise to case wealthy homes for jewels. *Dracula* is also evoked with its theme of mesmeric influence (like Lugosi, Barrymore spends significant time lingering below windows, projecting his will). *West of Zanzibar* and *The Road to Mandalay* are also thrown into the mix, with their themes of revenge and concealed identities between fathers and daughters.

To create the illusion of miniaturized humans and animals, the studio employed double-exposure optical printing techniques, but achieved far greater success by simply building gigantically oversize sets on the biggest M-G-M facility, sound stage no. 12. Browning shot *The Devil-Doll* in thirty-eight days, exactly the schedule of *Mark of the Vampire.* In contrast to Basil Wrangell's unpleasant experience with *Freaks,* film editor Frederick Y. Smith had no difficulties working with Browning. "Tod, to me at least, was very affable and thoughtful. He treated me with a lot of respect and was very cordial. I had no trouble cutting his film."

Frank S. Nugent of the *New York Times* enjoyed *The Devil-Doll.* "Not since *The Lost World, King Kong* and *The Invisible Man* have the camera wizards enjoyed such a field day. By use of the split screen, glass shots, over-sized sets, and other trick devices cherished of their kind, they have pieced together a photoplay which is grotesque, slightly horrible, and consistently interesting." The *Times* praised Browning for investing "essentially ridiculous episodes with a menacing, chilling quality which makes it impossible for you to consider them too lightly."

The Devil-Doll cost $391,000 and made a $68,000 profit, virtually the same cost-to-profit ratio as *Mark of the Vampire*. It came nowhere near the performance of his earlier work for Metro; by commercial comparison, even *The Thirteenth Chair* was a triumph. Browning's films were simply not earning. In the eyes of the studio, he had ceased to be a player.

Nine weeks after the release of *The Devil-Doll,* Irving Thalberg, Browning's longtime ally, died of a pulmonary infection his weakened heart could not withstand. Prior to his death, Thalberg and Mayer's professional relationship had become strained, but Thalberg's demise formally signified the end of an era that had, perhaps, already ended. Mayer biographer Bosley Crowther described the dark ritual undercurrents of the changing command. "Mayer, with appropriate formality, went to the Thalberg home as soon as word reached him of Irving's passing. He spoke his condolences to Norma and cried a few facile tears." But later that night, "a distinguished director whose integrity and temperance are unimpeachable was shocked to discover Mayer at the Trocadero, a Hollywood nightclub, dancing violently, frenziedly. . . . almost as though he was performing some barbaric rite."

Browning spent two long, inactive years trying to launch another project. Shortly following the release of *Mark of the Vampire,* Horace McCoy's caustic dance marathon novel, *They Shoot Horses, Don't They?,* was published. McCoy, a screenwriter who contributed to the script of *King Kong* (1933), had worked as a bouncer at the same Santa Monica marathon Browning had frequented. The *New Republic* called the book "a deliberate shocker . . . sordid, pathetic, senselessly exciting. It will be read, however. It has the immediacy—and significance—of a nerve-shattering explosion." McCoy had written a novel filled with characters and situations that could have been plucked from any number of Browning films; it is not difficult to understand how Browning found the carnivalesque story of dehumanized predation an attractive subject for the screen. He unsuccessfully attempted to persuade M-G-M to buy him the rights.

In 1938 Browning read a mystery novel, *Death from a Top Hat,* by

Clayton Rawson, featuring a retired magician devoted to exposing phony occultists. It was clearly a "Browning" property, and the director convinced M-G-M production manager J. J. Cohn to take a chance on it. Browning was not given a screenplay credit; the script was assigned to Harry Ruskin, Marion Parsonet, and James Edward Grant. And, for the first time since the early 1920s, the picture would not be billed as "A Tod Browning Production." He would be given only director's credit, for a demeaning flat fee of $10,000, later increased by E. J. Mannix to $15,000. Released as *Miracles for Sale* in the summer of 1939, the picture starred Robert Young as the ex-magician and sleuth.

One piece of evidence that Browning had some unbilled influence on the script was the macabre opening set piece, in which a woman is captured by the Japanese Army, forced into a child's coffin from which her head and legs protrude, and summarily machine-gunned in half. The spectacle is immediately revealed as a grisly bit of stage magic exploiting growing war anxieties in the Pacific. It also was yet another variation on images of below-the-waist mutilation that had long fascinated Browning, from the Chaney films to *The Show* to *Freaks*.

The rest of *Miracles for Sale* amounted to a rather transparent comedy melodrama revolving around the non-mystery of Henry Hull's dual role in a murder (Hull uses contact lenses to change his eye color, but is otherwise obviously recognizable, spoiling any sense of suspense). Gloria Holden, who played the title role in *Dracula's Daughter* for Universal, essentially repeats the performance as a glassy-eyed fake spiritualist.

The story was fairly innocuous, but its many demonstrations of the inner workings of stage-magic paraphernalia drew the ire of professional tricksters. Loew's, Inc., had received a complaint from the Pacific Coast Association of Magicians, objecting to the revelation of stage-magic techniques in the film. I. H. Printzmetal of Loew's responded to the association's spokesman, Hubert Brill, in early August 1939: "Pursuant to your request, we have made arrangements to delete from foreign prints the scenes of *Miracles for Sale* in question. Although this will entail quite an expenditure, we are pleased to cooperate to this extent with your organization.''

Brill thanked Printzmetal by letter on August 11, adding, ''Were widespread exposures by the medium of motion pictures permitted, they would soon render many of the magicians of this country without means of making their livings. For with the disclosure of their secrets, public interest would be destroyed and their investments in time and costly equipment rendered a total loss.''

Miracles for Sale received perfunctory reviews, and a few positive notices from women's groups and other critics who liked their entertainment lukewarm to begin with. The *New York Times* noted ''enough loose ends to fringe a Spanish shawl,'' but nonetheless praised Browning's direction, perhaps just for old time's sake. The *New York Herald-Tribune* called it ''mildly mystifying and lively,'' commending Browning for having ''built up a melodramatic unity out of very ordinary subject matter.''

Most of the reviews didn't mention Browning at all.

The final bit of censor interference he would ever have to endure came with Sweden's rejection of *Miracles for Sale* because of ''felonious homicides [and] terror scenes of a gruesome nature.''

By the time Browning directed what would prove to be his last film, he had sold the Beverly Hills house and moved with Alice permanently to Malibu. In December 1940 E. J. Mannix approved Hunt Stromberg's employment of Browning as his direct employee, an arrangement that would allow him to work, while shielding him from the pressure of other demands and assignments. The arrangement obviously smacked of charity and raised eyebrows among the new administrative regime.

Samuel Marx, who had known Browning from the time of their mutual employment at Universal in the late teens, was saddened to witness the final days of the director's career, when he was unable to get a studio commitment for any picture at all:

In my job as story editor I kept feeding him the kind of horror mystery stories he specialized in, but he couldn't seem to get an okay to go ahead with one—a sure sign of handwriting on the wall. His best friend in the studio at that time was the General Manager, Eddie Mannix, and Tod began to haunt his office. . . . I remember him telling me how he and Mannix spent almost every Sunday together socially, but they had a protocol agreement that no business was to be discussed on these get-togethers. Consequently, he would hang around every weekday from about ten to five, trying to get in to discuss business with Mannix, then he would raise hell and party with him on weekends without being able to mention what he was so concerned about, and start all over again Monday mornings with another vain vigil.

"I'm not sure the Hollywoodish irony of it struck Tod, but it did me," said Marx. "Not long after, he left the studio. Perhaps he got the bad news when he finally got in to see Mannix."

Marx confirmed what Browning had bitterly told others: namely, that his firing had been engineered by the producer Carey Wilson, whose own career Browning had helped advance in the mid-twenties. At M-G-M Wilson started as a scriptwriter on such films as Lon Chaney's *He Who Gets Slapped* (1924) and *Ben-Hur* (1925), eventually working his way up the ranks to become a producer to be reckoned with in the 1940s, taking credit for the enormously successful *Andy Hardy* and *Dr. Kildare* series. According to William S. Hart, Jr., although Browning had championed Wilson with the studio, the producer later "turned on him for no reason," fabricating stories that "made trouble for him with Mayer and with everybody else."

Studio executives began making pointed inquiries about Browning's activities since he became attached to the Stromberg unit. He had done a fifty-two-page rough treatment as well as a thirty-two-page continuity for a film called *Ghost of the Thin Man* (released as *Shadow of the Thin Man* in 1941), and had begun a treatment adaptation of the Hungarian novel *Hotel Majestic,* by Eugen Heltai, previously filmed in 1937 in Hungary under the title *Room 111.* Fueled by skepticism that Browning was doing "any writing at all," internal scrutiny increased. At the end of October 1941 he was transferred from the Stromberg unit to the M-G-M writer pool, his salary reduced to $200 a week. A few weeks later he filed his last story treatment, *Equilibrium,* and went off the M-G-M payroll for good on January 3, 1942.

Browning retired to Malibu with Alice within weeks of the United States' entry into World War II, which made their long-standing fondness for European travel an impossibility. Their residence at 31 Malibu Colony, as well as its garage, was filled with souvenirs and curios gleaned from two previous decades of globe-trotting. Browning was especially proud of his collection of ornate ceramic beer steins gathered during numerous trips to Germany. (His tastes in things Teutonic didn't stop at beer mugs; in his garage, Browning housed one of the first Volkswagens ever imported to the United States.)

Because the Brownings still had money, investments, and real estate, Tod's dismissal by M-G-M was more an emotional than financial trauma. According to Browning's longtime carpenter and handyman, Herve Babineau, he felt he had been "blackballed" and, whatever the role of Carey Wilson, ultimately blamed Louis B. Mayer personally for the collapse of his career. Now he focused his life on Alice and the house. Instead of the tennis courts that were a fixture of most of the neighboring homes, Browning installed a duck pond and victory garden. He called the plot of land "Tod's Little Acre."

Winifred Hart recalled that Browning enjoyed concocting mystery stories as a creative outlet during his decline at M-G-M, and had written pseudonymously for pulp magazines. Once, Mrs. Hart said, he boasted of having written an entire issue of *Black Cat,* using several pen names.*

In the spring of 1944 Alice Browning was hospitalized in Santa Monica for a recurrent obstruction of the small intestine, but she rallied sufficiently to return home. Once back in Malibu, she had a relapse, complicated by pneumonia, again requiring hospital care. Herve Babineau recalled the ambulance drivers who came to retrieve her, and Alice's request that they carry her down to the

---

* While the Black Cat *anecdote cannot be verified, the December 1994 issue of the Italian literary magazine* Panta *published a translation of a 1935* Spicy Detective *story, "Out of the Tomb," by Charles R. Allen, a purported Browning pseudonym.*

beach, in order to view the house for what she understood would be the last time. Browning visited his wife in the hospital on May 12. By the time he returned home, Babineau had already received a phone call from the hospital asking him to return immediately.

Babineau stayed with Browning in the Malibu house the night Alice died. Browning took the loss hard—very hard. Alice was cremated, her ashes interred with those of her parents and brother in Rosedale Cemetery, Los Angeles. In the months that followed, Browning became reclusive. Allan Dwan recalled that he would sometimes "freeze up" and not see anyone for days. Leila Hyams and Phil Berg came to visit; although they were certain he was home, there was no answer to their knock. Browning draped Alice's shawl over her favorite rocking chair, assuring that no one else would sit in it.

Thirty-one Malibu Colony became a solitary fortress for Browning in the postwar years, its porch guarded by an impassive bronze statue of a fisherman, frozen in the act of peering at the ocean. The world rarely intruded, and usually only at Browning's invitation. But there were occasional surprises.

A retrospective appraisal of Browning's career—the only such article published in his lifetime—appeared in the October 1953 issue of *Films in Review*. It was a flattering piece which noted the "unexpected scenes of sheer pictorial beauty in almost all of Browning's films. . . . his techniques and devices for thrilling and chilling audiences have been copied by directors all over the world." Browning responded personally in an undated letter to Mrs. Henry Geltzer, whose husband had written the piece, a laudatory overview. It remains, perhaps, the only commentary on his career he ever put on paper after his retirement:

Dear Mrs. Geltzer,

Please forgive the delay of this letter. I assure you it was not neglect. Your article in Films in Review was very—very—good. *Thanks.* There were some errors but without an interview that's to be expected. Had to smile at age seventy one, that was passed some time ago. I retired in forty one and have been enjoying life on the cream saved off the milk received for flickers I enjoyed making—that is until I started making *Freaks* and from then on— well that's another story.

Wishing you the Best of luck.

Thanks Again
Tod Browning

Browning's comment about his age is intriguing, because it seems to confirm William S. Hart, Jr.'s statement that he was born much earlier than official records indicated. A question remains, however, whether "some time ago" refers to the two-year discrepancy of the *Films in Review* piece (which cited his birth year as 1882, rather than 1880) or the 1874 date Hart mentioned.

Although he claimed to occasionally receive feelers from studios for new treatments or scripts, and hinted to acquaintances that he still developed screen stories for his own amusement, there was little place for him in Hollywood of the 1950s, which was then experiencing convulsions analogous to the early sound era as the studios scrambled to compete with television with spectacular new technical innovations—CinemaScope, 3-D, VistaVision, and stereophonic sound.

Many of Browning's former coworkers, some dating back to the dawn of the medium, were beginning to pass away. D. W. Griffith had died in 1948, Lionel Barrymore in 1954. And, although he once listed the actor as one of his closest friends on a studio publicity questionnaire, Browning did not attend the August 1956 funeral of Bela Lugosi, dead after a decades-long drug addiction, a highly publicized recovery, and a sadly unsuccessful comeback attempt. But because he followed the trade papers avidly, Browning likely read of the Lugosi family's half-poignant, half-macabre decision (then attributed to Lugosi himself) to bury the actor in full costume and makeup as Dracula. One of Browning's Malibu neighbors was actor Brian Donlevy, who in the 1960s would marry Lugosi's fourth wife, Lillian. Another neighbor and friend was actress June Havoc, sister of Gypsy Rose Lee.

Browning kept very much to himself in Malibu, usually venturing out only to the barbershop or supermarket. A lifelong insomniac, he stayed up reading, watching television, or drinking beer all night, happy to take phone calls at four in the morning, if a caller was so disposed. "Loner" was a word used frequently by his acquaintances.

"He had a feeling for humanity," recalled Malibu neighbor Mrs. Edward de Butts. "Lots of times it wasn't a really *friendly* feeling, but he did have emotions." Like many crusty old men, he wasn't particularly fond of children, but he took a rare shine to the de Buttses' daughter. He generally detested the spoiled youngsters of the Malibu colony, turned over by their parents to the care of English nurses—"they'd just run wild," Mrs. de Butts remembered. But her daughter was particularly well mannered and "was taught to curtsey to older people—that's what Tod liked about her." Like Browning, the de Buttses were southerners, from Virginia, shared certain values, and he therefore seemed to be less guarded in his dealings with them. Edward de Butts was Browning's mail carrier and had also worked at M-G-M for a time as Clark Gable's stand-in.

Although Browning lavished their little girl from time to time with unusual gifts like cultured pearls, he nonetheless was still capable of a deep distrust of people who considered themselves his friends. The de Buttses once quite innocently invited him to see their daughter perform in a dance recital—only to have him call the next day and ask angrily if they were trying to use him to get their child into motion pictures.

"He seemed always to be afraid that he had something that somebody wanted," Mrs. de Butts said. "In Hollywood, everyone camped around the doorsteps of directors and producers, and would do anything onerous to get a part in a picture." Browning, she believed, "was almost afraid to make a new friend, because that friend might want something." As a result, he tended to deal with ordinary human kindnesses caustically. Mrs. de Butts recalled his treatment of one friend, who often visited him with gifts of food. He accepted the offerings but exacted his pound of flesh, as it were. "He would sit there and say mean things to her about being overweight—she was *very* overweight, more than three hundred pounds. He would taunt her very cruelly, but she would keep coming back, bringing him good things to eat.''

As Mrs. de Butts understood his character, Browning "didn't want anyone, ever, to say he owed them anything. If you did something for him, he'd pay you. And that was something he'd insist on," even for "some picayunish thing," like fixing the plug of an electrical cord.

In addition to delivering his mail, Edward de Butts provided another major service for Browning: carrying in cases of beer from the back porch and stocking the refrigerator. Browning was by this time hobbled by gout, one shoe cut open to relieve the pressure on his foot and ankle, and could no longer lift or carry much of anything. But he could still hold two dozen bottles of Coors every day, a feat that drew comments of amazement from most who knew him. No one suggested openly that he might have a problem with alcohol—after all, it was "only" beer; he never touched hard liquor. According to Mrs. de Butts, her husband treated the daily responsibility as almost a "religious ritual," and afterward might spend hours listening to Browning recount "amazing" tales of early Hollywood, intimate, entertainingly revealing anecdotes about people like D. W. Griffith, Louis B. Mayer, and countless others.

The de Buttses both realized that Browning had the makings of a major book on Hollywood, if he would only write his stories down. When he didn't respond to their suggestions to do so, Mr. de Butts proposed bringing over a tape recorder to make things easier for him. Instead, it just made the old man furious. His stories were his own, to be doled out to whomever he decided, whenever he decided—he had no regard for posterity, or history, and absolutely no intention of giving anything away to anyone. Mrs. de Butts found Browning to be an irritating enigma—now charming, now snappish; sometimes apparently cultured and sometimes downright coarse. At times she "thought he had a lot of education, and sometimes I thought he didn't have any at all—because of the insecurities that go with an uneducated person.''

Browning had always kept dogs, and his animal companions in the 1940s and '50s included two bulldogs, and a mynah bird that excitedly asked "Where's Dorothy?" whenever guests arrived. In 1946 Browning made the acquaintance of Dr. Harold Snow, a veterinarian just out of school who treated his bulldog Toby until the dog's death, which devastated him. Browning "was so upset about it that it upset me," said Dr. Snow, who found him a replacement bulldog puppy named Dusty. Browning initially rejected it, but the veterinarian left the dog with Browning's neighbor June Havoc, who finally persuaded him to accept it. Tod and Dusty became fast friends.

The Snows periodically took him to lunch at Armstrong Schroder, the venerable Beverly Hills café, where he would meet old cronies, or, more memorably, to the Miramar hotel in Santa Monica. "As he was getting older, people in Hollywood just didn't recognize him anymore," Dr. Snow remembered. But the Miramar's maître d' "always made a big fuss over him. And Tod would just beam."

Though he feigned indifference to the modern world of show business, Browning still read the trades regularly, and grew addicted to old movies on late-night television, a pastime that dovetailed perfectly with his lifelong penchant for "burning moonlight." And despite his purported statement "I wouldn't walk across the street to see a movie," he did permit the Snows to take him to Ingmar Bergman's *Wild Strawberries* in 1959. According to Dr. Snow, he responded quite favorably to the film, a study in old age and alienation that coincidentally starred one of Browning's directorial colleagues at M-G-M in the twenties, Victor Sjöström.* Sjöström (who, like Browning, had also been one of Lon Chaney's directors) gave a powerful performance as an elderly professor, Isak Borg, simultaneously confronting the disappointments of an emotionally isolated life and the terrifying imminence of death.

Browning himself adhered to no formal spiritual practices or beliefs other than the metaphysical precepts of Masonry. William S. Hart, Jr., called Browning "a very religious man" with a "profound feeling for God." According to Hart, Browning took the Masonic

---

* In Hollywood, Sjöström's name was Americanized to Seastrom.

rite "*extremely* seriously," and, like his brother Avery, had achieved the penultimate rank of the 32nd degree. He gave Hart a signed application card. "Someday you'll join the shrine," he said, "and I'll be gone, but I want you to use this when I'm gone." He could be "very sentimental," said Hart. "Strange. He was such a hard man, then he'd come out with extremely sentimental things like this." A member of the Henry S. Orme Lodge, Browning had been one of the few shriners who had not blackballed D. W. Griffith when he applied for membership. The term "blackball" was literal: when voting for candidates, the shriners deposited balls in a fishbowl, wooden balls for and black ones against. In the case of Griffith, Browning remembered that "there were so many black balls in that goldfish bowl you'd have thought a goat had been sitting there."

In 1958 Dusty developed a metastatic tumor and had to be put to sleep by Dr. Snow. Browning once more experienced the deep, distressing sadness he had felt at Toby's loss a decade earlier, and this time refused to make another emotional commitment to a pet. But his grief over Dusty was soon overtaken by a larger, human loss.

On December 14, 1958, Avery Browning was found asphyxiated at the old family home at 2227 West Main Street, Louisville, which had been converted to a duplex. An upstairs tenant, Owen Salzgaver, had smelled gas fumes and discovered Avery sitting dead at his breakfast table. Louisville Deputy Coroner Harry Elstone ruled the death an accident caused by an unvented water heater.

Tod Browning had not visited Louisville since 1925, and his brother had visited California only once. But in later life the two had talked almost daily by telephone, placing bets on ball games. Accompanied by Mrs. Yvonne West, who had assisted and finally taken over the practice of his longtime business manager, Charles E. Green, Browning made a melancholy pilgrimage back to Louisville on the Superchief.

The wake at Pearson's Funeral Home proved a grotesque spectacle. Mildred McAuliffe recalled that about two dozen people were in attendance, mostly Avery's Masonic brothers. The casket was closed. Jennie Block, the Brownings' foster sister, asked to see Tod, but he was determined to mourn in theatrical privacy. He sat silently behind a curtain, refusing to greet or even acknowledge the guests. Jennie "raised the roof," said McAuliffe, but Browning held fast, resisting even the most perfunctory human contact.

McAuliffe, who had never met her cousin, tracked him to his accommodations on the twelfth floor of the Kentucky Home Towers hotel, and tried phoning him. Mrs. West informed her that Browning was too sick to have visitors. McAuliffe's father made inquiries at the bank where Browning had gone to settle his brother's affairs—Avery, in his later years, had invested in several pieces of Louisville real estate. A banker told McAuliffe's father that Browning was being treated for cancer of the tongue and had undergone an operation that made it painful and embarrassing for him to speak. None of Browning's other acquaintances, however, recalled Browning's having cancer at this time.

A few months after Avery's death, McAuliffe and her family visited the Browning family gravesite at the Eastern Cemetery. They were shocked to find that Avery's ashes had not been buried in his mother's grave, as they had expected, but instead were unceremoniously dumped atop Lydia Browning's plot. Worse yet, McAuliffe recalled that Avery's remains had not been thoroughly cremated— his thighbones were clearly visible in the ashy pile. The incident was, unfortunately, typical of the cemetery's lax practices, which would result in its falling into receivership.

The trials of old age, failing health, and the realization that he was deeply and irretrievably dependent on other people seem to have softened Browning considerably in his final years. He became more generous with gifts and kindnesses. He gave Mrs. de Butts a treasured family heirloom—a crazy quilt knitted by his grandmother after the Civil War, as well as a pair of elegant purses he bought for Alice Browning in Paris in the late twenties, one covered with seed pearls, the other commemorating the Lindbergh flight with chip-diamond clasps stylishly fashioned in the form of airplanes. When the Snows were vacationing in Europe in 1959, they received a completely unexpected cable of money from him in Munich along with the note "Here, darlings—have a good time on me."

The Snows became concerned about a visible deterioration in Browning's health. Dr. Snow remembered the signs, which he believed were the result of a series of minor strokes. "I can recall going to knock at the door, and Tod would answer in a confused state of mind. He looked like someone who was taking tranquilizers or sedatives, and I knew he wouldn't take anything stronger than aspirin."

The couple suggested that he come to live with them. "At first he was reluctant to come," said Mrs. Snow. "He never wanted to leave home." She drove him to the dentist and doctors, sometimes stopping at their home on Westgate Avenue in Brentwood. At first he wanted to return to Malibu immediately. But slowly he began to look forward to the visits, asking to see their children and forgetting about getting home to the beach. Finally he moved in. "He was sorry that he didn't come to live with us earlier," Mrs. Snow remembered. Before, he had just been existing, waiting for the end. Dr. Snow found it "enjoyable to see the transformation."

He took to preparing meals for the Snows and was particularly fond of spicy extravaganzas involving seafood, especially shrimp. "If you could ever choose a parent, he would be the most wonderful father anyone could have," Mrs. Snow said.

Snow recommended that Browning see another doctor about his chronic throat problems; he agreed, and they took him to a physician in Brentwood. "It only took one look," said Snow. The doctor immediately diagnosed a cancer of the larynx that had gone long undetected. Browning had been a lifelong smoker, addicted to Lucky Strikes and a local Louisville brand called Clowns.

Snow made no mention of an earlier oral cancer, but did confirm that Browning had been treated inappropriately for a laryngeal disorder for a number of years. The effects of those treatments may well have been interpreted by the Louisville banker as indicating cancer of the tongue at the time of Avery's funeral.

"If it was my father," the Brentwood doctor told them frankly, "I'd have it taken out right away." Browning's larynx was removed in June 1962. Mute and mutilated, he had arrived at, or regressed to, the silent-movie state of speechless disfigurement that had been his obsession and his avatar.

A series of uncomfortable throat treatments, including a breathing tube, followed the operation, causing Browning to panic when he felt his breath was being cut off. Whatever stamina had sustained him a half century earlier, buried alive in a carnival coffin, was of little use to him now. His own body was becoming a sarcophagus; death, this time, was more than just a sideshow scam.

He repeatedly expressed concern that he was becoming too much of a burden. Recovering at the Snows' home, he suffered a debilitating stroke. Unable to speak because of the operation, his motor functions further impaired by the brain hemorrhage, he would sit in a chair before a television tray, frantically scribbling the words FIRE IS HOT over and over.

On August 26, 1962, Browning was able to write and sign a simple power-of-attorney document: "If I become unable to decide on what to do, then I leave that up to Mr. and Mrs. Harold Snow." A night nurse was engaged to care for him. It is unlikely that word reached him of the retrospective screening of *Freaks,* at the 23rd Venice Film Festival on the morning of September 6. The film, double-billed with Lloyd Bacon's *42nd Street* (1933), was enthusiastically received as part of a tribute series called "The Birth of American Talkies," a highlight of what most critics felt to be an otherwise lackluster festival. The screening of *Freaks* created a buzz among an international contingent of influential filmmakers and critics.

In early October, Browning visited the house at 31 Malibu Colony with the Snows for what would be the last time. Rather than remove the last of Browning's possessions, with all the finality the act would signify, Dr. Snow decided to leave behind one of Tod's favorite objects, a decorative bronze pheasant, on the pretext that they would return for it another time.

On Friday, October 5, Browning awoke in unusually good spirits. Mrs. Snow took him to lunch at the Miramar in Santa Monica. After returning to Brentwood, he wrote a note expressing his desire to take a nap and then go out once more for dinner. Mrs. Snow told him it probably wasn't a good idea to go out again. Browning became infuriated and scrawled his protest. Sometime after midnight, he woke up, went into the bathroom, and never came out.

Mrs. Snow got up in the middle of the night to check on him and found him slumped against the bathroom wall. The official record gave the time of his death, inaccurately, as 7:30 A.M.

In his will, filed with the Los Angeles County Clerk on October 15, Browning named Harold and Jackie Snow as chief beneficiaries, Dr. Snow receiving fifteen percent of his estate, and his wife thirty-five percent. The Snows additionally were bequeathed the contents of his bar, including liquors, wines, glasses, and accessories, as well as the contents of his china cabinet. William S. Hart, Jr., and his mother, Winifred, received the next largest bequests, each allotted twenty percent of Browning's estate, plus all the books in his library. Mrs. Yvonne West received the remaining ten percent share of the estate. Mrs. Erma Patratz, Alice Browning's niece, received a cash bequest of $15,000. Edward de Butts received Browning's 1941 Chrysler, plus $5,000. His housekeeper, Pearl Cleveland, was given his red cottage piano and stool, plus $5,000. Four charitable contributions of $10,000 each were made to the Korsair Crippled Children's Hospital in Louisville, the Shriners Hospitals for Crippled Children (for the exclusive use of its Los Angeles facility), the Motion Picture Country House and Hospital, and the Damon Runyan Memorial Fund for Cancer Research. His neighbors Robert and Gertrude Leonard received two bequests of $5,000, and other cash bequests ranging from $1,500 to $2,500 were made to Harold B. and Sue Ann Brenton of Barstow, California, to Louis Sauter of the Malibu Colony Patrol, to M. E. Lucas and Mrs. Mary Ellen Lucas of Malibu. A codicil to the will added a $2,000 bequest to Joseph G. Tejada, and, in the event that the total value of his estate be less than $100,000, reduced in half cash bequests to Mr. and Mrs. Leonard and to the charities.

No Louisville bequests were made except to the Korsair Hospital. Regarding his family, Browning was terse: "I have intentionally and with full knowledge omitted to provide for my heirs."

In accordance with his wishes, no service or memorial was held

—save the late-night vigil of his friend with the case of Coors. Post-mortem arrangements were handled, at his request, by the funeral directors Gates, Kingsley & Gates, Santa Monica. He was cremated in the Chapel of the Pacific Crematorium, his ashes placed in niche #677-N.C. at the Rosedale Cemetery on Washington Boulevard in Los Angeles, along with the ashes of Alice and her family.

Just as he had avoided the final rites of both his parents, and shielded himself with a curtain from his only brother, in the end Tod Browning managed to elude his own funeral, simply by refusing to have one.

ONE OF US

Belgian poster for Freaks. (Courtesy of Delbert Winans)

Thirty-three years dead, Tod Browning is still among us, his shadow world of freaks, vampires, and carnivalesque con men resonating eerily in a media-circus age of body-image angst, tabloid voyeurism, predatory capitalism, and blood-borne plagues. In the AIDS-saturated eighties and nineties, the vampire was resurrected as a major cultural icon, and memorabilia dealers and auctioneers watched as original posters for Browning's *Dracula* began to appreciate faster than impressionist paintings. Today, *Dracula* trails only the 1931 *Frankenstein* as a collectible title; films by acknowledged giants of world cinema don't even begin to rival it.

In certain circles, particularly in Europe, where the Browning-Chaney collaborations were admired by the surrealists, Browning has always had a following. In 1956 the French critic Louis Seguin went so far as to call him "one of the greatest directors who ever lived. . . . far superior to men like John Ford or Hitchcock." But in America the critical tone has tended to be dismissive. Iris Barry, founder of the Museum of Modern Art film library, offered an early explanation of the director's appeal: Browning, she wrote in 1926, "has a peculiar gift for managing dramatic suspense, only rivaled by some of the Germans, though achieved by methods less obvious than others'. He has whatever it was [that] made Stevenson a notable writer in spite of his being a very second-rate mind."

Before discussing further the ultimate merit and meaning of

Browning's work, it may be useful to follow the progress of his reputation from the years following his retirement to the present. In August 1947 M-G-M broke a long-standing policy by licensing *Freaks* to the legendary exploitation film impresario Dwain Esper. Esper later maintained that Alice Browning had initially acted as a go-between in making the deal; if this is true, then the negotiations must have stretched over a period of at least three years, since Alice died in 1944. The studio gave Esper a twenty-five-year license on *Freaks,* which he added to his repertoire of luridly preachy docudramas with titles like *Damaged Lives* (about venereal disease) and *The Wages of Sin* (about drug addiction) and his all-time camp classic, *Reefer Madness* (the final word about "the devil weed"). As *Variety* noted, "Although the tone of these vintage films was anti-sex, anti-vice, anti-crime and decried the mistreatment of sideshow monstrosities . . . a curious audience was drawn to these subjects in hopes of seeing 'forbidden fruits' in the guise of cinematic sermonettes."

One of Epser's young associates was David F. Friedman, a Mississippi native who would, in the 1960s, inaugurate the splatter genre with his taboo-breaking cult films *Blood Feast* (1963) and *Two Thousand Maniacs* (1964) and had long been a Browning fan. "I first saw *Freaks* when I was nine years old, in 1932, in a theatre in Birmingham. Although the city censor had banned the picture to anyone under eighteen years of age, my uncle owned the theatre, and I was allowed to watch it from the projection booth, while my mother and father sat in the auditorium. No movie has ever impressed me more."

Friedman recalled one of Esper's screenings of *Freaks*—advertised as *Forbidden Love*—in a drive-in theater in Charlotte, North Carolina, in the late forties. The audience came in a pouring rain to watch what they assumed would be an exotic skin flick, and nearly rioted when they were denied answers to the rhetorical advertising come-ons: "Can a full grown woman truly love a midget?" "Do Siamese twins make love?" and "What sex is the half-man, half-woman?" Esper, not wishing to anger the mob further, produced a worn reel of a nudist colony film from the trunk of his car and held the revolt at bay.

Esper added an awkward preamble to *Freaks,* which was retained even when the distribution rights reverted to M-G-M. It appears on show prints and video copies to this day. As a result, audiences and critics have assumed it is some kind of position statement by Tod Browning himself, instead of a distributor's cynical attempt to position the picture with a moralistic, "educational" defense—just like the pictures about sex and drugs:

> Before proceeding with the showing of this HIGHLY UNUSUAL ATTRACTION, a few words should be said about the amazing subject matter. BELIEVE IT OR NOT . . . STRANGE AS IT SEEMS . . . In ancient times anything that deviated from the normal was considered an omen of ill luck or representative of evil. Gods of misfortune and adversity were invariably cast in the form of monstrosities. . . . The revulsion with which we view the abnormal, the malformed and the mutilated is the result of long conditioning by our forefathers. The majority of freaks themselves are endowed with normal thoughts and emotions. Their lot is truly a heart-breaking one. . . . With humility for the many un-justices done (they have no power to control their lot) we present the most startling horror story of the ABNORMAL and the UN-WANTED.

The revival of *Freaks* at the 1962 Venice Film Festival followed a summer of horrific international headlines about the disastrous consequences of a morning-sickness drug called thalidomide, which triggered gross birth defects. Images of limbless, flippered babies turned tabloids in America and Europe into newsprint side-shows—an uneasy media stew of pity and morbid voyeurism. Given this backdrop, it was not surprising that the 1960s critical response to a thirty-year-old film was strongly colored by the events of the day. The influential *Cahiers du cinéma,* for instance, titled its appraisal "Humain, trop humain." "If the last scenes are horrific enough to satisfy the most ghoulish tastes, the revelation of the film

is its warmth and humanity," wrote Tom Milne in *Sight and Sound*.
"Browning manages to evoke the closed world of the freaks, the
intensely human emotions contained in inhuman exteriors, in such
a way that fascinated revulsion turns into tender comprehension."
In a review called "Freaks with Feeling" in the *Spectator,* Isabel
Quigley declared that the film "does what the cinema might do
more often—it enlarges one's sympathy by treating something unknown to us . . . with compassion and even tenderness. . . ." Andrew Sarris went so far as to call *Freaks* "one of the most compassionate films ever made."

In the socially tumultuous sixties, when issues of cultural disenfranchisement boiled over into the streets, *Freaks* became an odd
cinematic mirror for a decade in which social norms and values
were being increasingly challenged. The taboo-breaking photographer Diane Arbus, partly inspired by a 1960 art-house revival of
Freaks in New York City, embarked on a now-legendary career docu-
menting urban grotesques, including sideshow freaks; her first photographic encounter with Browning seems to have come in 1958,
when she trained her lens on the flickering reciprocal gaze of Bela
Lugosi in *Dracula* when it was first televised.

Arbus' work emblemized the emphasis on bizarre images that
swelled throughout the sixties, culminating in the zombie-like
Warhol "superstars," *Fellini Satyricon* (1969), and Alexandro
Jodorowsky's *El Topo* (1971), a surrealist exercise in ultraviolence
performed, like *Freaks,* by a cast including actors with congenital
anomalies. Both *El Topo* and *Freaks* became staples of the midnight-
movie circuit during the Vietnam era, when a disaffected counter-
culture reclaimed the word "freak" itself as a badge of belonging.

By the end of Dwain Esper's twenty-five-year contract for *Freaks,*
the copyright on the film had been reassigned several times, first
from Esper's Warwick Amusement Corporation to Willy Werby and
his W.W. Film Distributing Company (the exact date is unclear, and
at some point a New York firm called the Excelsior Picture Corporation also controlled foreign distribution) and, in October 1959,
from Werby to Raymond Rohauer, a freelance film distributor who
would serve as *Freaks'* ringmaster during its 1960s revival. Rohauer

was more than a distributor; he was an aggressive film pirate who swelled the collector's market with illegal prints, and an abrasive bully. As John Baxter wrote in a 1973 profile in the London *Times Magazine,* "Shrewdly exploiting the vague and often contradictory statutes, Rohauer has renewed lapsed copyrights in his own name, tracked down writers or their heirs and bought the literary rights to classic films, revived dead companies and signed dead contracts with old stars to distribute their work. . . . Watching his activities among the aged, infirm and sometimes senile survivors of 1920s Hollywood, a disgusted associate nicknamed Rohauer 'the carrion crow of Beverly Hills.' "

Anticipating the end of the original Esper license on *Freaks,* and knowing that Loew's, Inc., had filed a renewal copyright in 1959 (while copyright was still legally in the hands of Dwain Esper's assignees—potentially a fatal mistake under the convoluted copyright law of the time), Rohauer tried to make his slippery hold on *Freaks* permanent by purchasing the underlying rights in the short story "Spurs" from the widow and sons of Clarence Aaron "Tod" Robbins. But his legal blustering failed to impress M-G-M, which restored its trademark lion to the film's opening credits, as well as a long-lost epilogue in which the two midgets are emotionally reunited.

Revisionist assessments of *Freaks* culminated in 1988, when French stage director Geneviève de Kermabon, who had previously mounted a theatrical version of Federico Fellini's *La Strada,* adapted *Freaks* for the stage under the combined auspices of Le Théâtre Djighite, Le Printemps des Comédiens (Montpellier), Le Festival d'Avignon, Peter Brooks' Centre International de Créations Théâtrales, the Avignon Festival, and Le Carrefour Européen du Théâtre, with touring funded by the French bicentennial committee. A protégée of Brooks, de Kermabon credited the director with having inspired the project.

Jean-Claude Carrière, who wrote the text for Brooks' *The Mahabharata,* assisted de Kermabon with the script, which reconceived the Browning film as an evocative piece of stage magic. The technical coarseness of the film was replaced with an ethereal theatrical-

ity, illuminated with torches and blue light; the vaudeville inter-
ludes were jettisoned from the plot, retaining only the fairy-tale
simplicity of the midget's betrayal and revenge.

Nearly all of de Kermabon's actors were actually disabled: a
legless man, an armless, legless woman, a pair each of dwarves and
giants, a fat lady, etc. Unlike the freaks in the film, de Kermabon's
performers had considerable stage presence. "The cast of *Freaks*
displays a theatrical skill, beauty and grace, which would banish all
patronizing thoughts from even the most insensitive voyeur," wrote
the critic for the London *Times*. Kermabon—herself a trained acro-
bat—took the role of Cleopatra and performed on a trapeze. Judging from descriptions in a variety of press appraisals, the production contained numerous *coups de théâtre*, the most striking being
the revenge scene: Cleopatra falls from her trapeze into a net above
the audience, where the freaks swarm over her. "The sequence is
one of those moments when you realize the inadequacy of words in
the face of pure theatre," noted the *Times*.

The *Irish Times* offered its reaction to the production's inclusion
in the 1989 Dublin Theatre Festival:

> . . . the line between the great performer of circus tricks, who is
> admired and applauded as super-human, and the freak who is
> debased and derided as sub-human, is virtually nonexistent. . . .
> Herve Paillet as Phroso straddles both categories, making the dis-
> tinction between the sub-human and the super-human disappear;
> he is a great tightrope walker who happens to walk the wire with
> his arms because he has no legs. . . . the extraordinary bodies of
> some of the performers are as wonderful as the feats of the tra-
> peze artist. They can be seen as original, extraordinary, adding
> something to the world, rather than gawked at as something dark
> and fearful.

Fintan O'Toole, the *Irish Times* critic, called *Freaks* "a stunningly
original piece of theatre that goes further and becomes a great
work of humanity. . . . What it has to say—that nothing is ugly
except human evil—is simple, but the theatrical force it brings to
bear is breathtaking."

Although de Kermabon disavowed any purpose besides story-telling, her *Freaks* provided a final closure to the revisionist stance on the Browning film that had begun in the thalidomide summer of 1962. Since Browning's *Freaks* could never really support the tremendous load of humanitarian baggage projected onto it, it was inevitable that someone would find a way to remake the story in a manner conforming to the dominant critical opinion, however wrongheaded. De Kermabon's *Freaks* was undoubtedly fine theater, but whether it was Tod Browning is another question entirely.

A bitter pessimism about the possibilities of human interaction pervades Tod Browning's work, while raising questions—many unanswerable—about Browning himself. *Dark Carnival* has attempted to document previously unknown aspects of the director's life while avoiding excessive speculation about his inner personality. In today's overheated realm of pop psychology, Browning's flight from home, his characteristic reclusiveness and mistrust, his obsession with stories of fractured, poisonous parent-child relationships, might all be considered red flags for a snap diagnosis of traumatic childhood abuse. But since no nuanced documentation of Browning's early life exists—or likely will ever exist—such interpretations are best left to novelists, dramatists, and the free-form fringes of criticism.

But the obvious intersection of Browning's cinematic obsessions with twentieth-century cultural trends provides a richer area for consideration. For all their melodramatic excess, Browning's films nag at us because they distill large cultural themes to an imagistic pop shorthand. The stories he tells are awful, often inelegantly told, and yet they resonate deeply with the relentless reductionism of modern times. His attraction to scams involving phony occultists and their ever-gullible prey cynically evokes the spirit of a materialistic, despiritualized century. Browning's favored characters are reduced, debased, diminished—disfigured, in essence—by modernism. In the decade following World War I, when surrealist artists were distorting and rearranging the human form on canvas as a response to a shattering cataclysm, Browning, working far more instinctively than his contemporary artist-intellectuals, did something similar, on-screen, for the masses.

Browning brings us the bad news attendant on the most techno-
logically advanced century in history that is simultaneously the
cruelest. We are animals, con men, thieves, and vampires, Browning
tells us in film after film, driven by overpoweringly primitive emotions—beyond any real freedom, much less dignity. Pain and alienation teach no lessons: they only madden. In *Freaks* whatever tenu-
ous identification we have developed for the sideshow denizens as
the "decent" characters is cynically shattered when they, too, de-
scend into bestiality: half-human shapes wallowing in the primal
mud, animated only by spleen and bloodlust. To Tod Browning, the
ultimate image of a human being—the final distillation of his previous amputations and reductions—is Prince Randian, an armless,
legless bag of guts, wriggling through the muck of existence with a
knife in its teeth. The image, often cited as one of the most atrocious sights in the history of cinema, is a hideous indictment of
human life, despairing and Sadean. He never repeated such an
image; indeed, he was never permitted to.

One can—and, it is hoped, one will—argue with the validity of
Browning's monstrous worldview, at least as presented in his films.
But it is precisely the monstrousness that attracts and compels.
Browning's shadow circus offers a cathartic sideshow of modern
hypocrisies and illusions, a forbidden—and tantalizing—glimpse
into the collective heart of darkness.

Because Browning's themes are primal, largely bypassing intel-
lect, they resonate strongly, last, and renew themselves. In the 1930s
Freaks' parable of "big people" versus "little people" delivered an
exaggerated reflection of the unbalanced economics and widespread disenfranchisement that characterized the Depression. In
the Vietnam era *Freaks* became a rallying point for a profoundly
alienated generation. In the 1980s and '90s the huge cultural fixa-
tion on body image and cosmetic surgery suggests that untold
masses of people feel somehow freakish and outcast. And as the
social safety net begins to fray anew, Browning's themes of
scapegoating, alienation, and predation achieve a new urgency.

A 1994 retrospective of Chaney and Browning films drew capac-
ity crowds to the Film Forum in New York City, and direct and

indirect references to *Freaks* and Tod Browning continue to pop up everywhere, from Robert Altman's *The Player* (in which police detective Whoopi Goldberg, beginning to interrogate a murder suspect, finds it necessary to ask an associate the name of the movie "where they turn a woman into a chicken") to the films of David and Jennifer Lynch to TV's *The Simpsons* to cablecasts of the 1972 Hammer film *Blood from the Mummy's Tomb* (with a minor character named "Tod Browning") to plastic model kits of Schlitze and Johnny Eck (who also appears on a T-shirt) to the edgy music of the Ramones and their song "Pinhead," with its "gooble-gobble" refrain. Katherine Dunn's startling 1989 novel *Geek Love* is, on one level, a knowingly postmodern homage to Tod Browning's America. In Dunn's book a carnival family carries the American ideals of ingenuity and self-reliance to their ultimate extreme, deliberately twisting themselves into commercially viable freaks. Even a cursory glance at the offerings of daytime TV talk shows proves that sideshows are alive and well in one form or another, and that Dunn's bizarre family is hardly out of step with the inexhaustible hordes of Americans eager to debase themselves for the voyeuristic amusement of the masses.

In the final analysis, whatever Browning's shortcomings as an artist, his ability to craft unforgettably disturbing visions would alone secure him a permanent niche in the pantheon of American popular culture. In the words of the late critic Richard Roud, "cinema is something you look at, and Browning has that specifically cinematic genius that knows how to create images that defy the power of time." Roud wisely used the present tense. For Tod Browning is indeed with us—"one of us"—his dark carnival beckoning permanently from the fringes of an excessively rationalized, brightly lit world. The ticket booth may be swathed in shadows, but it's always open for business . . . and paying customers are never turned away.

TOD BROWNING
FILMOGRAPHY

TOD BROWNING: ACTOR

SCENTING A TERRIBLE CRIME

Biograph Company. 9 Oct 1913 [©Biograph Company; 7 Oct 1913; LU1346]. Silent; black & white. 549 feet.

Scenario   E. Lynn Summers.

Cast   Charles Murray (*Frenchy*), Tod Browning (*Undertaker*).

Farce   Newlywed Katrina makes some sauerkraut as a surprise for her husband, Frenchy. When they are unexpectedly called away on a month's vacation, the sauerkraut is left forgotten in a closet. Returning home before his wife, Frenchy unleashes a suspicious smell when he opens the apartment door. Leaving his home with a dull knife to hone, gossipy neighbors accuse him of murdering someone and leaving the corpse to decompose. Soon the police, an undertaker, and a coroner arrive. After the newlyweds are arrested, the coroner finds the sauerkraut, and, like a good German, begins to eat it. The police flee, the undertaker gets a face full of sauerkraut, while the coroner and Katrina enjoy the food.

Note   Split-reel with *Never Known to Smile* (450 feet).

A FALLEN HERO

Biograph Company. 23 Oct 1913 [©Biograph Company; 23 Oct 1913; LU1442]. Silent; black & white. 595 feet.

Scenario   Anita Loos.

Cast   Charles Murray, Tod Browning.

Farce   The Fourth of July in a rural village. Ex-judge Silas Wiggins and Chester Arnold, rival candidates for judge, are to speak before the assembled townspeople. Arnold hires the village band to play while Wiggins is speaking. However, Sammy Getup, Arnold's rival for the hand of village beauty Mathilda Jones, arranges a trap for Arnold as he mounts the podium, roping the candidate's feet so he can't move and then setting off a fireworks display from under the speaker's platform. When Getup yells fire, the crowd disperses. With Arnold helpless on the grandstand, Getup rescues the fair Mathilda from Arnold's side.

Note   Production #4204. Split-reel with *The Winning Punch* (400 feet).

AN INTERRUPTED SÉANCE
The Reliance Motion Picture Company/Mutual Film Corporation. 21 Feb 1914. Silent; black & white. One reel.

Director   Edward Dillon.

Cast   Tod Browning (*The actor*), Jimmy Young (*His pal*), Max Davidson (*The landlord*), Edward Dillon.

Farce   Thrown out of a job, two actors spend their last dollar for a reading at a séance by a famous clairvoyant. The clairvoyant gets their dollar so easily, the actors decide to make some easy money, too. They put up a sign under the clairvoyant's own, directing patrons to their boardinghouse a few doors below, and the crowds begin to flow in. The landlord hears the noise of the spirits rapping, and in the midst of it all, a patch of plaster drops on his head. He rushes upstairs and breaks in upon the "séance," discovering under the table the actor's pal who has jarred down the ceiling. Learning of the hoax, the real clairvoyant appears upon the scene. The impostors are unmasked, driven out of the house, and chased out of town.

AFTER HER DOUGH
Komic Company/Mutual Film Corporation. 25 Mar 1914. Silent; black & white. One reel.

Director   Edward Dillon.

Cast   Fay Tincher (*Fay Doughbags, "The Heiress"*), Tod Browning (*Leader of the Yeggs*), Baldy Belmont (*Chief bomb thrower*), Max Davidson (*Policeman*).

Farce   When heiress Fay Doughbags moves to Quietville, her immense fortune needs protection. News that police are stationed around the house attracts the Yeggs as well as the anarchists—haters of society. The Yeggs apply a sleeping injection to the policemen at their station, don their clothes, and send one of their own to rob the house of the heiress. They await word from him so they can carry off the loot without being suspected. Meanwhile a citizen oversees the anarchists plotting and phones the police. The impostors, thinking it is their pal, go to the heiress' house and run into the anarchists' den. After the heiress phones the real police, who have recovered, they arrive and catch the crook. The anarchists chase the impostors back to the police station and end their schemes with the aid of a bomb. When the police return to the station with their prisoner, they find his pals have departed for the sweet hereafter.

VICTIMS OF SPEED

Komic Company/Mutual Film Corporation. 1 Apr 1914. Silent; black & white. Split-reel.

Director   Edward Dillon.

Cast   Tod Browning (*Weary Willie*), Tammany Young (*Dusty Rhoades*), Baldy Belmont (*Dr. Speed*), Fay Tincher.

Farce   Hooligans Weary Willie and Dusty Rhoades discover Dr. Speed, the eminent radium "speedologist," at work on his latest accelerator preparation. Realizing the value of the doctor's formula, the two hoboes make off with the discovery and proceed to apply it to everyone they meet. All those who are inoculated with the speed germ perform their daily tasks with an amazing celerity. A paperhanger who is given an extra strong dose does forty-eight hours' work in an eight-hour day. Old Doc Speed, however, discovering the loss of his radium, comes to the rescue. By administering antidotes, he manages to bring the victims back to their normal condition.

Note   Split-reel with *The Vanderbilt Cup Race, Santa Monica, Cal.*

THE FATAL DRESS SUIT

Komic Company/Mutual Film Corporation. 8 Apr 1914. Silent; black & white. One reel.

Director Edward Dillon. *Scenario* Anita Loos.

Cast Fay Tincher (*Rosie Green, the Village Belle, the Queen of Podunk*), Edward Dillon (*Sam, her sweetheart*), James Young (*Walter, the villain*), Tod Browning.

Farce Fashionable Walter, the villain, and Sam, the hero, are in love with Rosie, the Queen of Podunk. Preparing for a party at town hall, Walter decides to wear a business suit. When he learns his rival will sport a dress suit, Walter sprinkles dynamite and powder in the lining of Sam's pockets, unaware that he is being observed by a maid. Sam creates a sensation at the ball in his metropolitan attire, impressing Rosie. After Sam narrowly escapes detonation a dozen times, Sam's servant warns him of his danger and Walter's treachery. Sam tries to escape from the hall but is captured and brought back by his sweetheart's father, who wants his daughter's dressy suitor as a son-in-law. Rosie's father announces the engagement, but when Sam backs away from a kiss from Rosie, he flies into a rage and starts after Sam. Sam, seeing that an explosion is due sooner or later, jumps on Walter with both feet. They both are blown into the alley, and Walter's treachery is exposed.

NEARLY A BURGLAR'S BRIDE

Komic Company/Mutual Film Corporation. 22 Apr 1914. Silent; black & white. One reel.

Director Edward Dillon. *Scenario* Anita Loos.

Cast Tod Browning (*Edgar*), Fay Tincher (*The Widow Murphy*).

Farce In the park, burglar Edgar meets the Widow Murphy and obtains the widow's permission to call. The next night Mrs. Murphy pays a short visit to her neighbor, Mrs. Dunn, thinking she can get back home before the flirtatious Edgar arrives. Edgar sees her sitting in Mrs. Dunn's window, thinking this is the widow's house. He robs the house next door to Mrs. Dunn's and presents the stolen objects d'art as gifts to the Widow Murphy. The widow pretends to be much pleased at the gifts but has Mrs. Dunn quietly call the police. She is not able to conceal her rising anger, however, and Edgar attempts to break away. The widow detains him by sitting on him as she awaits the arriving of authorities.

IZZY AND THE BANDIT

Komic Company/Mutual Film Corporation. 29 Apr 1914. Silent; black & white. One reel.

Scenario   Russell E. Smith.

Cast   Tod Browning.

Farce   While traveling by stage, salesman Izzy is robbed by Silver Hat Harry, who forces him to change clothing with him to facilitate his own escape. Carried on a stolen horse to a ranch, Izzy is made to go to work. Ignorant of ranch chores, Izzy instead helps the ranch owner's daughter with her household duties. He falls in love with her but is made the butt of many practical jokes. A stranger recognizes Izzy's clothing and says that the scullion is Silver Hat Harry. Because of the bandit's reputation, Izzy is waited upon by the cowboys and the girl. With the real bandit's arrest, the old order is restored, although the daughter helps him. After Izzy puts blanks in the cowboy's guns, he and the girl compel his tormentors, at gunpoint, to do stunts for his amusement.

THE SCENE OF HIS CRIME

Apollo Co.–Komic Company/Mutual Film Corporation. 10 May 1914. Silent; black & white. Split-reel.

Cast   Tod Browning, Tammany Young, Fay Tincher.

Farce   "A hip hurrah, full-of-action Farce." (*Moving Picture World*, May 23, 1914)

Note   Split-reel with *A Race for a Bride*. In early April 1914 Mutual announced it would discontinue the Komic "brand" following the release of *Izzy and the Bandit* and replace it with a one-reel Reliance drama. However, owing to public demand for comedy subjects, Mutual reconsidered and within several weeks had begun production on the Komic shorts again. This split-reeler was originally intended for release under the Apollo label but was reassigned to Komic when that company was restarted.

A RACE FOR A BRIDE

Apollo Co.–Komic Company/Mutual Film Corporation. 10 May 1914. Silent; black & white. Split-reel.

Cast Tod Browning, Tammany Young, Fay Tincher.

Comedy "This is a fair-to-middling comedy which embraces in its plot the Grand Prix races. . . . in places it is exciting." (*Moving Picture World*, May 23, 1914)

Note Split-reel with *The Scene of His Crime*. In early April 1914 Mutual announced it would discontinue the Komic "brand" following the release of *Izzy and the Bandit* and replace it with a one-reel Reliance drama. However, owing to public demand for comedy subjects, Mutual reconsidered and within several weeks had begun production on the Komic shorts again. This split-reeler was originally intended for release under the Apollo label but was reassigned to Komic when that company was restarted.

THE MAN IN THE COUCH

Komic Company/Mutual Film Corporation. 17 May 1914. Silent; black & white. One reel.

Director Edward Dillon. *Scenario* Anita Loos.

Cast Fay Tincher (*Mabel*), Edward Dillon (*Jack, the successful*), Tod Browning (*Ronald, the villain*).

Farce "Ronald, upon proposing to Mabel and being rejected, vows to discover his hated rival. Concealing himself in a folding couch, he has himself delivered in it to Mabel's house in order that he may spy upon the object of her affections. In due course, he hears someone enter the room. Lifting the lid of the couch, he finds her entertaining 'the other man.' Jack, the successful suitor, smokes many cigarettes during his call, and accidentally sets fire to the couch. To reassure his sweetheart, he throws the couch bodily out of the window, Ronald and all. It goes through the roof of an anarchists' den below. The anarchists throw it through their window into a police station. All along its disastrous route, it sets things afire, calling out the police and fire departments. Ronald gets quite a shaking up, resolves never again to force himself upon those who do not want him." (*Reel Life*, May 9, 1914)

Note Original and working title: *All for Mabel*.

NELL'S EUGENIC WEDDING

Komic Company/Mutual Film Corporation. 24 May 1914. Silent; black & white. One reel.

Director   Edward Dillon. *Scenario*   Anita Loos.

Cast   Tod Browning, Baldy Belmont (*Policeman*), Max Davidson, Edward Dillon, Fay Tincher.

Farce   "There is nothing funny or elevating in having a man eat soap and vomit all over creation as the result of his diet. Because most people will take this view it may be said that *Nell's Eugenic Wedding* does not belong." (*Moving Picture World,* June 6, 1914)

AN EXCITING COURTSHIP

Komic Company/Mutual Film Corporation. 31 May 1914. Silent; black & white. One reel.

Director   Edward Dillon.

Cast   Fay Tincher, Tod Browning, Baldy Belmont.

Farce   "An eccentric character farce. It makes good . . . because its characters are played by actors with the peculiar ability to be wooden and funny at the same time. Good clowns are not so numerous as blackberries in July and it takes a good deal of ability to mimic a marionette while doing the lively playing required by pictures of this kind. There are several burlesque characters in it and three cub bears, thin and lively." (*Moving Picture World,* June 13, 1914)

THE LAST DRINK OF WHISKEY

Komic Company/Mutual Film Corporation. 7 Jun 1914. Silent; black & white. One reel.

Director   Edward Dillon. *Scenario*   Anita Loos.

Cast   Tod Browning (*Desperate Rudolph*), Tammany Young (*The sheriff*), Fay Tincher (*Rudolph's wife*), Baldy Belmont and Max Davidson (*Rudolph's gang*).

Farce   "It is a rattling burlesque, showing the efforts of Desperate Rudolph, the Terror of Red Gulch, to get the only three fingers of firewater in the camp. He has to kill twelve armed men before he gets it but does not hesitate. Unfortunately he hesitates before drinking and the sheriff seizes the bottle from his lips. Desperate Rudolph regains the bottle but is too busy defending it to drink it and his youthful son finally gets it—as a medicine.'' (*Reel Life*, June 6, 1914)

HUBBY TO THE RESCUE

Komic Company/Mutual Film Corporation. 14 Jun 1914. Silent; black & white. One reel.

Director   Edward Dillon. *Scenario*   Russell E. Smith.

Cast   Fay Tincher (*Jane Mersey*), Tod Browning (*John Mersey, her husband*), Max Davidson (*Jerry Harcourt*), Teddy Sampson (*Stenographer*), Baldy Belmont (*John's pal*), Edward Dillon, Miss Ainslee, Charles Rice, Frank Fisher Bennett.

Farce   Jane Mersey is ignored by John, her husband, who is always too busy to take her anywhere. She accepts a lunch date with Jerry, an agreeable young man, whose last name she does not quite catch on introduction, and he is equally vague as to the identity of his new acquaintance. Jane and Jerry meet incognito and enjoy their luncheon. When the waiter gives him the check, Jerry discovers that he has left his money at home. Concealing his agitation, he telephones his old acquaintance, John Mersey, begging ten dollars. Mersey promises to run around to the café directly with the sum. However, upon his arrival, John changes his mind, dragging Jane away and leaving Jerry to be plundered of watch and clothing by the restaurant keeper.

THE DECEIVER

Komic Company/Mutual Film Corporation. 21 Jun 1914. Silent; black & white. One reel.

Director   Edward Dillon. *Scenario*   Anita Loos.

Cast   Edward Dillon (*Clancy, the cop*), Tod Browning (*Simon Jenks*), Fay Tincher (*Bridgeen, the cook*), Baldy Belmont.

Farce   Simon Jenks is always out of cash. In love with Bridgeen, an enterprising cook, she refuses his affections until he is rich. By nature opposed to work, Simon pretends to be blind and succeeds in collecting quite a bit of silver. Clancy, a policeman and Simon's rival for Bridgeen, calls on the cook off his beat. Witnessed by Simon, the loafer tips Clancy's superior, causing the cop's transfer to a lonely part of town. After marrying Simon, Bridgeen refuses to work anymore, and Simon is forced to sham blind man again. In picking an unfamiliar quarter of the town, Simon chances into Clancy's precinct. His ex-rival recognizes him, beats him up, and takes him in. Bailed out of jail by Bridgeen, she sentences him to work for both of them the rest of his life.

THE WHITE SLAVE CATCHERS

Komic Company/Mutual Film Corporation. 28 Jun 1914. Silent; black & white. One reel.

Director   Edward Dillon. *Scenario*   Anita Loos.

Cast   Fay Tincher (*Sadie*), Edward Dillon (*Sam*), Tod Browning (*Anthony Gumstalk, the detec-a-tive*), Baldy Belmont, Frank Fisher Bennett, Tammany Young.

Farce   Sam is suicidal. Repeatedly kicked out of his girlfriend Sadie's house by her father, Sam is further reduced in spirits when Sadie tells him that her father has threatened to have him arrested as a white slaver if he shows up around her home again. Sam and Sadie elope, pack their telescopes, and set out for the pastorage in the next town. Sadie's dad calls in the police, and detectives are summoned. Sam and Sadie find the minister's house, but he is not home. Sadie foils the detectives by blacking her face and posing as the rector's maid. The weary detectives lie down in the pastor's parlor for a nap. With the minister's return, Sadie washes her face, explains matters to him, and while the sleuths of the law sleep, Sam and Sadie are wed. As Sadie's father arrives, the newlyweds are leaving with their marriage certificate.

Note   Working title: *The Wild Girl.*

BILL'S JOB [BILL #1]

Komic Company/Mutual Film Corporation. 5 Jul 1914. Silent; black & white. One reel.

Director Edward Dillon. *Author* Paul West.

Cast Tammany Young (*Bill, the office boy*), Tod Browning (*Mr. Hadley, the boss*), Fay Tincher (*Ethel, the stenographer*), Andy Rice (*The client*), Baldy Belmont (*Bill's father*), Mae Washington (*Bill's mother*), George A. Beranger.

Farce "Bill, a fourteen-year-old city-bred boy, answers an advertisement for an office boy. He finds a dozen other applicants for the place but manages to trick them into leaving in such clever fashion that James Hadley, the young lawyer who advertised, is delighted and engages him at once. Bill resolves to make business for his boss and corrals an old man in the hall who is looking for a certain lawyer. Despite the old man's protests, Bill hustles him into Hadley's office where the young lawyer quickly convinces the old fellow that he is just the man to handle the important case. Hadley gets a libel retainer from the corporation which the old man represents and handles the case so well that he is appointed chief of the legal staff of the concern." (*Reel Life*, July 11, 1914)

Note First on the *Bill* series, adapted from Paul West's weekly newspaper column, which first appeared in the *New York World* and was modeled on the antics of Tammany Young (who portrays his own character in this series), once West's office boy at the *World*.

WRONG ALL AROUND
Komic Company/Mutual Film Corporation. 12 Jul 1914. Silent; black & white. One reel.

Cast Tod Browning (*Mr. "Spotty" Jones*), Fay Tincher (*Mrs. Jones*), Baldy Belmont (*Mr. Hicks*), Tammany Young (*The father-in-law*), Mrs. Arthur Mackley, Mrs. W. H. Brown.

Farce "Spotty Jones abuses his wife, and she determines to be revenged. She calls her mother to her aid. Jones, apprised of her coming, changes nameplates in the hall, and when the mother-in-law arrives she goes to the wrong apartment. Never having seen her son-in-law, she opens hostilities on the occupant of the apartment, the hen-pecked Mr. Hicks. Mrs. Hicks, returning unexpectedly home, finds a strange woman beating her husband. Mrs. Hicks is busy lambasting the intruder when the father-in-law bursts open the door and sees Mr. Hicks beating his wife. Jones tries to square things, but his explanations don't clear him, and the film ends with Jones attacked from all sides." (*Reel Life*, July 11, 1914)

HOW BILL SQUARED IT WITH HIS BOSS [BILL #2]

Komic Company/Mutual Film Corporation. 19 Jul 1914. Silent; black & white. One reel.

Director Edward Dillon. *Author* Paul West.

Cast Tammany Young (*Bill, the office boy*), Fay Tincher (*Ethel, the stenographer*), Tod Browning (*Mr. Hadley, the boss*), Baldy Belmont, Mrs. Arthur Mackley, Mrs. W. H. Brown, Miss Carson, Miss Crawford.

Farce "Mr. Hadley, Bill's employer, shows Bill a picture of Alice Mordaunt, his fiancée, and tells his office boy to admit her at once when she arrives. Bill goes out to lunch and returns to find his employer kissing Ethel, Hadley's sister. Bill is properly horrified at such duplicity, but, faithful at all times to his employer, attempts to slip in a note warning his boss to get the 'other dame' out of the way when Alice arrives. Alice, however, intercepts the note, sees Hadley kissing a strange woman and leaves in a rage. Hadley hurriedly explains things to Bill and sends him after Alice, who, when everything is explained, is mollified and greets Ethel affectionately." (*Reel Life,* July 18, 1914)

LEAVE IT TO SMILEY

Komic Company/Mutual Film Corporation. 26 Jul 1914. Silent; black & white. One reel.

Director Edward Dillon. *Author* Marc Edmond Jones.

Cast Tod Browning (*The tragedian*), Baldy Belmont (*The manager*), Tammany Young (*Smiley*), Fay Tincher (*The ingenue*).

Farce "With the opening performance a fizzle, the members of Nigh[t]ingale Light Opera Company are decidedly on their uppers. Smiley and the tragedian, however, decide upon a plan whereby they may eat and drink. After the tragedian has finished a thirteen-course dinner in the city's best restaurant, Smiley enters and bangs him on the head with a wicked looking club. The tragedian hurries from the restaurant to chase his assailant and incidentally forgets to pay his bill. The same trick is played elsewhere successfully. Finally the tragedian and Smiley are discovered by their irate dupes reinforced by two of the village cops. A long chase follows and at the finish Smiley and the tragedian get theirs." (*Reel Life,* July 25, 1914)

BILL TAKES A LADY OUT TO LUNCH (—NEVER AGAIN!) [BILL #3]

Komic Company/Mutual Film Corporation. 2 Aug 1914. Silent; black & white. One reel.

Director Edward Dillon. *Author* Paul West.

Cast Tammany Young (*Bill, the office boy*), Miss Gaston (*Genevieve Reilly, his "lady friend"*), Tod Browning (*Mr. Hadley, the boss*), Fay Tincher (*Ethel, the stenographer*).

Farce Bill is about as untidy a young man as one could imagine until Genevieve Reilly attracts his attention. Bill gradually transforms himself into a regular guy and summons enough courage to ask Genevieve out to lunch. All goes merrily until Izzy, another suitor, and some of the other boys poke their heads through the door and begin to annoy Bill unmercifully. In his anger, Bill hurls the dishes and food at his tormentors, who promptly throw them back. Bill and his lady friend are ejected, but Bill is somewhat solaced when he discovers that in their excitement the restaurant forgot to collect for the lunch.

ETHEL'S TEACHER

Komic Company/Mutual Film Corporation. 9 Aug 1914. Silent; black & white. One reel.

Director Edward Dillon. *Author* William J. Woodley.

Cast Baldy Belmont (*Deacon Titus*), Fay Tincher (*Ethel*), Edward Dillon (*The teacher*), Tod Browning (*Hugh, her sweetheart*).

Farce "Deacon Titus takes Ethel to the seashore. Hugh, her sweetheart, dons woman's clothes and follows, introducing himself as Ethel's teacher. Ethel's real teacher arrives later and when all go into the water Hugh's deception is discovered. Hugh puts his 'female riggin' in the deacon's bathhouse and goes home in the latter's clothes with Ethel, while the deacon is obliged to put on the discarded lady's costume. He is chased away by the irate merry-makers." (*Reel Life,* July 25, 1914)

BILL [BILL SAVES THE DAY] [BILL #4]

Komic Company/Mutual Film Corporation. 16 Aug 1914. Silent; black & white. One reel.

Director   Edward Dillon. *Author*   Paul West.

Cast   Tammany Young (*Bill, the office boy*), Tod Browning (*Mr. Hadley, the boss*), Fay Tincher (*Ethel, the stenographer*), Edward Dillon (*Policeman*).

Farce   "Bill persuades the boss to order an electric fan. The electrician who installs it shows Jimmy how to number the blades and have a little gambling game. One by one the office boys in the building drop in and put their nickels on the numbers of the blades. One youngster who loses heavily complains to a policeman. Before the patrolman's arrival Bill's boss discovers the game going on and takes the fan into his private office, where a meeting of trust magnates is in session. The magnates become interested in the game just as the patrolman arrives. Bill's boss fixes the cop and business is finally resumed." (*Reel Life*, August 15, 1914)

A PHYSICAL CULTURE ROMANCE
Komic Company/Mutual Film Corporation. 23 Aug 1914. Silent; black & white. One reel.

Director   Edward Dillon.

Cast   Margaret Edwards (*The athletic girl*), Fay Tincher (*Fay*), Tod Browning and Max Stanley (*The boys*), Edward Dillon.

Farce   "Fay is so unattractive that none of the boys will look at her. Seeing her sister breaking hearts right and left, she gets morose and despondent. The teacher of physical culture at school takes a strong personal interest in Fay, who makes her, her confidante. She tells Fay that if she will do exactly as she tells her, everything will be different. The teacher actually does inject some kind of magic into the girl, who finally succeeds in turning the tables on her pretty sister and all her beaux." (*Reel Life*, August 8, 1914)

BILL ORGANIZES A UNION [BILL #5]
Komic Company/Mutual Film Corporation. 30 Aug 1914. Silent; black & white. One reel.

Director   Edward Dillon. *Author*   Paul West.

Cast   Tammany Young (*Bill, the office boy*), Tod Browning (*Mr. Hadley, the boss*), Fay Tincher (*Ethel, the stenographer*), "Fatty" Crame (*Izzy, Bill's pal*), Edward Dillon, Baldy Belmont, Max Davidson.

Farce "Bill gets careless about his duties, and the boss arranges a set of rules for his observance. Bill and his pal, Izzy, decide to right their wrongs by organizing a union. They chip in a nickel apiece and buy themselves badges. The next day Izzy loses his job and calls on Bill to strike in his behalf. They parade through the building, demanding that Izzy be pardoned and taken back on pay. The boss has the fire department turn the hose on the rebels who are dragged back to work in disgrace." (*Reel Life*, August 15, 1914)

THE MASCOT

Komic Company/Mutual Film Corporation. 6 Sep 1914. Silent; black & white. One reel.

Director Edward Dillon. *Author* Russell E. Smith.

Cast Tod Browning (*Tom Gaylord, the suitor*), Fay Tincher (*Fay, the girl*), Max Davidson (*Fay's father*).

Farce "Tom Gaylord, suitor for Fay's hand, is repulsed by her father because he has no money. Soon after a traveler comes to town with a Hindu image, a mascot of the gods. He is trailed by two Hindu priests who are sworn to kill the person who has stolen the precious idol. Closely pursued, the traveler throws the image in Fay's father's window, who, being a collector of antiques, is delighted with his windfall. But later, when he finds that the priests are seeking to kill the possessor of the mascot, he is terrified. After trying vainly to get the image off on numerous persons, he is glad to let a mysterious Hindu take it off his hands in return for a considerable sum of money and the promise of his daughter in marriage. When the 'Hindu' removes his disguise, the father finds that Tom Gaylord has made capital of the mascot scare." (*Reel Life*, August 15, 1914)

IN BUSINESS FOR HIMSELF [BILL #6]

Komic Company/Mutual Film Corporation. 13 Sep 1914. Silent; black & white. One reel.

Director Edward Dillon. *Author* Paul West.

Cast Tammany Young (*Bill, the office boy*), Fay Tincher (*Ethel, the stenographer*), Tod Browning (*Mr. Hadley, the boss*), "Fatty" Crame (*Izzy, Bill's pal*), Paul Willis (*Bill's other pal*), Max Davidson (*Lunch counter proprietor*).

Farce "Bill on arriving at the lunch counter where he has been a steady customer, finds that the proprietor has boosted his prices, much to the disgust of Bill. To show his hatred for the proprietor, Bill, with Izzy as a partner and Ethel as manageress, decides to open a lunch room in an unoccupied office. They procure all the food and coffee at home, while mothers and fathers are not looking, and open up to what promises to be a rushing business. Alas, in the midst of their successes the rival lunchman happens along and notifies the janitor, also Bill's boss, who comes and puts an end to Bill's aspirations as a connoisseur of rare dishes. Bill and Izzy are compelled to clean up the office, after which they decide they are better fitted for office boys." (*Reel Life*, August 29, 1914)

FOILED AGAIN

Komic Company/Mutual Film Corporation. 20 Sep 1914. Silent; black & white. One reel.

Director Edward Dillon. *Author* Russell E. Smith.

Cast Fay Tincher (*Moitle Perry*), Tod Browning (*Ralph Coises, the villain*), Edward Dillon (*Percy Basker, the boob*).

Farce Stage villain Ralph Coises falls in love with Moitle Perry. Farmhand Percy Basker is accepted as her future husband as soon as she has enough money saved up. When Moitle repulses Ralph's advances, he swears revenge in the manner of a typical stage villain. Percy foils him again by shaving his curling black mustache, without which he cannot work at the trade of villain. Grown again, Ralph seizes the scornful Moitle and ties her to the railroad tracks, only to learn that the tracks haven't been used in years. Next he puts Moitle in an abandoned cistern. As the water rises higher and higher, Moitle keeps herself from drowning by drinking the water as fast as it comes in. Later Ralph seeks to blow her up, but having no match to light the fuse, borrows one from the unsuspicious Percy. Just at the climactic moment, Ralph receives word from the Villains' Union that they had made a mistake and sent him after the wrong girl— Moitle hasn't a cent.

BILL MANAGES A PRIZEFIGHTER [BILL #7]

Komic Company/Mutual Film Corporation. 27 Sep 1914. Silent; black & white. One reel.

Director   Edward Dillon. *Author*   Paul West.

Cast   Tammany Young (*Bill, the office boy*), Fay Tincher (*Ethel, the stenographer*), Tod Browning (*Mr. Hadley, the boss*), Edward Dillon (*Spike*), Hobo Dougherty (*Mike*), Max Davidson.

Farce   Ambitious to make a name for himself, Bill decides to become a prizefight manager. Being impressed by the vigor with which bootblack Sylvest' shines shoes, Bill assures him that his fortune will be made. Figuring that Ethel, the attractive stenographer, ought to help a lot, he persuades her to be present at the ringside of a bout between his protégé and Knock 'em Dead Kelly using all her wiles to divert the opponent. This scheme works until Kelly, awaking to the fact that he has been double-crossed, ends Sylvest's hopes of becoming a champion.

THE MILLION DOLLAR BRIDE

Komic Company/Mutual Film Corporation. 4 Oct 1914. Silent; black & white. One reel.

Director   Edward Dillon. *Author*   Anita Loos.

Cast   Tod Browning (*Henry*), Edward Dillon (*The fiancé*), Fay Tincher (*The elder sister*), Max Davidson (*The minister*).

Farce   Henry, a high-class crook, knocks a newsboy down in the park, confiscates his papers, and sits down on a bench to read. Reading the headline that heiress Ethel Van Rocks will get a million dollars the day she chooses a husband, Henry swears that she shall be his. After stealing a bouquet, he goes to the heiress' mansion, where he waits in the parlor. Carried in the arms of her maid, Miss Van Rocks makes her appearance— an eighteen-month-old toddler. Nothing daunted, Henry fells the maid and escapes with Ethel. Disguising himself in a long linen duster, a hat, and a veil, he starts for the house of a minister who is deaf and almost blind. With the police tracking the kidnaper, Ethel drops her rattle, which leads to her rescue at the parsonage.

BILL SPOILS A VACATION [BILL #8]

Komic Company/Mutual Film Corporation. 11 Oct 1914. Silent; black & white. One reel.

Director   Edward Dillon. *Author*   Paul West.

Cast   Tammany Young (*Bill, the office boy*), Fay Tincher (*Ethel, the stenographer*), Tod Browning (*Mr. Hadley, the boss*), Baldy Belmont (*The millionaire*), Howard Gage, Max Davidson, Maxfield Stanley.

Farce   Mr. Hadley gives Ethel a vacation, advancing her a month's pay. Off to show Newport what life really is, Ethel meets a millionaire, who quickly proposes. Accepting, she wires her boss that she has no intention of returning to dictation. Hadley goes wild and sends Bill to find Ethel and bring her back. Bill locates her as she is about to dine and decides to butt in on the meal. The millionaire begins to doubt whether Ethel is a wise choice after all, and excusing himself for a few moments, makes up his mind he will not return. The waiter must have his check paid, and the big haul comes on Ethel, who is left with just her fare back to New York.

DIZZY JOE'S CAREER

Komic Company/Mutual Film Corporation. 18 Oct 1914. Silent; black & white. One reel.

Director   Edward Dillon. *Author*   C. Allan Gilbert.

Cast   Edward Dillon (*Dizzy Joe*), Tod Browning (*Circus manager*), Baldy Belmont (*The "coon"*), Tammany Young, Maxfield Stanley, Max Davidson.

Farce   While Dizzy Joe, a tramp, is resting behind a stone wall, a black wagon driver from a hospital drives up and deposits for burning a good suit of clothes from a man dead of smallpox. While he goes to get a match, Dizzy Joe wakes and, seeing the clothes, exchanges his ragged old duds for the good set before learning their origins. The tramp rushes into a lake, shedding clothes at every step. After staying all night, he ventures out in the morning and makes himself a garment out of cornstalks. Discovered by a circus freak manager, he is hired as a wild man. A romance develops between him and the bearded lady, and their elopement concludes Dizzy Joe's career.

Note   Adapted from A. B. Frost's series of cartoons that appeared in *Century Magazine*.

BILL JOINS THE W.W.W.'S [BILL #9]

Komic Company/Mutual Film Corporation. 25 Oct 1914. Silent; black & white. One reel.

Director   Edward Dillon.   *Author*   Paul West.

Cast   Tammany Young (*Bill, the office boy*), Fay Tincher (*Ethel, the stenographer*), Tod Browning (*Mr. Hadley, the boss*), Max Davidson (*Police captain*), Mae Gaston (*Minnie*), Edward Dillon.

Farce   "On his way to work Bill is attracted by a meeting of the W.W.W.'s, and becomes so absorbed that he forgets business. That same day, Bill's boss, while motoring with his lady love, neglects to notice the speedometer which had developed about forty-five miles an hour. The result is, he is landed in jail, and, unable to secure bail, he phones Bill the combination of the safe. That young man starts to follow instructions, but, unfortunately, the combination slips his mind, and he hastily goes and secures a pal who is quite adept at opening safes. . . . But when Hadley learns the character of Bill's accomplice who now shares the secret of the combination, he is not a little perturbed." (*Reel Life*, October 10, 1914)

CASEY'S VENDETTA

Komic Company/Mutual Film Corporation. 1 Nov 1914. Silent; black & white. One reel.

Director   Edward Dillon.

Cast   Edward Dillon (*Casey, the policeman*), Fay Tincher (*Nina*), Tod Browning (*Pedro*), Max Davidson (*Police captain*), Sylvia Ashton (*Casey's wife*).

Farce   Casey, a policeman, has everybody bluffed except his wife, who rules over Casey. Pedro runs a fruit stand on Casey's beat, and Nina, sweetheart of the former, also sells fruit. Casey eats Pedro's fruit and refuses to pay. Then he flirts with Nina, who likes it. Pedro, a member of the Black Hand, vows revenge. He sends Casey a note, demanding $500, or the Black Hand will take his life. The opportunistic Casey changes the word "life" to "wife," and shows her the letter. After telling her to keep out of sight, Casey returns to Nina. Enraged, Pedro captures Casey and locks him up. Nina alerts the police, just as the wife, missing Casey, also appeals to them. Being rescued, Casey rushes to his wife, while Nina is restrained from attacking him. After his wife learns the truth about the note, she strips Casey of his uniform and drags him home.

ETHEL'S ROOF PARTY [BILL #10]

Komic Company/Mutual Film Corporation. 8 Nov 1914. Silent; black & white. One reel.

Director Edward Dillon. *Author* Paul West.

Cast Tammany Young (*Bill, the office boy*), Fay Tincher (*Ethel, the stenographer*), Tod Browning (*Mr. Hadley, the boss*), Anna May Walthall, Mae Gaston, Baldy Belmont, Maxfield Stanley (*Guests at the party*).

Farce In her boss's absence, Ethel decides to give a luncheon on the roof. When Bill and his pal crash the party, Ethel is not at all pleased at their butting in. At her request her male friends kick the office boy and his chum off the roof and lock them out. Bill nails up the exit and starts some old rags smoldering. While Bill and his pal depart for lunch, the janitor smells smoke and soon locates the fire. The partygoers, in their wild desire to reach safety, smash a window and receive the full force of the fire hose. Luncheon and gowns are ruined—but Ethel and her guests are rescued.

OUT AGAIN—IN AGAIN

Komic Company/Mutual Film Corporation. 15 Nov 1914. Silent; black & white. One reel.

Director Edward Dillon.

Cast Fay Tincher (*Mrs. Henpeck*), Tod Browning (*Mr. Henpeck*), Tammany Young (*The crook*), Baldy Belmont, Max Davidson (*Mr. Henpeck's pals*).

Farce "Mr. Henpeck, being anxious to join the boys, arranges with two pals to disguise themselves as policemen and he will feign insanity. At a certain signal, they are to rush in and take him into custody. Meanwhile, a crook, pursued by two cops, takes refuge in Mr. Henpeck's kitchen. Mrs. Henpeck gets wise to hubby's game, locks him in the kitchen, and gives the signal herself. The crook forces Henpeck to exchange clothes with him, so that when the friends arrive they find themselves looking into the muzzle of a thirty-eight gun. When the real policemen reach the house they find Henpeck dressed in the crook's clothes and decide he is their man. They rush him off to the cooler, and after much business of mistaken identity, he finally is released, promising never again to try to put one over on his clever spouse." (*Reel Life,* October 31, 1914)

ETHEL HAS A STEADY [BILL #11]

Komic Company/Mutual Film Corporation. 22 Nov 1914. Silent; black & white. One reel.

Director   Edward Dillon. *Author*   Paul West.

Cast   Tammany Young (*Bill, the office boy*), Fay Tincher (*Ethel, the stenographer*), Tod Browning (*Mr. Hadley, the boss*), Anna May Walthall (*Bill's girl*), Edward Dillon (*Ethel's beau*), Mae Gaston (*Mr. Hadley's fiancée*), Lucille Brown (*The divorcée*), Max Davidson (*The janitor*), May Gaston (*The janitor's girl*), Walter Long.

Farce   Bill, smitten with a pretty stenographer in another office, writes her a love letter. Before he has finished, however, he is sent on another errand, leaving his billet-doux in the typewriter. Ethel, busy with office work, is unable to meet her steady for lunch. He comes to Ethel's office, sees Bill's love missive in the typewriter, and concludes that this is the explanation. Then Mr. Hadley's fiancée arrives and also discovers the letter. From Hadley's office she hears the sobbing from an unhappy wife trying for a divorce, and suspects the worst. When the letter reaches the woman for whom it was intended, it falls into the hands of her sweetheart, who promises that a recurrence of the offense will be painful for Bill. The luckless office boy explains all around, and decides he is better off single. "Fay Tincher has the best stenog costume yet . . . the piece makes an unusually laughable comic offering." *Moving Picture World,* December 5, 1914, p. 1384.

A CORNER IN HATS

Komic Company/Mutual Film Corporation. 29 Nov 1914. Silent; black & white. One reel.

Director   Edward Dillon. *Author*   Anita Loos.

Cast   Tod Browning (*Henry*), Fay Tincher (*Dolores, his wife*), Baldy Belmont, Sylvia Ashton, Tammany Young.

Farce   "Henry's wife is so scared of him that she scarcely dares breathe while he is around. She buys a little dog for a companion, but fearing that her husband will kick the animal out, she hides it whenever Henry comes home. Now the dog has a mania for collecting gentlemen's hats. When Henry finds various masculine 'lids' around the house—and no explanation of how they came there forthcoming from Dolores, his wife—he becomes insanely jealous. He beats up a dozen claimers of the hats, only to discover on each return home—more hats. The anteroom of the police station yields the dog a harvest [and Henry] . . . finding the parlor full of policemen's headgear, leaps to the conclusion that his wife has been entertaining the entire force. He goes with a bomb and blows up the police station, utterly ruining a quiet game of pinochle going on around the blue coats. Then, rushing home, he drags Dolores forth by the hair of her head and tells her to prepare to die. While he is sharpening his knife, however, the police are on the way. They reach the spot just in time. And as they are dragging Henry off, the dog runs in with another hat." (*Reel Life*, November 21, 1914)

Note   Original story title: *His Hated Rivals*.

MR. HADLEY'S UNCLE [BILL #12]

Komic Company/Mutual Film Corporation. 6 Dec 1914. Silent; black & white. One reel.

Director   Edward Dillon. *Author*   Paul West.

Cast   Tod Browning (*Mr. Hadley, the boss*), Baldy Belmont (*His uncle*), Tammany Young (*Bill, the office boy*), Fay Tincher (*Ethel, the stenographer*), Max Davidson (*Mr. Muchmoney*), Edward Dillon.

Farce   "Mr. Hadley, anxious to put through a big deal, writes his uncle, whom he has never seen, advising him to invest some of his money. The uncle wires Mr. Hadley that he will call on him and bring the money in person. Meanwhile, Mr. Muchmoney, who has a mania for writing checks, gets away from his keepers and sneaks out of the sanitarium. He wanders along, and then, deciding to visit an office building, presents himself in Mr. Hadley's establishment while that gentleman is out. Thinking that he is the rich uncle, Ethel entertains him until the boss returns. He writes a small fortune in checks, buys a few automobiles, and keeps everything lively—until his keepers succeed in tracing him to the office. On the arrival of the real uncle, after many painful experiences en route, things are squared." (*Reel Life*, November 28, 1914)

THE HOUSEBREAKERS

Komic Company/Mutual Film Corporation. 13 Dec 1914. Silent; black & white. One reel.

Director   Edward Dillon.

Cast   Tod Browning (*Bunko Bill, the crook*), Fay Tincher (*The girl*), Edward Dillon (*Harris, the girl's beau*), Max Davidson (*The commissioner*), Sylvia Ashton (*The commissioner's wife*), Ed Rice.

Farce   Bunko Bill takes a job as a gardener to set up a robbery. He selects the home of the police commissioner, whose daughter loves Harris, a young man she has refused to marry until he has caught a burglar red-handed. Harris gets the supposed gardener into a scheme to burglarize the house and be caught by Harris. He would pretend to hand him over to the authorities, but in reality arrange for his escape. Bunko Bill steals the silverware several nights before the mock burglary, and Harris actually does catch him. Discovered by the commissioner's wife, an uncompromising woman, she holds them both at gunpoint and delivers them to the police, who recognize Bunko Bill as a famous crook. The commissioner's wife, ashamed to have her husband know that she hired the crook, allows Harris to pose as the hero who has captured the thief, and win the heart of the daughter.

BILL AND ETHEL AT THE BALL [BILL #13]

Komic Company/Mutual Film Corporation. 20 Dec 1914. Silent; black & white. One reel.

Director   Edward Dillon. *Author*   Paul West.

Cast   Tammany Young (*Bill, the office boy*), Fay Tincher (*Ethel, the stenographer*), Tod Browning (*Mr. Hadley, the boss*), Edward Dillon (*Ethel's beau*), Maisie Radford, Florence Crawford.

Farce   When the stenographers decide to give a masked ball, they call upon Ethel to persuade Mr. Hadley to attend as guest of honor. Consenting, he sends Bill to procure a certain costume, phoning his sweetheart to meet him at the ball, where she may identify him by the costume he describes to her. Meanwhile, Ethel's admirer laments the fact that having no costume, he cannot act as her escort. Bill, always resourceful, gives him Mr. Hadley's and runs out to get the boss another. At the dance Ethel's beau is taken for Mr. Hadley by the latter's sweetheart, and the boss is taken for Ethel's beau. After additional complications, Bill comes forward with the explanation.

THE RECORD BREAKER

Komic Company/Mutual Film Corporation. 27 Dec 1914. Silent; black & white. One reel.

Director   Edward Dillon.

Cast   Edward Dillon (*Eddie Pullen*), Fay Tincher (*Nell*), Tod Browning (*John, Eddie's rival*), Max Davidson (*The gambler*).

Farce   "Nell persuades her father to take her to the Corona auto races. There she and Eddie Pullen, speed champion, have a case of love at first sight. John, a jealous rival, however, decides to ruin Eddie's chances of winning the race by interchanging the signs on the water and oil cans. It happens that a gambler, who has made a bet with Nell's father, has the same brilliant thought. So, after John has arranged matters, the gambler mistakenly restores the signs—and Eddie wins the race in record time, also the hand of Nell." (*Reel Life,* December 19, 1914)

ETHEL'S FIRST CASE [a.k.a. ETHEL GETS THE EVIDENCE] [BILL #14]

Komic Company/Mutual Film Corporation. 3 Jan 1915. Silent; black & white. One reel.

Director   Edward Dillon. *Author*   Paul West.

Cast   Fay Tincher (*Ethel, the stenographer*), Tammany Young (*Bill, the office boy*), Tod Browning (*Mr. Hadley, the boss*), Mrs. Anderson (*Mrs. Jones*), Chester Withey (*Mr. Jones*), Bobby Feuhrer.

Farce   "Mr. Hadley is sought by a heart-sick bride who pleads with him to secure her a divorce. Ethel, meanwhile, has been invited out to luncheon, by a new beau. She returns with a necklace which he has presented to her, and when the unhappy bride emerges from the private office, she instantly recognizes Ethel's latest ornament as the jewels which her faithless husband has stolen from her that very morning. She hastens to enlighten Ethel, and they conspire to lure Mr. Jones to the office to visit the stenographer. He rises to the bait, and then Ethel uses her powers on him to such good purpose that Hadley, watching with the wife from the inner office, considers the evidence sufficient to start divorce proceedings at once." (*Reel Life,* December 26, 1914)

LOVE AND BUSINESS

Komic Company/Mutual Film Corporation. 10 Jan 1915. Silent; black & white. One reel.

Director   Edward Dillon.

Cast   Tod Browning (*Fred Gates*), Fay Tincher (*Mrs. Gates*).

Farce   "Fred Gates is an attorney for a patent derrick and windlass concern. One day while demonstrating the windlass the hook catches in the dress of a woman, lifting her several feet from the sidewalk. She is a very proper spinster person, president of the Anti-Cigarette League. She files a claim against Fred's company and becomes a regular pest at his office. One morning at breakfast Fred and his wife have a little misunderstanding. After reaching the office he becomes penitent. He writes two letters— one a curt business note to the spinster, advising her that he will settle all claims against him for $500, and the other a tender missive, asking forgiveness, to his wife. The office boy gets the two letters exchanged in the envelopes, and on their arrival both ladies have hysterics. The spinster lady and Fred's wife arrive simultaneously at the office. Poor Fred gets all he ever deserved in his life. But when, at last, he effects the exchange of the two letters everybody is happy." (*Reel Life,* January 2, 1915)

A FLYER IN SPRING WATER [BILL #15]

Komic Company/Mutual Film Corporation. 17 Jan 1915. Silent; black & white. One reel.

Director   Edward Dillon. *Author*   Paul West.

Cast   Fay Tincher (*Ethel, the stenographer*), Tammany Young (*Bill, the office boy*), Tod Browning (*Mr. Hadley, the boss*), Bobby Feuhrer (*Izzy*), Sylvia Ashton (*Wife who notices scented water on husband's coat*), Edward Dillon, Max Davidson.

Farce   "Ethel's sweetheart makes her a present of a large bottle of perfume. Bill and Izzy hit upon the brilliant scheme of filling empty bottles and selling them for spring water. But when they turn the faucet they discover that the odor is not precisely what might be expected from nature's crystal wells, so they steal Ethel's perfume and doctor their bum goods. It chances that another office holder who has bought water from Bill and Izzy spills some on his coat. His wife notices the odor, becomes suspicious, and traces it to Ethel. Ethel does a little detective work, and the two office boys are caught in the act. But his latest venture costs Bill his job." (*Reel Life,* January 9, 1915)

A FLURRY IN ART
Komic Company/Mutual Film Corporation. 24 Jan 1915. Silent; black & white. One reel.

Director   Edward Dillon. *Author*   Anita Loos.

Cast   Edward Dillon (*Harry Gregg*), Fay Tincher (*Maisie Gillespie*), Baldy Belmont (*Mr. Gillespie*), Sylvia Ashton (*Mrs. Gillespie*), Tod Browning (*Thief*).

Farce   Multimillionaire Gillespie hires penniless young artist Harry Gregg to paint his daughter, Maisie. When the youngsters fall in love, Gillespie orders Harry out of the house forever. Two thieves break into the Gillespie mansion and steal a diamond necklace, which they slip between the frame and the canvas of Maisie's portrait, which Gillespie soon orders returned to the artist. Due to his financial condition, Harry's works are being auctioned off. The thieves bid against each other for Maisie's portrait, and subsequent canvases receive enthusiastic bids from other bidders. Informed that the portrait is not for sale, the thief who bought it engages Harry in a fight. Gillespie, informed by the losing bidder of the necklace's whereabouts, arrives with Maisie and finds an embattled Harry clasping the canvas. Gillespie, at sight of the hatful of money the auctioneer produces, gives the pair his blessing.

CUPID AND THE PEST
Komic Company/Mutual Film Corporation. 31 Jan 1915. Silent; black & white. One reel.

Director   Edward Dillon.

Cast   Max Davidson (*Tony, the printer*), Billie West (*Maryola*), Fay Tincher (*Estelle*), Tod Browning (*Ed*), Anna May Walthall, Chester Withey.

Farce   Tony, a printer, tries to fascinate Maryola, the cook at his boardinghouse, but is repulsed. He butts in upon two happy couples, who prove to him that they are in no mood to be disturbed. In revenge, he switches the dates of their wedding ceremonies in the local paper. The nervous grooms forget the hour of their weddings, refer to the newspaper, and on arriving at the church each meets the wrong young woman. Their common misfortune, however, draws them together and they are married. In the café, the interchanged couples take adjoining tables, and when Tony enters, the grooms thank him. Braving a volley of kitchen utensils from Maryola, Tony seizes her and persuades her to marry him.

BILL TURNS VALET [BILL #16]

Komic Company/Mutual Film Corporation. 7 Feb 1915. Silent; black & white. One reel.

Director   Edward Dillon. *Author*   Paul West.

Cast   Fay Tincher (*Ethel, the stenographer*), Tod Browning (*Mr. Hadley, the boss*), Bobby Feuhrer (*Bill, the office boy*), Max Davidson (*The tailor*), Edward Dillon.

Farce   "Hadley engages a new office boy by the name of Bill. Ethel comes down that morning in a new skirt which she displays to Mabel across the hall. She decides that it is too long, and is wondering how she can get it shortened in time to keep a twelve o'clock luncheon engagement, when Bill comes out of the inner office bound for the tailor's with his boss's ink-stained trousers. Ethel gives him her skirt and tells him to hurry. Bill finds the tailor out and decides to make good by doing the repairing himself. Meanwhile, Hadley and Ethel, their nether persons clad in newspapers, are suffering many embarrassments, which finally lead to a visit from the police. But in the nick of time Bill returns with the missing garments— though what he has done to them, under any other circumstances, would have cost him his job." (*Reel Life,* January 30, 1915)

Note   Working title: *Bill Becomes a Valet.* For the character Bill, Tammany Young was replaced by Bobby Feuhrer in this and future episodes.

MUSIC HATH CHARMS

Komic Company/Mutual Film Corporation. 14 Feb 1915. Silent; black & white. One reel.

Director   Edward Dillon.

Cast   Fay Tincher (*Nell*), Tod Browning (*Jim*), Max Davidson (*Nell's father*), Baldy Belmont (*Jed*), Augustus Carney (*Tony, the laborer*), Eleanor Washington (*The maid*).

Farce Aspiring singer Jim and brilliant pianist Jed, rivals for the hand of Nell, both ask her father's consent. She is in love with the latter, but her father favors Jim. It is decided to let the matter rest six months, and then try out the suitors on the strength of their musical abilities. Jim, realizing his chances are slim, hires Tony, an Italian laborer, with the voice of an opera singer, to be his proxy. On the evening of the contest, Tony, concealed behind a curtain, sings while Jim goes through the motions in dumb show. Jim is the clear "winner," until Tony is moved to sing on his own account and the ruse is discovered.

ETHEL GETS CONSENT [BILL #17]

Komic Company/Mutual Film Corporation. 21 Feb 1915. Silent; black & white. One reel.

Director Edward Dillon. *Author* Paul West.

Cast Fay Tincher (*Ethel, the stenographer*), Tod Browning (*Mr. Hadley, the boss*), Bobby Feuhrer (*Bill, the office boy*), Baldy Belmont (*Ed Sr., the father*), Edward Dillon (*Ed Jr., Ethel's beau*), Eleanor Washington (*Ed Sr.'s wife*).

Farce Ethel writes Ed, her beau, a note to meet for lunch. Ed's mother finds the note and thinks it is intended for Ed's father. After Ed Sr. notes his disapproval of his son's intention to marry Ethel, Ed Jr. calls on Ethel for lunch. Ed Sr. enters Hadley's office, mistakes a client for Ethel, and follows her. She chances to enter the same restaurant where Ed and Ethel are. Ed slips under the table, and is delighted to hear his father entering into animated conversation with Ethel, who evidently is making a hit. Meanwhile, Ed's mother has traced her husband to Hadley's office and then to the café. At her approach, it is Father's turn to hide under the table, where he and Ed are brought face-to-face. Ed Sr. gives his consent to the match, and in return Ed Jr. squares things for Father with Mother.

Note Also reviewed as *Ethel Gains Consent*.

A COSTLY EXCHANGE

Komic Company/Mutual Film Corporation. 28 Feb 1915. Silent; black & white. One reel.

Director Edward Dillon. *Author* Eugene Spofford.

Cast   Chet Withey (*Fred Moore*), Fay Tincher (*Mrs. Moore*), Edward Dillon (*Ned Bates*), Eleanor Washington (*Miss Clara Morrison*), Max Davidson (*Schmultz, the detective*).

Farce   Fred Moore has a jealous wife, and fellow office worker Ned Bates an engagement ring. Both have identical overcoats. Ned meets fiancée Clara, who puts her gloves in his overcoat pocket, which also contains the ring. While stopping at his office, Ned exchanges the overcoats. When Ned and Clara discover that the ring and the gloves are "missing," they notify the police. The next morning Fred's wife discovers the gloves dangling from his coat pocket; the husband rushes off to the office without his coat. He drops into Ned's office and absentmindedly picks up the identical coat. While Mrs. Moore threatens divorce over the phone, Ned and some hired detectives arrive at the Moore house. When Fred returns and the two men find the two coats, they realize the mix-up.

Note   Working title: *In a Pickle*. Although mentioned as an actor in this film during production, it appears Browning's role was assumed by Chet Withey (according to an intertitle sheet), who also replaced Browning (who had been promoted to a director at Mutual) as Mr. Hadley in the *Bill* series.

TOD BROWNING:
DIRECTOR, PRODUCER, SCENARIST

THE LUCKY TRANSFER
Reliance Motion Picture Corporation/Mutual Film Corporation. 10 Mar 1915. Silent; black & white. One reel.

Director Tod Browning. *Author* Russell E. Smith.

Cast Mary Alden (*Helen Holland*), Tom Wilson (*Ford*), Thomas Hull (*Ransom*), Vester Pegg (*The clerk*), Margery Wilson (*The little girl*), Jack Hull (*Jim Dodson*), W. E. Lowery (*Fields, the detective*), William Hinckley.

Drama Although he had spent over a year acting in one-reel comedies, Browning's first venture as a director displayed his dramatic instincts with this detective tale of Helen, a reporter, who discovers the facts in a jewelry store robbery. Tracking the thieves to their hideout, Ford, one of the crooks, catches her. Ford gives Ransom, the other crook, the address of the shack and the hiding place of the loot, writing it on a trolley transfer slip. Ransom drops the transfer, and Jim Dodson, a poor workman, who is in the habit of begging transfers on which to ride home at night, picks it up and jumps on the car. The conductor is talking to Fields, a detective, and shows the transfer with its message to him. Fields raids the crooks' den and rescues Helen.

THE SLAVE GIRL
Reliance Motion Picture Corporation/Mutual Film Corporation. 20 Mar 1915. Silent; black & white. Two reels.

Director Tod Browning. *Author* George Hennessey.

Cast Otto Lincoln (*Bob West*), Teddy Sampson (*Ida West, his daughter*), Mary Alden (*Sally, a mulatto*), W. E. Lawrence (*Fred Gilbert*), O. R. MacDiarmid, Miriam Cooper, Jennie Lee.

Drama Browning was given an extra reel to tell this story about a homesteader, killed by Indians, whose little daughter Ida is captured, then traded to Morgan, a slave trader. He substitutes Ida for a mulatto slave child, who recently has died. Neighbors Mr. and Mrs. Marks, out of pity for Ida, buy her. Twelve years later, Fred Gilbert, the Markses' nephew, visits and falls in love with Ida. The Markses are horrified, believing that the girl has Negro blood. Sally, a mulatto slave for Morgan, produces a letter Ida's father had written before his death. By a fingerprint test of the smudged letter, Ida's identity is confirmed, and her white blood proved. The young people marry. Morgan is shot dead by a posse.

Note Working title: *The White Slave*. Otto Lincoln was later known as Elmo Lincoln. One source credits O. R. MacDiarmid playing the role of Fred Gilbert.

AN IMAGE OF THE PAST
Majestic Motion Picture Corporation/Mutual Film Corporation. 30 Mar 1915. Silent; black & white. One reel.

Director Tod Browning.

Cast Signe Auen (*Jessie Dexter*), J. H. Allen (*Jack Dexter, her husband*), Charles Cosgrave (*Mr. Curtis, Jessie's father*).

Drama Jessie Curtis elopes with artist Jack Dexter. Furious, her wealthy father disinherits her and repulses any attempts at a reconciliation. Ten years later, Jack has fallen very ill, the family is penniless, and their three children, dressing themselves in costumes and masks, go out to sing in the street. They happen beneath the windows of their grandfather's house, and the lonely old man calls the youngsters in. Hearing their story, he promises to help the family. One of the children sees a portrait of Jessie painted by Jack at the wealthy man's order from a photograph of her when she was seven years old. The small boy asks why a picture of his sister is in the house. When the mask hiding little Jessie's face is removed, the grandfather learns the truth. He returns with the children to the rescue of his daughter and her husband.

Note Signe Auen was later known as Seena Owen.

THE HIGHBINDERS

Majestic Motion Picture Corporation/Mutual Film Corporation. 18 Apr 1915. Silent; black & white. Two reels.

Director Tod Browning.

Cast Signe Auen (*Ah Woo*), Eugene Pallette (*Hop Woo*), Walter Long (*Pat Gallagher*), Tom Wilson (*Jack Donovan*), Billie West (*Maggie Gallagher*).

Melodrama A trade item in the March 26, 1915, issue of *Variety* mentioned that "Tod Browning now speaks Chinese." Hence this atmospheric tale of San Francisco's Chinatown mixed with an intermarriage theme. Maggie, to avoid a forced marriage with a gangster protégé of her father, Pat Gallagher, a brutal saloonkeeper, takes refuge in a nearby shop and is persuaded to marry its Chinese owner. She exchanges a miserable existence for one even more repugnant. Twenty years later finds Hop Woo selling Ah Woo, his daughter by Maggie, into slavery. The girl's brother and Donovan, a young Irishman, rescue her from the law and the Chinese secret societies. Maggie commits suicide. Donovan sells his saloon and buys a ranch, where he takes his bride, Ah Woo, and her brother. "As a straight melodrama of the old school this is a particularly fine bit of work. It consists of one thrill after another, and should make a big hit." (*Motion Picture News,* May 1, 1915)

Note Signe Auen was later known as Seena Owen.

THE STORY OF A STORY

Majestic Motion Picture Corporation/Mutual Film Corporation. 20 Apr 1915. Silent; black & white. One reel.

Director Tod Browning.

Cast Eugene Pallette (*John Penhallow*), Miriam Cooper (*His daughter*), Claire Anderson, Frankie Newman, Charles Lee.

Melodrama An idealistic, yet impoverished, author writes a trashy, misleading story about the underworld, then dreams that his published book has fallen into the hands of a weary girl, who is ruined and disgraced by a man and is denied refuge by her mother. The author awakens just as his daughter picks up the manuscript to read it. He snatches it from her, his dream still vivid in his mind, and burns it. He rewrites the manuscript, giving it a moral ending. Browning's first venture into special effects. "In his dream the two leading characters of the man's book, a man and woman of evil repute, step out from the book. They are in miniature, and when the story is over they grow small again and step back. Again they are seen when the script is burning in the fire, wildly gesticulating for help." (*Motion Picture News,* May 1, 1915)

THE SPELL OF THE POPPY

Majestic Motion Picture Corporation/Mutual Film Corporation. 9 May 1915. Silent; black & white. Two reels.

Director   Tod Browning.

Cast   Eugene Pallette (*Manfredi*), Lucille Young (*Zuletta*), Joseph Henabery (*John Hale*).

Melodrama   Manfredi, an opium addict, is a piano player in a Chinese café. Sent abroad to study, he promises Zuletta, his common-law wife, that he will marry her when he comes back. Five years later he returns, still addicted. Under its spell he is accounted a genius. Breaking his promise to Zuletta, he becomes infatuated with society girl Margery Rhodes, who studies music with him. So strongly is Margery influenced by her teacher that she also acquires a taste for opium. John Hale, her lover and a Secret Service man, learns about Manfredi's opium den from the vengeful Zuletta. Manfredi is shot and killed, and Margery rescued. "There is considerable that is interesting, but the picture has little if any moral backing, and could not be highly recommended." (*Moving Picture World,* May 22, 1915)

THE ELECTRIC ALARM

Majestic Motion Picture Corporation/Mutual Film Corporation. 18 May 1915. Silent; black & white. One reel.

Director   Tod Browning.

Cast   Charles Gorman (*Dick Ray, the electrician*), Lillian Webster (*Mary, his sweetheart*), Lucy Payton (*Her mother*), A. E. Freeman (*Ryley*).

Melodrama   Dick Ray, a young electrical engineer, is installing a fire alarm system in a Pennsylvania town. All that yet remains to be done is to connect the wires from the alarm boxes with the bell in the Town Hall tower. While Ray is waiting for some more wire, he discovers that a distant railroad trestle is afire. Remembering that his sweetheart and her mother are on the train due in a few minutes, Dick grasps the loose ends of the wire with his hands, completing the circuit with his body. The alarm is sounded and the train saved. The young engineer recovers from his injuries, and receives a check from the railroad company big enough to permit him and his sweetheart to marry.

Note   The character portrayed by Charles Gorman is called Tom Elby in one source.

THE LIVING DEATH

Majestic Motion Picture Corporation/Mutual Film Corporation. 6 Jun 1915. Silent; black & white. Two reels.

Director   Tod Browning.

Cast   Fred A. Turner (*Dr. Farrell*), Billie West (*Naida Farrell, his daughter*), Edward J. Peil (*Tom O'Day*).

Melodrama   "A drama of great strength, well acted and staged, and consequently most effective." (*Motion Picture News,* June 19, 1915) Dr. Farrell, embittered by the deaths of his wife and son, loves with consuming selfishness his only child, Naida. He moves to a remote place on the California coast, but a neighbor, Tom O'Day, falls deeply in love with Naida. After Tom digs up a man's skull, the doctor purposefully diagnoses a poison-ivy rash on Tom's wrist as leprosy. In despair, Tom rushes to his motorboat to go to a leper colony on an offshore island. Naida flings herself into the water, and Tom is obliged to take her into the boat to save her from drowning. Dr. Farrell overtakes them, confesses, and gives them his blessing to marry.

THE BURNED HAND

Majestic Motion Picture Corporation/Mutual Film Corporation. 13 Jun 1915. Silent; black & white. Two reels.

Director Tod Browning.

Cast Miriam Cooper (*Marietta*), William Hinckley (*Billy Rider*), W. E. Lowery (*Marietta's father*), Cora Drew (*Marietta's mother*), Jack Dillon, William Wolbert (*Billy's pal who burns his hand*), Fred A. Turner, Charles West, Violet Wilkey, Jack Hull.

Melodrama Domestic difficulties cause Marietta's father and mother to divorce. The court refuses the father custody, so he kidnaps Marietta and takes her to another state, where he becomes prominent in politics. College graduate Billy Rider, in love with Marietta, and two companions trace the girl. In stealing her from her father, Billy burns his hand with a red-hot poker, and the father uses this scar to track him. One of Billy's pals, to save him from arrest, burns his own hand in the same manner to conceal Billy's identity.

THE WOMAN FROM WARRENS

Majestic Motion Picture Corporation/Mutual Film Corporation. 30 Jun 1915. Silent; black & white. Two reels.

Director Tod Browning.

Cast Lucille Younge (*Wynona Ware*), Fred A. Turner (*Fred Thompson, the landlord*), "Billy" Hutton (*Alice Thompson, his daughter*), Charles West (*Hanson Landing*).

Melodrama When Wynona Ware, who had been tricked years earlier by libertine Hanson Landing, discovers he is wooing Alice, a hotelkeeper's daughter, her suspicions are aroused. Her betrayer's threats to expose her past force a silent game, but Wynona sends the crook on his way on the evening that he had planned to carry out a mock marriage with the trusting girl.

LITTLE MARIE

Reliance Motion Picture Corporation/Mutual Film Corporation. 3 Jul 1915. Silent; black & white. Two reels.

Director Tod Browning.

Cast Charles West (*Beppo Puccini*), Signe Auen (*Bianca Pastorell*), Tom Wilson (*Sam Coggini*), Walter Long.

Melodrama Ignorant Beppo Puccini, a railroad laborer, asks Bianca, whom his little daughter Marie loves, to marry him. Bianca takes his proposal as a joke, and, later, when he sees Sam Coggini, his foreman, talking with her, the Sicilian believes that Sam is standing between him and his baby's desire. He decides to kill his foreman and places a bomb in the gate of Bianca's house. A tragedy is narrowly averted and Sam explains that Bianca is his own sister. Beppo, Bianca, and Marie become one family.

Note Signe Auen was later known as Seena Owen.

THE QUEEN OF THE BAND

Reliance Motion Picture Corporation/Mutual Film Corporation. 10 Oct 1915. Silent; black & white. Two reels.

Director Ray Myers. *Story* Tod Browning.

Cast Adoni Fovieri (*Zoah, the international criminal*), George Walsh (*Ramar, the detective*), Frank Fisher Bennett (*Jack Lyle*), Gladys Field (*Ethel Dawn*), Jack McDermott, O. R. MacDiarmid, Jack Cosgrove, Phil Gastrock.

Crime Melodrama Browning's story concerns the theft by Zoah, queen of a band of crooks, of a priceless Kaffir diamond. While the police seize upon the wrong suspect, Ramar, a celebrated detective, seizes upon a clue which leads to the crooks' hangout. Later he and his assistant enter the house as paperhangers and hear a conversation that incriminates the gang. The two men are discovered and barely escape a horrible fate by the timely arrival of the police.

SUNSHINE DAD

Fine Arts Film Company/Triangle Film Corporation. 23 Apr 1916 [©Triangle Film Corporation; 17 Apr 1916; LP8603]. Silent; black & white. Five reels.

Director Edward Dillon. *Scenario* F. M. Pierson and Chester Withey. *Story* Tod Browning and Chester Withey. *Camera* Alfred G. Gosden.

Cast De Wolf Hopper (*Alonzo Evergreen*), Fay Tincher (*Widow Marrimore*), Chester Withey (*Count Kottschkojff*), Max Davidson (*Mystic seer*), Raymond Wells (*Mystic doer*), Eugene Pallette (*Alfred Evergreen*), Jewel Carmen (*Charlotte, Alfred's fiancée*), William De Wolf Hopper, Jr. (*The baby*), Leo (*The lion*).

Comedy Many of the stars who worked with Browning during his Komic comedy days are featured in this comedy starring De Wolf Hopper (then making $125,000 a year) "in the role of a gay parent whose broad shoulders refuse to be burdened with anything savoring of seriousness. As Alonzo Evergreen, widower and possessor of a dutiful son, the bulky comedian wins out in a dash for the dashing widow. Mr. Hopper has the support of a good cast . . . but not so with the story. *Sunshine Dad* is amusing, but it lacks that elusive something that makes a picture funny. . . . a mixture of slapstick and straight comedy and though the blending is not of the cleverest, the picture is undeniably entertaining." (*Motography,* April 8, 1916)

Note Working title: *A Knight of the Garter.*

THE MYSTERY OF THE LEAPING FISH
Keystone Komedy/Triangle Film Corporation. 11 Jun 1916. Silent; black & white. Two reels.

Director John Emerson. *Story* Tod Browning. *Fish floats patented by* J. P. McCarty.

Cast Douglas Fairbanks (*Coke Ennyday*), Bessie Love (*Inane, the Little Fish Blower of Short Beach*), Alfred D. Sears (*Gent rolling in wealth*), Alma Reubens (*His female confederate*), Charles Stevens and George Hall (*The two Japanese accomplices*), Tom Wilson (*I. M. Keene, the chief*), Bennie Zeidman (*Himself, a scenario editor*).

Farce "Laying aside the sort of parts for which he has become famous, Douglas Fairbanks goes in for pure farce here, his role being that of a 'nut' detective, whose characteristics are well described by his name— Coke Ennyday. It is near slapstick, without a trace of the heart interest which Fairbanks handles with such distinction, and in fact is a burlesque of Fairbanks' own style of acting, to a degree, and more emphatically, a burlesque of the know-it-all scientific detective and his methods." (*Motion Picture News,* July 15, 1916)

Note Working title: *The Detective.*

PUPPETS
Fine Arts Film Company/Triangle Film Corporation. 13 Aug 1916. Silent; black & white. Two reels.

Director   Tod Browning.

Cast   De Wolf Hopper (*Pantaloon*), Kate Toncray (*The widow*), Jack Bram-mall (*Harlequin*), Robert Lawlor (*Clown*), Pauline Starke (*Columbine*), Ed-ward Bolles (*Pierrot*), Max Davidson (*Scaramouche*).

Fantasy Drama   Finally recovered from his near-fatal automobile acci-dent, Browning displayed his directorial creativity with this poetic fantasy of the harlequinade, a story of mismatched loves told in actual panto-mime, filmed at Venice-by-the-Sea. The settings were an innovation in themselves, being designed in pure blacks and whites, and all the charac-ters were dressed like puppets with their pantaloons, Pierrot costumes, ballet effects, and tights.

Note   Working title: *The Mummy.*

INTOLERANCE [THE MODERN STORY sequence]
Wark Producing Corporation. 5 Sep 1916 [©David Wark Griffith; 24 Jun 1916; LU8570; ©David Wark Griffith; 5 Sep 1916; LP9934]. Silent; black & white. Thirteen to fourteen reels.

Presented by   D. W. Griffith. *Producer-Director-Story*   D. W. Griffith. *Photog-raphy*   G. W. Bitzer. *Assistant Directors*   George Siegmann, W. S. Van Dyke, Erich von Stroheim, Edward Dillon, Elmer Clifton, Joseph Henabery, Tod Browning.

Cast (The Modern Story)   Mae Marsh (*The Little Dear One*), Robert Harron (*The Boy*), Miriam Cooper (*The Friendless One*), Vera Lewis (*Miss Mary T. Jenkins*), Sam De Grasse (*Arthur Jenkins*), Clyde Hopkins (*His secretary*), Fred A. Turner (*The Girl's father*), Walter Long (*The Musketeer of the Slums*), Tom Wilson (*The kindly policeman*), Ralph Lewis (*The governor*), Edward Dillon (*Chief detective*), A. W. McClure (*Father Farley*), Lloyd Ingraham (*The judge*), William Brown (*The warden*), Max Davidson (*The kindly neighbor*), Alberta Lee (*The wife*), Frank Brownlee (*The brother of the Girl*), Barney Bernard (*Attorney for the Boy*), Luray Huntley, Eleanor Washington, Lucille Brown, Mary Alden, Pearl Elmore, Mrs. Arthur Mackley (*Self-styled "Uplift-ers"*), Margaret Marsh (*Debutante at ball*), Tod Browning (*Owner of racing car*), Kate Bruce (*The city mother*).

Social Melodrama   Wallflower Mary Jenkins, whose brother owns a pros-perous mill, is easily seduced by reformers into leading their group. To provide their funds, Jenkins cuts his workers' wages. Using machine guns, the militia and company guards quell the resultant strike, leaving the Boy's father dead, and the Little Dear One and her father unemployed. In the city, the Boy joins a criminal band. After marrying the Dear One, he tries to leave the gang, but its leader, the Musketeer, gets him arrested. The Dear One has a child which the reformers tear away from her, insisting that she is an unfit mother. The Musketeer, trying to seduce the Dear One, promises help, but the baby dies from neglect in an institution. When the Boy returns, he fights the Musketeer, who is killed by his jealous mistress. After she confesses, a racing car speeds to catch the governor's train, and the Boy, about to hang, is pardoned.

Note Production began in 1914. Browning apparently worked as an assistant director on *The Modern Story* sequence of this four-part photoplay; his participation occurred prior to his June 1915 car accident. As *The Mother and the Law,* this segment was expanded and reedited into a separate seven-reel film released in August 1919. Browning also appeared in a bit role.

EVERYBODY'S DOING IT
Fine Arts Film Company/Triangle Film Corporation. Oct 1916. Silent; black & white. Two reels.

Director Tod Browning.

Cast Tully Marshall (*A crook*), Howard Gaye (*A society youth*), Lillian Webster (*A young woman*), George Stone and Violet Radcliffe (*Messengers*), Richard Cummings, Jack Brammall, Carmen De Rue.

Crook Farce This appears to be a film within a film, with the framing story concerning two children writing movie scenarios, and the story they write is of a crook who corrupts a society youth and induces him to help in a bold robbery by making him believe he is aiding a woman in distress.

Note Working title: *The Rescuers.* Filmed in September 1916; the official release date is not mentioned in the film trades.

THE DEADLY GLASS OF BEER
Fine Arts Film Company/Triangle Film Corporation. Oct 1916. Silent; black & white. Two reels.

Director Tod Browning. *Story* Anita Loos.

Cast Teddy Sampson (*Nell*), Tully Marshall (*Henry*), Jack Brammall (*John*), Elmo Lincoln.

Farce John, a noble lad, and his villainous cousin Henry learn that John will inherit a million dollars if he has not taken a drink of beer before reaching the age of twenty-one. Henry, who stands to get the inheritance if John takes a drink, desperately schemes to trick his cousin, including kidnaping him on his twenty-first birthday, but Nell, a young woman who knows of Henry's plotting, rescues John.

Note Alternate title: *The Fatal Glass of Beer.*

ATTA BOY'S LAST RACE

Fine Arts Film Company/Triangle Film Corporation. 5 Nov 1916. Silent; black & white. Five reels.

Director George Siegmann. *Story and Script* Tod Browning.

Cast Dorothy Gish (*Lois Brandon*), Keith Armour (*Jim Spencer, owner of a small "string" of horses*), Carlton Stockdale (*Jarvis Johnson, a gambler*), Adele Clifton (*Lucille Stone, his consort*), Loyola O'Connor (*Mrs. Brandon, Lois' mother*), Fred A. Turner (*Phil Strong*), Tom Wilson (*Bill Golden, a trainer*), Joe Neery (*Jockey*).

Drama Browning used the old horse-racing theme in this average tale, with most of the story's background being supplied from memories of his days as an exercise boy at Churchill Downs. The simple plot dictated that the decent people's horse win out against the villain, allowing the mortgage to be paid off and the young couple to be married.

Note Working title: *The Best Bet.* The film was to have been fashion model Raymond Jerome Binder's screen debut; he was replaced by Keith Armour. Racetrack scenes filmed at Exposition Park in Los Angeles and in San Francisco. Additional exteriors filmed at the California State Fair in Sacramento and in Tijuana, Mexico.

JIM BLUDSO

Fine Arts Film Company/Triangle Distributing Corporation. 4 Feb 1917. Silent; black & white. Five reels.

Director/Scenario Tod Browning. *Codirector* Wilfred Lucas (see note). *Camera* Alfred G. Gosden. Based on the poems "Jim Bludso of the Prairie Belle" and "Little Breeches," by John Hay, collected in his *Pike County Ballads* (Boston, 1871), and the play *Jim Bludso of the Prairie Belle,* by I. N. Morris, as produced by Robert Hillard at the 14th Street Theatre in New York, opening on January 5, 1903 [closed after forty performances].

Cast   Wilfred Lucas (*Jim Bludso, captain of the Prairie Belle*), Olga Grey (*Gabrielle, Jim's wife*), George Stone (*Little Breeches, their son*), Charles Lee (*Tom Taggart*), Winifred Westover (*Kate Taggart*), Sam De Grasse (*Ben Merrill*), James O'Shea (*Banty Tim*), Monte Blue (*Joe Bowers*), Al Joy (*Riverboat gambler*).

Drama   This action-packed picturization of the old Mississippi River era, recalling the rivalry that existed between the famous riverboats, was Browning's first exposure to feature-length direction. In delivering this story of a picturesque community of antebellum days, there was no sacrifice of realism, especially during the climactic scenes, which included a fire aboard one of the steamers, the breakup of the town levee during a thunderstorm, and the flooding of the riverside village. "With many thrills and a plot of the heart interest variety, *Jim Bludso,* a picture based on the poem by John Hay, makes an excellent release. . . . The production given it by Tod Browning is quite without the bounds of averse criticism. . . ." (*Motion Picture News,* February 10, 1917) "The screen retains the Mississippi River scenes and for a climax brings forward the episode of the race, the fire, and the heroism of the engineer who held the boat's nose against the bank 'Till the last galoot's ashore.' " (*Variety,* February 2, 1917)

Note   Several sources cite Wilfred Lucas as codirector; this appears to be contractual in nature. Location scenes filmed in San Francisco, Rio Vista (on the Sacramento River), and "Nigger Slough," a marshy depression near Los Angeles.

A LOVE SUBLIME

Fine Arts Film Company/Triangle Distributing Corporation. 11 Mar 1917. Silent; black & white. Five reels.

Director Tod Browning. *Codirector* Wilfred Lucas (see note). *Scenario* Tod Browning and Wilfred Lucas, based on the short story "Orpheus," by Samuel Hopkins Adams (*Collier's Weekly,* November 11, 1916). *Camera* Alfred G. Gosden.

Cast   Wilfred Lucas (*Philip*), Carmel Myers (*Toinette, the girl*), Fred A. Turner (*The professor*), Alice Rae (*Bonnie Lassie, the sculptress*), George A. Beranger (*Her husband*), Jack Brammall (*Piney the Rat*), James O'Shea (*Terry, the cop*), Bert Woodruff (*The Little Red Doctor*), Mildred Harris (*Eurydice*), Rev. Alexander W. McClure.

Drama As a modern allegory of the legendary Greek *Orpheus,* this film concerns the affections of a philanthropic Greek steelworker, Philip, toward French waitress Toinette. A story of love found, lost, and happily regained, the photoplay features Carmel Myers in her first starring role. "Wilfred Lucas is a sterling actor and his impersonation of the seemingly half crazed flute-playing Greek in *A Love Sublime* is indeed a work of art." (*Variety,* March 9, 1917)

Note Working title: *Orpheus in Our Square.* Several sources cite Wilfred Lucas as codirector; this appears to be contractual in nature. Actress Alice Rae, also known as Alice Wilson, later married Tod Browning. Elmer Clifton was originally announced as a member of the cast; he appears to have been replaced by George A. Beranger. Location scenes filmed in Los Angeles.

HANDS UP!

Fine Arts Film Company/Triangle Distributing Corporation. 29 Apr 1917. Silent; black & white. Five reels.

Director Tod Browning. *Scenario* Wilfred Lucas. *Story* Al Jennings.

Cast Wilfred Lucas (*John Huston*), Colleen Moore (*Marjorie Houston, his daughter*), Monte Blue (*Dan Tracy*), Beatrice Van (*Elinor Craig, John's fiancée*), Rhea Haynes (*Rosanna*), Bert Woodruff (*Tim Farley*), Kate Toncray (*Mrs. Farley*), Sam De Grasse.

Drama "This picture, credited to the authorship of Al Jennings, ex-holdup man, gets away to a fine start, the promise of which is in no way fulfilled by the finish. It takes up the difficult plot of a brother and sister who are unaware of their relationship—being in love with one another. At least, such is the supposition until a last minute discovery reveals the fact that the relationship came not through blood, but through marriage. The young man, however, after acting like a hero for four reels, suddenly reverts to type and shows his villainous nature. He is killed finally." (Peter Milne, *Motion Picture News,* May 5, 1917)

Note Several sources cite Wilfred Lucas as co-director; this appears to be contractual in nature. Location scenes filmed in the Santa Ynez Canyon, California, and in the Hotel Alexandria in Los Angeles.

PEGGY, THE WILL O' THE WISP

Rolfe Photoplays, Inc./Metro Pictures Corporation. 9 Jul 1917 [©Metro Pictures Corporation; 10 Jul 1917; LP11069]. Silent; black & white. Five reels.

A Metro Wonderplay. Presented by B. A. Rolfe. *Director* Tod Browning. *Story* Katherine Kavanaugh (loosely based on the Irish folktale "The Will o' the Wisp"). *Camera* John Bauman. *Technical (Set) Director* Edward J. Shulter. *Assistant Technical Director* Robert Farrell. *Casting Director* Ben Weiss.

Cast Mabel Taliaferro (*Peggy Desmond*), Thomas J. Carrigan (*Captain Neil Dacey*), W. J. Gross (*Anthony Desmond, Peggy's father*), Sam J. Ryan (*Squire O'Malley*), Nathaniel Saxe (*Terence O' Malley, his nephew and rent collector*), Thomas F. O'Malley (*Shamus Donnelly*), Florence Ashbrooke (*Sarah*), Clara Blandick (*Mrs. Donnelly*), J. J. Williams (*Muldoon*).

Drama Shortly after D. W. Griffith's departure from Triangle, Browning switched to Metro Pictures, which brought him back to New York, where he had started his film career as an actor. The story concerns one Peggy Desmond who masquerades as a modern-day highwayman playing an Irish Robin Hood who helps the suffering tenants of a misery landlord. "Talented Mabel Taliaferro as star of this picture, and director Tod Browning, who was alive to every possibility in the script, have made it a worthwhile production despite its almost deplorable lack of story." (*Motion Picture News*, August 4, 1917)

Note Also reviewed as *The Will o' the Wisp*.

THE JURY OF FATE

Metro Pictures Corporation. 6 Aug 1917 [©Metro Pictures Corporation; 9 Aug 1917; LP11234]. Silent; black & white. Five reels.

A Metro Wonderplay. Presented by B. A. Rolfe. *Director* Tod Browning. *Adaptation* June Mathis. *Story* Finis Fox. *Camera* Charles W. Hoffman.

Cast Mabel Taliaferro (*Jeanne Labordie and Jacques Labordie, twins*), William Sherwood (*Donald Duncan*), Frank Fisher Bennett (*François Leblanc*), Charles Fang (*Ching*), Albert Tavernier (*Henri Labordie, the father*), Bradley Barker (*Louis Hebert*), H. F. Webber (*Duval Hebert*), Dee Dorsey.

Drama Twins Jeanne and Jacques Labordie live in the Canadian north woods with their widowed father, Henri. When Jacques is accidentally drowned, Jeanne cuts her hair and masquerades as her brother, the favorite of their father, so that the shock will not kill him. Donald Duncan, Jeanne's secret fiancé, is sent into despair believing her dead. After Henri's death, Jeanne learns her father had arranged for her marriage to Louis Hebert, the dissipated son of an old family friend. After learning of Jeanne's love for Duncan, Louis, in a drunken attack on François, a faithful half-breed devoted to Jeanne, is killed. Duncan and Jeanne are reunited. "The direction is excellent and finished. *The Jury of Fate* will hold an audience. It's just like a breeze in the warm weather, with its [scenes] nearly all out of doors. . . ." (*Variety,* August 17, 1917)

Note   Location scenes filmed at Saranac Lake and the Saint Lawrence River, New York.

THE EYES OF MYSTERY

Metro Pictures Corporation. 21 Jan 1918 [©Metro Pictures Corporation; 14 Jan 1918; LP11950]. Silent; black & white. Five reels.

Presented by B. A. Rolfe. *Director* Tod Browning. *Adaptation* June Mathis, based on the short story "The House in the Mist," by Octavus Roy Cohen and John U. Geisy (*People's Magazine,* August 10, 1917). *Camera* Harry L. Keepers. *Assistant Director* James J. Dunne.

Cast   Edith Storey (*Carma Carmichael/her mother*), Bradley Barker (*Jack Carrington*), Harry S. Northrup (*Roger Carmichael*), Frank Andrews (*Quincy Carmichael, Carma's uncle*), Kempton Greene (*Steve Graham*), Frank Fisher Bennett (*Seth Megget, the overseer*), Louis R. Wolheim (*Brad Tilton*), Anthony Byrd (*Uncle George*), Pauline Dempsey (*Aunt Liza*).

Mystery   A melodramatic offering complete with sliding doors, secret stairways, "seeing" portraits, and other similar gadgetry, was a forerunner of some of Browning's later work. Schoolgirl Carma Carmichael's overbearing father, Roger, causes the death of her mother (also portrayed by Edith Story) by neglect. After being adopted by her uncle Quincy, Carma tries to elude her father, who wants her back. A pretended death by Quincy allows for a happy ending. "The direction is particularly noteworthy. Due to Mr. Browning's able work, an even continuity has been supplied that presents the story at its best. . . . The atmosphere of the South has been ably maintained and the photography and lighting effects could not be improved upon whatsoever.'' (*Exhibitor's Trade Review*, February 2, 1918)

Note Working titles: *The House in the Mist* and *The Maid of the Mist*.

THE LEGION OF DEATH

Metro Pictures Corporation. A Metro Special De Luxe Production. 8 Feb 1918 [©Metro Pictures Corporation; 1 Feb 1918; LP12028]. Silent; black & white. Seven reels.

Presented by B. A. Rolfe. *Director* Tod Browning. *Scenario and Story* June Mathis. *Camera* Harry L. Keepers. *Assistant Director* Abe Cantor. *Technical (Set) Director* J. E. Newman. *Casting Director* J. C. Richardson. *Props* Danny Hogan.

Cast Edith Storey (*Princess Marya*), Philo McCullough (*Captain Rodney Willard*), Fred Malatesta (*Grand Duke Paul*), Charles Gerard (*Grand Duke Orloff*), Pomeroy Cannon (*Dmitri*), Norma Nichols (*Draya*), R. O. Pennell (*Czar*), Grace Aide (*Czarina*), H. L. Swisher (*Kerensky*), Francis Marion (*Little Czarevitch*), Harry Moody (*Makar*), Irene Aldwin, Junior Beckner.

Mystery With the leasing of the old Charlie Chaplin studios in Hollywood, Browning, with producer, cast, and crew, relocated to California to film this spectacular romance of the Russian Revolution. As the first feature to be produced by Metro's West Coast studio, a great effort was made to accurately record the real-life adventures of the women revolutionary fighters and their part in battling the autocratic states of Germany during World War I.

Note Location scenes filmed in San Pedro, Monrovia, and the San Fernando Valley, California.

REVENGE

Metro Pictures Corporation. A Metro All-Star Production. 25 Feb 1918 [©Metro Pictures Corporation; 18 Feb 1918; LP12074]. Silent; black & white. Five reels.

Presented by B. A. Rolfe. *Director* Tod Browning. *Scenario* H. P. Keeler and William Parker, based on the novel *Hearts Steadfast*, by Edward Moffat (New York, 1915). *Camera* William C. Thompson.

Cast Edith Storey (*Alva Leigh*), Wheeler Oakman (*Dick Randall*), Ralph Lewis (*"Sudden" Duncan*), Alberta Ballard (*Tiger Lil*), Charles West (*Donald Jaffray*).

Western Set in a small town in the Arizona desert, Edith Storey returns to the type of role that first endeared her to the screen. She is Alva Leigh, a vengeful easterner who sets out to find the murderer of her fiancé. It was announced in early February 1918 that Browning would return to New York to film two features for Metro, possibly with either Ethel Barrymore or Mme Nazimova, but the projects never reached fruition, as the director signed a contract with Universal the following month.

Note Location scenes filmed in Pine Crest (near Bear Lake Valley) and Pleasanton, California.

WHICH WOMAN
Bluebird Photoplays, Inc./Universal Film Manufacturing Company, Inc. 10 Jun 1918 [©Bluebird Photoplays, Inc.; 10 Jun 1918; LP12494]. Silent; black & white. Five reels.

Director Tod Browning. *Original Director* Harry Pollard. *Scenario* Anthony W. Coldeway, based on the novelette "Nobody's Bride," by Evelyn Campbell (*All-Story Weekly*). *Camera* John Webster Brown.

Cast Ella Hall (*Doris Standish*), Priscilla Dean (*Mary Butler*), Eddie Sutherland (*Jimmy Nevin*), Edward Jobson (*Cyrus W. Hopkins*), Andrew Robson (*Peter Standish, Doris' uncle*), Harry Carter (*The butler*).

Crime Drama "An interrupted wedding in which the unwilling bride flees and afterward becomes entangled with a band of crooks are the chief features. The story is a good one, and contains both thrills and humor." (*Moving Picture World*, June 29, 1918) "Only an average program picture, which will appeal mostly to children. The story reads more or less like a dime novel, with a hero and a heroine and jewels and crooks and, of course, policemen to arrest them. It is very improbable and the kind grown-ups will not believe." (P. S. Harrison, *Motion Picture News*, June 15, 1918)

Note Working titles: *Nobody's Bride* and *Woman Against Woman*. Original director Pollard took ill during filming and Browning completed the production. Remade in 1923 by Universal as *Nobody's Bride*. A treatment prepared by Alice Catlin in 1918 may have been used, but she does not receive screen credit.

THE DECIDING KISS

Bluebird Photoplays, Inc./Universal Film Manufacturing Company, Inc. 22 Jul 1918 [©Bluebird Photoplays, Inc.; 9 Jul 1918; LP12642]. Silent; black & white. Five reels.

Director Tod Browning. *Scenario* Bernard McConville, based on the novel *Turn About Eleanor,* by Ethel May Kelley (Indianapolis, 1917). *Camera* John Webster Brown.

Cast Edith Roberts (*Eleanor Hamlin*), Winifred Greenwood (*Beulah Page*), Hal Cooley (*Jimmy Sears*), Thornton Church (*Peter Bolling*), Lottie Kruse, Edwin Cobb.

Drama "There is something distinctly novel in this amusing little story. . . . It is a gentle satire on a theory called 'cooperative parentage,' one of the numerous new methods of child-rearing usually indulged in by people who have no children of their own. At the same time the story itself is delightfully human and intermingles humor and pathos effectively." (Robert C. Elravy, *Moving Picture World,* July 27, 1918) "The first reel is pathetic indeed, and shows Eleanor Hamlin severing home ties with her grandparents to be 'adopted' by a party of idle rich on the cooperative plan. The parties adopting her are single, and one of them, Beulah Page, has her own ideas on the subject of raising the young—these ideas absolutely precluding the main requisite, love. And on this the story hangs. The climax is rather unexpected, but is wholesome and refreshing. . . . The direction of Tod Browning leaves nothing to be desired." (F. G. Spencer, *Motion Picture News,* July 20, 1918)

THE BRAZEN BEAUTY

Bluebird Photoplays, Inc./Universal Film Manufacturing Company, Inc. 9 Sep 1918 [©Bluebird Photoplays, Inc.; 31 Aug 1918; LP12804]. Silent; black & white. Five reels.

Director Tod Browning. *Scenario* William Everett Wing, based on the novelette "The Magnificent Jacala," by Louise Winter (*Parisienne,* May 4, 1918). *Camera* Alfred G. Gosden. *Assistant Director* Fred Tyler.

Cast Priscilla Dean (*Jacala*), Gertrude Astor (*Mrs. Augusta Van Ruysdael*), Thurston Hall (*Kenneth Hyde*), Katherine Griffith (*Aunt Ellen*), Alice Wilson (Kate Dewey), Leo White (*Tony Dewey, her brother*), Thornton Church (*Bruce Edwards*), Rex de Rosselli.

Comedy Drama As a rising star, Priscilla Dean was quickly becoming one of the more popular attractions for Universal's patrons. Browning took advantage of her dynamic acting ability and repeatedly cast her in the energetic, carefree leads that suited her so well. In *The Brazen Beauty* she is Jacala, a temperamental Montana ranch woman who inherits her father's fortune and moves to New York. In her efforts to join society, she only learns that she must cast it aside for the man she loves. ". . . a knockout. It is one of those occasional subjects that please the observer in so many ways that it leaves him tingling with admiration." (*Motion Picture News,* October 5, 1918)

Note Working title: *The Magnificent Jacala.* Also referred to as *The Beautiful Jacala* prior to release. The underlying story was purchased for $1,000.

SET FREE

Bluebird Photoplays, Inc./Universal Film Manufacturing Company, Inc. 9 Dec 1918 [©Bluebird Photoplays, Inc.; 2 Dec 1918; LP13093]. Silent; black & white. Five reels.

Director Tod Browning. *Scenario* Rex Taylor and Tod Browning. *Story* Joseph Franklin Poland. *Camera* Alfred G. Gosden. *Assistant Camera* Fred Leahy. *Assistant Director* Edward Laemmle.

Cast Edith Roberts (*Roma Wycliffe*), Harry Hilliard (*John Roberts*), Harold Goodwin (*Ronald Blair*), Molly McConnell (*Mrs. Roberts, John's mother*), Blanche Gray (*Aunt Henrietta*).

Comedy Drama Another bored-heiress story has Roma Wycliffe disguising herself as a "Gypsy Nan." John Roberts, the son of the woman who takes Roma on as a boarder, cures her of her Gypsy airs. He pretends to abduct her and involves her with a gang planning a fake robbery. When the ruffians actually rob a bank, John has them arrested. All is settled happily as Roma settles down to a quieter life with John. "This is another one of those things that altogether misses fire because of its apparent and forced attempt to get laughs. . . . However, it can be said of this that it has been given a very artistic production." (*Wid's Daily,* December 10, 1918)

Note Working titles: *Romance for Roma* and *Double Crossed.*

THE WICKED DARLING

Universal Film Manufacturing Company, Inc. A Universal Special Attraction. 24 Feb 1919 [©Universal Film Manufacturing Company, Inc.; 3 Feb 1919; LP13356]. Silent; black & white. Six reels.

Director Tod Browning. *Scenario* Harvey H. Gates and Waldemar Young, based on the story "The Moth," by Evelyn Campbell. *Camera* Alfred G. Gosden. *Assistant Camera* Harold Janes. *Assistant Director* Clifford Elfelt.

Cast Priscilla Dean (*Mary Stevens*), Wellington Playter (*Kent Mortimer*), Lon Chaney (*Stoop Connors*), Spottiswoode Aitken (*Fadem*), Gertrude Astor (*Adele Hoyt*), Kalla Pascha (*The bartender*).

Crime Drama Although this was the first appearance for Lon Chaney in a Tod Browning film, it would not be until many years later, at MGM, that the pair would become famous as evangelists of the macabre. Chaney portrays a character villain in this metropolitan melodrama in which Priscilla Dean is a guttersnipe whose heart goes out to an ailing young man, leading to her reformation and subsequent marriage. "This . . . should be a success in every way. . . . The picture is well enough directed and the actors never have any difficulty in registering that which they wish to convey." (*Variety,* February 7, 1919)

Note Working titles: *The Gutter Rose, The Gutter Bride, The Rose of the Dark,* and *The Rose of the Night.* Sources conflict on scenario credit; Gates' version may have been rewritten by Young.

THE EXQUISITE THIEF

Universal Film Manufacturing Company, Inc. A Universal Special Attraction. 28 Apr 1919 [©Universal Film Manufacturing Company, Inc.; 4 Apr 1919; LP13573]. Silent; black & white. Six reels.

Presented by R. H. Cochrane. *Director* Tod Browning. *Scenario* Harvey H. Gates and Waldemar Young, based on the short story "Raggedy Ann," by Charles W. Tyler (*Detective Stories Magazine*). *Camera* Alfred G. Gosden. *Assistant Directors* Fred Tyler and K. C. Stewart. *Props* E. Dyer.

Cast Priscilla Dean (*Blue Jean Billie*), Thurston Hall (*Algernon P. Smythe, alias Lord Harry "English Harry" Chesterton*), J. Milton Ross (*Detective Wood*), Sam De Grasse (*Shaver Michael, Billie's accomplice*), Jean Calhoun (*Muriel Vanderflip*), Andrew Robson, Mary Gunn, Wilton Taylor, Sam Polo.

Crime Drama Another "super-crook" adventure with Priscilla Dean as Blue Jean Billie, a thief who crashes a fashionable party and carries off an English lord, intending to ask ransom for his return. Billie inadvertently falls in love with her captive and vows to reform, beginning with the return of the stolen merchandise. The nobleman is revealed as a notorious English thief who thwarts Billie's former accomplice's attempt to double-cross her, then decides to reform with his lover. "The picture is really the result of a strong and intelligent combination of star, director, author. The suspense, instead of being worked up gradually, starting somewhere from the middle of the picture, is in full force right from the beginning and is kept up all the way through to the last scene. . . . It seems that director Browning has staked his all to produce a picture that is distinctive, and he has succeeded." (P. S. Harrison, *Motion Picture News,* April 19, 1919)

Note Working title: *Raggedy Ann*. Location scenes filmed in the San Bernardino Valley, California.

THE UNPAINTED WOMAN

Universal Film Manufacturing Company, Inc. A Universal Special Attraction. 23 May 1919 (New York opening) [©Universal Film Manufacturing Company, Inc.; 9 May 1919; LP13698]. Silent; black & white. Six reels (5,427 feet).

Director Tod Browning. *Scenario* Waldemar Young, based on the short story "Prairie Gold," by Sinclair Lewis (*Saturday Evening Post*). *Camera* Allen G. Siegler. *Original Camera* Alfred G. Gosden. *Assistant Directors* Fred Tyler and K. C. Stewart. *Props* E. Dyer.

Cast Mary MacLaren (*Gudrun Trygavson*), Thurston Hall (*Martin O'Neill*), David Butler (*Charley Holt*), Laura Lavarnie (*Mrs. Holt, Charley's mother*), Fritzie Ridgeway (*Edna*), Willard Louis (*Heine Lorber*), Carl Stockdale (*Pliny*), Lydia Yeamans Titus (*Mrs. Hawes*), Mickey Moore (*Olaf*), Sam De Grasse.

Rural Drama Charley Holt, son of one of the town's "best families," marries beneath himself. Estranged from his family, ridiculed by the townspeople, and driven to alcohol, Charley dies in a drunken melee. His wife, Gudrun, is determined to make a better place in the world for herself and her son. She makes her farm a paying proposition and reforms a drunken tramp, who, after rescuing Gudrun and her child from a blazing fire, marries her. "In certain respects [*The Unpainted Woman*] breaks virgin soil in the presentation of American farm life in the Middle West. It is a tale of the wheat country, firm in its portrayal of varied rural types and gripping and vivid in its pathetic picture of the heroine's struggle to find happiness in her difficult environment." (Robert C. McElravy, *Moving Picture World,* May 31, 1919)

Note   Working title: *Prairie Gold.* Location scenes filmed in the Imperial Valley, California.

THE PETAL ON THE CURRENT
Universal Film Manufacturing Company, Inc. A Universal Special Attraction. 28 Jul 1919 [©Universal Film Manufacturing Company, Inc.; 18 Jul 1919; LP13967]. Silent; black & white. Six reels.

Presented by   R. H. Cochrane. *Director*   Tod Browning. *Scenario*   Waldemar Young, based on the novelette "The Petal on the Current," by Fanny Hurst (*Cosmopolitan Magazine,* June 1918). *Camera*   William Fildew. *Assistant Director*   Fred Tyler. *Props*   W. Kegker.

Cast   Mary MacLaren (*Stella Schump*), Gertrude Claire (*Stella's mother*), Fritzie Ridgeway (*Cora Kinealy*), Robert Anderson (*John Gilley*), Beatrice Burnham (*Gertie Cobb*), Victor Potel (*Skinny Flint*), David Butler (*Ed Kinealy*).

Rural Drama   Moving the background of the original Fanny Hurst story from New York to San Francisco, Browning relates the story of an innocent woman sentenced in night court by the erroneous testimony of a police officer. Fortunately, a helpful hero arrives to aid the lady in distress. "A drama portraying the difficulties of the poor working girl after she took her first glass of beer. The star is very effective in a role that fits her style of acting and the cast is entirely satisfactory. The story . . . will hold the attention to the last. However, the director and continuity writer did not rise to the heights demanded by the story in the last reel and this takes away from what promised to be a real smashing picture." (Tom Hamlin, *Motion Picture News,* August 9, 1919)

Note   Location scenes filmed in San Francisco, California.

BONNIE, BONNIE LASSIE
Universal Film Manufacturing Company, Inc. A Universal Special Attraction. 5 Oct 1919 [©Universal Film Manufacturing Company, Inc.; 1 Oct 1919; LP14258]. Silent; black & white. Six reels.

Director Tod Browning. *Scenario* Violet Clark and Tod Browning. *Original Scenario* Waldemar Young, based on the novelette "Auld Jeremiah," by Henry Cottrell Rowland (*Ainslee's Magazine*). *Camera* William Fildew. *Assistant Director* Fred Tyler.

Cast Mary MacLaren (*Ailsa Graeme*), Spottiswoode Aitken (*Jeremiah Wishart*), David Butler (*David*), Arthur Edmund Carewe (*Archibald Loveday*), Fred A. Turner, Clarissa Selwyn, Eugenie Forde.

Comedy "They don't make them as good as this one very often nowadays. Comedy, drama, romance—all these elements have been combined to make *Bonnie, Bonnie Lassie* a picture that is enjoyable, amusing, and entertaining. The story is simple, but it is in this very simplicity that its charm lies. It depicts a millionaire (Jeremiah Wishart), a very old man, who hates his relatives, because they all wish him to die so that they can inherit his millions. The only one he likes is his nephew (David), a jolly young man, who always succeeds in getting some change out of his uncle. A young lassie (Ailsa Graeme) comes from Scotland to her aunt in America. At the request of her father, she visits the old millionaire, an old friend of his. The millionaire is charmed with this young girl. He decides she would make a good wife for his nephew. The nephew, before seeing the girl, refuses, telling his uncle he would rather have the money without a wife." (*Harrison's Reports,* November 8, 1919)

Note Working title: *Auld Jeremiah.* Location scenes filmed in San Francisco, California.

THE POINTING FINGER

Universal Film Manufacturing Company, Inc. 1 Dec 1919 [©Universal Film Manufacturing Company, Inc.; 10 Dec 1919; LP14525]. Silent; black & white. Five reels (4,800 feet).

Supervised by Tod Browning. *Director* Edward Kull. *Original Director* Edward Morrissey. *Scenario* Violet Clark, based on the short story "No Experience Required," by Frank R. Adams (*Munsey's Magazine,* January 1917). *Camera* Howard Oswald and William Fildew. *Assistant Director* Duke Lee.

Cast Mary MacLaren (*Mary Murphy*), David Butler (*David*), Johnnie Cook (*William Saxton*), Carl Stockdale (*Grosset*), Lydia Knott (*Matron*), Charlotte Woods (*Matron's assistant*).

Drama   This film's critical drubbing could have been the result of a director change during production or due to Browning's preoccupation with completing *The Virgin of Stamboul.* "Universal probably didn't intend this for a comedy, but it's so darned nonsensical all the way through that folks will feel inclined to laugh at it instead of sympathizing with the poor little orphan girl played by Mary MacLaren. . . . The story of the little girl, who, tired of the orphanage drudgery, makes her escape, is coupled with another familiar picture idea, that of the eccentric bug-collector." (*Wid's Daily,* December 7, 1919) "The only wonder of it is that Mary MacLaren would consent to play in such a feature as *The Pointed [sic] Finger.* Certain it is that if she was imposed upon, and certain it is that everyone who pays good money to see the picture will feel themselves imposed upon. It only has a few moments which are not drenched in stupidity." (Helen Rockwell, *Exhibitor's Trade Review,* December 6, 1919)

Note   Working title: *No Experience Required.* Location scenes filmed in the Wrigley Mansion, Pasadena, California. Paul Powell was originally announced to direct this film.

THE VIRGIN OF STAMBOUL

Universal Film Manufacturing Company, Inc. A Universal-Jewel De Luxe Production. 21 Mar 1920 (New York City premiere) [©Universal Film Manufacturing Company, Inc.; 23 Mar 1920; LP14919]. Silent; black & white. Eight reels (preview length); seven reels (release length).

Presented by   Carl Laemmle. *Director* Tod Browning. *Scenario* Tod Browning and William Parker, based on the story "Undraped," by H. H. Van Loan. *Camera* William Fildew. *Supervising Editor* Edward M. Roskam. *Editor* Viola Lawrence. *Assistant Directors*   Fred Tyler, Frank Messenger, and Leo McCarey. *Music Accompaniment arranged by*   Max Winkler.

Cast   Priscilla Dean (*Sari, the beggar girl*), Eugenie Forde (*Sari's mother*), Wheeler Oakman (*Captain Carlisle Pemberton, in charge of the Black Horse Troop*), Wallace Beery (*Achmet Hamid*), E. Alyn Warren (*Yusef Bey, bazaar keeper*), Edward Burns (*Hector Baron, an American tourist*), Nigel de Brulier (*Kaptain Kassan*), Ethel Ritchie (*Resha*), Clyde Benson (*Diplomat*), Yvette Mitchell.

Drama   "*The Virgin of Stamboul* is 7,000 feet of satisfaction. If you shouldn't know what 7,000 feet of satisfaction is—why, just go to the Strand theater this week. . . . Tod Browning has done some really remarkable directing. He handled the crowd scenes skillfully and made the actors live their characterizations. The settings are elaborate—extremely so—and everything about it bespeaks lavishness." (*San Francisco Chronicle,* May 10, 1920) "It isn't the sort of play to win the favor of those who lean toward the aesthetic in films, but the folk who delight in ardent love-making, snappy action, sinister villains and hand-to-hand combat will surely pronounce it as the real thing in thrills and spectacular punch. . . . The Oriental atmosphere is wonderfully developed and maintained." (*Exhibitor's Trade Review,* April 20, 1920)

Note Working titles: *Undraped* and *The Beautiful Beggar.* Location scenes filmed in Oxnard, California, and in Arizona.

OUTSIDE THE LAW
Universal Film Manufacturing Company, Inc. A Universal-Jewel De Luxe Production. 20 Dec 1920 (Los Angeles opening); Jan 1921 (general release) [©Universal Film Manufacturing Company, Inc.; 25 Jan 1921; LP16049]. Silent; black & white. Eight reels (7,754 feet).

Carl Laemmle *offers A Tod Browning Production. Producer-Director* Tod Browning. *Scenario* Lucien Hubbard and Tod Browning. *Story* Tod Browning. *Additional Story (uncredited)* Garrett E. Fort. *Camera* William Fildew. *Assistant Director* Leo McCarey. *Subtitles* Gardner Bradford. *Art Director* E. E. Sheeley. *Art Titles* Lewis Lipton and Fred Archer. *Consultant* Tom Gubbins. *Still Photographer* Roman Freulich. *Props* Joe Cooke.

Cast Priscilla Dean (*Molly "Silky Moll" Madden*), Wheeler Oakman (*"Dapper Bill" Ballard*), Lon Chaney (*"Black Mike" Sylva/Ah Wing*), Ralph Lewis (*"Silent" Madden*), E. Alyn Warren (*Chang Low, a Chinese philosopher*), Stanley Goethals (*"That Kid Across the Hall"*), Melbourne MacDowell (*Morgan Spencer*), Wilton Taylor (*Inspector*), John George (*Humpy, a member of Black Mike's gang*).

Crime Drama ". . . as Tod Browning has written, cast, and directed *Outside the Law,* there is practically a thrill a minute guaranteed . . . [there is also] a sprinkling of morals as a kind of thematic deodorant. . . . Priscilla Dean is a convincingly human sort of crook, and she is splendidly assisted by Lon Chaney. . . ." (*Photoplay,* April 1921) "Those who like crook melodrama with scenes in Chinatown are certainly going to like *Outside the Law,* for it is much bigger than anything of the kind we have seen." (*New York Tribune,* January 16, 1921) ". . . thoroughly attractive to the eye and it is also exceptionally fine from a photographic standpoint

. . . [but] an artificial story of this type, even when sumptuously mounted, will doubtless prove tiring to many spectators." (*Moving Picture World,* January 22, 1921)

Note Rereleased on May 9, 1926, in a slightly recut form with new titles. Remade in 1930 (see later entry). Location scenes filmed in San Francisco, California.

SOCIETY SECRETS
Universal Film Manufacturing Company, Inc. 21 Feb 1921 [©Universal Film Manufacturing Company, Inc.; 18 Feb 1921; LP16166]. Silent; black & white. Five reels (4,795 feet).

Presented by Carl Laemmle. *Supervised by* Tod Browning. *Director* Leo McCarey. *Scenario* Douglas Z. Doty. Based on the story "It's Never Too Late to Mend," by Helen Christine Bennett. *Camera* William Fildew. *Assistant Director* William Tummel.

Cast Eva Novak (*Louise Kerran*), Gertrude Claire (*Mrs. Kerran, her mother*), George Berrell (*Amos Kerran, her father*), Clarissa Selwyn (*Aunt*), William Buckley (*Arthur*), Ethel Ritchie (*Maybelle*), L. C. Shumway (*George*), Carl Stockdale (*Squire*), Lucy Donahue (*Squire's wife*), Harris Gordon.

Drama "This picture has been given excellent treatment. The characters act as if they were human beings. But the story can hardly be called complete; it is really one big situation, depicting how a son, engaged to a society girl, is ashamed of his parents, who lived in the country, because they are illiterate and have no manners. His fiancée takes a trip to that town, and accidentally becomes acquainted with the old folks. They engage her to teach them manners. She proves a good teacher, and surprises her sweetheart, when she takes them along to the city. The young folk eventually marry." (*Harrison's Reports,* February 26, 1921)

Note Working title: *Plain Folks.*

NO WOMAN KNOWS
Universal Film Manufacturing Company, Inc. A Universal-Jewel De Luxe Production. 4 Sep 1921 (New York premiere) [©Universal Film Manufacturing Company, Inc.; 17 Sep 1921; LP16969]. Silent; tinted deep dark blue. Seven reels (7,031 feet).

Carl Laemmle   *offers A Tod Browning Production. Producer-Director* Tod Browning. *Scenario* Tod Browning and George M. Yohalem, based on the short story "Fanny Herself," by Edna Ferber (*Cosmopolitan Magazine,* 1917). *Camera* William Fildew. *Assistant Director* Leo McCarey.

Cast Mabel Julienne Scott (*Fanny Brandeis*), Stuart Holmes (*Michael Fenger*), John Davidson (*Theodore Brandeis*), Grace Marvin (*Molly Brandeis, the mother*), Max Davidson (*Ferdinand Brandeis, the father*), E. Alyn Warren (*Rabbi Thalman*), Dick Cummings (*Father Fitzpatrick*), Snitz Edwards (*Herr Bauer*), Joseph Swickard (*Shaublitz, the famous violinist*), Danny Hoy (*Aloysius*), Earle Schenk (*Clarence Heyl*), Raymond Lee (*Little Theodore Brandeis*), Bernice Radom (*Little Fanny Brandeis*), Joseph Stearns (*Little Clarence Heyl*), Dorothy Dein (*Little Bella*).

Drama A tear-jerking family drama, adapted from a best-selling story/ novel. The story of a Jewish mother's sacrifice for her children. "Its sole important fault lies in the fact that the occasional humor that comes into even the most pathetic lives is not brought in for relief. The power that is already in the picture would be increased if the drabness were relieved now and again in a natural way . . . the utter somberness just escapes taking the edge off the picture. Nevertheless, there are many who like their pathos raw." (*Moving Picture World,* September 24, 1921)

Note Working title: *Fanny Herself.* Edna Ferber's story was also published in book form in 1917. Originally purchased as a vehicle for Carmel Myers.

THE WISE KID
Universal Film Manufacturing Company, Inc. A Universal Special Attraction. 3 Mar 1922 (St. Louis premiere) [©Universal Film Manufacturing Company, Inc.; 22 Feb 1922; LP17577]. Silent; black & white. Five reels (4,606 feet).

Presented by Carl Laemmle. *Director* Tod Browning. *Scenario* Wallace Clifton, based on the short story "Kind Deeds," by William Slavens McNutt (*Metropolitan Magazine,* September 1921). *Camera* William Fildew. *Assistant Director* Leo McCarey.

Cast Gladys Walton (*Rosie Cooper*), David Butler (*Freddie Smith, the baker boy*), Hallam Cooley (*Harry*), Hector V. Sarno (*Tony Rossi*), Henry A. Barrows (*Jefferson Southwick*), C. Norman Hammond (*Mr. Haverty*).

Comedy Drama "Rosie Cooper is cashier in a cheap restaurant and among those she favors is . . . Smith, the bakery boy. Rose is a 'wise kid' all right, but it takes her some time to see through a shiny young thin model gent. . . . The girl entertains his advances because he means romance to her. But he proves his shallow character and Rosie is glad to turn to Jimmy, the bakery youth." (*Motion Picture News Booking Guide*, October 1922) "A more than pleasant reaction from the tiresome Pollyanna fairy tales . . . the continuity writer and director have made the most of every situation and character. . . ." (*Moving Picture World*, March 4, 1922) "Some jazz, a few clever titles, a slightly mutilated story. . . . Not much to think about, but fairly good entertainment. It will teach the children new slang." (*Photoplay*, May 1922)

Note Working title: *Kind Deeds*. Henry B. Walthall may also have appeared in the film.

THE MAN UNDER COVER

Universal Film Manufacturing Company, Inc. A Universal Special Attraction. 10 Apr 1922 [©Universal Film Manufacturing Company, Inc.; 4 Apr 1922; LP17728]. Silent; black & white. Five reels (4,566 feet).

Presented by Carl Laemmle. *Director* Tod Browning. *Scenario* Harvey H. Gates, based on the original story "Peterman," by Louis Victor Eytinge. *Camera* Virgil E. Miller. *Assistant Director* Leo McCarey.

Cast Herbert Rawlinson (*Paul Porter*), George Hernandez (*Martin "Daddy" Moffat*), Barbara Bedford (*Margaret Langdon*), William Courtwright (*Mayor Harper*), George Webb (*Colonel E. Jones Wiley*), Edwin Booth Tilton (*"Coal Oil" Chase*), Gerald Pring (*Holt Langdon*), Willis Marks (*Colonel Culpepper*), Betty Eliason, Betty Stone (*The Kiddies*).

Comedy Drama "This 'crook' story is convincing—perhaps because L. V. Eytinge, the author, is serving a life sentence in prison. . . . There are quite a few nice comfy thrills and the ending is quite satisfactory. For the family." (*Photoplay*, June 1922) "Tod Browning . . . has caught the atmosphere of the story so well that the action proceeds like clockwork." (*Motion Picture News*)

Note Working title: *Peterman*.

UNDER TWO FLAGS

Universal Film Manufacturing Company, Inc. A Universal-Jewel De Luxe Production. 24 Sep 1922 (New York premiere) [©Universal Film Manufacturing Company, Inc.; 21 Sep 1922; LP18229]. Silent; black & white. Eight reels (7,407 feet).

Presented by Carl Laemmle. *Director* Tod Browning. *Scenario* Edward T. Lowe, Jr. and Elliott Clawson. *Adaptation* Tod Browning and Edward T. Lowe, Jr., based on the novel *Under Two Flags,* by Ouida (Philadelphia, 1867) and the stage play of the same name, as first produced in New York at the Garden Theatre, opening on February 5, 1901 [closed after 133 performances]. *Camera* William Fildew. *Film Editor* Errol Taggart. *Art Director* E. E. Sheeley. *Assistant Director* Leo McCarey. *Titles* Gardner Bradford.

Cast Priscilla Dean (*Cigarette*), James Kirkwood (*Bertie Cecil, alias Corporal Victor*), John Davidson (*Sheik Ben Ali Hammed*), Stuart Holmes (*Marquis de Chateauroy*), Ethel Grey Terry (*Princess Corona d'Amaque*), Robert Mack (*Rake*), Burton Law (*The sheik's aide*), Albert Pollet (*Captain Tollaire*), W. H. Bainbridge (*The colonel*).

Melodrama With the craze brought on by *The Sheik* for more desert epics, Browning's effort to transform Priscilla Dean into a female Rudolph Valentino was, at best, a second-rate adventure tale. "The public's recent craze for desert atmosphere manifests itself in the adaptation of another popular story. . . . For those who expect a picture full of thrills and action from start to finish, *Under Two Flags* will prove a big disappointment. It moves slowly at the start, emphasizing many unimportant sequences, but reaches a fiery climax. . . ." (*Detroit News,* December 4, 1922) ". . . a vivid bit of screen portraiture. Mr. Browning, who directed it, managed to get every ha-penny's worth of good work there was to get out of a cast of capable people. . . . That wildfire of the silversheet, Miss Priscilla Dean, never had a role that suited her better." (*Chicago Daily Tribune,* September 26, 1922)

DRIFTING
Universal Film Manufacturing Company, Inc. A Universal-Jewel De Luxe Production. 19 Aug 1923 (New York premiere) [©Universal Film Manufacturing Company, Inc.; 31 Jul 1923; LP19262]. Silent; black & white. Eight reels (7,394 feet).

Presented by Carl Laemmle. *Director* Tod Browning. *Scenario* A. P. Younger, based on the stage play *Drifting,* by John Colton and Daisy N. Andrews, as first produced by William A. Brady in New York at the Playhouse Theatre, opening on January 2, 1922 [closed after 63 performances]. *Camera* William Fildew. *Film Editor* Errol Taggart. *Titles* Gardner Bradford. *Assistant Director* Leo McCarey.

Cast Priscilla Dean (*Cassie Cook, alias Lucille Preston*), Matt Moore (*Captain Arthur Jarvis*), Wallace Beery (*Jules Repin*), J. Farrell MacDonald (*Murphy*), Rose Dione (*Madame Polly Voo*), Edna Tichenor (*Molly Norton*), William V. Mong (*Dr. Li*), Anna May Wong (*Rose Li, his daughter*), Bruce Guerin (*Billy Hepburn*), Marie De Albert (*Mrs. Hepburn*), William Moran (*Mr. Hepburn*), Frank Lanning (*Chang Wang*), Tully Marshall.

Melodrama Priscilla Dean is the "Poppy Queen," an opium smuggler in Indochina who falls in love with the government agent sent to break up her operation. "The Chinese atmosphere of *Drifting*, the film presentation this week at the Capitol, has been unusually well carried out, and although the story has a somewhat abrupt termination, it is nevertheless interesting and in spots quite thrilling." (*New York Times,* August 20, 1923) "If we remember correctly, *Drifting* was not received with any great enthusiasm when it was presented here on the stage. We did not see it, but if it was half as dull as the picture, which opened yesterday, we have no regrets on that score. . . . The man who viewed *Drifting* with us had seen very few pictures and he kept asking questions similar to 'Daddy, what is that?' 'That, my son, is a cow.' 'Daddy, why?' And we couldn't answer that." (*New York Tribune,* August 20, 1923)

THE DAY OF FAITH

Goldwyn Pictures Corporation/Goldwyn-Cosmopolitan Distributing Corporation. 21 Oct 1923 [©Goldwyn Pictures Corporation; 11 Nov 1923; LP19742]. Silent; black & white. Seven reels (6,557 feet).

Director Tod Browning. *Scenario* June Mathis and Katherine Kavanaugh, based on the novel *The Day of Faith,* by Arthur Somers Roche (Boston, 1921). *Camera* William Fildew. *Additional Camera* Paul Kerschner. *Assistant Director* Errol Taggart. *Art Director* Cedric Gibbons. *Titles* Tom Miranda.

Cast Eleanor Boardman (*Jane Maynard*), [Frederick] Tyrone Power (*Michael Anstell*), Raymond Griffith (*Tom Barnett*), Wallace MacDonald (*John Anstell*), Ford Sterling (*Montreal Sammy*), Charles Conklin (*Yegg Darby*), Ruby Lafayette (*Granny Maynard*), Jane Mercer (*Red Johnson's child*), Edward Martindell (*Uncle Mortimer*), Winter Hall (*Bland Hendricks*), Emmett King (*Simmons*), Jack Curtis (*Red Johnson*), Frederick Vroom (*Marley May-*

nard), John Curry (*Isaac, Red Johnson's child*), Henry Hebert (*Samuel Jackson*), Myles McCarthy (*Kelly*), Robert Dudley (*Morris*), Mattie Peters (*Maid*), Frances Hatton (*Trained nurse*), William Star, Ina Anson, Carmel Myers (?), Wallie Van (?).

Melodrama With his departure from Universal, Browning took on a one-picture contract with Goldwyn, directing this minor work, undoubtedly affected by his deteriorating mental condition. "A melodramatic story based upon the psychology that faith will cure anything, superbly directed and unusually cast. . . . The picture drags immeasurably in spots, but is exceptionally well acted." (*Variety,* November 29, 1923) "*The Day of Faith* is a fine picture—unafraid of being forceful to achieve its points, and aiming to do something more than just amuse." (*Morning Telegraph,* November 26, 1923)

Note The source novel for this film was originally published serially in *Collier's Weekly* in 1921. Filmed between May 14 and August 10, 1923.

WHITE TIGER
Universal Film Manufacturing Company, Inc. A Universal-Jewel De Luxe Production. 20 Dec 1923 (San Francisco premiere) [©Universal Film Manufacturing Company, Inc.; 13 Nov 1923; LP19608]. Silent; black & white. Eight reels (7,177 feet).

Presented by Carl Laemmle. *Director* Tod Browning. *Scenario* Charles Kenyon and Tod Browning. *Story* Tod Browning. *Camera* William Fildew. *Film Editor* Errol Taggart. *Titles* Gardner Bradford. *Art Director* E. E. Sheeley. *Assistant Director* Leo McCarey.

Cast Priscilla Dean (*Sylvia Donovan*), Matt Moore (*Detective Dick Longworth*), Raymond Griffith (*Roy Donovan*), Wallace Beery (*Bill Hawkes, alias Count Donelli*), Alfred Allen (*Mike Donovan*).

Crime Drama Sylvia Donovan, Roy Donovan, and Count Donelli are international crooks who come to the United States to swindle high society with a mechanical chess player. While Sylvia falls in love with Dick Longworth, one of their intended victims, she learns that Ray is actually her brother and that Donelli is Bill Hawkes, who murdered their father. Fate allows for Hawkes' disposal and the Donovans are reformed. "Tod Browning's latest crook drama for Universal is somewhat of a departure. For the greater part, it is minus the expected action and thrills. . . . *White Tiger* is not altogether satisfying as an attraction for the majority. It is vague in purpose and passive in mood, compared to the Universal-Jewel standard." (*Moving Picture World,* November 23, 1923)

Note   Working title: *Lady Raffles.* Filmed before *Drifting,* this film was actually released after Browning's Universal contract had expired and he had moved to Goldwyn. Location scenes filmed in Manhattan and at Coney Island in Brooklyn, New York.

THE DANGEROUS FLIRT

Gothic Pictures/Film Booking Offices of America. 19 Oct 1924 [©R-C Pictures Corporation; 19 Oct 1924; LP20795]. Silent; black & white. Six reels (5,297 feet).

Director   Tod Browning. *Adaptation*   E. Richard Schayer, based on the story "The Prude," by Julie Herne. *Photography*   Lucien Andriot and Maynard Rugg. *Assistant Director*   Fred Tyler.

Cast   Evelyn Brent (*Sheila Fairfax*), Edward Earle (*Dick Morris*), Sheldon Lewis (*Don Alfonso*), Clarissa Selwynne (*Aunt Prissy [Priscilla Fairfax]*), Pierre Gendron (*Captain Ramon José Gonzales*), Ben Deely.

Melodrama   In her first starring performance in an FBO attraction, Evelyn Brent is seen as a naïve woman who was reared by a puritanical spinster aunt. She is fearful of marriage to the man she loves, and on her wedding night her husband mistakes her timidity for disgust. He leaves, but she chases him to South America, where they are reunited. "This drama is well-acted, with Evelyn Brent as the girl scoring repeatedly . . . her scenes where the husband, played by Edward Earle, misunderstands her timidity are marvels of realism and dramatic force, and the point the story sets out to make is unmistakably accomplished." (*Moving Picture World,* November 29, 1924)

Note   Working title: *The Prude.* British title: *A Dangerous Flirtation.*

SILK STOCKING SAL

Gothic Pictures/Film Booking Offices of America. 30 Nov 1924 [©R-C Pictures Corporation; 30 Nov 1924; LP20927]. Silent; black & white. Six reels (5,367 feet).

Director   Tod Browning. *Scenario and Story*   E. Richard Schayer. *Photography*   Silvano Balboni. *Assistant Director*   Fred Tyler.

Cast Evelyn Brent (*"Stormy" Sal Martin*), Robert Ellis (*Bob Cooper*), Earl Metcalfe (*Bull Reagan*), Alice Browning (*Bargain Basement Annie [The Wop]*), Virginia Madison (*Mrs. Cooper, Bob's mother*), Marylynn Warner (*Miss Cooper*), John Gough (*The Gopher, a member of the gang*), Louis Fitzroy (*Abner Bingham*).

Melodrama Browning was on the wagon by the time this film was begun, having sworn off hard liquor. To celebrate his reconciliation with his wife, the director gave her a small role as a member of a gang of jewel thieves. The dramatic punch of the story evolves from a murder, the identity of the killer being a mystery to the players. ". . . there is not only considerable action, but real hair-trigger suspense developed because of the good work of the players, excellent direction, and the clever manner in which the heroine uses all of her feminine wiles to taunt the crook into making the desired confession. . . . *Silk Stocking Sal* should provide good entertainment for patrons who like plenty of punch and suspense." (*Moving Picture World*, January 3, 1925)

THE UNHOLY THREE

Metro-Goldwyn-Mayer Corporation. 30 May 1925 (San Francisco premiere) [©Metro-Goldwyn-Mayer Corporation; 24 Jun 1925; LP21593]. Silent; black & white, with tinted sequences. Seven reels (6,948 feet).

Presented by Louis B. Mayer. *A Tod Browning Production. Director* Tod Browning. *Scenario* Waldemar Young, based on the novel *The Unholy Three,* by Clarence Aaron "Tod" Robbins (New York, 1917). *Photography* David Kesson. *Settings* Cedric Gibbons and Joseph Wright. *Film Editor* Daniel J. Gray.

Cast Lon Chaney (*Professor Echo, the ventriloquist*), Mae Busch (*Rosie O'Grady*), Matt Moore (*Hector McDonald*), Victor McLaglen (*Hercules*), Harry Earles (*Tweedledee*), Matthew Betz (*Regan*), Edward Connelly (*Judge*), William Humphreys (*Defense attorney*), E. Alyn Warren (*Prosecuting attorney*), John Merkyl (*Jeweler*), Percy Williams (*Butler*), Charles Wellesley (*John Arlington*), Marjorie Morton (*Mrs. Arlington*), Violet Cane (*Their little girl*), Lou Morrison (*Police commissioner*), Walter Perry (*Announcer in dime museum*), Alice Julian (*Fat lady deluxe*), Walter P. Cole (*Human skeleton*), Peter Kortos (*Sword swallower*), Vera Vance (*Dancer*), John Millerta (*Wild Borneo man*), Delmo Fritz (*Sword swallower[?]*), Mickey McBan (*Boy watching Hercules' act*), Louis Shank (*Newsboy*).

Melodrama ". . . one of the finest pictures ever made, due to the able and clever direction of Tod Browning." (*Photoplay,* July 1925) "Not often does one see so powerful a photodrama as *The Unholy Three.* . . . a stirring story stocked with original twists and situations, a picture that teems with surprises. . . . the suspense is kept as taut as the string of a bow." (*New York Times,* August 4, 1925) "[Browning] has risen far above the story, which is, especially at the end, as full of holes as a sieve and again has proved the old Shakespearian adage that 'the direction's the thing.' " (*New Yorker,* August 1925)

Note Principal photography: December 22, 1924, to January 20, 1925. French title: *Le Club des Trois.* Robbins' novel was first published in story form in *New York Magazine* in 1917.

DOLLAR DOWN

Tiffany Productions, Co-Artists Productions/Truart Film Corporation. 16 Aug 1925 [©Truart Film Corporation; 19 Oct 1925; LP21917]. Silent; black & white. Six reels (6,318 feet).

Director Tod Browning. *Scenario* Frederick Stowers. *Story* Jan Courthope and Ethel Hill. *Photography* Allen Thompson.

Cast Ruth Roland (*Ruth Craig*), Henry B. Walthall (*Alec Craig*), Maym Kelso (*Mrs. Craig*), Earl Schenck (*Grant Elliot*), Claire McDowell (*Mrs. Meadows*), Roscoe Karns (*Gene Meadows*), Jane Mercer (*Betty Meadows*), Lloyd Whitlock (*Howard Steele*), Otis Harlan (*Norris*), Edward Borman (*Tilton*), Michael Dark, Madison Wing, Toby Wing, Sonnie Walker.

Melodrama Although slated for release in July 1924, this was the first of the three films Browning directed at FBO, the others being *The Dangerous Flirt* and *Silk Stocking Sal* (see above). The reportedly poor quality of the production held up its release until after Browning scored with *The Unholy Three.* "It's possible that this story looked quite good on paper. It doesn't work out that way. . . . Any exhibitor may sidestep this with perfect safety. It's guaranteed to irritate any audience." (*Variety,* August 12, 1925)

THE MYSTIC

Metro-Goldwyn-Mayer Corporation. 30 Aug 1925 (New York premiere) [©Metro-Goldwyn-Mayer Corporation; 11 Sep 1925; LP21824]. Silent; black & white. Seven reels (6,147 feet).

Presented by Louis B. Mayer. *A Tod Browning Production. Director* Tod Browning. *Scenario* Waldemar Young. *Story* Tod Browning. *Photography* Ira H. Morgan. *Assistant Camera* Willard Sheldon. *Settings* Cedric Gibbons and Hervey Libbert. *Gowns* Erté. *Film Editor* Frank Sullivan. *Assistant Director* Errol Taggart. *Titles* Joseph W. Farnham.

Cast Aileen Pringle (*Zara*), Conway Tearle (*Michael Nash*), Mitchell Lewis (*Zazarack*), Robert Ober (*Anton*), Stanton Heck (*Carlo*), David Torrence (*James Bradshaw*), Gladys Hulette (*Doris Merrick*), DeWitt Jennings (*Inspector of police*).

Melodrama ". . . interesting in spite of the flaws in the story. Mr. Browning is an expert in such tales, which he unfolds with delightful originality. He has a tendency, however, to forget the hand of the law, and he has matters turn out rather too easily for his criminals." (*New York Times*, September 6, 1925) "While I was still under the spell of *The Unholy Three* I announced with great fervor that Mr. Browning was henceforth this department's favorite supervisor of motion picture thrillers. I now reserve decision on the question, for if Mr. Browning is going to repeat a formula in his various movies—as is the occasional habit of D. W. Griffith—he isn't as bright and original a master of the wicked, the untrue, and the beautiful as I thought he was. This may or may not put him in the hospital with despairing grief, but movie critics must have their say. . . ." (*New York Sun*, September 1, 1925)

Note Principal photography: April 8 to May 11, 1925.

THE BLACK BIRD

Metro-Goldwyn-Mayer Corporation. 10 Jan 1926 [©Metro-Goldwyn-Mayer Corporation; 29 Jan 1926; LP22381]. Silent; black & white. Seven reels (6,688 feet).

Presented by Louis B. Mayer. *A Tod Browning Production. Director* Tod Browning. *Scenario* Waldemar Young. *Story* Tod Browning. *Photography* Percy Hilburn. *Settings* Cedric Gibbons and A. Arnold Gillespie. *Wardrobe* Kathleen Kay and Maude Marsh [André-Ami]. *Film Editor* Errol Taggart. *Titles* Joseph W. Farnham.

Cast Lon Chaney (*Dan Tate, alias the Black Bird and the Bishop of Limehouse*), Renée Adorée (*Fifi Lorraine*), Owen Moore (*Bertram P. Gladye, alias West End Bertie*), Doris Lloyd (*Limehouse Polly, Dan's ex-wife*), Andy MacLennan (*Ghost, the Shadow*), William Weston (*Red*), Eric Mayne (*Sightseer*), Sid-

ney Bracy (*Bertie's no. 1 man*), Ernie S. Adams (*Bertie's no. 2 man*), Cecil
Holland (*Old man at mission*), Louise Emmons (*Old lady at mission*), Eddie
Sturgis (*The bartender*), Polly Moran (*Flower woman*), Frank Norcross (*English music-hall announcer*), Willie Fung (*Chinese man*), Lionel Belmore,
James T. Mack, Peggy Best.

Melodrama Chaney in a role playing two characters, the straight-shaped
crook and his crippled brother, the Bishop of Limehouse. "Mr. Browning
here glibly refutes the accusation that he is a flash-in-the-pan or an accident. The introduction of this film story is excellent with a series of close-
ups of greedy and wicked faces fading in and out in a light fog. This
director not only has a keen eye for detail, but he gives a good reason for
everything that is done." (*New York Times,* February 1, 1926) "There is no
one working in the medium of the screen who has the ability of Mr.
Browning to cast a fitful, horrendous, evil glow over a given motion picture melodrama." (*New York Sun,* February 2, 1926)

Note Working title: *The Mocking Bird.* Principal photography: October 29
to November 28, 1925.

THE ROAD TO MANDALAY

Metro-Goldwyn-Mayer Corporation. 26 Jun 1926 [©Metro-Goldwyn-Mayer
Corporation; 12 Jul 1926; LP22907]. Silent; black & white. Seven reels
(6,551 feet).

Presented by Louis B. Mayer. *A Tod Browning Production. Director* Tod
Browning. *Scenario* Elliott Clawson and Waldemar Young. *Story* Tod
Browning and Herman J. Mankiewicz. *Photography* Merritt B. Gerstad.
Settings Cedric Gibbons and A. Arnold Gillespie. *Film Editor* Errol Taggart. *Titles* Joseph W. Farnham. *Still Photographer* Longworth. *Chaney's
Eye Shield* Dr. Hugo Kiefer.

Cast Lon Chaney (*Singapore Joe*), Lois Moran (*Rosemary, Joe's daughter*),
Owen Moore (*The admiral, Edward Herrington*), Henry B. Walthall (*Father
James Stevens, Joe's brother*), Kamiyama Sojin (*"English Charlie" Wing*), Rose
Langdon (*Pansy*), John George (*Yakmo, the servant*), Willie Fung (*Chinese
man at bar*), Eddie Sturgis (*Bartender*), Virginia Bushman, Lenore Bushman, Robert Seiter, Eric S. Mayne.

Melodrama "True, it gives Lon Chaney another opportunity to tuck a
weird characterization away in his gallery, but the plot is so sordid and
morbid that were it not for the grip of the star's uncanny performance it

would in all likelihood be dismissed as a crass caricature of life. . . . Tod Browning can be depended upon for thrilling melodramas. . . . If his story was as good as his direction, he would have another *Unholy Three* on his hands." (*Motion Picture Magazine,* October 1926) "This picture is quite tedious, and it strikes one that Mr. Browning did not quite know what to do with the players in a number of scenes. They show themselves and talk to one another, employing conventional actions that are helped out by the title writer." (*New York Times,* June 29, 1926)

Note Principal photography: March 29 to April 29, 1926.

THE SHOW

Metro-Goldwyn-Mayer Corporation. 22 Jan 1927 [©Metro-Goldwyn-Mayer Corporation; 24 Jan 1927; LP23586]. Silent; black & white. Seven reels (6,309 feet).

Presented by Louis B. Mayer. *A Tod Browning Production. Director* Tod Browning. *Scenario* Waldemar Young, based on the novel *The Day of Souls,* by Charles Tenney Jackson (Indianapolis, 1910). *Photography* John Arnold. *Settings* Cedric Gibbons and Captain Richard Day. *Film Editor* Errol Taggart. *Wardrobe* Lucia Coulter. *Titles* Joseph W. Farnham. *Casting Director* Cliff Robertson.

Cast John Gilbert (*Cock Robin*), Renée Adorée (*Salome*), Lionel Barrymore (*The Greek*), Edward Connelly (*The Soldier, Salome's blind father*), Gertrude Short (*Lena*), Andy MacLennan (*The Ferret*), Agostino Borgato (*Wise old politician of Budapest*), Dorothy Sebastian (*Salvation Army girl*), Zalla Zarana (*Zela, the Living Half-Lady*), Betty Boyd (*Neptuna, Queen of the Mermaids*), Edna Tichenor (*Arachnida, the Human Spider*), Francis Powers, Jules Cowles, Cecil Holland, Jacqueline Gadsden, Dorothy Seay, Billy Seay, Ida May, Barbara De Bozoky.

Melodrama "*The Show* is an exceptionally tense, forceful, well-constructed melodrama, but its reception by the average patron will depend on whether this outweighs the sordidness of the characters and the story itself, and the gruesomeness of a number of the situations." (*Moving Picture World,* March 19, 1927) "With plenty of action and a colorful background to build upon, Mr. Browning has proceeded in his usual unsentimental fashion to turn out a picture now gay, now sad, always absorbing and at the same time conducive to involuntary shrieks in the audience." (*New York Evening Post,* March 14, 1927)

Note Working titles: *Cock o' the Walk* and *The Day of Souls*. Principal photography: October 11 to November 11, 1926.

THE UNKNOWN

Metro-Goldwyn-Mayer Corporation. 4 Jun 1927 [©Metro-Goldwyn-Mayer Corporation; 27 Jun 1927; LP24123]. Silent; black & white. Six reels (5,517 feet).

Presented by Louis B. Mayer. *A Tod Browning Production. Director* Tod Browning. *Scenario* Waldemar Young. *Story* Tod Browning. *Photography* Merritt B. Gerstad. *Settings* Cedric Gibbons and Captain Richard Day. *Film Editors* Harry Reynolds and Errol Taggart. *Wardrobe* Lucia Coulter. *Titles* Joseph W. Farnham.

Cast Lon Chaney (*Alonzo, the Armless*), Norman Kerry (*Malabar, the Strong Man*), Joan Crawford (*Estrellita*), Nick De Ruiz (*Zanzi, the circus manager, Estrellita's father*), John George (*Cojo, Alonzo's servant*), Frank Lanning (*Costra, a renegade Spanish Gypsy lover*), Billy Seay (*The little waif*), Louise Emmons (*Gypsy woman*), Polly Moran (*Landlady [cut from release version]*), Bobbie Mack (*Gypsy [cut from release version]*), Paul Dismute (*Lon Chaney's stunt double*), John St. Polis.

Melodrama "Mr. Browning's methods of picture making; his avoidance of exteriors and sunlit scenes in favor of black, cavernous interiors, with hideous shadows groping menacingly; his preoccupations with sideshow freaks; his love for the Grand Guignol manner in story telling, have long been recognized, but never before have these traits been as strongly emphasized." (*New York Herald-Tribune,* June 19, 1927) "Like most films in which Lon Chaney and Tod Browning have been associated as star and director, it is artistically acted and skillfully directed. But those facts do not atone for the offense given by the feature to every normal-minded moviegoer. From beginning to end the picture is one horror after another." (*Harrison's Reports,* June 25, 1927) "[*The Unknown*] can hardly be recommended even as moderate entertainment. A visit to the dissecting room in a hospital would be quite as pleasant, and at the same time more instructive." (*New York Evening Post,* June 13, 1927)

Note Working title: *Alonzo, the Armless*. Principal photography: February 7 to March 19, 1927.

LONDON AFTER MIDNIGHT

Metro-Goldwyn-Mayer Corporation. 11 Dec 1927 (New York premiere) [©Metro-Goldwyn-Mayer Distributing Corporation; 3 Dec 1927; LP25289]. Silent; black & white. Six reels (5,687 feet).

Presented by Louis B. Mayer. *A Tod Browning Production. Director* Tod Browning. *Scenario* Waldemar Young and Tod Browning. *Story* Tod Browning. *Camera* Merritt B. Gerstad. *Assistant Photography* Wallace Chewning. *Settings* Cedric Gibbons and Captain Richard Day. *Film Editor* Harry Reynolds. *Wardrobe* Lucia Coulter. *Titles* Joseph W. Farnham. *Unit Manager* George Noffka. *Assistant Director* Harry Sharrock.

Cast Lon Chaney (*Detective Edmund Burke [the Man in the Beaver Hat], alias Colonel Yates, alias Mooney, the vampire man*), Marceline Day (*Lucille Balfour*), Henry B. Walthall (*Sir James Hamlin*), Percy Williams (*Butler*), Conrad Nagel (*Arthur Hibbs*), Polly Moran (*Miss Anne Smithson*), Edna Tichenor (*Lunette, the bat girl*), Claude King (*The Stranger*), Andy McLennan (*One of Burke's Scotland Yard detectives*), Jules Cowles (*Gallagher, the Irish chauffeur*).

Melodrama "Since the screen began some months ago to get itself all worked up over mystery melodramas, no more satisfying, pleasantly gruesome, and, presumably, blood-curdling example of its school has yet been revealed." (*New York Herald-Tribune,* December 12, 1927) "Mr. Chaney's make-up is at times hideous—enough to make one sick in the stomach. The picture succeeds in giving one a creepy feeling." (*Harrison's Reports,* December 24, 1927) "Will add nothing to Chaney's prestige as a trouper, nor increase the star's box office value. With Chaney's name in lights, however, this picture, any picture with Chaney, means a strong box office draw. . . ." (*Variety,* December 14, 1927)

Note Working (and British release) title: *The Hypnotist.* Principal photography: July 23 to August 24, 1927. Browning story was serialized and novelized by Marie Coolidge-Rask. Remade by Browning in 1935 as *Mark of the Vampire* (see below).

THE BIG CITY

Metro-Goldwyn-Mayer Corporation. 18 Feb 1928 [©Metro-Goldwyn-Mayer Distributing Corporation; 18 Feb 1928; LP25205]. Silent; black & white. Seven reels (6,838 feet).

Presented by Louis B. Mayer. *A Tod Browning Production. Director* Tod Browning. *Scenario* Waldemar Young. *Story* Tod Browning. *Photography*

Henry Sharp. *Settings*   Cedric Gibbons and Captain Richard Day. *Film Editor*   Harry Reynolds. *Wardrobe*   Lucia Coulter. *Titles*   Joseph W. Farnham. *Assistant Director*   Harry Sharrock.

Cast   Lon Chaney (*Chuck Collins*), Marceline Day (*Sunshine*), James Murray (*Curly*), Betty Compson (*Helen*), Matthew Betz (*Red Watson*), John George (*The Arab*), Virginia Pearson (*Tennessee*), Walter Percival (*Grogan*), Lew Short (*O'Hara*), Eddie Sturgis (*Blinkie*), Clinton Lyle (*Mobster*), Alfred Allen (*Policeman*), F. Finch-Smiles (*Sunshine's father*), Betty Egan, Dolores Brinkman, Della Peterson (*Ballet dancers*), George H. Redd (*Black waiter*), Nora Cecil.

Melodrama   "Not much better than a light-weight underworld picture for a Metro-Goldwyn-Mayer program release, but with the possible novelty of showing Lon Chaney playing a human being in modern dress. . . . On that score *The Big City* should at least bring the week's average to any house without undue stage assistance." (*Variety*, March 28, 1928) "Browning and Chaney have reached the point of turning out pictures with hammer and saw. Every situation in *The Big City* is a manufactured one, with corners so poorly cut that it does not fit into the one next to it. . . . One absurd scene follows another until the only feature of the picture that is entertaining is the speculation it arouses as to how long the absurdities can last." (*Film Spectator*, April 14, 1928)

WEST OF ZANZIBAR

Metro-Goldwyn-Mayer Corporation. 16 Nov 1928 (Los Angeles premiere) [©Metro-Goldwyn-Mayer Distributing Corporation; 24 Nov 1928; LP25865]. Silent or sound effects with music score; black & white. Seven reels (6,150 feet).

Presented by   Louis B. Mayer. *A Tod Browning Production. Director*   Tod Browning. *Scenario*   Elliott Clawson, based on the stage play *Kongo*, by Chester De Vonde and Kilborne Gordon, as produced at the Biltmore Theatre in New York, opening on March 30, 1926 [closed after 135 performances]. *Photography*   Percy Hilburn. *Settings*   Cedric Gibbons and Captain Richard Day. *Film Editor*   Harry Reynolds. *Wardrobe*   David Cox. *Titles*   Joseph W. Farnham. *Assistant Director*   Harry Sharrock.

Cast   Lon Chaney (*Professor Phroso, a.k.a. "Dead Legs" Flint*), Lionel Barrymore (*Crane*), Mary Nolan (*Maizie*), Warner Baxter (*Doc*), Jane Daly [formerly known as Jacquelin Gadsden] (*Anna*), Roscoe Ward (*Tiny*), Kalla Pasha (*Babe*), Curtis Nero (*Bumba*), Fred Gambold (*Vaudeville comedian in*

English dance hall), Edna Tichenor (*Dancing girl in African dive [cut from release print]*), Rose Dione (*Madam who ran Zanzibar dive*), Art Winkler (*Phroso's assistant*), Chaz Chase (*Music hall performer*), Louise Emmons (*Old woman on the street*), Emmett King (*Stage manager*), Dan Wolheim (*Man in dive [cut from release print]*), Mae Busch, Anita Page (?), Richard Cummings, Ida May, Dick Sutherland, June Riley.

Melodrama   ". . . a grim, ingenious, but somewhat artificial tale . . . Mr. Chaney gives one of his most able and effective portrayals. . . ." (*New York Times*, December 31, 1928) "Mr. Chaney's latest picture . . . is revolting from start to finish and leaves a bad taste to which no amount of clever acting—and there is considerable—can reconcile you." (*Chicago Sunday Tribune*, December 16, 1928) "It's getting so that Lon Chaney's name warns theatergoers of a bad picture, and with Tod Browning an atrocity is assured. . . . Chaney's once considerable acting ability has been atrophied by the parts he has had to play until he has about three expressions left." (*Film Spectator*, January 5, 1929)

Note   Working title: *South of the Equator*.

WHERE EAST IS EAST

Metro-Goldwyn-Mayer Corporation. 4 May 1929 [©Metro-Goldwyn-Mayer Distributing Corporation; 13 May 1929; LP362]. Silent or sound effects with music score; black & white. Seven reels (6,294 feet/sound version; 6,000 feet/silent version).

Presented by   Louis B. Mayer. *A Tod Browning Production. Producer*   Hunt Stromberg. *Director*   Tod Browning. *Adaptation*   Waldemar Young. *Continuity*   E. Richard Schayer. *Story*   Tod Browning and Henry Sinclair Drago. *Photography*   Henry Sharp. *Settings*   Cedric Gibbons and James Havens. *Film Editor*   Harry Reynolds. *Wardrobe*   David Cox. *Titles*   Joseph W. Farnham. *Assistant Director*   William Ryan.

Cast   Lon Chaney (*"Tiger" Haynes*), Estelle Taylor (*Madame de Sylva*), Lupe Velez (*Toyo, their daughter*), Lloyd Hughes (*Bobby Bailey*), Louis Stern (*Father Angelo*), Mrs. Wong Wing (*Ming, the grandmother*), Duke Kahanamoku (*Wild-animal trapper*), Willie Fung (*Servant*), Richard R. Neill (*Rangho, the gorilla*).

Melodrama   "The alliance of the Messrs Lon Chaney and Tod Browning, the two cinema apostles of the engagingly morbid, is usually indicative of amusing things for the devotee of screen horror tales. Their latest screen vehicle, however . . . is a pretty feeble tale, brightened only by the brilliant performance that the striking Miss Estelle Taylor brings to it. . . . Some of Mr. Browning's touches, in suggesting the atmosphere of Indo-China, are impressive, and Mr. Chaney is always interesting to watch, but the story is too much in the mood of a cheap magazine sex tale of the Orient to be anything more than ordinary melodrama." (*New York Herald-Tribune*, May 27, 1929)

THE THIRTEENTH CHAIR

Metro-Goldwyn-Mayer Corporation. 19 Oct 1929 [©Metro-Goldwyn-Mayer Distributing Corporation; 28 Oct 1929; LP794]. Silent or sound effects with music score; black & white. Seven reels (6,571 feet/sound version; 5,543 feet/silent version).

Presented by Louis B. Mayer. *A Tod Browning Production. Director* Tod Browning. *Screenplay and Dialogue* Elliott Clawson, based on the stage play *The Thirteenth Chair,* by Bayard Veiller, as produced at the 48th Street Theatre in New York, opening on November 20, 1916 [closed after 328 performances]. *Photography* Merritt B. Gerstad. *Settings* Cedric Gibbons and Captain Richard Day. *Film Editor* Harry Reynolds. *Gowns* Adrian. *Recording Engineers* Douglas Shearer and Paul Neal. *Titles* Joseph W. Farnham. *Assistant Director* William Ryan.

Cast Conrad Nagel (*Richard Crosby*), Leila Hyams (*Helen O'Neill*), Margaret Wycherly (*Madame Rosalie La Grange*), Helene Millard (*Mary Eastwood*), Holmes Herbert (*Sir Roscoe Crosby*), Mary Forbes (*Lady Crosby*), Bela Lugosi (*Inspector Delzante*), John Davidson (*Edward Wales*), Charles Quartermaine (*Dr. Philip Mason*), Moon Carroll (*Helen Trent*), Cyril Chadwick (*Brandon Trent*), Bertram Johns (*Howard Standish*), Gretchen Holland (*Grace Standish*), Frank Leigh (*Professor Feringeea*), Clarence Geldert (*Commissioner Grimshaw*), Lal Chand Mehra (*Chotee*), Henry Daniell.

Melodrama "While the picture is running we are quite sure it is a murder-mystery story, but with his final clinch fadeout Browning reveals the fact he thought it was a romance. A clinch ending to such a picture is more than absurd. It is idiotic. . . . *The Thirteenth Chair* is a murder-mystery-drama which should have ended on a dramatic note, not a romantic one." (*Film Spectator,* November 2, 1929) "Happily, the end is exciting enough to justify all the fuss over achieving it, and to excuse the middle portion of the film, which sags a trifle under all the conversation." (*San*

Francisco Chronicle, December 14, 1929) "The picture meanders and isn't nearly as thrilling as was the play. There's too much dialogue and footage. You are moderately interested in development when you should be excitedly so." (*Chicago Daily Tribune,* December 27, 1929)

OUTSIDE THE LAW

Universal Pictures Corporation. A Universal Special Production. 29 Aug 1930 (New York premiere) [©Universal Pictures Corporation; 25 Aug 1930; LP1517]. Sound; black & white. Nine reels (7,116 feet).

Presented by   Carl Laemmle. *A Tod Browning Production. Associate Producer* E. M. Asher. *Director*   Tod Browning. *Screenplay*   Tod Browning and Garrett Fort. *Adaptation (uncredited)*   Wells Root. *Story*   Tod Browning. *Photography*   Roy Field Overbaugh. *Settings*   William R. Schmidt. *Film Editor* Milton Carruth. *Recording Engineer*   C. Roy Hunter. *Sound Technician* William W. Hedgecock. *Synchronization and Score*   David Broekman. *Assistant Director*   Jay Marchant.

Cast   Mary Nolan (*Connie*), Edward G. Robinson (*"Cobra" Collins*), Owen Moore (*"Fingers" O'Dell*), Edwin Sturgis (*Jake*), John George (*Humpy*), Delmar Watson (*That Kid, O'Reilly's son*), DeWitt Jennings (*Police captain*), Rockliffe Fellowes (*Officer O'Reilly*), Frank Burke (*District attorney*), Sidney Bracy (*Assistant*), Matthew Betz (*Stage manager*), Jack Mower (*Policeman*), Mabel Mayo, Louise Beavers (?).

Melodrama   "It is old-fashioned, but it is so well directed and acted that it results in exciting, constantly interesting entertainment. Certainly Tod Browning deserved praise for his skill in sustaining suspense throughout the picture and in much of his camera work. He maintains his silent picture technique, which always was original and pictorial, in the 'talkie,' combining with it rapid action and snappy, sometimes intense, dialogue." (*New York Herald-Tribune,* September 1, 1930) "Competent acting by the principals . . . fails to atone for a flow of incredible incidents." (*New York Times,* September 2, 1930) "No excuse for this. It's one of the worst examples of clap trap since sound came in. Not a thread of continuity. The thing rants on, an on-the-cuff script, players obviously as bewildered as the director." (*Variety,* September 3, 1930)

Note   Previously filmed in 1920 by Browning (see above).

DRACULA

Universal Pictures Corporation. A Universal Special Production. 12 Feb 1931 (New York premiere) [©Universal Pictures Corporation; 2 Feb 1931; LP1947]. Sound; black & white. Nine reels (6,738 feet).

Presented by Carl Laemmle. *A Tod Browning Production. Producer* Carl Laemmle, Jr. *Associate Producer* E. M. Asher. *Director* Tod Browning. *Screenplay* Tod Browning and Garrett Fort. *Treatment and concert hall dialogue (uncredited)* Louis Bromfield. Based on the novel *Dracula,* by Bram Stoker (London, 1897), and the stage play *Dracula,* by Hamilton Deane and John Lloyd Balderston, as produced by Horace Liveright at the Fulton Theatre in New York, opening on October 5, 1927 [261 performances]. Also based on (uncredited) the play *Dracula* adapted by Charles Morrell, as produced in England in 1927. *Dialogue* Dudley Murphy. *Photography* Karl Freund. *Assistant Photography* King Gray and Frank Booth. *Second Unit Photography* Joseph Bretherton. *Art Direction* Charles D. Hall. *Set Designers* Herman Rosse, John Ivan Hoffman. *Scenery Supervisor* Charles A. Logue. *Set Decorator* Russell A. Gausman. *Editorial Supervisor* Maurice Pivar. *Film Editor* Milton Carruth. *Makeup* Jack Pierce. *Costumes* Ed Ware and Vera West. *Recording Engineer* C. Roy Hunter. *Music Conductor* Heinz Roemheld. *Script Girl* Aileen Webster. *Assistant Director* Scotty R. Beal. *Second Assistant Director* Herman Schlom. *Still Photographer* Roman Freulich. *Art Titles* Max Cohen. *Casting* Phil M. Friedman. *Research* Nan Grant.

Cast   Bela Lugosi (*Count Dracula*), Helen Chandler (*Mina Seward*), David Manners (*Jonathan Harker*), Dwight Frye (*Renfield*), Edward Van Sloan (*Dr. Van Helsing*), Herbert Bunston (*Dr. Seward*), Frances Dade (*Lucy Weston*), Charles Gerrard (*Martin*), Joan Standing (*Briggs*), Moon Carroll (*Maid*), Josephine Velez (*English nurse*), Donald Murphy (*Coach passenger*), Daisy Belmore (*English-woman passenger*), Nicholas Bela (*Transylvanian passenger*), Michael Visaroff (*Innkeeper*), Carla Laemmle (*Girl in coach*), Dorothy Tree, Jeraldine Dvorak, Cornelia Thaw [a.k.a. Mildred Peirce] (*Dracula's vampire wives*), John George (*Van Helsing's assistant*), George Hill Mailes (*Operating room doctor [?]*), Tod Browning (*Voice of the harbormaster*).

Horror Melodrama   ". . . only Tod Browning, specialist in the macabre, was properly equipped to direct this grotesque, fantastic, slightly unhealthy melodrama with proper forcefulness and conviction. . . . [The story] is presented in the photoplay with a skilled reliance on both the stage version and the novel. Some of the details are perhaps a bit complicated, but Browning manages both story and mood, with striking resourcefulness." (*New York Herald-Tribune,* February 11, 1931) "On the stage it was a thriller carried to such an extreme that it had a comedy punch by its very outre aspect. On the screen it comes out as a sublimated ghost story related with all surface seriousness and above all with a remarkably effective background of creepy atmosphere. . . . the mute perfection of the settings carries the conviction that the characters lack." (*Variety,* February 14, 1931) "Had the rest of the picture lived up to the first sequence in the ruined castle in Transylvania, *Dracula* . . . would have been a horror and thrill classic long remembered. . . . Lugosi outdoes any of the performances of the undead count we have seen him give on the stage. . . . His cruel smile—hypnotic glance—slow, stately, tread—they make *Dracula.* . . . Tod Browning directed—although we cannot believe that the same man was responsible for both the first and latter parts of the picture." (*Hollywood Filmograph,* April 14, 1931)

Note   Principal photography: September 29 to November 15, 1930. Additional scenes filmed on December 13, 1930, and January 2, 1931. Location scenes filmed in Vasquez Rocks, Chatsworth, California. A treatment by Fritz Stephani and an adaptation by Louis Stevens were also submitted to Universal; none of their material was used.

IRON MAN

Universal Pictures Corporation. A Universal Special Production. 17 Apr 1931 (New York premiere) [©Universal Pictures Corporation; 11 Apr 1931; LP2135]. Sound; black & white. Eight reels (6,736 feet).

Presented by   Carl Laemmle. *A Tod Browning Production. Producer* Carl Laemmle, Jr. *Associate Producer* E. M. Asher. *Director* Tod Browning. *Screenplay and Dialogue* Francis Edward Faragoh, based on the novel *Iron Man,* by William Riley Burnett (New York, 1930). *Photography* Percy Hilburn. *Art Direction* Charles D. Hall. *Editorial Supervisor* Maurice Pivar. *Film Editor* Milton Carruth. *Assistant Director* Scotty R. Beal.

Cast   Lew Ayres (*"Kid" Mason*), Robert Armstrong (*George Regan, his manager*), Jean Harlow (*Rose Mason*), John Miljan (*Paul H. Lewis*), Mary Doran (*The showgirl*), Mildred Van Dorn (*Gladys DeVere*), Eddie Dillon (*Jeff*), Ned Sparks (*Riley*), Mike Donlin (*McNeill*), Sammy Blum (*Mandl*), Morrie Cohan (*Rattler O'Keefe*), Sammy Gerron (*Trainer*), Angelo Rossitto (*Card player*), Claire Whitney.

Drama   ". . . an earnest and interesting motion picture. It is, however, just good enough to make you wish that it were better; just honest and skillful enough to fill you with regret that more honesty and skill had not gone into its manufacture, and to end by leaving you with a definite sense of disappointment." (*New York Herald-Tribune,* April 20, 1931) ". . . vastly more bracing than the usual romantic claptrap. Where *Iron Man* falls down is not being quite cruel enough. It fails to bring up the real and purposeful atmosphere of the training camp and prize ring, and as a result fails to impress you, as W. R. Burnett's book so overpoweringly did, with the savage struggle awaiting the fighter. Nor is Lew Ayres the best choice to play Kid Mason. . . . Jean Harlow, who has one of the best figures on the screen and continues to be almost embarrassingly candid about it, plays the wife." (*San Francisco Chronicle,* April 30, 1931)

Note   Principal photography: January 19 to February 20, 1931.

FREAKS

Metro-Goldwyn-Mayer Corporation. 10 Feb 1932 (Los Angeles opening) [©Metro-Goldwyn-Mayer Distributing Corporation; 23 Feb 1932; LP2870]. Sound; black & white. Seven reels (64 minutes).

Tod Browning's Production. Producer (uncredited)   Irving Thalberg. *Director* Tod Browning. *Screenplay*   Willis Goldbeck and Leon Gordon, based on the short story "Spurs," by Clarence Aaron "Tod" Robbins (*Munsey's Magazine,* February 1923). *Dialogue*   Edgar Allan Wolf and Al Boasberg. *Photography*   Merritt B. Gerstad. *Additional Photography*   Paul C. Vogel and Oliver T. Marsh. *Assistant Camera*   David S. Horsley. *Art Direction* Cedric Gibbons and Merrill Pye. *Film Editor*   Basil Wrangell. *Recording Engineer*   Gavin Burns. *Production Manager*   Harry Sharrock. *Assistant Director*   Errol Taggart. *Second Assistant Director*   William Ryan. *Script Clerk/ Third Assistant Director*   Willard Sheldon.

Cast   Wallace Ford (*Phroso*), Leila Hyams (*Venus*), Olga Baclanova (*Cleopatra*), Rosco Ates (*Roscoe*), Henry Victor (*Hercules*), Harry Earles (*Hans*), Daisy Earles (*Frieda*), Rose Dione (*Madame Tetrallini*), Daisy and Violet Hilton (*Siamese twins*), Schlitze (*Herself*), Josephine Joseph (*Half-woman– Half-man*), Johnny Eck (*Half-boy*), Frances O'Connor (*The Living Venus de Milo [armless girl]*), Peter Robinson (*Human skeleton*), Olga Roderick (*Bearded lady*), Koo Koo (*Herself*), Prince Randian (*Living torso*), Martha Morris (*Armless girl*), Elvira Snow, Jennie Lee Snow, Zip and Pip (*Pinheads*), Elizabeth Green (*Stork Woman*), Angelo Rossitto (*Angeleno*), Edward Brophy and Matt McHugh (*Rollo Brothers*), Albert Conti (*Monsieur Duval, the landowner*), Michael Visaroff (*Jean, the caretaker*), Ernie S. Adams (*Side-*

show patron), Louise Beavers (*Maid [cut from release print]*), Murray Kinnell (*Sideshow barker*).

Circus/Horror Melodrama "Whatever else may be said of the latest contribution to the growing list of 'shocker' dramas, there has never been another like it. Daring in conception, repellant in much of its content and at times infinitely pathetic . . . it is all a matter of taste whether the thwarted loves, ambitions and physical aspirations of these strange people impress the spectator as valid entertainment or merely a gratuitous overemphasis of hideous affliction." (*Washington Post*, February 20, 1932) "Planned by Metro to be one of the sensation pictures of the season, *Freaks* failed to qualify in the sure-fire category and has been shown in most parts of the country with astonishingly variable results. In spots it has been a cleanup. In others it was merely misery. . . . It has been sumptuously produced, admirably directed, and no cost was spared, but . . . the story is not sufficiently strong to get and hold the interest, partly because the interest cannot easily be granted for a too fantastic romance." (*Variety*, July 12, 1932) "The ghastly part of it is that the horrible thing may become a swell box office success. With the public taste lower than it has been in generations, not only will it attract the inframen of Main Street, who like snakes, two-headed calves, Chambers of Horrors and Halls of Anatomy, but the morbidly curious and psychically sick whose libidos are stimulated by contemplating the sex-life of abnormalities and monsters." (*Rob Wagner's Script*, February 20, 1932)

Note Working title: *Spurs*. Dwain Esper acquired the film's distribution rights in 1948 and subsequently exhibited it through his Excelsior Pictures under the titles *Nature's Mistakes*, *The Monster Show*, and *Forbidden Love*.

FAST WORKERS

Metro-Goldwyn-Mayer Corporation. 10 Mar 1933 [©Metro-Goldwyn-Mayer Distributing Corporation; 23 Mar 1933; LP3744]. Sound; black & white. Seven reels (66 minutes).

Tod Browning's Production. Director Tod Browning. *Continuity* Karl Brown and Ralph Wheelwright. *Dialogue* Laurence T. Stallings, based on the unproduced play *Rivets*, by John W. McDermott. *Photography* J. Peverall Marley. *Art Direction* Cedric Gibbons and A. Arnold Gillespie. *Film Editor* Ben Lewis. *Recording Director* Douglas Shearer. *Sound Mixer* Fred Morgan. *Assistant Director* Errol Taggart.

Cast John Gilbert (*Gunner Smith*), Robert Armstrong (*Bucker Reilly*), Mae Clarke (*Mary*), Muriel Kirkland (*Millie*), Vince Barnett (*Spike*), Virginia Cherrill (*Virginia*), Muriel Evans (*Nurse*), Sterling Holloway (*Pinky Magoo*), Guy Usher (*Scudder*), Warner Richmond (*Feets Wilson*), Robert Burns (*Alabam*), Elaine Line, Robert Graves.

Comedy Drama "In his new picture John Gilbert is a dashing riveter with an enormous talent for persuading young women to make fools of themselves. A temperamental and sometimes sullen lover, he drinks freely in after-midnight dives, punches men he does not like, mistreats his women, deceives his friends and shows himself to be an intolerable brag-gart. It requires witty writing to make an audience feel any affection for such a character, and there is little wit in *Fast Workers*." (*New York Times*, March 20, 1933) "The story is thoroughly spiced from beginning to end, in theme and dialogue, both essentially metropolitan. Flipping silver dol-lars at girls, in the street and in the hospital, scarcely encourages mothers to bring the 'dear kiddies.' "(Unidentified publication)

Note Working title: *Not the Marrying Kind*.

MARK OF THE VAMPIRE
Metro-Goldwyn-Mayer Corporation. 15 Apr 1935 [©Metro-Goldwyn-Mayer Distributing Corporation; 15 Apr 1935; LP5490]. Sound; black & white. Six reels (59 minutes).

Tod Browning's Production. Producer Edward J. Mannix. *Director* Tod Browning. *Screenplay* Guy Endore and Bernard Schubert. *Contributors to Dialogue* H. S. Kraft, Samuel Ornitz, and John L. Balderston. *Story* Tod Browning. *Photography* James Wong Howe. *Camera Operator* Charles Sa-lerno. *Photographic Effects–Matte Paintings* Warren Newcombe. *Photo-graphic Effects–Camera* Thomas Tutwiller. *Art Direction* Cedric Gibbons. *Art Direction Associates* Harry Oliver and Edwin B. Willis. *Film Editor* Ben Lewis. *Makeup* Jack Dawn. *Makeup Assistant* William Tuttle. *Gowns* Adrian. *Recording Director* Douglas Shearer. *Sound Mixer* Gavin Burns. *Effects Mixers* T. B. Hoffman, James Graham, and Mike Steinore. *Assistant Director and Stand-in for Carroll Borland* Harry Sharrock. *Still Photographers* Jimmy Rowe and Clarence Sinclair Bull.

Cast Lionel Barrymore (*Professor Zelin*), Elizabeth Allan (*Irena Borotyn*), Lionel Atwill (*Inspector Neumann*), Bela Lugosi (*Count Mora*), Jean Hersholt (*Baron Otto Von Zinden*), Henry Wadsworth (*Fedor Vincente*), Donald Meek

(*Dr. Doskil*), Jessie Ralph (*Midwife*), Ivan Simpson (*Jan*), Franklyn Ardell (*Chauffeur*), Leila Bennett (*Maria*), June Gittelson (*Annie*), Carroll Borland (*Luna Mora*), Holmes Herbert (*Sir Karell Borotyn*), Michael Visaroff (*Innkeeper*), Rosemary Glosz (*Innkeeper's wife*), Eily Malyon (*Sick woman [cut from release print]*), Zeffie Tilbury (*Grandmother [cut from release print]*), Guy Bellis (*Englishman*), Claire Vedera (*Englishwoman*), Baron Hesse (*Bus driver [cut from release print]*), Mrs. Lesovosky (*Old woman in inn*), Egon Brecher (*Coroner*), Christian Rub (*Deaf man [cut from release print]*), Robert Greig (*Fat man [cut from release print]*), Torben Meyer (*Card player*), James Bradbury, Jr., Lionel Belmore, Henry Stephenson, James Mercer, Doris Lloyd, Greta Meyer.

Horror/Mystery Melodrama "A genuine horror film in which the director's effects are sometimes so weird that they provide laughter instead of shudders. For the moderately impressionable, however, it will provide first-rate entertainment until the time comes for the mystery to be solved. The solution provides a marked anti-climax." (*Monthly Film Bulletin*, May 1935) "The straight melodrama of the film is accomplished with somewhat heavy handed, but none the less effective adroitness, and a number of young things at the Rialto yesterday found occasion to clutch each other in hasty search for mutual assurance, as Mr. Lugosi practiced visual frightfulness in his most approved manner. . . . Thrill seekers who can overlook the blemishes of the film, added in the name of comic relief, will have no cause to complain. . . ." (*New York Herald-Tribune*, May 3, 1935) "Although directed by Tod Browning, a director of considerable distinction, and written in part by Guy Endore, a specialist in things creepy and gruesome, *Mark of the Vampire* emerges as an inconsequential little piece of synthetic movie-making, which will probably go on record as the horror film to end all horror films." (*New York World-Telegram*, May 3, 1935)

Note Working titles: *The Vampires of Prague* and *Vampires of the Night*. Remake of the 1927 Browning film *London After Midnight* (see above).

THE DEVIL-DOLL

Metro-Goldwyn-Mayer Corporation. 10 Jul 1936 [©Metro-Goldwyn-Mayer Distributing Corporation; 7 Jul 1936; LP6486]. Sound; black & white. Eight reels (79 minutes).

A Tod Browning Production. Producer Edward J. Mannix. Director Tod Browning. *Screenplay* Garrett Fort, Guy Endore, Eric von Stroheim, and

Tod Browning. *Contributor to Dialogue* Richard Schayer. *Story* Tod Browning, inspired by the novel *Burn, Witch, Burn!*, by Abraham Merritt (New York, 1933). *Photography* Leonard Smith. *Additional Photography* Willard Vogel. *Art Direction* Cedric Gibbons. *Art Direction Associates* Stan Rogers and Edwin B. Willis. *Film Editor* Frederick Y. Smith. *Musical Score* Franz Waxman. *Wardrobe* Dolly Tree. *Recording Director* Douglas Shearer. *Sound Mixer* James K. Brock. *Rerecording Mixers* S. J. Lambert, Ralph Pender, R. L. Stirling, and Don T. Whitmer. *Effects Mixers* T. B. Hoffman and Mike Steinore. *Musical Mixer* M. J. McLaughlin. *Assistant Director* Harry Sharrock. *Apache Dance* Val Raset. *Stunt Double for Arthur Hohl* Paul Foltz.

Cast Lionel Barrymore (*Paul Lavond, a.k.a. Madame Mandelip*), Maureen O'Sullivan (*Lorraine Lavond*), Frank Lawton (*Toto*), Rafaela Ottiano (*Malita*), Robert Greig (*Emil Coulvet*), Lucy Beaumont (*Mme. Lavond*), Henry B. Walthall (*Marcel*), Grace Ford (*Lachna*), Pedro de Cordoba (*Charles Matin*), Arthur Hohl (*Victor Radin*), Juanita Quigley (*Marguerite Coulvet*), Claire du Brey (*Mme Coulvet*), Rollo Lloyd (*Detective*), E. Allyn Warren (*Commissioner*), Billy Gilbert (*Butler*), Eily Malyon (*Laundry proprietor*), Christian J. Frank, Sherry Hall, Francis McDonald (*Detectives*), Robert Graves (*Gendarme*), Edward Keene (*Gendarme*), Nick Thompson (*Police sergeant*), Robert Du Couedic (*Policeman*), Inez Palange (*Concierge*), Evelyn Selbie (*Flower woman*), Paul Foltz, Jean Alden (*Apache dancers*), Wilfred Lucas (*Voice*), Henry Daniell, Paul Sotoff, Billy Dooley, King Baggott.

Fantasy Melodrama   "*The Devil-Doll* is the most ambitious effort ever undertaken in the long-known but seldom-employed technique of photographic disproportion. . . . Unlike Director Tod Browning's *Freaks,* or most of the famed Lon Chaney silents which he made, *The Devil-Doll*'s hobgoblinery beguiles rather than frightens." (*Time,* July 20, 1936) "In *The Devil-Doll,* Mr. Browning is hardly at his best. Yet in a dramatic medium that is too much given to health and vitality, it is always pleasant to run across one of his slyly unwholesome melodramas if only for the sake of contrast." (*New York Herald-Tribune,* August 8, 1936) "The miniature humans of the film, instead of appearing sinister, are only cute. Even the crimes they are forced to commit are quaint rather than horrible. *The Devil-Doll* isn't likely to scare any one but children, whom it might affect most seriously. It is, for those over twelve, a fairly entertaining novelty. . . . Mr. Barrymore, disguised as an old lady, is astonishingly believable." (*New York Sun,* August 8, 1936)

Note   Working title: *Witch of Timbuctoo.*

MIRACLES FOR SALE

Metro-Goldwyn-Mayer Corporation. 4 Aug 1939 [©Loew's, Inc., 1 Aug 1939; LP9038]. Sound; black & white. Eight reels (71 minutes).

Producer (uncredited) J. J. Cohn. *Director* Tod Browning. *Screenplay* Harry Ruskin, Marion Parsonnet, and James Edward Grant, based on the novel *Death from a Top Hat: A Merlini Mystery,* by Clayton Rawson (New York, 1938). *Photography* Charles Lawton. *Additional Photography* Alfred Gilks. *Art Direction* Cedric Gibbons. *Art Direction Associate* Gabriel Scognomillo. *Set Decorations* Edwin B. Willis. *Film Editor* Frederick Y. Smith. *Makeup* Jack Dawn. *Wardrobe* Dolly Tree. *Recording Director* Douglas Shearer. *Unit Manager* Jerry Bresler. *Assistant Director* Harry Sharrock.

Cast   Robert Young (*Michael Morgan*), Florence Rice (*Judy Barclay*), Frank Craven (*Dad Morgan*), Henry Hull (*Dave Duvallo*), Lee Bowman (*La Claire*), Cliff Clark (*Inspector Gavigan*), Astrid Allwyn (*Mrs. Zelma La Claire*), Walter Kingsford (*Colonel Watrous*), Frederic Worlock (*Dr. Cesare Sabbatt*), Gloria Holden (*Madame Rapport*), William Demarest (*Quinn*), Harold Minjir (*Tauro*), Charles Lane (*Hotel clerk*), Richard Loo (*Chinese soldier*), John Picorri (*Colonel*), Suzanne Kaaren (*Girl*), Armand Kaliz (*François*), Harry Tyler (*Taxi driver*), Frank Sully (*Bus driver*), Claire McDowell (*Woman*), Edward Earle (*Man*), Chester Clute (*Waiter*), Truman Bradley (*Master of ceremonies*), Alphonse Martell (*Headwaiter*), E. Allyn Warren (*Dr. Hendricks*), Monte Vandergrift (*Bergin*), James C. Morton (*Electrician*), Edward Kilroy (*First attendant*), Phillip Terry (*Master of ceremonies*), Paul Sutton (*Captain R. Z. Storm*), Eddie Acuff (*Taxi driver*), John Davidson (*Weird voice*), Harry Vejar (*Citizen*), Frances McInerney (*Magician's assistant*), Manuel Paris (*Sinister man*), William Norton Bailey (*Man in box*), Margaret Bert (*Mary*), Cyril Ring (*Numbers man*), Fred Warren (*Police surgeon*).

Mystery Comedy   "While it has enough loose ends to fringe a Spanish shawl, this tale has been rather ingeniously contrived and jogs along briskly under Tod Browning's direction. . . . The identity of the murderer is fairly obvious from the start, but the motive and methods are not —not even, we are bound to add, after the crime-solver Robert Young has explained it all." (*New York Times,* August 10, 1939) "This whodunit has some background color that tickles the imagination, but beyond that there isn't much to excite the customers. What little comedy there is meanders through the proceedings and is well handled . . . even though the film runs thin in dramatic sock and mystery elements, it manages to leave a pleasant impression. The plot stumbles over itself most of the time and the solution is anything but clear, although director Tod Browning does succeed in keeping the narrative nicely paced and the mood interestingly pitched throughout." (*Variety*, August 16, 1939)

INSIDE JOB

Universal Pictures Company. 28 Jun 1946 [©Universal Pictures Co., Inc., 6 Jun 1946; LP362]. Sound; black & white. Seven reels (65 minutes).

Producers Ben Pivar and Jean Yarbrough. *Director* Jean Yarbrough. *Screenplay* George Bricker and Jerry Warner, based on a story by Tod Browning and Garrett E. Fort. *Photography* Maury Gertsman. *Art Direction* Cedric Gibbons. *Art Direction Associate* Jack Otterson and Abraham Grossman. *Film Editor* Otto Ludwig. *Music Director* Frank Skinner.

Cast Preston Foster (*Bart Madden*), Alan Curtis (*Eddie Norton*), Ann Rutherford (*Claire Gray*), Joe Sawyer (*Captain Thomas*), Joan [Shawlee] Fulton (*Ruth*), Milburn Stone (*District Attorney Sutton*), Jimmie Moss (*Skipper*), Samuel S. Hinds (*Judge Kinkaid*), Howard Freeman (*Mr. Wickle*), John Berkes (*Freddie*), Harry Brown (*Pop Hurley*), Joe Kirk (*Fenway*), Oliver Prickett (*Man*), Ruby Dandridge.

Melodrama A remake of Browning's 1930 version of *Outside the Law*. "Well produced, directed and acted, but the story is somewhat demoralizing. It is of the 'cheating cheaters' type, showing one of the principals planning and committing a robbery and getting away with it. In the last reel, of course, the crook reforms and pays for his crime, but showing him to become a good fellow does not offset the harm done in the first five reels." (*Harrison's Reports*, June 22, 1946)

TOD BROWNING:
OTHER PROJECTS

The following are projects conceived by or assigned to Browning but not ultimately realized by him. Years above titles refer to Browning's period of involvement.

1919
ROUGE AND RICHES

Universal Film Manufacturing Company, Inc. 9 Feb 1920 [©Universal Film Manufacturing Company, Inc.; 15 Jan 1920; LP14650]. Silent; black & white. Six reels.

Browning was announced to direct this Mary MacLaren dramatic vehicle, which dealt with New York stage life, originally entitled *Myself, Becky* (and based on the W. Carey Wonderly short story of the same name in *Life Stories Magazine*) in the August 9, 1919 issue of *Camera,* to follow his recently completed *Bonnie, Bonnie Lassie.* A week later it was reported that Browning was supervising the erection of the elaborate sets required for this new production. As MacLaren's next film became *The Pointing Finger* (see above), this project was shelved until October 1919 and retitled *Rouge and Riches.* Harry Franklin, a recent addition to the Universal directorial staff, handled directing chores, and Browning was no longer involved in the project.

1919
THE INCORRIGIBLE
Universal Film Manufacturing Company, Inc. Unproduced.

Universal purchased this original story by E. Mangus Ingleton on September 8, 1919, for $1,000. A continuity by H. Tipton Steck was submitted, and Priscilla Dean was to star in this proposed eight-reel melodrama. According to internal Universal records, Browning was to direct this modern tale about Susanna Blake, a misguided woman whose father died in prison. After several terms in correctional institutions herself, she has earned the title of "Incorrigible." She promises Bob Raywood, a crusading young attorney, to reform, but, when refused work because of her past, instead becomes the mistress of Max Wyndham, the prison warden's son. Eventually, after she is freed from Max' persistent machinations by his death from a heart attack, Susanna withstands an effort to make her act against the attorney's interests. She and Bob are brought together again and marry.

1920
PINK TIGHTS
Universal Film Manufacturing Company, Inc. 4 Oct 1920 [©Universal Film Manufacturing Company, Inc.; 25 Sep 1920; LP15577]. Silent; black & white. Five reels.

Another project originally announced as a possible Priscilla Dean feature to be directed by Browning. The March 20, 1920, issues of *Moving Picture World* and *Motion Picture News* carried nearly identical announcements that "coincident with Tod Browning's arrival in New York with . . . *The Virgin of Stamboul* . . . Universal announced the purchase of . . . 'Out of the Clear Sky,' a short story by [John U. Geisy], which appeared in the March number of *Telling Tales,* [and] will offer the plot for Browning's next production." Geisy had cowritten the story that became Browning's Metro feature *The Eyes of Mystery*. Throughout May and June, Philip Rosen was slated to direct and Edith Roberts to star; Doris Schroeder and later Philip Hurn had each finished continuities. In late June, Reeves Eason was working with the manuscript department on this circus story. Gladys Walton and Jack Perrin ultimately starred, with direction handled by Eason and the script credited to Hurn. Just prior to release, the film was retitled *Pink Tights*.

1920

THE WOMAN WHO WALKED ALONE

Famous Players–Lasky. Paramount Pictures. 11 Jun 1922 [©Famous Players–Lasky Corporation; 7 Jun 1922; LP17948]. Silent; black & white. Six reels (5,947 feet).

Universal purchased John Colton's screen story, originally entitled *The Cat That Walked Alone*, in early 1920, and announced a feature under that title as a Carmel Myers vehicle to be directed by Rollin Sturgeon. A continuity was submitted by Doris Schroeder on May 3, 1920. In the May 15, 1920, issue of *Moving Picture World*, it was now to star Priscilla Dean and be directed by Browning. R. H. Cochrane, vice-president of Universal, in an interview in the May 15, 1920, issue of *Motion Picture News* stated that "perhaps the most important of our recent purchases is an original screen story called *The Cat That Walked Alone*, by John Colton, who has turned from the magazine field to the film world. In [it] we have found an ideal vehicle for Miss Priscilla Dean. It is admirably suited to display the many facets of her volatile screen temperament. Universal will lose no time putting it into production." Two weeks later, Universal had engaged Colton to write stories solely for Dean, and he was on his way to Los Angeles to "work side by side with Miss Dean and her director in the construction of suitable plots for the star." By the end of June, this was announced as the follow-up feature for Browning after *Outside the Law* and that Colton's story had originally been written for Geraldine Farrar and was to have been produced by Goldwyn. The project was given back to director Sturgeon, according to an interview in *Motion Picture News* (August 28, 1920): "Already I have had many fruitful conferences with Miss Dean and Colton over the script." The property was sold to Paramount and released as a Dorothy Dalton vehicle directed by George Melford.

1921

SLIPPY McGEE

Oliver Morosco Productions/Associated First National Pictures. 11 Jun 1923. Silent; black & white. Seven reels (6,399 feet).

A trade item in *Camera* (January 15, 1921, "Pickups by the Staff," p. 7) indicated that Browning "may be borrowed from Carl Laemmle by Oliver Morosco to produce *Slippy McGee* as a screen drama, according to reports." The film was eventually directed by Wesley Ruggles and starred Wheeler Oakman and Colleen Moore.

1923
THE HUNCHBACK OF NOTRE DAME

Universal Pictures. 2 Sep 1923 (New York premiere) [©Universal Pictures Corporation; 6 Sep 1923; LP19381]. Silent; black & white. Twelve reels.

Universal first announced Browning as director of this silent classic starring Lon Chaney, but Browning's concurrent slide into alcoholism may have prompted Irving Thalberg, then Universal's production head, to withdraw him. Wallace Worsley directed in his stead.

1925
THE FOUR STRAGGLERS / HATE

Metro-Goldwyn-Mayer Pictures. Unproduced.

Based on a novel by Frank L. Packard, author of *The Miracle Man*, *The Four Stragglers* was announced by M-G-M as Browning's follow-up to *The Black Bird* in January 1926. The story had earlier been described as "a gripping mystery laid about four odd characters whose apparent shortcomings are proved to mask a very remarkable purpose in life." (*Hollywood Filmograph*, September 13, 1925) In 1927 the story was being developed under the title *Hate*. The project was dropped in May 1928 when Browning was assigned *The Big City*. (*Harrison's Reports*, May 12, 1928, p. 73)

1926
POLLY OF THE CIRCUS

Metro-Goldwyn-Mayer. 27 Feb 1932 [©Metro-Goldwyn-Mayer Distributing Corporation; 27 Feb 1932; LP2912]. Silent; black & white. Eight reels.

In May 1926 M-G-M announced Browning would direct the second screen adaptation of Margaret Mayo's stage play (the first was a 1917 version by Goldwyn Pictures), to star Norma Shearer (*Moving Picture World*, May 8, 1926, p. 119; July 10, 1926, p. 24; *Film Mercury*, May 28, 1926, p. 16, supplement). The film was not made until 1932, in a production directed by Alfred Santell and starring Marion Davies and Clark Gable.

1928
THE OLD AGE HANDICAP

Pacifica Features Corporation, Frank Mattison Productions/Trinity Pictures. 18 May 1928 (New York premiere). Silent; black & white. Six reels (5,573 feet).

While most references credit this dramatic story to Tod Underwood, the initial production release carried in *Moving Picture World* noted the story was authored by Tod Browning. Browning could have used Underwood as a pseudonym, as the plot for this film bears a passing resemblance to *Atta Boy's Last Race* (see above). It's very likely that Browning's M-G-M contract precluded him from using his name on any other work at that time. Frank S. Mattison directed, with adaptation by Charles A. Taylor and Cecil Burtis Hall. Alberta Vaughn and Gareth Hughes starred. "A youth (played by Gareth Hughes) from a large, poor family prefers a shantytown girl (Alberta Vaughn), who becomes a popular cabaret dancer, to the daughter of the banker. The dancer saves the youth's sister from being molested by the town bad boy—at some danger to her own reputation—and rides the family's horse to victory and a $5,000 purse in a handicap rigged by the banker. (*American Film Institute Catalog, Feature Films, 1921–1930*)

1928
FOUR WALLS

Metro-Goldwyn-Mayer Pictures. 11 Aug 1928 [©Metro-Goldwyn-Mayer Distributing Corporation; 4 Aug 1928; LP25604]. Silent; black & white. Eight reels (6,620 feet).

Several unsourced trade items indicate Browning was the initial choice to direct this adaptation of the stage melodrama by Dana Burnet and George Abbott. William Nigh directed; John Gilbert and Joan Crawford starred.

1929
THE SEA BAT

Metro-Goldwyn-Mayer Pictures. 5 Jul 1930 [©Metro-Goldwyn-Mayer Distributing Corporation; 7 Jul 1930; LP1401]. Silent; black & white. Eight reels (6,570 feet).

In spring 1929 M-G-M announced Browning as the director of a "weird story of tropical life and jungle voodoo" to star Lon Chaney. (*Hollywood Filmograph,* June 1, 1929, p. 34) The project was instead helmed by Wesley Ruggles and featured Charles Bickford and Raquel Torres in the cast.

1930
THE SCARLET TRIANGLE
Universal Pictures. Unproduced.

The Scarlet Triangle was heralded as Browning's first film for Universal upon his return to that studio (*Universal Weekly,* March 15, 1930). The title does not appear in Universal's catalog of literary properties, and may have been an original, unscripted (and unsold) idea by Browning.

1930
THE YELLOW SIN
Universal Pictures. Unproduced.

Another title announced as a Browning idea around July 1930, according to unsourced trade clippings.

1931
RECKLESS LIVING
Universal Pictures. 20 Oct 1931 [©Universal Pictures Corporation; 30 Sep 1931; LP2521]. Sound; black & white. Seven reels.

According to *Variety* (October 20, 1930, p. 12), Browning "will go into production at once" on this comedy drama, based on the stage play *The Up and Up,* by Eva K. Flint and Martha Madison. Browning, however, was just beginning *Dracula,* and the film was instead directed by Cyril Gardner. Ricardo Cortez and Mae Clarke starred.

1931
ARSÈNE LUPIN
Metro-Goldwyn-Mayer Corporation. 5 Mar 1932 [©Metro-Goldwyn-Mayer Corporation; 8 Feb 1932; LP2827]. Sound; black & white. Nine reels.

Although M-G-M wanted Browning to direct an adaptation of this 1908 play by Maurice Leblanc and Francis de Crisset, Browning instead convinced the studio to allow him to film *Freaks.* Jack Conway took over this project, which featured John and Lionel Barrymore.

1932
CHINA SEAS

Metro-Goldwyn-Mayer Corporation. 16 Aug 1935 [©Metro-Goldwyn-Mayer Corporation; 6 Aug 1935; LP5770]. Sound; black & white. Nine reels.

First announced by M-G-M as Browning's follow-up to *Freaks,* Crosbie Garston's novel was delayed in preproduction for many months (the Hays Office rejected the project, citing objectionable aspects of the novel, including the interracial love affair central to the original story, the resulting illegitimate child, and references to opium use [*American Film Institute Catalog, Feature Films, 1931–1940*]). The *Hollywood Reporter* noted in various trade items between August and October 1932 that the picture would begin filming in mid-November 1932. After producer Eddie Mannix submitted a revised script to the Hays Office in September 1933, Jack Conway was now the director associated with the film. After several other script rewrites, Tay Garnett finally took over direction, with Clark Gable, Jean Harlow, and Wallace Beery starring.

1932
REVOLT OF THE DEAD

Metro-Goldwyn-Mayer Corporation. Unproduced.

Novelist Gouverneur Morris, author of *The Penalty,* was hired by M-G-M to collaborate with Browning on this story, described by *Variety* (November 8, 1932) as dealing with reincarnation.

1933
LAZY RIVER

Metro-Goldwyn-Mayer Corporation. 16 Mar 1934 [©Metro-Goldwyn-Mayer Corporation; 7 Mar 1934; LP4549]. Sound; black & white. Eight reels.

Lea David Freeman's unproduced play *Dance Hall Daisy* was the basis for this rural drama which started production as *Louisiana Lou.* Also called *Bride of the Bayou,* this Cajun-country fiasco was shut down by M-G-M while on location in the Louisiana swamps. William Faulkner and Erskine Caldwell contributed to the script. See Chapter 6, "Malibu After Midnight," for full discussion. The story was eventually produced, from scratch, as *Lazy River,* directed by George B. Seitz and featuring Jean Parker and Robert Young.

1935
THEY SHOOT HORSES, DON'T THEY?
Metro-Goldwyn-Mayer Corporation. Unproduced.

According to Elliott Stein ("Tod Browning" in Richard Roud, ed., *Cinema: A Critical Dictionary*, vol. 2 [New York: Viking Press, 1980], p. 166), Browning tried unsuccessfully to convince M-G-M to purchase Horace McCoy's excoriating dance-marathon novel after its publication in 1935. Sydney Pollack filmed the property in 1969, with Gig Young winning an Academy Award for best supporting actor and the film receiving nine nominations.

1941
SHADOW OF THE THIN MAN
Metro-Goldwyn-Mayer Corporation. 20 Nov 1941 (New York premiere) [©Loew's Inc.; 21 Oct 1941; LP10854]. Sound; black & white. Nine reels.

It is possible that material from Browning's 32-page continuity for his property (then called *Ghost of the Thin Man*) was used in the released version of this work, based on characters created by Dashiell Hammett. W. S. Van Dyke II directed from a screenplay by Irving Brecher and Harry Kurnitz. William Powell and Myrna Loy starred in this fourth *Thin Man* film.

1941
HOTEL MAJESTIC
Metro-Goldwyn-Mayer Corporation. Unproduced.

According to a March 24, 1941, internal office communication at M-G-M, Browning was working on a new treatment for this project, which was based on the 1920 Hungarian novel by Eugen Heltai and earlier filmed in Hungary as *Room 111* by Steve Falus (as scripted by Heltai and Steve Milhaly).

1941
EQUILIBRIUM
Metro-Goldwyn-Mayer Corporation. Unproduced.

Although Browning signed over all rights to this original story to M-G-M on November 18, 1941, the project was never filmed.

ALICE BROWNING: ACTRESS

THE CHILDREN IN THE HOUSE

Fine Arts Film Company/Triangle Film Corporation. 30 Apr 1916. Silent; black & white. Five reels.

Directors C. M. Franklin and S. A. Franklin. *Scenario* Roy Somerville.

Cast Norma Talmadge (*Cora*), Alice Rae (*Alice*), Jewel Carmen (*Jane Courtenay*), William Hinckley (*Charles Brown*), W. E. Lawrence (*Fred Brown*), George Pearce (*Jasper Vincent*), Eugene Pallette (*Arthur Vincent*), Walter Long (*Al Fellowes*), Alva D. Blake (*Gaffey*), George Stone, Violet Radcliffe, Carmen de Rue, Francis Carpenter, Ninon Fovieri (*The children*).

A LOVE SUBLIME

Fine Arts Film Company/Triangle Distributing Corporation. 11 Mar 1917. Silent; black & white. Five reels.

See full entry in Tod Browning filmography.

SHOULD SHE OBEY?

Arizona Film Co./State Rights. 6 May 1917. Silent; black & white. Seven to nine reels.

Director George A. Siegmann. *Scenario* Walter C. Howey.

Cast George A. Siegmann (*Allegorical types*), Norbert Myles (*William Gordon*), Gene Genung (*Lorna Gordon*), J. Webster Dill (*Henry Blake*), Billie West (*Mamie Blake*), Andrew Arbuckle (*Uncle John*), Alice Wilson (*Marie Gibson*), James Harrison (*William Gordon, Jr.*), Robert Lawlor (*The vulture*), Herbert Sutch, Laura Winston, Margaret McQuarrie.

PARENTAGE

Hobart Henley/State Rights/Frank S. Seng. 8 Jul 1918. Silent; black & white. Seven reels.

Producer-Director Hobart Henley. *Scenario* Hobart Henley and Martin G. Chandler.

Cast Anna Lehr (*Mrs. Brown*), Hobart Henley (*Robert Smith, Jr., as a man*), Barbara Castleton (*Agnes Melton, as a woman*), William Welsh (*John Brown*), Bert Busby (*Robert Smith*), Mary Grey (*Mrs. Smith*), Matty Roubert (*Horace Brown, as a boy*), Gilbert Rooney (*Horace Brown, as a man*), Frank Goyette (*Robert Smith, Jr., as a boy*), Alice Alexander (*Agnes Melton, as a girl*), W. DeShields (*Samuel Melton*), Alice Wilson (*Mrs. Melton*).

THE FACE IN THE DARK

Goldwyn Pictures Corporation/Goldwyn Distributing Corporation. 21 Apr 1918. Silent; black & white. Six reels.

Director Hobart Henley. Based on the short story "The Web," by Irvin S. Cobb.

Cast Mae Marsh (*Jane Ridgeway*), Niles Welch (*Richard Grant*), Alec B. Francis (*Charles Ridgeway*), Harry C. Myers (*Jim Weaver*), Donald Hall (*Nixon*), Joseph Smiley (*Charles Hammond*), Isabelle Lamon (*Rosalind Hammond*), Alice Wilson (*Mrs. Hammond*), Willard Dashiell.

THE EYES OF JULIA DEEP

American Film Co./Pathé Exchange, Inc. Aug–Sep 1918. Silent; black & white. Five reels.

Director Lloyd Ingraham. *Scenario* Elizabeth Mahoney, based on the short story by Kate L. McLaurin.

Cast Mary Miles Minter (*Julia Deep*), Alan Forrest (*Terry Hartridge*), Alice Wilson (*Lottie Driscoll*), George Periolat (*Timothy Black*), Ida Easthope (*Mrs. Turner*), Eugenie Besserer (*Mrs. Lowe*), Carl Stockdale (*Simon Plummet*).

THE BRAZEN BEAUTY

Bluebird Photoplays, Inc./Universal Film Manufacturing Company, Inc. 9 Sep 1918. Silent; black & white. Five reels.

See full entry in Tod Browning filmography.

LA BELLE RUSSE

Fox Film Corporation. 21 Sep 1919. Silent; black & white. Six reels (5,400 feet).

Director/Scenario Charles J. Brabin. Based on the 1882 play by David Belasco.

Cast Theda Bara (*La Belle Russe/Fleurette*), Warburton Gamble (*Phillip Sackton*), Marian Stewart (*Phillip Sackton, Jr.*), Robert Lee Keeling (*Sir James Sackton*), William B. Davidson (*Brand*), Alice Wilson (*Lady Sackton*), Robert Vivian (*Butler*), Lewis Broughton.

THE WILLOW TREE

Screen Classics/Metro Pictures Corporation. Jan 1920. Silent; black & white. Six reels.

Director Henry Otto. *Scenario* June Mathis, based on the 1917 play by J. H. Benrimo and Harrison Rhodes.

Cast Viola Dana (*O-Riu*), Edward Connelly (*Tomotada*), Pell Trenton (*Ned Hamilton*), Harry Dunkinson (*Jeoffrey Fuller*), Alice Wilson (*Mary Fuller*), Frank Tokunago (*John Charles Goto*), Togo Yamamato (*Itomudo*), George Kuwa (*Kimura*), Tom Ricketts (*The priest*), Jack Yutaka Abbe (*Nogo*).

WHAT'S YOUR HUSBAND DOING?

Thomas H. Ince Productions/Famous Players–Lasky Corporation/Paramount-Artcraft Pictures. 25 Jan 1920. Silent; black & white. Five reels (4,692 feet).

Director Lloyd Ingraham. *Scenario* R. Cecil Smith, based on the 1917 play by George V. Hobart.

Cast Douglas MacLean (*John P. Widgast*), Doris May (*Beatrice Ridley*), Walter Hiers (*Charley Pidgeon*), William Buckley (*Robert Ridley*), Norris Johnson (*Helen Widgast*), Alice Elliott (*Gwendolyn Pidgeon*), Alice Wilson (*Sylvia Pennywise*), Marguerite Livingston (*Madge Mitchell*), J. P. Lockney (*Tyrus Trotman*).

PASSION'S PLAYGROUND

Katherine MacDonald Pictures Corp./First National Exhibitors Circuit. Apr 1920. Silent; black & white. Five reels.

Directors Sam E. Rork and J. A. Barry. *Scenario* C. N. Williamson and A. M. Williamson, based on the 1912 novel *The Guests of Hercules*, by Charles Norris Williamson and Alice Muriel Williamson.

Cast Katherine MacDonald (*Mary Grant*), Norman Kerry (*Prince Vanno Della Robbia*), Nell Craig (*Marie Grant*), Edwin Stevens (*Lord Dauntry*), Virginia Ainsworth (*Lady Dauntry*), Rudolph Valentine (*Prince Angelo Della Robbia*), Alice Wilson (*Dodo Wardropp*), Howard Gaye (*James Hanaford*), Fanny Ferrari (*Idina Bland*), Sylvia Jocelyn (*Molly Maxwell*), Walt Whitman (*Cure of Roquebrune*).

THE DREAM CHEATER

Robert Brunton Productions/W. W. Hodkinson Corporation. 4 Apr 1920. Silent; black & white. Five reels.

Director Ernest C. Warde. *Scenario* Jack Cunningham, based on the 1831 novel *La Peau de Chagrin*, by Honoré de Balzac.

Cast J. Warren Kerrigan (*Brandon McShane*), Wedgewood Nowell (*Angus Burton*), Alice Wilson (*Mimi Gascoigne*), Joseph J. Dowling (*Shib Mizah*), Thomas H. Guise (*Patrick Fitz-George*), Fritzi Brunette (*Pauline Mahon*), Aggie Herring (*Mrs. Mahon*), Sam Sothern (*Shamus McShane*).

THE LITTLE WANDERER

Fox Film Corporation. Aug 1920. Silent; black & white. Five reels (5,240 feet).

Director Howard M. Mitchell. *Scenario/Story* Denison Clift.

Cast Shirley Mason (*Jenny*), Raymond McKee (*Larry Hart*), Cecil Vanauker (*Joe Farley*), Alice Wilson (*Kit*), Jack Pratt (*Tully*).

PAYMENT GUARANTEED
Lois Zellner Production Co./American Film Co./Pathé Exchange, Inc. Mar 1921. Silent; black & white. Five reels.

Director George L. Cox. *Story* Lois Zellner.

Cast Margarita Fisher (*Emily Heath*), Cecil Van Auker (*Stephen Strange*), Hayward Mack (*Harry Fenton*), Harry Lonsdale (*Jim Barton*), Harvey Clark (*Reporter*), Marjorie Manners (*Myrtle*), Alice Wilson (*Gertie*).

MAKING THE GRADE
David Butler Productions/Western Pictures Exploitation Co. Sep 1921. Silent; black & white. Five reels (4,735 feet).

Director Fred J. Butler. *Adapter* A. P. Younger. Based on the short story "Sophie Semenoff," by Wallace Irvin.

Cast David Butler (*Eddie Ramson*), Helen Ferguson (*Sophie Semenoff*), William Walling (*Mr. Ramson*), Lillian Lawrence (*Mrs. Ramson*), Jack Cosgrove (*Captain Carleton*), Alice Wilson (*Mrs. Garnie Crest*), Otto Lederer, Jack Rollins.

SILK STOCKING SAL
Gothic Pictures/Film Booking Offices of America. 30 Nov 1924. Silent; black & white. Six reels (5,367 feet).

See full entry in Tod Browning filmography.

GENEALOGY

BROWNING FAMILY

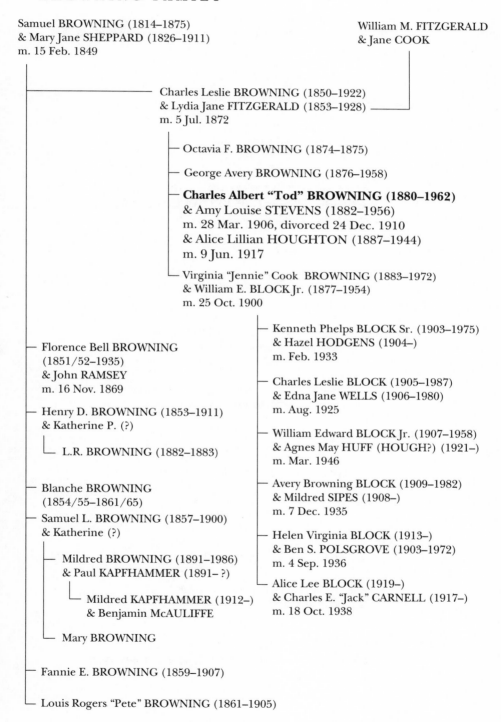

Samuel BROWNING (1814–1875)
& Mary Jane SHEPPARD (1826–1911)
m. 15 Feb. 1849

William M. FITZGERALD
& Jane COOK

Charles Leslie BROWNING (1850–1922)
& Lydia Jane FITZGERALD (1853–1928)
m. 5 Jul. 1872

— Octavia F. BROWNING (1874–1875)

— George Avery BROWNING (1876–1958)

— **Charles Albert "Tod" BROWNING (1880–1962)**
& Amy Louise STEVENS (1882–1956)
m. 28 Mar. 1906, divorced 24 Dec. 1910
& Alice Lillian HOUGHTON (1887–1944)
m. 9 Jun. 1917

— Virginia "Jennie" Cook BROWNING (1883–1972)
& William E. BLOCK Jr. (1877–1954)
m. 25 Oct. 1900

— Kenneth Phelps BLOCK Sr. (1903–1975)
& Hazel HODGENS (1904–)
m. Feb. 1933

— Charles Leslie BLOCK (1905–1987)
& Edna Jane WELLS (1906–1980)
m. Aug. 1925

— William Edward BLOCK Jr. (1907–1958)
& Agnes May HUFF (HOUGH?) (1921–)
m. Mar. 1946

— Avery Browning BLOCK (1909–1982)
& Mildred SIPES (1908–)
m. 7 Dec. 1935

— Helen Virginia BLOCK (1913–)
& Ben S. POLSGROVE (1903–1972)
m. 4 Sep. 1936

— Alice Lee BLOCK (1919–)
& Charles E. "Jack" CARNELL (1917–)
m. 18 Oct. 1938

— Florence Bell BROWNING
(1851/52–1935)
& John RAMSEY
m. 16 Nov. 1869

— Henry D. BROWNING (1853–1911)
& Katherine P. (?)

  └─ L.R. BROWNING (1882–1883)

— Blanche BROWNING
(1854/55–1861/65)
— Samuel L. BROWNING (1857–1900)
& Katherine (?)

  — Mildred BROWNING (1891–1986)
  & Paul KAPFHAMMER (1891– ?)

    └─ Mildred KAPFHAMMER (1912–)
    & Benjamin McAULIFFE

  └─ Mary BROWNING

— Fannie E. BROWNING (1859–1907)

— Louis Rogers "Pete" BROWNING (1861–1905)

STEVENS FAMILY

Frederick E. STEVENS Sr. (1857–1941)
& Emma Louise HUMBERT (1862–1939)
m. 5 Oct. 1880

└─ Kathryn B. STEVENS (1881–1978)
   & Sam HUDGINS
   m. Feb. 1902

     └─ Amy Louise HUDGINS (1904–1994)
       & Mr. HADDEN
       & Leo W. McCOMBS

├─ Amy Louise STEVENS (1882–1956)
   & Charles Albert "Tod" BROWNING (1880–1962
   m. 28 Mar. 1906, div. 24 Dec. 1910

├─ Wilbur STEVENS

└─ Frederick E. STEVENS Jr. (1887–1979)
   & Marie Esther IRWIN (1889–1969)
   m. 18 Jun. 1908

     └─ Marie Louise "Stevey" STEVENS (1909–1981)
       & William "Buster" COLLIER Jr. (1902–1987)
       m. 31 Dec. 1934

         └─ Constance "Chatty" COLLIER (1937–)
          & Don ELIASON (1936–)

HOUGHTON FAMILY

George W. HOUGHTON (1857–1916)
& Effie L. VOSBERGH (1860–1938)

├─ Nathan Fay HOUGHTON (1883–1923)

├─ Alice Lillian HOUGHTON (1887–1944)
   & J. Douglas WILSON
   m. 20 Mar. 1907, div. 11 Dec. 1916

└─ Alice Lillian HOUGHTON (1887–1944)
   & Charles Albert "Tod" BROWNING (1880–1962
   m. 9 Jun. 1917

ACKNOWLEDGMENTS

This work is a product of a decades-long fascination with the work of Tod Browning by both authors, who separately discovered *Dracula* and *Freaks* in the late 1960s and early 1970s and have been on the director's trail, obsessively, ever since.

Thanks are due primarily to the men and women who knew and worked with Tod Browning and who graciously provided interviews to Elias Savada in person and by telephone during a three-month-long research trip to Los Angeles in 1972: Mr. and Mrs. Lucien Andriot, Herve Babineau, Phil Berg, Margaret Booth, Carroll Borland, Evelyn Brent, David W. Butler, Mr. and Mrs. Edward de Butts, J. J. Cohn, Howard Dietz, Allan Dwan, Louis F. Edelman, Henrietta Endore, A. Arnold Gillespie, William S. Hart, Jr.; Winifred Westover Hart, Leila Hyams, Mary MacLaren, David Manners, George Marshall, Samuel Marx, Harry Oliver, Merrill Pye, Bernard Schubert, Frederick Y. Smith, Dr. and Mrs. Harold Snow, Ed Stone, and Basil Wrangell. The following individuals answered Mr. Savada's inquiries by correspondence: Karl Brown, Kevin Brownlow, Joan Crawford, Eleanor Boardman D'Arrast, Priscilla Dean, Lillian Gish, Willis Goldbeck, Joseph Henabery, John Robbins, and King Vidor.

Mr. Savada also conducted interviews in 1994 with Browning's foster nieces Alice Carnell and Helen Polsgrove, his first cousin once removed Mildred McAuliffe, and with the grandniece of Browning's first wife, Chatty Eliason. David J. Skal conducted on-site and

328   ACKNOWLEDGMENTS

telephone interviews with Carroll Borland, David Manners, Mildred McAuliffe, and Willard Sheldon.

Research institutions consulted include the American Film Institute Catalog Project; Elmer Holmes Bobst Library of New York University; Cave Hill Cemetery; Commonwealth of Kentucky Department for Health Services, Vital Statistics; Filson Club; Free Library of Philadelphia Theatre Collection; Margaret Herrick Library, Academy of Motion Picture Arts and Sciences; Highlands Funeral Home; Jefferson County, Kentucky, Division of Public Properties, Historic Preservation and Archives; Kentucky Department for Libraries and Archives, Public Records Division, State Archives Center; Kentucky Historical Society; Library of Congress; Louisville Free Public Library; Louisville Consistory, Ancient and Accepted Scottish Rite; Louis B. Mayer Library, American Film Institute; National Archives; Billy Rose Theatre Collection, New York Public Library at Lincoln Center; Southern Baptist Theological Seminary; University of Louisville, Archaeology Department.

Both authors thank the following individuals for assistance, information, advice, photographs, and various indispensable forms of inspiration related to this project: Forrest J Ackerman, Dr. Gordon Beck, Michael F. Blake, Robert Bloch, Richard Bojarski, Ron and Margaret Borst, Nick Bougas, R. E. Braff, Kevin Burns, Jonathan Sinclair Carey, Mike Damian, Philip J. DiBlasi, William K. Everson, Scott Eyman, Elinor Fitzgerald, Mark Frank, Robert F. Freedman, Leonardo Gandini, George Geltzer, Sam Gill, Hilary Hinzmann, Richard Lamparksi, Bela Lugosi, Jr., Scott MacQueen, Howard and Ron Mandelbaum (Photofest), Dion McGregor, William G. Obbagy, Richard Peterson, Richard Platt, George C. Pratt, John Reid, Gary Don Rhodes, Gene Ringgold, Laura Ross, Leonard Schrader, Don Shay, Charles Silver, Takashi Teshigawara, Johanne Tournier, Tony Villone, Tom Weaver, Delbert Winans, and Bret Wood.

Penultimately, both authors thank their editor, Charles Conrad, their agents, Malaga Baldi and Steve Fisher, and, finally, each other, for providing the closest approximation of Siamese twinship to which a pair of sane writers should ever aspire.

NOTES

Prologue: The Director Vanishes

4   REPEATEDLY EMPHASIZE SPECIFIC THOUGHTS. Stuart Rosenthal, "Tod Browning," in Peter Cowie, ed., *The Hollywood Professionals,* vol. 4 (New York: A. S. Barnes & Co., 1975), pp. 8–9.

5   WHEN I QUIT A THING, I QUIT. Quoted by Rory Guy, "Horror: The Browning Version," *Cinema,* June 1963.

6   THE DEAD MAN'S REQUEST. William S. Hart, Jr., interview by Elias Savada, Los Angeles, California, April 8, 1972.

6   ADOLPH COORS. Elias Savada, miscellaneous research notes, January–April 1972.

6   OUT-AND-OUT SADIST. Budd Schulberg, *Moving Pictures: Memories of a Hollywood Prince* (New York: Stein & Day, 1981), p. 314.

7   SUBJECTS FOR FURTHER RESEARCH. Andrew Sarris, *The American Cinema: Directors and Directions, 1929–68* (New York: E. P. Dutton & Co., 1968), pp. 227–29.

One: Certified Public Spectacles

11   LYDIA JANE FITZGERALD BROWNING. Lydia's middle name appears as "Jane" or the initial "J." on all official records, except for Tod Browning's second marriage certificate, where it is entered as "Lydia Virginia Fitzgerald." The name "Virginia" also appears on her death certificate, crossed out and replaced by "Jane."

11 REMARKABLY THIN MAN. Charles Leslie Browning 1922 interment records, Lee E. Cralle Funeral Home, Louisville, Kentucky.

11 HER HEIGHT IN DEATH. Lydia Browning 1928 interment records,
Lee E. Cralle Funeral Home, Louisville, Kentucky.

12 BROWNING CLAN. Genealogical information on the Browning
family is drawn from *Gabriel Collins' Louisville and New Albany Directory*
(1848); *Caron's Louisville Directory*, 1880–1916; records of the Jefferson County Health Department, Louisville; the Commonwealth of
Kentucky Registrar of Vital Statistics, Frankfort; Kentucky census
records, 1850–1920; records of the Lee E. Cralle Funeral Home
(Browning family undertakers), currently maintained by the Highland Funeral Home, Louisville. Information on Browning family
burial sites was also provided by Philip J. DiBlasi, staff archaeologist
at the University of Louisville.

14 MORE THAN A DECADE JOUSTING. Philip Von Borries, "Re-
quiem for a Gladiator," *Baseball Research Journal* (1983).

14 LITTLE BEER WAS LEFT. "Pete Browning 'Out' of Life's Game,"
Louisville Times, September 11, 1905.

14 ALCOHOLIC MICROBES. John Thorn and Pete Palmer, eds., *Total
Baseball*, 3rd. ed. (New York: HarperPerennial, 1993), p. 208.

15 INTENSE DISGUST OF THE SPECTATORS. Unsourced clipping,
October 12, 1887, Louis R. Browning file, National Baseball Hall of
Fame Library, Cooperstown, New York.

15 OTHER PECULIARITIES. Miscellaneous clippings and documents,
ibid.

16 ULCERATION OF THE STOMACH. Although the Jefferson County
Clerk Register of Deaths cites this as the cause of death, the obituary
for his wife, Mary J. Browning, stated her husband "was killed in a
cyclone thirty-seven years ago," *Louisville Courier-Journal*, April 7,
1911, p. 8.

16 OBSESSIVELY ORGANIZED PERSONALITY. Helen Polsgrove and
Alice Carnell, interview by Elias Savada, Louisville, Kentucky, August
15, 1994.

17 PERFORMANCES TO ASTOUND. "Famous Mystery Pictures Are
Work of Native Louisvillian," *Louisville Herald-Post*, July 18, 1928.

17 FAMILY'S SECOND HOUSE. Property conveyance cited in a deed
filed in the matter of the estate of Charles L. Browning, by George
Avery Browning, executor, recorded on June 24, 1922, at the Jefferson County Court House.

18 MILDRED McAULIFFE. Telephone interview by David J. Skal, August 19, 1994.

18 INFANT PHENOMENON. "Famous Mystery Pictures," *op. cit.*

18 RECEIVED FOR BAPTISM. Handwritten records of the 26th and Market Street Baptist Church, 1891–93, at the Baptist Tabernacle Church, Louisville, Kentucky.

18 RECALLS ATTENDING CHURCH. Polsgrove and Carnell interview, *op. cit.*

19 THE SATELLITES OF MERCURY. Isabel McLennan McMeekin, *Louisville: The Gateway City* (New York: Julian Messner, Inc., 1946), pp. 172–73.

19 STRONG WINE, FAST MUSIC. Peter Chew, *The Kentucky Derby: The First 100 Years* (Boston: Houghton Mifflin Co., 1974), p. 10.

19 YOU AIN'T NEVER SEEN NOTHIN'. Irvin S. Cobb, 1936 program for the Kentucky Derby, p. 52.

19 GYPSY ENCAMPMENTS. Richard Clemensen, "When Radio and Film Were Young," *Louisville Magazine,* June 1977, pp. 21–22.

19 DEVASTATING TORNADO. McMeekin, *op. cit.*, p. 173.

19 MASSIVE FUNNEL. *New York Times,* March 28 and 29, 1890, p. 1.

20 MAURICE "OLE HOSS" KIRBY. Eustace Williams, *That Old Rivalry: Manual vs. High School 1893–1900* (Louisville: John P. Morton & Co., 1940), p. 4.

21 HE BEGAN EARNING MONEY. Mrs. Robert Z. Leonard, interview by Elias Savada, Los Angeles, California, February 18, 1972.

22 ENVY OF HIS BARKING BRETHREN. "Tod Browning Rejoins Universal," *Universal Weekly,* March 15, 1930, p. 10.

22 INFATUATION WITH THE SIDE SHOW QUEEN. "Tod Browning's Varied Career," *Louisville Herald-Post,* February 27, 1921.

24 SHOWMEN KNEW THEY WERE NOT TRUSTED. Robert Bogdan, *Freak Show: Presenting Human Oddities for Amusement and Profit* (Chicago and London: University of Chicago Press, 1988), pp. 80–81.

24 SNOOTY. Polsgrove and Carnell interview, *op. cit.*

24 BROWNING WAS "PROUD." William Hart interview, *op. cit.*

24 ON BETTER TERMS WITH HIS GRANDMOTHER. Mrs. Edward de Butts, interview by Elias Savada, Malibu, California, April 21, 1972.

25 ST. LOUIS WORLD'S FAIR. Obituary of Roy C. Jones, *Variety,* December 22, 1948.

25 WHEN THE CELEBRATED HYPNOTIST. "The Personal Side of the Pictures," *Reel Life,* July 25, 1914, p. 19.

25 TRADITIONAL INDIAN VERSION. Joseph Dunninger, *Dunninger's Complete Encyclopedia of Magic* (New York: University Books/Carroll Publishing Group, 1967), p. 127.

26 HOUDINI, HAD HE LIVED. James Randi, *Conjuring* (New York: St. Martin's Press, 1992), p. 173.

26 WHEN I HEARD THE DIRT. "Tod Browning's Varied Career," *op. cit.*

27 FANTASTICALLY EMBROIDERED KIMONO. H. J. Moulton, *Houdini's History of Magic in Boston 1792–1915* (Glenwood, Ill.: Meyerbooks, 1983), p. 125.

28 RENOWNED CHINESE MAGICIAN. William Hart interview, *op. cit.*

28 EVERY CITY OF IMPORTANCE. "Clever Screen Director Was Side Show Barker," *New York Times,* February 7, 1926, sec. 7, p. 4.

30 ANDREW MELLON OF RACING ACTIVITIES. Unsourced, undated obituaries of Milton Meffert from Louisville newspapers contained in the effects of Amy Louise McCombs, niece of Amy Louise Stevens.

31 EXCEPT WHEN THEY WERE TRAVELING. Statement of Emma L. Stevens, brief for plaintiff in divorce proceeding, *Browning v. Browning* (Case No. 61806), Chancery Branch, First Division, Jefferson Circuit Court, Louisville, Kentucky, November 25, 1910.

31 BORROWED SUMS OF MONEY. Statement of Emma L. Stevens, Jefferson Circuit Court (Case No. 77721), Common Pleas Branch; *Emma Stevens, plaintiff, v. C. A. Browning, alias Tod Browning, defendant,* Louisville, Kentucky, January 17, 1913.

31 WAS A SHIFTLESS MAN. *Browning v. Browning, op. cit.*

31 FONTAINE FERRY PARK. *Fontaine Ferry Park: A Time of Innocence* (Louisville: Tim Young Productions, Inc., 1992). Video documentary.

32 1910 DIVORCE. *Browning v. Browning, op. cit.*

33 LIVED WITH A WOMAN IN CHICAGO. McAuliffe interview, *op. cit.*

33 THE DARKER SIDE OF THEATRICAL BOARDINGHOUSES. Mary MacLaren, interview by Elias Savada, Los Angeles, California, April 15, 1972.

34 HIS GRANDMOTHER'S DEATH. Obituary of Mrs. Mary J. Browning, *Louisville Courier-Journal,* April 7, 1911, p. 8.

34 LOUISVILLE CONNECTION. Obituaries of John H. Whallen, *Variety,* December 12, 1913, p. 22, and *Louisville Courier-Journal,* December 4, 1913, p. 1.

34 A BETTER DRESSED SHOW. "Burlesque News—*The Whirl of Mirth*" (review), *New York Clipper,* August 24, 1912, p. 16.

34 WAXWORKS AT THE EDEN MUSÉE. David J. Skal recalls viewing the original Eden Musée figures at the Cedar Point amusement park in Sandusky, Ohio, in the early 1960s.

34 PRAISED HIS PERFORMANCE. Review of *The Whirl of Mirth, Variety,* August 23, 1912, p. 22.

34 AN ABUNDANCE OF LAUGHS. "Burlesque News," *New York Clipper,* August 24, 1912, p. 16.

34 NEARLY FORTY SEPARATE ENGAGEMENTS. "Burlesque Routes" listings, *Variety,* August 1912–April 1913.

35 VERY AMUSING. "At the Theater," *Louisville Courier-Journal,* January 6, 1913, p. 4.

35 A COURT CHALLENGE. "Burlesque Men in Court," *Variety,* September 6, 1912, p. 17.

35 AFFIDAVIT FILED. *Emma Stevens v. C. A. Browning, op. cit.*

36 QUEER MAKE-UP EFFECTS. *Moving Picture World,* November 8, 1913, p. 611.

37 LITTLE GIRL FRESH FROM A DEPARTMENT STORE. Mary Pickford, *Sunshine and Shadows* (New York: Doubleday & Co., 1955), p. 146.

37 TOD BROWNING USED A CANE. Karl Brown, *Adventures with D. W. Griffith* (New York: Farrar, Straus & Giroux, 1973), p. 167.

38 NOTHING FUNNY OR ELEVATING. Review of *Nell's Eugenic Wedding, Moving Picture World,* June 6, 1914, p. 1409.

38 DOES NOT HESITATE TO MAKE HERSELF GROTESQUE. "The Personal Side of Pictures," *Reel Life,* September 19, 1914, p. 14.

39 IN HIS EARLY THIRTIES. Anita Loos, *Cast of Thousands* (New York: Grosset & Dunlap, 1977), p. 25.

40 LARGELY A SCHOOLGIRL INFATUATION. Winifred Hart, interview by Elias Savada, Los Angeles, California, April 8, 1972.

40 WILLFULLY, WITHOUT CAUSE. Interlocutory decree of divorce, *J. Douglas Wilson v. Alice Lillian Wilson,* Superior Court of the State of California, City and County of San Francisco, July 1, 1915 (Case No. 66108, no. 7).

41 ALWAYS ALICE BROWNING TO ME. George E. Marshall, interview by Elias Savada, Los Angeles, California, April 14, 1972.

41 EARLIER MAJOR INVOLVEMENT. Allan Dwan, interview by Elias Savada, Los Angeles, California, February 26, 1972.

41 DIRECTOR RAOUL WALSH. Alanna Nash, "The Man Who Unearthed Count Dracula—Louisville Runaway Tod Browning," *Louisville Courier-Journal,* April 2, 1978.

42 BOUGHT A FRENCH RACING CAR. "Reel Tales About Reel Folks," *Reel Life,* August 29, 1914, p. 18.

42   SPEEDING MANIA. "The Personal Side of the Pictures," *Reel Life,* July 25, 1914, p. 19.

43   TALL, SKINNY, VERY REMARKABLE MAN. Miriam Cooper, interview in *Classic Film Collector* (undated clipping).

Two: Shadows of Babylon

48   ALSO IN THE VEHICLE. The Los Angeles County Coroner's Office records of June 18, 1915, list as witnesses to the accident Edward Joseph Booth, S. E. Harrison, "Tod Albert Browning," E. L. Terry, H. H. Jones, and George A. Siegmann.

48   WAFFLE OFF THE GRILL. "Investigating Ride to Death," *Los Angeles Times,* June 17, 1915, part 2, p. 1.

48   RECOVERY "DOUBTFUL." "Film Stars in Auto Wreck; One Killed, Two Hurt," *San Francisco Chronicle,* June 17, 1915.

49   I WASN'T FAR BEHIND. Dwan interview, *op. cit.*

49   DENTURES NEVER FIT PROPERLY. Dr. and Mrs. Harold Snow, interview by Elias Savada, Los Angeles, California, February 19, 1992.

49   IMPROMPTU EULOGY. "Funeral of Elmer Booth," *Moving Picture World,* July 10, 1915, p. 289; Grace Kingsley, "At the Stage Door," *Los Angeles Times,* June 21, 1915, part 3, p. 4; "In and Out of Los Angeles Studios," *Motion Picture News,* July 10, 1915, p. 55.

49   LACK OF PRECAUTION. Los Angeles County Coroner's Office records, *op. cit.*

50   IN BED FOR ALMOST A YEAR. MacLaren interview, *op. cit.*

50   PICTURESQUELY CALLED DEAD MEN. Richard Schickel, *D. W. Griffith: An American Life* (New York: Simon & Schuster, 1984), p. 319.

51   ACTIVITY WAS PERMANENTLY LIMITED. Dwan interview, *op. cit.*

52   HOFFMAN CAFÉ. William S. Hart, *My Life East and West* (Boston: Houghton Mifflin Company, 1929), p. 227.

52   WITHOUT THE LIMITS OF ADVERSE CRITICISM. Review of *Jim Bludso,* by Peter Milne, *Motion Picture News,* February 10, 1917, p. 922.

52   WITCHERY OF THE RIVER SCENES. Review of *Jim Bludso, New York Dramatic Mirror,* February 3, 1917, p. 28.

53   NIGGER SLOUGH, CALIFORNIA. Winifred Hart interview, *op. cit.*

54   DIVORCE PAPERS. *Ibid.*

54   RATIONAL LIGHTING. "Tod Browning Discusses Lighting," *Moving Picture World,* June 23, 1917.

55 TREMENDOUS LEGS. Samuel Marx, interview by Elias Savada, Los Angeles, California, April 4, 1972.

57 BOTH PARENTS WERE DEAF. For the most comprehensive documentation of the facts of Lon Chaney's life and career, see Michael F. Blake, *Lon Chaney: The Man Behind the Thousand Faces* (Vestal, N.Y.: Vestal Press, Ltd., 1993).

57 ATTEMPTED SUICIDE. "Drinks Poison Behind Scenes," *Los Angeles Times,* May 1, 1913, part 2, p. 7.

57 HABITUAL INTEMPERANCE. Chaney divorce papers, December 19, 1913, cited by Blake, *op. cit.,* p. 40.

58 MY PROPERTY MAN. Dwan interview, *op. cit.*

60 THEY WERE BOTH THIEVES. MacLaren interview, *op. cit.*

60 CARNY TECHNIQUES. Fred Pasley, "What a Life! Directing Freaks Is a Man's Job in the 'Talkies,' " *Philadelphia Evening Bulletin,* February 11, 1932, p. 16.

60 EMERGING DIRECTORIAL TECHNIQUE. David Butler, interview by Elias Savada, Los Angeles, California, April 4, 1972.

60 THE ACTUAL COST OF *INTOLERANCE.* Schickel, *op. cit.,* p. 326, reports the negative cost of Griffith's film as $385,906.77.

62 CALLED FOR A CAMEL RACE. "Tod Browning Brings His Own Big Picture, *The Virgin of Stamboul,* Across Continent to Show Here," *New York Tribune,* March 21, 1920.

62 IT FINALLY TURNED AND WINKED. *Ibid.*

62 A HEALTHY CALIFORNIAN. Review of *The Virgin of Stamboul, Photoplay,* May 1920, pp. 112–13.

63 FEMININE SPELLING OF HIS NAME. "This Is the Banner Press Agent Stunt: A Sheik in Search of Sari Stirs Town Like Milk Baths Did in Good Old Days," *Moving Picture World,* March 27, 1920, p. 2117.

64 RECOVER FROM HER HYSTERIA. "Hotel Ousts Sari: 'Pearl of Stamboul' Can Recover in a Studio, Says Manager," *New York Times,* March 11, 1920, p. 3.

64 QUALIFIED PRAISE. Review of *The Virgin of Stamboul, New York Times,* March 28, 1920.

64 AS A PICTURE OF ORIENTAL LIFE AND CHARACTER. Review of *The Virgin of Stamboul, Bioscope* (U.K.), May 8, 1920.

65 FIVE-ROOM CHATELET. "Hollywood Hokum" (column), *Motion Picture News,* December 18, 1920, p. 4648.

65 BURNING MOONLIGHT. Ray Davidson, "Little Trips to Los Angeles Studios," *Screen World,* October 23, 1920, p. 757.

65   RELEASED CHANEY FROM THE COMMITMENT. "Tod Browning, Who Used to Cut Corners at the Louisville Race Track, Now Tells How to Cut Non Essentials Out of Films," *Moving Picture World,* December 25, 1920, p. 1021.

65   HORROR OF HORRORS, "FRISCO." Tom W. Baily, "San Francisco Story Is Filmed for Tivoli," *San Francisco Chronicle,* February 28, 1921, p. B2-3.

66   LIKE A HUMMINGBIRD. Pete Martin, *Hollywood Without Make-Up* (New York: J. B. Lippincott Company, 1948), p. 107.

66   BROWNING WAS ILL. Leo McCarey, interview by Peter Bogdanovich, Louis B. Mayer Foundation Oral History Program, American Film Institute.

67   WHY DO WE GO TO THE CINEMA. David Thomson, *A Biographical Dictionary of Film,* 2nd ed. rev. (New York: William Morrow & Co., Inc., 1981), p. 93.

68   MISSING ITS LAST REEL. "*Outside the Law,* Universal's Big Production to Be Revived," *Moving Picture World,* May 15, 1926, p. 240.

68   BILLBOARD MESSAGES. "Exploitation of *Outside the Law,* Universal Feature, Has Attracted Unusual Attention," *Exhibitor's Trade Review,* January 22, 1921, p. 771.

68   STAGE PRODUCTION. *Motion Picture News,* November 13, 1920, p. 3778.

69   HE DIDN'T PUT HIS NAME ON IT. McCarey interview, *op. cit.*

69   SOME MEASURE OF PHYSICAL THERAPY. Polsgrove and Carnell interview, *op. cit.*

70   A REAL SANDSTORM BURIED THE WIND MACHINES. Samuel Marx, *Mayer and Thalberg: The Make-Believe Saints* (New York: Random House, 1975), p. 34.

71   ODDLY WORDED TRADE PAPER ITEMS. *Camera,* June 24, 1922, p. 17, and July 8, 1922, p. 4.

72   HADN'T THE REMOTEST IDEA. Mae Tinee, "Just a Movie That Rates Non-Essential: Even Miss Dean Can't Put Over *White Tiger,*" *Chicago Daily Tribune,* January 10, 1924, p. 15.

72   QUEEN OF THE LOT. Marx interview, *op. cit.*

72   WORLD-WEARY HOMOSEXUAL. Marx, *Mayer and Thalberg, op. cit.,* p. 43.

72   A HARD, RATHER UNWOMANLY ROLE. Mary Kelly, "Stirring Melodrama of China, a Universal-Jewel Production," *Moving Picture World,* September 1, 1923, p. 57.

73   VITUPERATIVE HEROINE OF THE SCREEN. Harriette Underhill, "On the Screen," *New York Tribune,* August 20, 1923, p. 8.

73   DAUGHTER OF A CHINATOWN LAUNDRYMAN. Biographical information drawn from Anna May Wong clippings file, Billy Rose Theater Collection, New York Public Library for the Performing Arts at Lincoln Center.

74   LIQUOR UNDER HIS BED. Dwan interview, *op. cit.*

74   HE WAS IN LOVE WITH HER. J. J. Cohn, interview by Elias Savada, Los Angeles, California, February 3, 1972.

75   SOMETHING DIFFERENT. Butler interview, *op. cit.*

75   UNIVERSAL LAID HIM OFF. Dwan interview, *op. cit.*

75   MADE AN ASS OF MYSELF. Myrtle Gebhart, "Because a Woman Believed," *Picture Play Magazine,* December 1925, pp. 32–33, 100.

75   GO BITE YOURSELF. Pasley, *op. cit.*

Three: "Murderous Midgets, Crippled Thieves . . ."

79   A ONE-PICTURE DEAL WITH GOLDWYN. Memo from Goldwyn Pictures business department to Mott and Cross, February 7, 1923.

80   I WENT TO SMASH. Gebhart, *op. cit.*

80   LISTENED POLITELY TO BROWNING'S IDEA. Interoffice communication, Goldwyn Producing Corporation, June Mathis to Mr. Lehr, March 3, 1923.

81   SOMETIME AT YOUR CONVENIENCE. Interoffice communication, Abraham Lehr to Mr. [Harry] Edington, March 5, 1923.

81   FORCED TO EDIT THE FILM REPEATEDLY. Interoffice communication, Goldwyn Producing Corporation, T. N. Miranda to Mr. [Harry] Edington, August 27, 1923.

81   I WAS BRAND NEW. Eleanor Boardman D'Arrast, letter to Elias Savada, February 26, 1972.

81   A GREAT DEAL OF SLUSH. Review of *The Day of Faith, New York Herald,* November 26, 1923.

82   WHAT NEEDLES ARE FOR. Dialogue quoted in *Film Fun: A Magazine of Real Merriment,* October 1922, p. 5.

83   ALL THE BAD LIQUOR IN THE WORLD. Joan Dickey, "A Maker of Mysteries: Tod Browning Is a Specialist in Building Thrills and Chills," *Motion Picture Classic,* April 1928, pp. 33, 80.

85   MRS. LUCIEN ANDRIOT. Interview by Elias Savada, Palm Springs, California, March 27, 1972.

85   I WAS SCARED. Evelyn Brent, interview by Elias Savada, Los Angeles, California, April 10, 1972.

86 ATTEMPTS TO ARRANGE A MARRIAGE. Marx, *Mayer and Thalberg, op. cit.*

86 YOU CAN'T MAKE AN AUDIENCE SERIOUSLY BELIEVE. Dickey, *op. cit.*

87 NOT A DETECTIVE STORY. Review of *The Unholy Three, New York Times Book Review,* October 21, 1917.

87 THE GREEN MOULD OF EVIL COVERED EVERYTHING. C. A. "Tod" Robbins, *The Unholy Three* (New York: John Lane Co., 1917), p. 14.

88 UNRECOGNIZABLE BLOODY HEAPS. *Ibid.*

89 PAID HALF THAT AMOUNT. John Robbins, letter to Elias Savada, February 23, 1972.

89 SOMETHING OF A FREAK. Roland Flamini, *Thalberg: The Last Tycoon and the World of M-G-M* (New York: Crown Publishers, 1994), p. 224.

89 ONE-PICTURE CONTRACT. Interoffice communication, Chas. A. Greene to Messrs Mayer, Thalberg, Rapf, Mannix, Clark, Craig, and Cohn, February 23, 1925. Undated attachment of budget estimate for *The Unholy Three.*

91 TOO INTENSE FOR 1925 AUDIENCES. Blake, *op. cit.,* p. 145.

91 A STARTLING ORIGINAL ACHIEVEMENT. Mordaunt Hall, "An Excellent Drama," *New York Times,* August 4, 1925.

91 WEALTH OF CINEMATIC IMAGINATION. Quoted in display advertisement, *New York Times,* August 9, 1925.

92 KICK EQUIVALENT TO A COCKTAIL. Review of *The Unholy Three, New Yorker,* August 1925.

92 SPECTACULAR PROFIT. Production figures drawn from E. J. Mannix ledgers of M-G-M expenses, revenues, and profits, Margaret Herrick Library, Special Collections, Academy of Motion Picture Arts and Sciences, Beverly Hills, California.

94 FLAT PAYMENT. Last Will and Testament of Charles L. Browning, dated February 10, 1917; Inventory in the Matter of the Estate of Charles L. Browning, deceased, dated April 28, 1922; and Final Settlement in the matter of the estate of Charles L. Browning, dated June 2, 1922, as stated by George Avery Browning, executor, as filed in the Jefferson County Court House, Louisville, Kentucky.

94 AN AUBREY BEARDSLEY WHO MASTERED THE FOXTROT. *New York Times* critic John Canady (1967), quoted in Charles Spencer, *Erté* (New York: Clarkson N. Potter, Inc., New York), 1970.

94   TO SAY THE LEAST, OUTRÉ. Charles Higham, *Merchant of Dreams: Louis B. Mayer, M.G.M. and the Secret Hollywood* (New York: Donald I. Fine, Inc., 1993), p. 90.

95   CLOTHES LACKED ALLURE. Erté, *Things I Remember: An Autobiography* (New York: Quadrangle/New York Times Book Co., 1975), p. 83.

95   ACTORS BECAME BORED. *Ibid.*, p. 84.

95   MY DREAM WAS TO MAKE A FILM FANTASY. *Ibid.*, p. 80.

96   DIDN'T KNOW ANYTHING ABOUT DRESSES. Elliott Stein, letter to Elias Savada describing conversation with Aileen Pringle, February 1972.

97   WILLARD SHELDON. Mr. Sheldon was interviewed, separately by telephone, on December 6 and 7, 1994, by David J. Skal and film historian Michael F. Blake. Mr. Blake provided a transcript of his interview, which has been integrated into the present text.

98   PROFIT OF $52,000. Mannix ledgers, *op. cit.*

98   THE AMAZING EVENTS. "Another Good Crook Melodrama Is Underground at the Capitol," *New York Evening Post,* September 1, 1925.

98   LEGITIMATE RIGHTS. "Stage Calls *The Mystic,*" *Moving Picture World,* September 26, 1925, p. 344.

98   CHANEY WAS PREPARING TO TOUR. 1924 press release on stage plans for *The Hunchback of Notre Dame,* Free Library of Philadelphia Theatre Collection.

99   DARK, CONTROLLED AMBIANCE. "Picture Plays and Players," *New York Sun,* February 2, 1926.

100   POSTED A PROFIT OF $263,000. Mannix ledgers, *op. cit.*

100   PHANTOM OF THE OPERA. Profit figure cited in Blake, *op. cit.*, p. 345.

100   REALLY LOOKED FOR MATERIAL. Phil Berg, interview by Elias Savada, Los Angeles, California, April 4, 1972.

101   FAST, WITTY WRITERS. Pauline Kael, "Onward and Upward with the Arts: Raising Kane—I," *New Yorker,* February 20, 1971, p. 49.

101   PERVERSENESS. "Poor Singapore," by Mordaunt Hall, *New York Times,* July 4, 1926.

102   IT OPENS WITH LON CHANEY. Howard Dietz, *Dancing in the Dark: An Autobiography* (New York: Quadrangle/New York Times Book Co., 1974), p. 160.

102 WHAT BUSINESS IS HE IN. Dietz' published recollections vary somewhat from those given to Elias Savada during a taped interview in Los Angeles on February 3, 1972. In his autobiography, the anecdote provides a pretext for Dietz introducing Browning to Herman Mankiewicz. In the interview, Dietz related the story as being told by Browning to Mankiewicz.

102 MILLIONS ARE TO BE GRABBED. Mankiewicz telegram, quoted in Ann Douglas, *Terrible Honesty: Mongrel Manhattan in the 1920s* (New York: Farrar, Straus and Giroux, 1995), p. 61.

103 FAMILIAR WITH THE CURRENTS. Stephen Farber and Marc Green, *Hollywood on the Couch: A Candid Look at the Overheated Love Affair Between Psychiatrists and Moviemakers* (New York: William Morrow & Co., Inc., 1993), p. 27.

103 FILTERED THROUGH THE SUCCESSIVE MINDS. Frederick Lewis Allen, *Only Yesterday: An Informal History of the Nineteen-Twenties* (New York: Harper & Row, 1931), p. 28.

104 BOARDWALK ASTROLOGER. Farber and Green, *op. cit.*, p. 23.

104 AMERICA IS A MISTAKE. Ernest Jones, *The Life and Work of Sigmund Freud* (New York: Basic Books, 1955), vol. 2, p. 60.

104 A STUDY OF DREAMS. Sigmund Freud, "The 'Uncanny,'" in James Stratchey, ed., *Complete Psychological Works,* vol. 17 (London: Hogarth Press, 1955), p. 231.

105 $267,000 PROFIT. Mannix ledgers, *op. cit.*

105 THE PICTURE IS QUITE TEDIOUS. Review of *The Road to Mandalay,* by Mordaunt Hall, *New York Times,* June 29, 1926, p. 21.

105 A SLUMMING PARTY. Review of *The Road to Mandalay, Variety,* June 30, 1926.

106 CLASHED REPEATEDLY WITH MAYER. Marx, *Mayer and Thalberg, op. cit.*, p. 74.

106 JUST FUCK HER AND FORGET ABOUT IT. Leatrice Gilbert Fountain, with John R. Maxim, *Dark Star: The Untold Story of the Meteoric Rise and Fall of the Legendary John Gilbert* (New York: St. Martin's Press, 1985), p. 131.

106 IF IT COSTS ME A MILLION DOLLARS. *Ibid.*

108 DISMEMBERED LIMBS, A SEVERED HEAD. Freud, *op. cit.*, p. 244.

108 LONG-STANDING HOLLYWOOD RUMOR. The present authors have been unable to pinpoint the origin of the castration story, though it seems to come from the period following the enthusiastic rediscovery of *Freaks* by psychologizing critics of the 1970s. It is cited most recently by John McCarty in his book *The Fearmakers* (New York: St. Martin's Press, 1994), pp. 4–5.

109   STARTS OFF LIKE A HOUSE AFIRE. Review of *The Show, New York Morning Telegram,* March 14, 1927.

109   SNAPPY AND UNUSUAL STORY. Review of *The Show, New York Daily Mirror,* undated clipping, March 1927.

109   ANY ONE WHO IS TIRED. Wilella Waldorf, "New Photoplays," *New York Evening Post,* March 14, 1927, p. 16.

109   LIKE MOST OF MR. BROWNING'S HEROES. Review of *The Show,* by Mordaunt Hall, *New York Times,* March 14, 1927.

109   A POSITIVE EVALUATION. Richard Watts, Jr., "A Glance at Tod Browning, an Original of the Cinema," *New York Herald-Tribune,* March 20, 1927, sec. 6, p. 3.

112   A SADISTIC CHARACTER. Curt Siodmak, letter to David J. Skal, February 18, 1991.

112   I WAS SO EAGER TO LEARN. Joan Crawford, letter to Elias Savada, March 11, 1972.

112   SUCH NUMBNESS, SUCH TORTURE. Joan Crawford, with Jean Kesner Ardmore, *A Portrait of Joan: The Autobiography of Joan Crawford* (New York: Doubleday & Co., 1962), p. 30.

112   MOST TENSE, EXCITING INDIVIDUAL. *Ibid.*

113   AS IF GOD WERE WORKING. *Ibid.*

113   HE WAS VERY PATIENT WITH ME. Crawford letter to Savada, *op. cit.*

113   I'LL NEVER FORGET ONE INCIDENT. "Miss Joan Crawford Has a Word to Say About Screen Stars: Playing with Man Before Camera Good Index to His Character, Actress Asserts," *New York Herald-Tribune,* August 26, 1928.

113   THIS TIME A LEG COMES OFF. Dickey, *op. cit.*

113   A REAL ARMLESS MAN. Blake, *op. cit.,* p. 195.

114   THE CASE OF MR. TOD BROWNING. Review of *The Unknown,* by Richard Watts, Jr., *New York Herald-Tribune,* June 19, 1927.

114   WRITTEN BY NERO, DIRECTED BY LUCRETIA BORGIA. John S. Cohen, Jr., "The New Photo Plays," *New York Sun,* June 13, 1927.

115   IF YOU LIKE TO TEAR BUTTERFLIES APART. Review of *The Unknown,* by Dorothy Herzog, *New York Daily Mirror,* June 13, 1927.

115   MR. CHANEY HAS BEEN TWISTING JOINTS. Wilella Waldorf, "New Photoplays," *New York Evening Post,* June 13, 1927.

115   ONE CAN IMAGINE A MORAL PERVERT. Review of *The Unknown, Harrison's Reports,* June 25, 1927, p. 103.

115   DESPITE THE POPULARITY. Review of *The Unknown*, by Donald Thompson, *New York Telegram*, June 13, 1927.

116   AN UNBRIDLED ROMANTIC. 1929 review of *The Unknown*, by Jacques B. Brunius, reprinted in program notes of the National Film Theatre, London, undated.

116   THOUGHT TO BE A LOST FILM. Anecdote related by James Card at screening of *The Unknown* at the Museum of Modern Art, New York, January 14, 1970.

117   CHANEY WANTED TO ACT DRACULA. "Vampires, Monsters, Horrors!" *New York Times*, March 1, 1936.

118   GROUCHO MARX. Forrest J. Ackerman, foreword to Philip J. Riley, ed., *London After Midnight* (New York, London, Toronto: Cornwall Books, 1985), p. 15.

118   ARMADILLOS. Robert Bloch, conversation with David J. Skal, Van Nuys, California, 1993. Armadillos are not mentioned in the script for *London After Midnight*, but Bloch's recollection is supported by references to the animal in both publicity clippings and reviews.

118   GROSSING MORE THAN A MILLION. Mannix ledgers, *op. cit.*

118   DISTINGUISHED TALENTS. Review of *London After Midnight*, *New York Herald-Tribune*, December 12, 1927.

119   ENOUGH TO MAKE ONE SICK. Review of *London After Midnight*, *Harrison's Reports*, December 24, 1927, p. 206.

119   THEIR THROATS SLASHED. "Man and Woman with Throats Cut," *Times* (London), October 25, 1928, p. 10.

119   HUNG JURY. "Hyde Park Murder Trial: Jury Unable to Agree," *Times* (London), December 21, 1928, p. 16.

119   A VISION OF LON CHANEY. "Hyde Park Murder: Verdict of 'Guilty' at Second Trial," *Times* (London), January 11, 1929, p. 7.

119   HORRIFYING AND TERRIBLE SPECTACLE. Justice Travers Humphreys, quoted in obituary of Lon Chaney, *Times* (London), August 27, 1930, p. 12.

120   WAS ISSUED A REPRIEVE. "Reprieve in Hyde Park Murder Case," *Times* (London), January 28, 1929, p. 14.

120   ATTEMPTED TO ENGAGE SOPHIE TUCKER. *Photoplay*, January 1928.

120   TRITE AND UNINTERESTING. Betty Compson, letter to Elias Savada, February 17, 1971.

120   THE FILM DID WELL. Mannix ledgers, *op. cit.*

120   A WIZ OF A DIRECTOR. "Among Month's Movies These Are Rated Best," *Chicago Sunday Tribune*, April 1, 1928.

120 DIRECTED WRETCHEDLY. "We Have a Close-up of Some Ham and Eggs," *Film Spectator*, April 14, 1928.

121 THE CLEAN LOVE OF A GOOD WOMAN. Review of *The Big City*, by Richard Watts, Jr., *New York Herald-Tribune*, March 25, 1928.

121 ONLY DOCUMENTATION OF A PASSPORT. Browning's birth certificate, filed only in 1947, lists as documentation a U.S. passport dated December 21, 1927. A formal request to the National Archives for any supplemental information or earlier passports turned up nothing.

122 WAS HANGING CLOTHES. Polsgrove and Carnell interview, *op. cit.*

122 FUNERAL ARRANGEMENTS. Lydia Browning interment records, *op. cit.*

123 OUTPOURING OF THE CESSPOOLS. F. S. Harrison, lead editorial, *Harrison's Reports*, January 5, 1929, pp. 1, 4.

124 WORLDWIDE BILLINGS. Mannix ledgers, *op. cit.*

124 CHANEY'S NAME WARNS THEATREGOERS. Donald Beaton, "As They Appeal to Youth," *Film Spectator*, January 5, 1929, pp. 10–11.

125 BIGGEST HIT OF ALL. Mannix ledgers, *op. cit.*

125 $399,000 IN THE BLACK. *Ibid.*

125 A PROFIT OF $450,000. *Ibid.*

125 POLITELY DISMISSIVE. "The True Life Story of Lon Chaney," *Photoplay*, February 1928.

125 USED TO ARGUE A BIT. Adela Rogers St. Johns, "Lon Chaney: A Portrait of the Man Behind a Thousand Faces (Part Five)," *Liberty*, May 30, 1931, p. 41.

126 WERE VERY SIMPATICO. Berg interview, *op. cit.*

126 WEREN'T EXACTLY BOSOM BUDDIES. Michael F. Blake, quoting Taggart, telephone conversation with David J. Skal, December 1994.

127 BEASTLY EXHIBITION OF POOR TASTE. "*Where East Is East* Good Example of Pictorial Effect," *Film Spectator*, July 15, 1929, p. 6.

127 WEANED ON A POGO STICK. Donald Beaton, "Another Point of View," *Film Spectator*, July 27, 1929.

127 MORE THAN SLIGHTLY INCREDIBLE. Review of *Where East Is East*, by Mordaunt Hall, *New York Times*, May 27, 1929, p. 22.

127 CHANEY'S ILLNESS. Blake, *op. cit.*, pp. 254–55.

128 THE SEA BAT. *Hollywood Filmograph*, June 1, 1929, p. 34; *Film Spectator*, July 27, 1929, p. 17.

128 AN UNKNOWN, A SORT OF COWBOY. Leila Hyams, interview by Elias Savada, Los Angeles, California, April 4, 1972.

128 BROWNING OFFERED AN EXPLANATION. Pressbook for *The Thirteenth Chair.*

130 W. F. WILLIS, ADVISING M-G-M. Memo dated October 1, 1929; MPPDA case file on *The Thirteenth Chair,* Margaret Herrick Library, Academy of Motion Picture Arts and Sciences, Beverly Hills, California.

131 HALF THE PROFIT. Mannix ledgers, *op. cit.*

132 NEW DRINK OF CHOICE. Leila Hyams clearly remembered Browning's fondness for beer during the period she worked with him, 1929–32. Hyams interview, *op. cit.*

Four: Transylvania

135 FROM BLOOD POISONING. Obituary of Paul Leni, *Variety,* September 11, 1929.

137 TOYED WITH AN IDEA OF A FILM. For a complete documentation of the endless intrigue surrounding Universal's negotiations for the rights to *Dracula,* see David J. Skal, *Hollywood Gothic: The Tangled Web of "Dracula" from Novel to Stage to Screen* (New York: W. W. Norton & Co., 1990).

137 READERS' REPORTS. Philip J. Riley, ed., *MagicImage Filmbooks Presents "Dracula"* (Atlantic City, N.J., and Hollywood, Ca.: MagicImage Filmbooks, 1990), p. 30.

137 FIVE-YEAR CONTRACT. "Tod Browning Rejoins Universal," *op. cit.*

138 TALKING REMAKE. Unsourced Los Angeles clipping, Margaret Herrick Library, Academy of Motion Picture Arts and Sciences, Beverly Hills, California. In " 'U' Plans Talker Version of Two Silent Successes" (*Film Daily,* November 17, 1929, p. 10), *The Virgin of Stamboul* was announced as a remake, but no director was mentioned for the project.

138 SIGNED A NEW CONTRACT. Blake, *op. cit.,* p. 259.

138 A GOOD PICTURE. Margaret Tazelar, "On the Screen," *New York Herald-Tribune,* September 1, 1930, p. 6.

139 ONE OF THE WORST PIECES OF CLAP TRAP. Review of *Outside the Law, Variety,* September 3, 1930.

140 WARNING FLAGS. "Director Wants 'Mikes' Marked with Red," publicity article in Universal Pictures pressbook for *Outside the Law,* 1930.

141 THE UNNECESSARY SUBTITLE. "Tod Browning, Who Used to Cut Corners at the Louisville Race Track, Now Tells How to Cut Non Essentials Out of Films," *op. cit.*

141 FOR PURPOSES OF DESTRUCTION. See Skal, *op. cit.,* for complete documentation of the *Nosferatu* affair.

141 TO AVOID NUISANCE LITIGATION. *Ibid.* pp. 108–9.

142 LAVISH FIRST TREATMENT. Bromfield's incomplete treatment is reproduced in Riley, *Dracula, op. cit.*

143 BROWNING LEANED HEAVILY. William Hart interview, *op. cit.*

144 ASKED FOR NUMEROUS CHANGES. Riley, *op. cit.,* p. 56.

145 UNIVERSAL'S FINAL CHOICES. "Ian Keith to Play Dracula; Bela Lugosi, William Courtenay Also Considered," *Hollywood Filmograph,* undated clipping.

145 A STRANGER FROM EUROPE. Untitled item, *Los Angeles Examiner,* July 2, 1930.

145 JOHN WRAY. "Wray, the Neck-Biter," *Variety,* June 2, 1930.

145 CHESTER MORRIS. Scott MacQueen, "Roland West," in Frank Thompson, ed., *Between Action and Cut* (Metuchen, N.J.: Scarecrow Press, 1985), p. 146.

145 PAUL MUNI. "No Dracula Yet," *Variety,* September 3, 1930, p. 8.

146 JOSEPH SCHILDKRAUT. Harold Freedman, letter to Verne Porter, Universal Pictures, March 13, 1930.

148 HONORARY PALLBEARER. "Lon Chaney Dies After Brave Fight," *New York Times,* August 27, 1930, p. 25.

148 AMEREECAN PEOPLE. Fred Johnson, "Dracula Escapes Coffin, Revels in S.F.," *San Francisco Call and Post,* August 25, 1928.

148 NEVER ABLE TO THINK. Bela Lugosi, Jr., conversation with David J. Skal, Orlando, Florida, October 21, 1994.

148 A PAIN IN THE ASS. Jonathan Sinclair Carey, conversation with David J. Skal, December 31, 1994.

148 REMEMBERED THE ACTOR. David Manners, interview by David J. Skal, Santa Barbara, California, March 1991.

148 AFTER I HAD BEEN IN THE PLAY. "Lugosi at High Emotional Pitch in *Dracula* Role," Universal Pictures pressbook for *Dracula,* 1931.

149 "UNLEARNING" FAST. "Bela Lugosi Praises Director Tod Browning," *Hollywood Filmograph,* October 18, 1930, p. 12.

149 EXTREMELY DISORGANIZED. Manners interview, *op. cit.*

149 FUNNY YOU SHOULD ASK. David Manners, telephone conversation with Elias Savada, Pacific Palisades, California, April 9, 1972.

150 AS LUGOSI REMEMBERED. Tom Hutchinson and Roy Pickard, *Horrors: A History of Horror Movies* (Secaucus, N.J.: Chartwell Books, 1984), pp. 15–16.

150 MINUSCULE BUDGET. Comparative production logs for the English- and Spanish-language versions of *Dracula*; Riley, *MagicImage Filmbooks Presents "Dracula," op. cit.*, p. 62.

151 SET RENDERINGS WERE EXHIBITED. Ralph Wilk, "A Little from 'Lots' " (column), *Film Daily*, October 19, 1930, p. 4.

151 TRADE PAPER PREVIEW. "Universal Has a Winner in *Dracula* Spanish Version," *Hollywood Filmograph*, January 10, 1931, p. 21.

153 FORTY-EIGHT HOURS OF BUSINESS. "*Dracula* Draws 50,000 in Two Days at Roxy," *Film Daily*, February 16, 1931, p. 1.

153 $700,000. Figure from Universal documents submitted as evidence in the antitrust case *U.S. v. 20th Century Fox Film Corporation*, December 5, 1955.

153 $1.2 MILLION. *Cinema Digest*, August 22, 1932, p. 8.

154 EXCITING GRAND GUIGNOL PRODUCTION. Mordaunt Hall, "*Dracula* as a Film," *New York Times*, February 22, 1931.

154 TRAGIC DIGNITY. Ada Hanifin, "Dracula Film Wins Acclaim: Vampire Tale Has 'Tragic Dignity,' " *San Francisco Examiner*, March 28, 1931.

154 GLOOMINESS IN EXCELSIS. "*Dracula*: Talkie Version of Famous Vampire Story," *Era* (London), February 25, 1931.

154 TOD BROWNING DIRECTED. Review of *Dracula*, by Harold Weight, *Hollywood Filmograph*, April 4, 1931.

154 IT WOULD BE DIFFICULT TO THINK. Review of *Dracula*, *Variety*, February 18, 1931.

154 TOD BROWNING WAS PERHAPS THE FIRST. Edgar G. Ulmer, quoted in *Midi-minuit fantastique*, no. 13, November 1965. Trans. by Elliott Stein.

155 PRELIMINARY SET SKETCHES. Reproduced in Riley, *Dracula, op. cit.*, pp. 74–75.

156 AMBIVALENCE IS THE KEYNOTE. Maurice Richardson, "The Psychoanalysis of Ghost Stories," *Twentieth Century*, December 1959.

157 THREE WALLS OF A STAGE SET. Review of *Iron Man*, *New York Times*, April 18, 1931, p. 17.

157 AS A STORY OF THE RING. Review of *Iron Man*, *Variety*, April 22, 1931, p. 18.

157 A NEW PHASE OF REALISM. Katherine Hill, "Realism of Fight Film," *San Francisco Chronicle*, May 1, 1931.

157 SMALL ITEM APPEARED. *Los Angeles Times,* March 30, 1931.

158 WHETHER *DRACULA* IS JUST A FREAK. "U Has Horror Cycle All to Self," *Variety,* April 8, 1931, p. 2.

Five: "Offend One and You Offend Them All"

161 $8,000. Robbins letter to Savada, *op. cit.*

163 AVENGED HIMSELF UPON A GIANT. Watts, "A Glance at Tod Browning," *op. cit.*

164 WELL, IT'S HORRIBLE. Willis Goldbeck, letter to Elias Savada, February 22, 1972.

165 CHANEY IS VISITED. Lon Chaney, "The Most Grotesque Moment of My Life," *Motion Picture Classic,* June 1930.

167 I WAS IN TOD'S OFFICE. Hyams interview, *op. cit.*

167 AMONG THE REJECTS. Résumé photographs of freaks submitted to M-G-M for the film can be viewed in the *Freaks* still photo collection of the Margaret Herrick Library, Academy of Motion Picture Arts and Sciences, Beverly Hills, California.

168 ARRAY OF FREAKS ASSEMBLED. Grace Mack, "Venus and the Freaks," *Screenplay,* April 1932.

168 DID NOT ATTRACT GAWKERS. Merrill Pye, interview by Elias Savada, Los Angeles, California, April 21, 1972.

168 WITHOUT THROWING UP. Marx interview, *op. cit.*

168 SCOTT TURNED PEA-GREEN. Dwight Taylor, *Joy Ride* (New York: G. P. Putnam's Sons, 1969), pp. 247–48.

169 STARTED WEARING SUNGLASSES. Joe Collura, "Johnny Eck— Beyond Measure," *Classic Images,* no. 139, July 1991, p. 51.

169 VERY GRAND AND RITZY. Mack, *op. cit.*

169 JEALOUSY WAS AMAZING. Harrison Carroll, "Queerest Hollywood Cast Turns Out to Be All 'Stars,' " *Los Angeles Herald and Express,* February 13, 1932, p. A-7.

170 BLOODCURDLING YELL. Sheldon interview, *op. cit.*

170 A TRIUMPH OF PERSONALITY. Faith Service, "The Amazing Life Stories of the Freaks!" *Motion Picture,* April 1932, p. 100.

170 SCHLITZE WAS FILTHY RICH. Hyams interview, *op. cit.*

170 DYING IN CALIFORNIA. Daniel P. Mannix, *Freaks: We Who Are Not as Others* (San Francisco: Re/Search Publications, 1990).

171 LIKE A MONKEY, SHE GO CRAZY. John Kobal, "Olga Baclanova," in *People Will Talk* (New York: Alfred A. Knopf, 1985).

171 I WAS BITTEN ONCE. Muriel Babcock, "Freaks Rouse Ire and Wonder: Horrified Spectators Write Scathing Letters," *Los Angeles Times*, February 14, 1932, part 3, p. 9.

171 I WAS TRYING TO SHOOT. Carroll, *op. cit.*

171 I WAS A VERY YOUNG BOY. Basil Wrangell, interview by Elias Savada, Los Angeles, California, April 9, 1972.

172 HORRIBLY POCKMARKED FACE. Hyams and Berg interviews, *op. cit.*

172 A PARTICULAR SHINE TO JOHNNY ECK. Johnny Eck, interview by Mark Feldman, *Pandemonium*, no. 3, 1989, p. 169.

172 BROWNING WAS WONDERFUL. Collura, *op. cit.*

172 COMPREHENSIVE SERIES OF PHOTOGRAPHS. Stills of Alice Browning with the freaks are included in the *Freaks* photo collection of the Margaret Herrick Library, Academy of Arts and Sciences, Beverly Hills, California.

173 TOUGHEST ONE I'VE WORKED ON. David S. Horsley, letter to *Photon*, no. 24, 1977, p. 46.

173 BROWNING WANTED RAIN. Sheldon interview (Skal segment), *op. cit.*

174 THEY *RAN* OUT. Pye interview, *op. cit.*

174 MISCARRIAGE. Cohn interview, *op. cit.*

175 FILM DID SURPRISINGLY WELL. Weekly box-office reports from *Motion Picture Herald*, Spring 1932.

176 ABOUT THAT OFFENSIVE FILM. Mrs. Ambrose Nevin Diehl, letter with attachment to Will H. Hays, February 26, 1932, in Douglas Gomery, ed., *Will H. Hays Papers, Part II: April 1929 to September 1945* (Frederick, Md.: University Publications of America, Indiana State University, 1986), microfilm, reel 6 of 35.

176 A GREAT HUMANIST. Louis F. Edelman, interview by Elias Savada, Los Angeles, California, April 5, 1972.

177 A LANDMARK IN SCREEN DARING. *Washington Post* advertisement for the premiere of *Freaks*, February 19, 1932, p. 11.

177 UNKIND AND BRUTAL. "The Pay-Off," *Motion Picture Daily*, April 11, 1932, p. 2.

177 TONE DOWN 'FREAKS.' *Motion Picture Daily*, February 29, 1932, p. 1.

178 LOATHSOME, OBSCENE, GROTESQUE AND BIZARRE. "M-G-M *Freaks* Banned by Atlanta Censors," *Hollywood Herald*, March 8, 1932, p. 2.

178 TRANSCENDS THE FASCINATINGLY HORRIBLE. Frank Daniel, "Abhorrent and Akin," *Atlanta Journal,* February 19, 1932.

178 IT TOOK A WEAK MIND. Review of *Freaks, Kansas City (Missouri) Star,* quoted in *"Freaks* Neither Amusing or Entertaining," *Cinema Digest,* August 8, 1932, p. 17.

178 TOD BROWNING CAN NOW RETIRE. Review of *Freaks,* by Elinor Hughes, *Boston Herald,* February 20, 1932.

179 THE VENGEANCE PORTION. Harold Hunt, "Circus Sideshow Oddities Give Unusual Twist to Fox Broadway Talkie," *Oregon Daily Journal,* February 17, 1932, p. 14.

179 SOMEBODY BLUNDERED. Review of *Freaks, Boston Evening Transcript,* February 20, 1932.

179 IF THEY REFUSED TO SHOW IT. "What to Do with *Freaks,*" *Harrison's Reports,* April 9, 1932, p. 60.

180 MUCK FOR MONEY'S SAKE. Review of *Freaks, Rob Wagner's Script,* February 20, 1932, pp. 8–9.

180 TECHNIQUE OF CRIME. *What Shocked the Censors: A Complete Record of Cuts in Motion Picture Films Ordered by the New York State Censors from January, 1932 to March, 1933* (New York: National Council on Freedom from Censorship, 1933).

180 ONE OF THE FEW TRULY INDIVIDUAL DIRECTORS. "Cinema," *Time,* April 18, 1932, p. 17.

180 MERELY MISERY. Review of *Freaks, Variety,* July 12, 1932.

180 SECOND, SUNDAY PIECE. *New York Times,* July 10, 1932.

181 WHIMSICAL NURSERY TALES. Review of *Freaks,* by Richard Watts, Jr., *New York Herald-Tribune,* July 9, 1932, p. 6.

181 DISGUSTED WITH THE MAN. Wrangell interview, *op. cit.*

181 COMMERCIAL DISASTER. Mannix ledgers, *op. cit.*

181 LAUGH THE WHOLE THING OFF. Marx interview, *op. cit.*

Six: Malibu After Midnight

185 USE HIM IN ANOTHER HORROR FILM. Johnny Eck, "Johnny Eck" (autobiography fragment), *Pandemonium,* no. 3, 1989, p. 160.

185 SAWING-IN-HALF TRICK. *Ibid.,* pp. 161–62.

186 REINCARNATION THEME. *Variety,* November 8, 1932.

186 REVISIONS WOULD BE NEEDED. Jason S. Joy, letter to Irving Thalberg, November 10, 1930, MPPDA case file on *Fast Workers,* Special Collections, Margaret Herrick Library, Academy of Motion Picture Arts and Sciences, Beverly Hills, California.

186   HIGHLY OFFENSIVE, UTTERLY UNPRINCIPLED. L. Trotti, Production Code reader, comments on synopsis of *Rivets* submitted by the Caddo Company, January 30, 1931, *ibid.*

186   UNTIL HE FAINTED. Fountain, *op. cit.*, p. 228.

187   WILL HAYS COMPLAINED DIRECTLY. MPPDA case file on *Fast Workers, op. cit.*

188   COST $525,000. Mannix ledgers, *op. cit.*

188   TITANIC BOX-OFFICE DISASTER. *Ibid.*

188   THE SUSPICION GROWS. Review of *Fast Workers, New York Times,* March 20, 1933, p. 18.

188   VIVID MYSTERY. "Bayou Shots Made for New Barrymore Film," *Loew's Weekly,* vol. 14, no. 51, August 18, 1933, p. 4.

188   WEIRD TRADITIONS. "Natives in Bayou Drama," *Loew's Weekly,* vol. 14, no. 48, July 28, 1933, p. 1.

189   GET A GOOD NIGHT'S SLEEP. "William Faulkner," in Malcolm Cowley, ed., *Writers at Work: The Paris Review Interviews* (New York: Viking Press, 1958), p. 127.

189   TOD BROWNING'S EXPEDITION. "Mysterious Goings On," *Los Angeles Times,* May 4, 1933.

190   INCOMPREHENSIBLE ACTIVITY. Cowley, *op. cit.,* p. 128.

190   WHAT IS THE STORY? Robert Coughlan, *The Private World of William Faulkner* (New York: Avon Books, 1953–54), p. 91.

190   THAT SON OF A BITCH. *Ibid.*

190   BROWNING BLEW UP. *Ibid.*

190   BRILLIANT CAPABLE MAN. Joseph Blotner, *Faulkner: A Biography* (New York: Random House, 1974), p. 802.

191   BEING IN A PROHIBITION STATE. William Faulkner, letter to Tod Browning, May 14, 1933; Bruce F. Kawin, ed., *Faulkner's MGM Screenplays* (Knoxville: University of Tennessee Press, 1982), p. xxxvi.

191   WE WILL BE MOST HAPPY. Mark telegram to Faulkner, *op. cit.*

191   PRIVATE COLLECTOR. *Ibid.,* p. xxxv.

191   HEARD THAT THE CAJUN PEOPLE. Cowley, *op. cit.*

191   LOVED COMPETITIVE SPORTS. Dwan interview, *op. cit.*

192   FEEL SORRY FOR SOMEONE. Arnold Gingrich, "Poor Man's Nightclub," *Esquire,* Autumn 1933, p. 61.

192   EVEN MORE APPALLING. Schulberg, *op. cit.*

192   SEEING THEM GO "SQUIRRELLY." Unsourced clipping.

193   BLACKFACE COMEDIANS. Dwan interview, *op. cit.*

194   STRANGE, WISPY LITTLE MAN. Florabel Muir, "Methinks Guy En-
      dore's a Strange Little Guy," *Hollywood Citizen News,* February 13,
      1946.

194   DISPLACED INCEST FANTASIES. Ernest Jones, "The Vampire," in
      On the Nightmare (1931; reprint, New York: Liveright Publishing
      Corp., 1951), pp. 98–130.

195   RITA HAYWORTH. James Wong Howe, interview in Charles
      Higham, *Hollywood Cameramen* (Bloomington, Ind., and London: In-
      diana University Press, 1970), p. 87.

195   JUST DOWN FROM BERKELEY. Carroll Borland, interview by Elias
      Savada, Los Angeles, California, January 23, 1972.

197   QUITE A CHARACTER. Howe interview, *op. cit.*

197   WASN'T GETTING THE EFFECTS RIGHT. Cohn interview, *op. cit.*

198   WHEN TOD BROWNING WAS CHASING COWS. Schubert inter-
      view, *op. cit.*

198   ESPECIALLY IN CLEVELAND. "Human Trailer Announced *Mark of
      the Vampire* in Cleve.," *Film Daily,* May 15, 1935, p. 9.

198   MINIMALLY PROFITABLE. Mannix ledgers, *op. cit.*

199   FANTASTIC VOODOO RITES. M-G-M advertisement announcing
      1935–36 season, *Film Daily,* June 12, 1935.

199   COMPLETED A SCRIPT. Bret Wood, "The Witch, the *Devil,* and the
      Code," *Film Comment,* November–December 1992, pp. 52–53.

200   HAD QUIET TALK WITH CENSOR. Dave Blum, telegram to Sam-
      uel Marx, November 11, 1935, MPPDA case file on *The Devil-Doll,*
      Margaret Herrick Library, Academy of Motion Picture Arts and Sci-
      ences, Beverly Hills, California.

201   MY GOD! IT'S ETHEL! "Cinema: The New Pictures," *Time,* July 20,
      1936, p. 36.

201   IN THIRTY-EIGHT DAYS. Mannix ledgers, *op. cit.*

201   NO TROUBLE CUTTING HIS FILM. Frederick Y. Smith, interview
      by Elias Savada, Los Angeles, California, April 22, 1972.

201   SLIGHTLY HORRIBLE, AND CONSISTENTLY INTERESTING. Re-
      view of *The Devil-Doll,* by Frank S. Nugent, *New York Times,* August 8,
      1936, p. 5.

201   BARBARIC RITE. Bosley Crowther, *Hollywood Rajah: The Life and
      Times of Louis B. Mayer* (New York: Holt, Rinehart & Winston, 1960),
      p. 204.

202   A DELIBERATE SHOCKER. Review of *They Shoot Horses, Don't They?
      New Republic,* September 11, 1935.

202   HE ATTEMPTED TO PERSUADE M-G-M. Elliott Stein, "Tod Browning," in Richard Roud, ed., *Cinema: A Critical Dictionary* (New York: Viking Press, 1980), vol. 2, p. 166.

203   PACIFIC COAST ASSOCIATION OF MAGICIANS. Correspondence in MPPDA case file, *op. cit.*

204   ENOUGH LOOSE ENDS TO FRINGE A SPANISH SHAWL. Review of *Miracles for Sale,* by Frank S. Nugent, *New York Times,* August 10, 1939, p. 15.

204   A MELODRAMATIC UNITY. Howard Barnes, "On the Screen," *New York Herald-Tribune,* August 11, 1939.

204   FELONIOUS HOMICIDES. MPPDA case file on *Miracles for Sale, op. cit.*

205   HOLLYWOODISH IRONY. Samuel Marx, letter to Elias Savada, February 10, 1972.

205   TURNED ON HIM FOR NO REASON. William Hart interview, *op. cit.*

206   ONE OF THE FIRST VOLKSWAGENS. Dwan interview, *op. cit.*

206   COMPLICATED BY PNEUMONIA. Alice L. Browning, Certificate of Death, State of California, Department of Public Health, May 12, 1944.

207   CARRY HER DOWN TO THE BEACH. Babineau interview, *op. cit.*

207   FREEZE UP. Dwan interview, *op. cit.*

207   NO ANSWER TO THEIR KNOCK. Hyams and Berg interviews, *op. cit.*

207   DRAPED ALICE'S SHAWL. Marshall interview, *op. cit.*

207   FLATTERING PIECE. George Geltzer, "Tod Browning: He Made Great Horror Films Because He Believed Horror Is Naturally Cinematic," *Films in Review,* October 1953, p. 416.

207   DEAR MRS. GELTZER. Letter courtesy of George Geltzer.

209   A FEELING FOR HUMANITY. Mrs. Edward de Butts, interview by Elias Savada, Malibu, California, April 21, 1972.

209   CLARK GABLE'S STAND-IN. William Hart interview, *op. cit.*

211   REPLACEMENT BULLDOG. Dr. and Mrs. Harold Snow, interview by Elias Savada, February 14 and 19, 1972, Los Angeles, California.

211   A VERY RELIGIOUS MAN. William Hart interview, *op. cit.*

212   AVERY BROWNING WAS FOUND ASPHYXIATED. "Man's Death Laid to Fumes from Heater," *Louisville Courier-Journal,* December 15, 1958.

213   RAISED THE ROOF. McAuliffe interview, *op. cit.*

213 CANCER OF THE TONGUE. *Ibid.*

213 THIGHBONES. *Ibid.*

214 DETERIORATION IN BROWNING'S HEALTH. Snow interview, *op. cit.*

Epilogue: "One of Us"

221 ONE OF THE GREATEST DIRECTORS. Quoted in Roud, *op. cit.*, p. 166.

221 SECOND-RATE MIND. Iris Barry, *Let's Go to the Movies* (New York: Payson & Clarke Ltd., 1926), p. 277.

222 CINEMATIC SERMONETTES. Charles Teitel, "Vintage 'Message' Shocker Pics Yanked from Grave by Homevid," *Variety,* May 8, 1985.

222 NO MOVIE HAS EVER IMPRESSED ME MORE. David F. Friedman, letter to David J. Skal, July 8, 1993.

223 HELD THE REVOLT AT BAY. David F. Friedman, with Don DeNevi, *A Youth in Babylon: Confessions of a Trash-Film King* (Buffalo, N.Y.: Prometheus Books, 1990), p. 63.

223 *CAHIERS DU CINEMA.* Jean-Pierre Oudart, "Humain, Trop Humain," *Cahiers du cinéma,* no. 210, March 1969, pp. 57–58.

224 TENDER COMPREHENSION. Review of *Freaks,* by Tom Milne, *Sight and Sound,* vol. 32, no. 3, Summer 1963, p. 145.

224 WHAT THE CINEMA MIGHT DO MORE OFTEN. Isabel Quigley, "Freaks with Feeling," *Spectator* (U.K.), June 21, 1963.

224 ONE OF THE MOST COMPASSIONATE FILMS EVER MADE. Sarris, *op. cit.*

224 FLICKERING RECIPROCAL GAZE. Arbus' photo of Lugosi was included in her retrospective exhibition *The Movies* at the Robert Miller Gallery, New York, in January 1995.

225 CARRION CROW OF BEVERLY HILLS. John Baxter, "The Silent Empire of Raymond Rohauer," *Times Magazine* (London), January 19, 1973, p. 32.

226 EVEN THE MOST INSENSITIVE VOYEUR. Review of *Freaks,* by Alasdair Cameron, *Times* (London), March 6, 1990.

226 SOMETHING DARK AND FEARFUL. Fintan O'Toole, "Women Steal the Stage," *Irish Times,* September 30, 1989.

229 CINEMA IS SOMETHING YOU LOOK AT. Richard Roud, "Tod Browning Version," *Guardian* (U.K.), undated clipping, 1963.

INDEX

ABOUT THE AUTHORS

DAVID J. SKAL is the author of *Hollywood Gothic* (called "the ultimate book on Dracula" by *Newsweek*) and *The Monster Show: A Cultural History of Horror*. His writing has appeared in the *New York Times*, in *The Village Voice,* and, for television, on *Biography*, the A&E Network's award-winning series. He lives in New York City.

ELIAS SAVADA, a film historian, copyright researcher, and archival programming consultant, is director of the Motion Picture Information Service in Bethesda, Maryland, where he lives with his wife and two children. He compiled the recently published *American Film Institute Catalog: Film Beginnings, 1893–1910.*